TURTLE WAS GONE
A LONG TIME

Volume Two

HORSEHEAD NEBULA NEIGHING

John Moriarty

THE LILLIPUT PRESS
Dublin

First published in 1997 by
THE LILLIPUT PRESS LTD
4 Rosemount Terrace, Arbour Hill,
Dublin 7, Ireland.

A CIP record for this
title is available from
The British Library.

ISBN 1 874675 90 2

Acknowledgments
To Anne Garvey for her composition.
The Lilliput Press receives financial assistance from
An Chomhairle Ealaíon/The Arts Council of Ireland.

Set in 11 on 13 Bembo
by Sheila Stephenson
Printed in Ireland
by Betaprint of Clonshaugh.

TURTLE WAS GONE
A LONG TIME

PRELUDE

In what way or ways does this second volume move forward from ground occupied or reached in the first?

Given that the concern of this book is with movement essential not movement local, it doesn't move forward in the obvious way that a narrative poem like 'The Ancient Mariner' does, episode by distinct episode. And yet, tacking this way and that, but mostly becalmed, it is a voyage, through shipwreck, to Buddh Gaia. Strangely, it is when we are standing still in the doldrums that we make most progress. Movement local denied us, we are plunged into the rough inner seas of movement essential, the paradigm of which in this book is the Triduum Sacrum. It isn't only the individuals on board who undergo this voyage of transformation, however. Their religion and their culture, each in its most fundamental assumptions and axioms, undergo it also. For this is the voyage of our Hebrew and Greek estimation of ourselves and of our world. Poetically imagined, it is a voyage in five tall ships – *Argo, Nave, Mayflower, Beagle* and *Pequod*. Pursuing the harpooned Cetus Dei, it sails self-destructively into the Sea of Typhoons, it sails out of Time into Tehom, and, in the long, acosmic night, it re-emerges as the Maidu raft.

One of the generating theses of this volume is that modern Western culture is *Pequod* culture. Portending doom as we rounded the Cape of Good Hope, a phantom laugh echoed upwards from the hold and, like Erinyes unafraid of our threatening clamour, sea ravens settled on the rigging. But, our purpose unaltered, we sailed on.

In all of this we are re-engaging with a central theme in the first volume. There, too, we dealt with this voyage into self-destruction. And there, too, continued in Big Mike rowing himself out into the Night of Brahma, it became a voyage of transformation:

> They that go down to the sea in ships
> And find, off course, no near landfall,
> Find more than Job, my dear brethren,
> The terrible scriptures of water and squall.

More numerous than the desert sand
A remnant shipped for the Promised Land
And swelling our sails two thousand leagues out
The wind was still all word of mouth.
The moon removed her dark half shawl –
Though our masts stood stately and tall
It was, if you like, an ominous sea
And like women the waves at a well in Galilee:
The troublous gossip of water, that's all
Our dreaming senses heard out there:
Birds left no footprints in the air.
Suddenly then the beasts were shod,
The sun came up like a firing squad
And as if our ship was a drifting wreck
The Beasts of the Zodiac walked the deck.
Into the waste, month after month,
The skyline pulled back the battlefront;
Though our prophets proclaimed
The Beasts were from God,
That our masts would lie down
With Yahweh's rod,
Flashing about the scything prow,
The rotted cords, the rusted nails,
Whoever made the distant plough
Wields it now
Like a cat-o-nine-tails.
Tomorrow at dawn the high ocean begins,
We shall know whether God or the water wins,
The only thing Christ deserved was our sins.

It is here, our voyage becalmed in these great waters, that this second volume begins. As it turns out, it isn't a negative calm. It is indeed the calm of Tehom and in it we hear the birth of the universe or, in cittamatra terms, the birth of awareness-of-self-and-other-than-self.

In it we hear the Horsehead Nebula neighing.

Does Western culture sailing into the Sea of Typhoons have its analogue, indeed its real meaning, in Narada walking into his initiation?

As phantoms went aboard the *Pequod* so, somehow, has Narada come aboard our voyage. Maybe he was always on board, biding his time below waterline. Hitherto suppressed or kept at bay by our cultural immune system, his time has come. Breached when the Beasts of the Zodiac walked the deck, that immune system was an open Thermopylae to him and there he is now, outcast no longer, standing before the mast. Looking at him, we know that he is portent. Looking at him, we know that what happens to him will happen to our voyage, will happen to our religion, will happen to our culture. Like Noah, Ahab anticipates:

All visible objects, man, are but as pasteboard masks.

Ahab's response to this – his diluvian insight, or, should we say, his response to the abyss he has broken into – is Mesopotamian. He turns this threat to his sense of himself and his world into a Tiamat that he must do battle with. But there is a better way, a Christian way, and this being so, it might be that, suppressed for three or four centuries now, Jesus will also come up from below the waterline, and looking at him we will see something of ourselves, something of our own transtorrentem destiny. Looking at him, we will see Tenebrae not Tiamat, moksha not Middle-Eastern myth. So yes, it is true. However careful we were to exclude them, some phantoms did come aboard our Titanic modern voyage. Could it be that religion will erupt among us again? Could it be that albatross and whale will return to guide us? Could it be that, for those who have eyes to see it, there it is, the Spirit-Spout:

It was while gliding through these latter waters that one serene and moonlight night, when all the waves rolled by like scrolls of silver; and by their soft suffusing seethings, made what seemed a silvery silence not a solitude: on such a silent night a silvery jet was seen far in advance of the white bubbles at the bow. Lit up by the moon, it looked celestial; seemed some plumed and glittering god uprising from the sea.

The Cetus Dei who would lead us to a vision of the Earth as Buddh Gaia, to a vision of the universe as Bodhi Tree.

It sounds like the pillar of cloud by day and the pillar of fire by night. Do you think of what you have written as a Book of Exodus?

Biblically, exodus suggests enormities of direct, divine intervention in human affairs:

For ask now of the days that are past, which were before thee, since the day that God created man upon the earth, and ask from the one side of heaven unto the other, whether there hath been any such thing as this great thing is, or hath been heard like it? Did ever people hear the voice of God speaking out of the midst of fire, as thou hast heard, and live? Or hath God assayed to go and take him a nation from the midst of another nation, by temptations, by signs, and by wonders and by war, and by a mighty hand, and by a stretched-out arm, and by great terrors, according to all the Lord your God did for you in Egypt before your eyes?

It is religiously difficult for me to claim it, but it is true that the Book of Exodus does underlie what I've attempted to do. This volume begins with a Horsehead Nebula – the one out of which I imagine that our solar system has evolved – it begins with this astronomical Equus Dei neighing a mahavakya into our cosmic origins. Hard upon this, two stories come into our world. Their coming is like the coming among us of Moses and Aaron. Like Aaron and his wand is Narada and his ropesnake. With his snake-wand, Aaron opened a path through the Red Sea. With his rope-snake, Narada opens a path through consciousness-of. Walking dryshod through the Red Sea, the Children of Israel came into the desert of Zin. Walking dryshod through the deluge of consciousness-of, or if you like, walking dryshod through the world-illusion, Narada would lead us into Nirvikalpasamadhi.

I often think of Cortez in Mexico. In our calendar, he went ashore there in AD 1519. In the Aztec calendar he came among them, they thinking of him as a God returning, in Year One Reed. Very obviously, Year One Reed was a year of awful transition for Aztecs. Could it be though that Europeans must now undergo a Year One Reed? Could it be that humanity at large must undergo a Year One Reed? If not, what chance does the Earth have? Imagine it: circling the sun, a terribly destroyed Gaia calling out, bury my heart at Wounded Knee.

It is in the shadow of two questions, not yet answered, that this volume was written:

Are we the iceberg the Earth has crashed into?
Have we lost, or did we ever acquire, evolutionary legitimacy?

Certain it is that we need to bring the Harrowing of Hell back into our repertoire. Not just into our theatrical repertoire. Into our sacramental repertoire. There is need for someone who is ordained to do so and who is therefore sacramentally protected to go down into the hold of our cultural unconscious and call out: 'Lift up your heads, O ye gates, and be ye lift up, ye everlasting doors, and the King of Glory shall come in.'

Assumptions and axioms of our Western way need to be harrowed. Our myths and our metaphors need to be harrowed.

In the forms of our sensibility and in the categories of our understanding we need to undergo a 1519.

Inwardly, in the depths of our being, we need to undergo a Year One Reed.

Initially, in this volume, Narada is our conquistador.

What, walking out of our Year One Reed, will we bring with us?

What seeds or intuitions of what new culture will we bring with us?

In a mood of revolutionary anguish and fervour, Shelley wrote his 'Ode to the West Wind' in a wood beside the Arno. The Oglala Sioux enacted Black Elk's vision on a bank of the Tongue River. In your search for cultural regeneration, you go more readily to the Tongue than to the Arno, the Ilissus and the Tiber. You go more readily to the Aurignacian way of the Navajo and the Sioux than to the classical way of the Greeks and the Romans. If this is so, why is it so?

In the West, in our century, if someone suffers a breakdown or is afflicted by neurotic symptoms, we tend to lie them on a psychiatrist's couch and take them back to their childhood, the hope being that we will discover an unintegrated experience or fantasy or trauma that is giving rise to the trouble. It isn't only individuals who break down, however. Civilizations break down. And so, standing under a hole in the ozone layer, it might be timely to lie our culture on a psychiatrist's couch or, better perhaps, it might be timely to take Europa to Uvavnuk's igloo or to Wolf Collar's Blue Thunder tipi, because sitting with her there, the old Pleistocene medicine woman or the old Aurignacian medicine man might soon see that our Western voyage to calamity in the Sea of Typhoons was charted for disaster from the beginning. In the first page of our holy book we gave ourselves a divine mandate to rule over and subdue. This estimation of ourselves and our prospects was corroborated among the Greeks in Sophocles' famous second stasimon. Second stasimon and Psalm eight, that is the chart we would work with, and so begins our *polla ta deina* voyage in five tall ships – the ship of aboriginal heroism, Herculean and Orphic; the ship that would be our cathedral nave, the cathedral nave that would be our ship taking us through time into eternity; the ship that would take us to the Willie Loman Land we would build elsewhere and build here at home; the ship of modern science, of the exploring mind becomes single in its vision; the vengeful, tusked ship that would strike through, sail through, the illusion or masquerade which, in Ahab's Hindu view of it, is what the empirical world is.

It is time, if we cannot yet harrow it, to nail our Psalm eight and second stasimon estimation of ourselves and our world to a Caucasus rockwall, or better, to a Golgotha rockwall.

I am of course reading these texts not as Heidegger would read them but as a capitalist would read them, or indeed as Prometheus would read them: eyes wide open to techne, closed to tolma, seeing the *Dreadnought* not the nought.

Biblically insensitive to all forms of life that aren't human, Habakkuk is outraged by demiurgic dominion only when it is exercised over other human beings. Speaking to his God, he says:

Thou art of purer eyes than to behold evil, and canst not look on iniquity: wherefore lookest thou upon them that deal treacherously, and holdest thy tongue when the wicked devoureth the man that is more righteous than he? And makest men as the fishes of the sea, as the creeping things, that have no ruler over them? They take up all of them with the angle, they catch them in their net, and gather them in their drag: therefore they rejoice and are glad. Therefore they sacrifice unto their net, and burn incense unto their drag: because by them their portion is fat, and their meat plenteous.

The net and the drag, the stasimon and the Psalm. And in the Spouter Inn, in an upstairs room lit by a spermaceti candle, Ishmael is looking at himself in a less than elegant mirror. Can you see him, David? And you Sophocles, can you see him? Can ye see that the harpooner's poncho he is wearing is the skin of a sperm whale's penis? Seeing him, can ye see the end of the whaleroad and the whale? Seeing him, can ye see the end of our Hebrew and Greek estimation of ourselves?

And as for Shelley – I imagine him writing his 'Prometheus Unbound' in the Whaleman's Chapel in New Bedford. It is with the quill of a very dead but very famous albatross that he writes it. It is by the light of a spermaceti candle that he writes it. But here they come, the first tumults of autumn and, even as he speaks them, the words of Prometheus gutter on the guttering page.

If harpoon-wounds alone were all that was necessary for it to be so, then our spermaceti candle would be our Paschal candle. But it isn't. And every time we light it, the universe is a darker place. Indeed, I sometimes imagine that to quench our galaxy, finally and forever, all we have to do is light a spermaceti candle in it.

> Agnus Dei
> Cetus Dei
> Albatross Dei

Longinus, Queequeg, Ancient Mariner: our three harpooners in their terrible Whaleman's Chapel chasubles. It is of course the last rites of our civilization that they are enacting. Last rites that cannot give release, cannot give requiem.

> When the whale's viscera go and the roll
> Of its corruption overruns this world
> Beyond tree-swept Nantucket and Wood's Hole
> And Martha's Vineyard, Sailor, will your sword
> Whistle and fall and sink into the fat?
> In the great ash-pit of Jehoshaphat
> The bones cry for the blood of the white whale,

The fat flukes arch and whack about its ears,
The death-lance churns into the sanctuary,
Tears the gun-blue swingle, heaving like a flail,
And hacks the coiling life out: it works and drags
And rips the spermwhale's midriff into rags,
Gobbets of blubber spill to wind and weather,
Sailor, and gulls go round the stoven timbers
Where the morning stars sing out together
And thunder shakes the white surf and dismembers
The red flag hammered in the masthead. Hide
Our steel, Jonas Messias, in Thy side.

Our Whaleman's Chapel in New Canaan. Our new nave. Nave in which we sacrifice to our net, and burn incense to our drag.

And having sacrificed we set sail in our whaler and as soon as we have reached the high seas, Ahab the captain comes up on deck and institutes a deadly eucharist. From the detached and upturned irons of the mate's harpoons the harpooners drink the terrible grog – Ahab's grog not Christ's wine. Christ's wine is Passover wine, it is the wine of our rite of passage from Fall to Recovery. Ahab's grog is in every sense the reverse.

Ahab isn't Antichrist but, letting the story grow as all great stories do, we can think of the ship as the Anti-ark, the Anti-nave, the Anti-ashram, the Anti-yana – its mission to eliminate the Spirit-Spout from the world and leave us to the wonders of our humanist devices.

O wild West Wind, thou breath of Autumn's being,
Thou from whose unseen presence the leaves dead
Are driven, like ghosts from an enchanter fleeing,

Yellow, and black, and pale, and hectic red,
Pestilence-stricken multitudes! O thou
Who chariotest to their dark, wintry bed

The wingèd seeds, where they lie cold and low,
Each like a corpse within its grave, until
Thine azure sister of the Spring shall blow

Her clarion o'er the dreaming earth …

Awaiting that clarion, we should know that ours is a civilization of *yu wei* works and days, a civilization of fantastic second-stasimon tricks:

… but man, proud man,
Dressed in a little brief authority,
Most ignorant of what he's most assured,
His glassy essence like an angry ape

> Plays such fantastic tricks before high heaven
> As makes the angels weep.

It reminds me of a haiku that could yet serve as an epitaph to our modern way of being in the world:

> The thief left it behind –
> The moon at the window.

So yes, I seek for healing by the Tongue altogether more readily than I seek for it by the Ilissus. But the Ilissus too. And the Arno. And yet, walking one day into the sixteenth-century Italian room in the Louvre, maybe we will find that, tired of being our humanist mirror, Mona Melencolia Europa will have walked back into the stupendous world she has for so long eclipsed. Rivers like the Tongue there are among those mountains. Among them are rivers like the Lena. But when I think of final healing and final hope, I turn to the Kedron. In the spiritual geography of this book all other medicine rivers are tributaries of the Kedron-Colorado.

Even the Yangtse and the Ganges?

The Yangtse and the Ganges have their gorges, their descents to Bright Angel. And the peoples of the Orient have religions that can watch with them. The Triduum Sacrum belongs to humanity, not just to Christians. It belongs as if by genetic inheritance to humanity in all ages, in all cultures. It belongs as much to Lucy as it does to Teresa of Avila. It belongs backwards in time as well as forward in time. It belongs to whatever depths, to whatever heights, Bright Angel Trail descends and ascends. Trilobite and toxodon crossed the Kedron with Jesus. Crossed it in him, he being Vishvarupa, he being Vishvayuga.

You don't only take Europa back to igloo or yurt. As though she were Lyca or Little Girl Lost, you find her and bring her to a Navajo hogan and laying her in a Navajo cradle you sing Uvavnuk's song to her. What's the reasoning here?

Elaborated for us in Hindu myth is the quite wonderful conception of Adityas and Danavas, releasers and restrainers. Eminent among the Danavas is a great dragon called Vritra. Hardly had the world come into existence when Vritra captured the waters and held them fast bound in his glittering coils. Indra, a great god and an Aditya, did battle with him. He won the day and in so doing he released the waters. Now again the earth flourished.

All too often our myths and our metaphors are Vritras to us. They are Vritras to eye and mind in us. They are Vritras to the source of life in us.

Think of one of the proverbs of Blake's hell: the cistern contains, the fountain overflows.

Berkeley, Blake and Black Elk are among the great Adityas of the modern Western world.

As Indra had, they have a fight on their hands.

Her myth is Vritra to Europa. His myth is Vritra to Prometheus. His story is Vritra to Noah. His romance is Vritra to Galahad.

The Aditya impulse is at work throughout this volume. Think for instance of how it attempts to release Theseus from our limiting image of him.

There is more to Europa than her abduction. She has it in her to undergo a re-birth and a re-education.

But why, you will ask, why in particular a Navajo education?

In a poem called 'Turkey-Cock', D.H. Lawrence looks Westward:

> Turkey-cock, turkey-cock,
> Are you the bird of the next dawn?
>
> Has the peacock had his day, does he call in vain, screecher,
> For the sun to rise?
> The eagle, the dove and the barnyard rooster, do they call in
> Vain, trying to wake the morrow?
> And do you await us, wattled father, Westward?
> Will your yell do it?

In the same poem, it being possible that 'the East [is] a dead letter and Europe moribund', he advises us to

> Take up the trail of the vanished American.

In this book it is assumed, with poetic licence, that in taking up the trail of the Native American we are also taking up the trail of our own Aurignacian ancestors. Beginning again after Gaia's collision with the iceberg, we find that we aren't wholly destitute. Our ancestral trail has brought us to a Navajo cradle, to a Blue Thunder tipi, to an Inuit medicine song, to the Oglala horsedance. It is assumed, again with poetic licence, that these elementary shaping shapes of culture belong to the Pleistocene, ancient and contemporary, indeed wherever and whenever it occurs. It is aboriginal ground here at home that we have come into. Here at home, now in our day, we can hear a Pleistocene song sung by a Pleistocene medicine woman in Altamira. Here at home, now in our day, a contemporary medicine man who is nevertheless Aurignacian can sit in a

Blue Thunder tipi in the Dordogne. Listening to the medicine song we know, sitting in Blue Thunder tipi we know, that neither Psalm eight nor the second stasimon is inevitable.

It is, in other words, a generating premise of this book that, after the collision, someone must dive to the floor of the abyss; after Auschwitz, Ta'doiko; after Hiroshima, the Navajo cradle and the Inuit medicine song. Inheriting these, we have as much maybe as Abraham had leaving Ur in the Chaldees or as Aeneas had leaving his burning town, or as Ishmael had, an ocean current carrying his raft out of the age of world's night. It might be that we will survive the collision, will also survive our Year One Reed.

If Narada comes bringing the ropesnake so will Jesus come bringing the Tenebrae harrow. Thinking of him as a culture hero, I have sometimes imagined him inaugurating a Tenebrae Temple ethos which, for as long as possible, will resist the impulse to be yet another civilization.

Are you doing what Plato did in The Republic? *Are you giving us the blueprint of a new socio-political order?*

No. It would never occur to me to design a society. What I am talking about is a ritual around which a people might religiously and culturally cohere. But this isn't designing. In Taoist terms, it is *wu wei* much more than it is *yu wei*.

What you have written is, however, vulnerable to the charge that it presumes to script-write history all the way to its denouement. Events didn't oblige Hegel's script or Marx's script. So why should we assume that they will oblige yours?

That's not how I understand what I've attempted to do. Very Western in their outlook, almost claustrophobically so, both Hegel and Marx believed there is such a thing as linear history. They believed that it is a pro-gression. They believed that this pro-gression is dialectical, a working out, in and through historical reality, of a succession of theses, antitheses and syntheses. For Hegel the denouement of all of this was the Prussian state, for Marx it was the stateless state that revolutionary, industrial workers would one day inaugurate.

How provincial of them to have assumed that our European way is paradigm.

How sinful of them to have projected a snake as hungry for human hearts as Aztec religion ever was into the rope.

And all of this in spite of Bacon's warnings about idols: idols of the tribe, the cave, the market-place and the theatre.

How gorged our idols are!

How gorged, as much in its secular as in its sacred form, is *heilsgeschichte*!

Oracularly, in his poem 'The Quaker Graveyard in Nantucket', Robert Lowell consoles us saying:

> The Lord survives the rainbow of his will.

He survives his biblical will as, after creating them, he communicated it to Adam and Eve; as, after the flood, he communicated it to Noah.

Not only does he survive it. In the Book of Job he reverses it. Job endures the reversal. In the deepest places of his psyche and soul he endures the crash of our civilization. In him it has crashed in its most fundamental assumptions and axioms. Questions this book asks are: what, walking away, will Job bring with him? And, given how rooted in us is our axiomatic opposition to it, can we hear his story?

Still reeling from the idea that our God might have survived our holy book, that the Divine might have survived all images of it in our smoking mirrors, I have myself opened the small gate to my own small yard to the one who comes riding a donkey. Religiously for me, the Triduum Sacrum is, in a phrase of Wallace Stevens, the fecund minimum. And, as I've already suggested, it might be that it is indeed the kind of minimum around which a people might organize themselves. I am thinking here of Pascal. Pascal distinguishes between a book accepted by a people and a book that creates a people. Could it be that, religiously and culturally, Tenebrae might yet be the strange attractor that we hear about in chaos theory? Could it be that, having Tenebrae, we have once again a centre that will hold?

Can we therefore conclude that you have written an old-fashioned, biblical Apocalypse? Or, in terms more resonant with Nordic myth: has the whole book been written with a moulted wing-quill of one of the Ragnarok cocks − with a wing-quill of Fjalar crowing from the cross-beam of a gibbet, or with a wing-quill of Rustred crowing at the bars of our ecological Hell-upon-Earth?

That isn't anything like the whole story, but there is, formally in the first volume, an apocalyptic calling to account. It occurs in a poem called 'Missa Tuba Mirum'.

> Tuba mirum spargens sonum
> Per sepulchra regionum
> Coget omnes ante thronum

Hebrews, Greeks and modern Europeans come before the throne. As founders, agents and carriers of a particular kind of civilization they come before it. The judgment is simple: we are off course. At the end of the poem we are back in the shamanic North, we are back in the Pleistocene. And yet, even though the church tower has become an igloo, even though the nave has become a raft, we are still not destitute. In the igloo a medicine woman sings a medicine song and on the raft there is someone who is willing to seek regeneration for all things on the floor of the Abyss. The Pleistocene means Pleistocene healing. It means a Navajo cradle for the new humanity. It means fire sent down not fire stolen. It means Wolf Collar's Blue Thunder tipi. It means Black Elk's theurgy. It means Black Elk, a Pleistocene thunder dreamer, praying for the Earth on a mountain peak in Paha Sapa. So yes, in some of its moods, the book is apocalyptically apprehensive. And that is why it wrestles at the foundations of Western civilization as a psychoanalyst such as Jung might wrestle at the foundations of an individual's psyche. Into ground no longer occupied by the old cultural assumptions and axioms there is an attempt to sow other myths, other metaphors – those, if you like, that A'noshma returns with.

Aeschulus also. He wrestled at foundations. And he tended to write trilogies. Is your trilogy a tribute? Does it attempt to continue his work?

I know that this will seem to contradict something I said in the Overture to the first volume, but I'll say it anyway: working our way into a flank of Golgotha, maybe we should chisel out a new Greek theatre in which to stage ourselves, in which to interrogate ourselves, all over again. I'm talking about an interrogation of ourselves as a species who have yet to evolve into evolutionary legitimacy.

Like Dionysus and his chorus of goatmen singing their goatsong, its beginnings could be, and maybe should be, primitive.

We could start with Jesus in Gethsemane. Jesus and a chorus of Grand Canyon seafloors. In song and in dance they suffer with him. In song and in dance they interpret and make visible his agony. In him and in them we see our inchoate but growing compatibility with the Earth as it so gloriously and ferociously is. In him and with him we acquire evolutionary legitimacy.

Are you saying that it is on the floor of the Grand Canyon, not on the moon or on Mars, that we will acquire it?

It is descending and ascending Bright Angel Trail that we will acquire it. It is because Bright Angel Trail brings us to what we have been, that it can bring us to what we will be. Bright Angel Trail is our way to the heart of the universe. The Good News is: Jesus has crossed the Torrent and that means Bright Angel Trail is aisle.

Am I right in assuming that this volume attempts to negotiate a way from the foundered Pequod *to a Navajo cradle?*

Yes, that among other things it attempts to do.

Are you not in this laying yourself open to the charge of romantic primitivism, of romantic faith in nature?

Looking at Christ in Gethsemane, I sense that we should evolve not from but with the Earth, not from but with Buddh Gaia.

Also, I in no wise intended to suggest that Uvavnuk's song and the Navajo cradle are the whole story.

The book ends at the door of a Tenebrae temple.

Emerging from that temple, some will say that Time isn't other than Turiya.

And there, although in another mode, we have it again, Uvavnuk's song.

Or should we say, Uvavnuk's Arctic Tao Te Ching.

If ever you are in Galway city, go to the Salmon Weir Bridge and you will see how, growing from its bed, the weeds flow and go with the little side-river.

A very unbiblical image, you might think, flourishing there between the Cathedral and the Mercy Convent.

But how unbiblical is it?

Recently, a friend of mine went to visit an old Taoist sage living on the steep side of a very high mountain in China. When Jesus was mentioned the old man smiled and, speaking from a mood of lovely and thankful recognition, he said, we think of him as a *wu wei* Master.

That said, we must of course insist that if Jesus was indeed a *wu wei* Master, it was in relation to a transcendent God not in relation to nature or to anything immanent in it that he was so.

Jesus wasn't a Taoist in the way that Chuang Tzu was, nor was he a Romantic poet in the way that the young Wordsworth was.

Uvavnuk wasn't an Arctic Lucy Gray. Arctic blizzards didn't mould her maiden form, but she did sing:

> The great sea has set me in motion,
> Set me adrift,

Moving me as the weed moves in a river.
The arch of sky and mightiness of storms
Have moved the spirit within me
Till I am carried away
Trembling with joy.

As metaphors of a way of being in the world, the Navajo cradle and the weed in the river aren't blind to all that is brutal and terrible in nature. Nor do they preclude prayerful recourse to the transcendent Divine.

Now, however, I feel I've conceded too much. So I will argue against myself.

Let me locate what I've been saying in its cultural context.

It was Whitehead's view that the last three centuries of European history and culture were provincial. That indeed is what he called them, the provincial centuries. To this I would add that Europe has been provincial not just in relation to cultures outside and beyond itself but also in relation to alternative possibilities of culture and growth within itself. Let me remind you of one such possibility. There were Stoics who believed in a *sumpatheia ton hollon* – a sympathy deep down in all things with all things.

So could it be that the antagonisms of the world aren't the full truth about the world? Could Wordsworth be right? Could there, deep down in their seemingly so separate natures, be a sympathy between Lucy Gray and the willow? Could there, in inner ground below ferocity and fear, be a sympathy between the leaping tiger and the tiring gazelle?

Presuming that it does exist, couldn't we live from that ground?

And how far are we now from the Navajo cradle?

How far are we now from Uvavnuk's song?

The consequence for our culture of being less inwardly provincial is evident: the shamanic north and the classical south are a twain that can meet. And when they do meet, as in some little way they do in this book, it won't only be the shamanic north that will have to cede ground.

Are we, in all of this, dealing with the old dialogue of body and soul? I am in particular thinking of the way Yeats and Marvell wrestled with the theme.

There are times when the dialogue is an agon. An agon between the Navajo cradle and the Christian cross, between Uvavnuk's song and Christ's cry of dereliction.

A night comes when, his eye glittering with new insight into his own story, the Ancient Mariner knocks on Lucy Gray's door. And there you have it, a new and a wiser preface to our lyrical reliance on nature.

The Mariner knows something Coleridge, his creator, never knew.

Have you imagined him, the Ancient Mariner I mean, have you imagined him walking through Uvavnuk's igloo door?

And there again, among combatants more evenly matched, you have it, the dialogue or *acallamh* of the Mariner and the Medicine Woman.

It is only on Easter morning, it seems to me, that the song and the cry are a rime.

Do you mean that they rime with each other or that they rime with how things are?

It is because they rime with how things are that they rime with each other. Towards the end of the rime there is only one song.

What I'm saying is this: when, returning from beyond the Torrent on Easter morning, Jesus sings it, then as it was in the beginning, it is one song. Only now it is altogether richer for having seemed for so long to have been two.

It isn't only once or twice that your text sings Uvavnuk's song for us. In the work as a whole repetition seems to be a structuring device. Is there justification for this?

It isn't by trying them on once in a shop that a new pair of boots will take on the shape of our feet or the shape of our walking. Similarly, it isn't in a single encounter with it that an unfamiliar idea will take on the shape of our seeing and knowing. Or better: it isn't in a single encounter with it that an unfamiliar idea will give new shape, new perceptive and cognitive shape, to our seeing and knowing. Particularly will this be so if the idea is subversively foreign to cultural and to personal predisposition.

Among wolves there are pack smells. Among cows there are herd smells. It isn't all at once and without challenge that such a smell is acquired. All the ideas, all the metaphors and tropes, and all the constituent parts of a book should have the herd smell or pack smell of that book. That a book should, in the literal sense, have such kindness among its parts is an essential aesthetic requirement. Think of the redactors who set themselves the task of giving to four distinct traditions that common, trans-individual ethos that we think of as biblical.

As with a book so with a culture. If new, challenging myths come into a culture, both the culture and the myths must be given a chance to adapt to each other, must be given a chance to acquire a new, common culture-smell. Otherwise, the new myths will be like animals in a zoo, fenced off from interaction with their environment. Another possibility of course is that the incoming myth will drive the indigenous myth underground.

Like a man intent on setting up the Christian Thousand-Year Reich, this is what Milton envisaged on the morning of Christ's nativity.

This book allows for a confrontation of myths, exotic and indigenous, and it fosters kindness, a growing into cultural kinship, among those that survive. Repetition in different contexts is a way of fostering such kindness. But this isn't the only nor most important reason for the repetition.

In intention, if not in achievement, this volume is liturgical not literary. It is a kind of cultural healing rite. Writing it, I had the Sings of the Navajo in mind. Sings are healing liturgies that go on, some of them, for nine nights. They aren't embarrassed, not in the least, by repetition. Indeed they rely on it for much of their effect and power. This they have in common with almost all liturgies, ancient and modern. To recite the Christian rosary in all its mysteries is to repeat the same pattern fifteen times. And it isn't only once in the course of the Mass that we will hear

> *Dominus vobiscum*
> *Et cum spiritu tuo.*

In this regard it would be instructive to read the hozhonji song in the body of the text. Equally instructive would be any session of shamanic healing in igloo, tipi, hogan or yurt.

Take the Maori story of origins as an example:

> Te Kore
> Te Kore-tua-tahi
> Te Kore-tua-rua –

I repeat these words as often as I do because I think of them as *hekau*, as words of power. In them is the hope of a new way of being in the world. In them is the birth of a world which by reason of its mode of emergence cannot but be hospitable to jnana yoga and Tenebrae. In them, speaking them backwards as sacredly as we speak them forwards, we seek to return divinely guided through night and void into the final exaltations that Sufis call *fana* and *baqa*.

It has been said that all art aspires to the condition of music. What I have written doesn't aspire to the condition of art but in its own proto-liturgical way it does now and then aspire to the condition of prayer, and in some of its moods prayer is incantation. Relevant, if only distantly in this regard, is something Ted Hughes has said:

Those Greek plays were close to liturgy. The gods and the underworld were still listening, and it was intended they should hear. And not only in ancient Greece, but all over the world, in all places, at all times, whenever men try to reach the ear of spirits, or of gods, or of God, they use incantatory speech. They abandon all workaday tones and inflections – without which we human beings can hardly understand each other – and resort to this more or less frenzied plainsong. As if those spirits had somehow let it be known that they will listen to nothing else. And this is inborn. We all discover it the moment we need to pray.

Think of this volume as the protoplasmic matrix out of which a European Sing might one day evolve. Already, it aspires to be the groundwork for a hozhonji song that will take us to Buddh Gaia. Encountering them in that context, the repetitions won't seem so noisome.

While your contemporaries travel by spaceship to the Moon and Mars you drift, longing for sacred sight of the sacred Earth, on a Maidu raft. Instead of giving wings to Icarus you weight A'noshma with a stone. Is it not a little like saying to the reptile, thus far and no further shall you evolve – into archaeornis you shall not evolve?

If, while I was in the womb, my umbilical cord had been cut, I would have been in trouble, wouldn't I? Similarly, if my connection with the Divine is severed, there is essential nourishment I am not getting and whether I acknowledge it or not I am in trouble, and in this condition it matters not at all whether I am adapted to how things are on the Earth, on the Moon or on Mars. In no matter what galaxy, indeed in no matter what universe, I am, I am in trouble, and a source of trouble to whatever environs me.

Of archaeornis and Icarus, or rather, of my attitude to them, I must ask: am I so excited by the plumage that I have forgotten the Mesozoic reptile in the singing or stooping bird?

In the hand is the fin. It is in it even when we are playing a piece by Mozart. And it is in the anguish of such self-awareness that we cross the Kedron.

For those who have crossed it, 'Gethsemane' and 'Golgotha' are big Darwinian words. But I should of course say, big post-Darwinian words, for although evolution has occurred and continues to occur, it hasn't occurred nor does it continue to occur only for the reasons that Darwin elaborated. As Australian Aborigines who have remained in touch with the Dreamtime know: fantasy fathers fact. And to make ourselves available to Dreamtime is to make ourselves available to evolution.

Even if his wings are genetically engineered, Icarus will still be impious, a freak who has separated himself from the whole. Modern humanity is increasingly freakish. And what is freakish does not survive.

I sometimes imagine it: Ishmael, our most recent Deucalion, returns to the Whaleman's Chapel. Invited to preach the sermon, he stands there, bleeding lance in hand, and says just that: what is freakish does not survive.

Heidegger says that in the age of the world's night someone must endure the abyss.

For purely human reasons, indeed for selfish reasons, Gilgamesh endured it and, as we would expect, he lost.

For universal reasons, Jesus crossed the Kedron and, as A'noshma Jesu, he endured it, and with him there came ashore a new way of seeing and being in the world. That way of being and seeing this book would promote.

But the diver myth is a myth, and isn't it therefore odd that you give it such a generative role in a book which attempts to grow into a truth?

Utnapishtim, Narada, Job, Jonah, Jesus, Julian of Norwich, Marguerite Porete and Teresa of Avila – they and the tremendous transitions they underwent are as real and inevitable as the more visible, more common, more expected transitions of birth, puberty and death.

Freud, bless his heart, didn't see much farther than Oedipus, Narcissus and the socially and economically successful person in whom, for the sake of pulling together, ego and id have buried the hatchet.

I think of Turtle's longing for worldly ground as the re-emergent phase of the Narada initiation.

Turtle was gone a long time. So long was he gone that by the time he returned bringing with him the seed or source intuitions of a world he could come ashore on – so long for all our sakes did he endure the abyss that he was covered, coming back, in green slime.

I imagine that as it dried out the slime shrivelled and shrank into a *mahavakya*, a permanent watermark in the inner and outer armature of his epistemological naive realism:

> *Yatra na anyat pasyati, na anyat srinoti,*
> *na anyad vijanati, sa bhuma.*

In other words, Turtle's experience of being grounded in and by a world was at best only provisional. A day would come when, as Narada did, he would hear the great question: did you bring the water?

I think of Descartes, Hume and Kant.

I think of Coleridge in dejection, of Arnold on Dover Beach and of Stevens in Key West.

Three philosophers and three poets. Their collective name is Ahab. And being who he desperately is, seeking most desperately to recover his dignity, Ahab will stake everything on the diluvian deed. Epistemologically dismasted he might be, but he will harpoon the world-mirage, he will harpoon the snake in the rope.

We have, I believe, integrated our Copernican revolution in astronomy altogether more successfully than we have integrated our Copernican revolution in epistemology.

Is Ahab dismasted humanity dismasted? Have we been possessed by Ahab's naught? Have we been possessed by a kind of *nacht und nebel* nihilism? Is the wake of the *Pequod* the wake of our culture? Have we sailed already through the Sunda Straits? And if so, for how long more can we refuse the terrible medicine of a walk with Vishnu? For how long more can we refuse the Narada initiation? For how long more can the Tenebrae harrow not be our astrolabe in the night where no stars shine?

If the voyage of the *Pequod* is in any sense an analogue of Western culture since Descartes, then, simplifying things, a future Hegel or Spengler or Marx might be able to declare: like the story of the famous whale ship the story of the modern West is the story of a tragically mislived insight:

All visible objects, man, are but as pasteboard masks.

Ahab didn't know Brahman. Nor did he know that the stupendous world that masks Brahman is also Brahman.

As for the implication in your question that myths are untrue. Certain it is that there are persons who endure the abyss. But the abyss isn't an abyss of waters. And it isn't godless.

Coming home at last to Noah in his ark the raven calls out

Tehom is Turiya

In the Ground of our being there is no enduring. There is only the One. Or should I say, in the Ground that grounds our being there is no enduring, there is only the One.

To call Jesus A'noshma Jesu is not, I believe, to falsely name him.

Is this the mythus that Carlyle called for? The myth that would clothe or reimagine the divine spirit in Christianity and make it religiously available to our perishing souls?

If only by way of initial or tactical concession to sceptical rationalists, maybe Carlyle was right to keep open or reopen a distinction between myth and matter-of-fact in Christianity. As I understand it, Christianity has its origin in experiential matter-of-fact – in the Gethsemane experience, the Golgotha-Borobudur experience and the Anodos or Easter experience, and just as it would be a poverty in our lives not to undergo puberty so would it be a poverty, altogether greater, not to undergo our transtorrentem evolution.

As experiential matter-of-fact, the Triduum Sacrum is as invulnerable as puberty is to rationalist attack by Voltaire, to Dionysian, instinctive attack by Nietzsche.

If, in imitation of Jesus crossing the Kedron, Dionysus decided to cross the Ilissus, and if, desiring to have someone to watch with him, he asked Nietzsche to drop his thyrsus and fawnskin and cross it with him, I think that by cockcrow next morning the philologists' bluff might well have been called. And as for Voltaire – well, his waistcoat didn't turn out to be as surprising as Pascal's.

Once we've established what is matter-of-fact in Christianity, then we can open a world-wide door in it to whatever shepherds' lantern might illuminate it for us.

Myths illuminate no less than lanterns do. And among the myths that will help us to articulate the Gethsemane experience will be those which are, in Jung's phrase, self-portraits of the instincts.

But, to cross from the Gethsemane phase to the Golgotha phase of the Triduum Sacrum is to cross from myth to mahavakya. In Tenebrae our myths and our lamps and our lanterns are quenched. As the Kena Upanishad has it:

There goes neither the eye nor speech nor the mind; we know it not; nor do we see how to teach one about it. Different it is from all that is known, and beyond the unknown it also is.

The Gethsemane phase of the Triduum Sacrum is an evolution, the Golgotha phase is an involution. On Golgotha the psychic pleroma of Gethsemane finds itself looking down into its own empty skull. We are carried back not just to psychic but to cosmic beginnings. And that's why, from the outset, this second volume so concerns itself with beginnings. That's why it rehearses so many stories of origin, among them the diver myth.

It isn't only among Native Americans that the diver myth is found. Different versions of it are widespread among the peoples of north-eastern Asia. And who knows! It might have been told by a campfire in the Aurignacian Dordogne.

This is how the Yenisei Ostyaks know it and tell it: in the beginning there was only water, and hovering above it, accompanied by swans, geese, ducks, loons and other water-birds, was the Great Shaman Doh. Thinking that it would be good if there was land for him to come down and walk on and rest on, he asked diverbird to bring him soil from the floor of the abyss. Diverbird dove but after a long, long time came back with nothing. He dove again and, from the morsel of mud he eventually returned with, Doh made the Earth, a great island in the midst of the waters.

Like Great Shaman Doh and the waterbirds, modern humanity hovers above the Earth. We are losing contact with it. But unless we are to go the way of the dinosaurs we must come down and set foot, set descending finfoot, on Bright Angel Trail. If we wish, we can be lungfish not just to another stage of evolution but to release from evolution.

Are you saying that a hitherto unheard-of angel, an angel called Bright Angel, has drawn near? If you are, there are questions of some importance that need to be asked. Given that it is on the floor of the Grand Canyon that the encounter must take place, who among us is able for it? Are we as little able for his brightness, as little able for a new phase of evangelization, as we were when it was Gabriel who approached?

Often when I think of Michelangelo's *Mouscron Madonna* I wonder what he felt and thought as he saw the new face of the Mother of God emerging from the stone. Like Mary herself in the presence of the announcing Angel, were there days when he was afraid? Did he sometimes think that a presence so heavenly might emerge that neither he nor we would be able for it? Were there days when he felt like Actaeon? Were there nights when he dreamed that he was a deer, howled at hugely, and then hunted down by his hounds?

And when he began to catch glimpses of the angel's face, of the angel's presence, in the *Virgin of the Rocks*, did Leonardo feel he had trespassed? Did he feel he had crossed a threshold too many? Thinking of the smouldering fire in ancient Thebes, did he sometimes fear that he had uncovered a realm that should always be hidden, always be out of bounds, to beings who are still incarnate? Even while he was still painting Mona and the background to Mona, were there days when he prayed and nights when he prayed that God would be merciful, would re-create him like others, would restore in him the veils of protective blindness?

The God of the Bible was kinder, wasn't he? He only called into being as much as we would be able for. But no, because that's the old flawed view, the view that makes Man measure and master of the created world. As we know, God tested Job in this regard and Job, the representative human, was found wanting. And Blake was sure:

The roaring of lions, the howling of wolves, the raging of the stormy sea and the destructive sword are portions of eternity too great for the mind of man.

It might indeed be that God's creative bounty has overflowed his mercy. And here we might recall that Hindus describe the origin of all things as a *sristi,* a pouring forth. The pouring forth of more than Arjuna was easily able for in Kurukshetra.

Arjuna and Job.

And Michelangelo? Was Michelangelo an Actaeon who painted his own portrait on his own flayed skin? And was that the price he had to pay for having lived so long with the seeing sibyls? For having seen what they saw?

It's hard, isn't it, to blame Mona Lisa for turning her back on it all. But that of course is a superficial way of seeing her.

She is the sibyl of what's behind her.

And for as long as she sits there, mystifying us, she protects us from too naked a vision of what's behind her. She makes what's behind her partially bearable.

Viewed against what's behind her, viewed against what's behind the Virgin in *The Virgin of the Rocks*, much of European history is an impertinence

These paintings are immense openings in our European Great Wall. Openings Marco Polo didn't walk through, Columbus didn't sail through.

In the backgrounds of these paintings, art anticipates history. Or should I say, looking at these backgrounds, it is obvious that history has yet to catch up with art, and when in this case it does, if it does, it might be run down by its own hounds.

Leonardo has opened the way to Canyon Country, and when we cross into it, if we cross into it, our only hope is that Bright Angel, the Angel of the place, will welcome us, will walk with us.

So the answer to your question is yes. I do sometimes think that a hitherto unheard-of angel is waiting, that a hitherto unseen face of God is emerging.

But here we must ask: who will bear the first, stupendous impact of the revelation? And how much of our Bible and how much of our religion will survive it?

As regards who will bear it, all I can say is what a Christian might say: once already, in the person of Jesus Transtorrentem, God himself has been our Actaeon, our Semele.

Hindus tell a story: once upon a time the earth was sorely afflicted by drought. There was wailing. Wailing for the corn that didn't sprout, for the rice that didn't strike root. Wailing by people too weak to perform the linga-sharira for their dead. Bhagiratha was a good and pious king. Leaving his dominions in charge of his chief minister, he walked out across the cracked earth. He built four fires in the four directions and sitting in the midst of them he practised the most frightful austerities, hoping in this way to win the favour of one of the Great Gods. The sun that sucked all moisture out of lizards' eggs sucked him dry, and at last, when his last delirium was crumbling, Brahma, the Great God, approached. Bhagiratha's request was as boundless as the famine: would it please his Divine Majesty to let Ganga, the heavenly river, descend and flow across the burning earth. Brahma reminded the fierce but pious ascetic that the unimpeded descent upon it of such a wide and mighty river would shatter the earth. Maybe, however, there was a way. Maybe the god Shiva could be persuaded to emerge from his yogic introversion high in the Himalyas and take the impact of the descent upon his head and shoulders. Bhagiratha resumed his austerities. In the end he was little more than a mirage of mantras:

> Shivo'ham
> Bhairavo'ham
> Sa'ham
>
> Shivo'ham
> Bhairavo'ham
> Sa'ham

Shiva acceded. And so it was. And so it is. Continuously now, coming down to us from on high, we have here on Earth a heavenly river. A medicine river.

Though he stood between heaven and earth, mediating, not a hair of Shiva's head was hurt. Jesus on the other hand was very badly damaged. And now again, in what looks like a collapsed Cumaean cave in Canyon Country, the angel is pointing to the Baptist who is looking towards Jesus.

And listening on behalf of a humanity that is hard of hearing, hard of spiritual hearing, maybe the angel can already hear a voice crying in that wilderness of geological sikharas that we see through the opening.

Could it be that there is a depth of nature that yearns with us, prays with us?

Could it be that we will come to the Kedron-Colorado?

Could it be that we will survive the impact?

Could it be that we are ready for Bright Angel?

Your text bristles with exotic words, among them the mantra you have just quoted. What are you up to? Are you showing off?

It is likely that a person who seriously sets out to study genetics will be willing to encounter and acquire a new vocabulary. If they are lucky, young people undergoing puberty will also acquire new words. In their case the words they acquire will help them to name what is happening to them. Although our culture of *yu wei* works and days will neither acknowledge, or accommodate them, there are puberties of spirit as well as puberties of body and mind. There is the Gethsemane experience and the Golgotha experience. There is an *itinerarium transmentem in Deo*. In Europe nowadays, persons caught up in such evolutions and egressions are unlikely to find a naming and enabling language immediately to hand. Like King Lear, they are out of doors. Mythically and verbally, they are out of doors. Little wonder if, in their destitution, they take shelter where they can. In igloo or tipi or hogan. In mosque or Amazonian myth. In the East Pagoda Hall of a Green Dragon Temple. In the neglected or rejected wisdom of their own culture. Nietzsche was acutely aware of such destitution among us:

Let us think of a culture that has no fixed and sacred site but is doomed to exhaust all possibilities and to nourish itself wretchedly on all other cultures – there we have the present age, the result of that Socratism which is bent on the destruction of myth. And now the mythless man stands eternally hungry, surrounded by all past ages, and digs and grubs for roots, even if he has to dig for them among the remotest antiquities.

So, yes, there are exotic words in the text. But they aren't there as a display of learning. They are there for the same reason that Indian meal was in Ireland during the famine. And it might be no harm to remember that during the sixteenth and later centuries not a few outlandish plants, among them the potato, were naturalized in Europe. This book does attempt to naturalize some of the mahavakyas and myths that Turtle brought back from the floor of the Abyss, that our Argonauts brought home from Outre Mere. It attempts to naturalize an exotic diagnosis of what ails us. It attempts to naturalize much that was once indigenous. The most exotic of the things it would naturalize is the Triduum Sacrum, is the Tenebrae harrow, and to do this it is glad of any helpful word that any Marco Polo will bring back from anywhere in the world. Spiritually, our condition brings Caliban to mind. Caliban is a landfish. And he is languageless. I am not unaware of how culturally amphibious the book is. I am sure that it does at times give the impression of being a disorganized Musée de l'Homme. But could it be, as Nietzsche divined, that that is how we are. In our Waste Land, is that how we are? En Attendant Godot, is that how we are?

And there is one further thing I'd like to say. Many of the words that I borrow are technical words. In the traditions from which they derive

they have, many of them, a sacredly exact meaning. Also, they aren't
words that are likely to be widely used in popular speech or in the popular press and lexically therefore they are reliable, even durable. They help
to stabilize a text and to protect it from misinterpretation.

And as for the myths that I've imported, I think of them as Magna
Cartas, inspiring, permitting and fostering a new way of being in the
world, enabling us, for instance, to welcome the Lord of Life who, on a
hot Sicilian day, comes to drink at our well. This surely is necessary
among a people in whose cultural assumptions and axioms lie the seeds of
ecological havoc. It wouldn't, I think, be altogether irresponsible to suggest that European culture must now run the risk of loosing its moorings
to the ancient Mediterranean – to Hebrew prophecy, Greek philosophy
and Roman law – in so far as we have thought of them as the normative
perspective within which we have for so long attempted to organize ourselves and our world. I'm not talking about an exodus away from our past.
I'm talking about not being deaf to the crakynge and cryynge of Pente-
costal thunder. I'm talking about a journey to Medicine River. I'm talking about a Pleistocene thunder dreamer praying on a peak in Paha Sapa.
I'm talking about Black Elk's restorative stroke redeeming the Earth from
the effect upon it of the Lascauvian stroke. I'm talking about a healing
backwards and well as forwards from the Triduum Sacrum. I'm talking
about a healing that has happened at the origins of Western consciousness.
It isn't always in indigenous ritual, myth and metaphor that we will inherit
that healing. It isn't always passively that we will inherit it. Some there are
who, like Jacob, will walk away lamed from the wrestling. Old indoctri-
nations, particularly when they have become habits of eye and mind, tend
to have a lot of pride in them, and fight in them, and never more so than
when their hegemony in us is threatened. To know this, even more dev-
astatingly than he did awake, Job had only to seek comfort in sleep. So no.
We shouldn't let words like Gethsemane and Golgotha fall into disuse.
Not yet. Not at this stage of our evolution. Rather should we try to naturalize them in ritual, myth and metaphor, whatever their provenance.
Hagia Sophia and Chartres Cathedral and all the rituals enacted within
them notwithstanding, European Christianity hasn't yet housed the
Triduum Sacrum. Maybe there is no religion that can. And yet how wonderful an attempt Tenebrae is. Religiously in Tenebrae we overcome the
linguistic and ethnic diversification of Babel. So how, in that context,
could the sacred words of other peoples sound like jargon? On the contrary, they are marvels of our mother tongue.

You have just mentioned Black Elk. Him and his vision you have also attempted to naturalize. But can it be done? Industrialized as we are, can we culturally integrate the healing ministrations, however heavenly, of a Pleistocene thunder dreamer?

Walking into Altamira or Lascaux, we see that Europe was once a vast Serengeti. How geographically vast it was we do not know, but the impression we come away with is that it teemed with wild animals. Stroke by stroke we wiped them out. That accumulation of strokes was a dolorous stroke. As dolorous in every way as the dolorous stroke we see in the pit in Lascaux. We built Europa's Europe above that pit, above that stroke. All over again, it is Minoan Crete built above a labyrinth. A labyrinth in which is impounded that in ourselves which we cannot accept or be hospitable to. What I'm saying is, I'm not at all sure that Europa's Europe is a good idea. Also, but not without trepidation, I believe it has run its course. The book is hospitable to Black Elk and his vision because with him, he being a Pleistocene medicine man, we can go down into our labyrinth and with his restorative stroke heal our dolorous stroke. Where Theseus merely intensified our trouble, making it more malignant, Black Elk resolves it and, in so doing, our sick or poisoned Dordogne becomes our Pleistocene Tongue River, and – this is stretching it, but I will stretch it – in so doing he has mystically revived and recalled our lost Serengeti. And now again, as if our ghost dance had succeeded, the herds are back. Now again we can live in the Great Memory with them. Now again, walking into our dreams, Rhinoceros and Birdman and Bull will leave their medicine bundles. Now again, the good will of all things coming with us, we can come forward into culture. And so, empowered as he was by the heavens, we can of course be healed by the healing ministrations of a Pleistocene thunder dreamer. If an individual is healed by them, if, returning to the primal world, some Job or other is healed by them, then in a sense the group is healed by them. Then psychically, if not yet culturally, the group has integrated them. Then, whether we know it yet or not, Tsetsekia has replaced the labyrinth. And, in a way that we previously didn't have, we have a chance. And, come to think of it, a Tsetsekia of sorts has already been enacted: in four great engravings by Picasso, a little girl with flowers in her arm, or with a dove in her arm, is leading the blind Minotaur among us. Where else but to Pasiphae's calving-ground is she leading him? Where else but there have we most need of the hospitalities of Kwakiutl firelight?

Who is she, the little girl? Is she a Virgil who guides us through our Underworld? Or is she a Beatrice who leads us to Paradise?

I call her Marie Therese, but only because Picasso gave her the profile of a woman of that name, a woman he loved.

More important than who she is is what she does. By leading the Minotaur back into our world, she, the child, reintroduces the theranthropic among us, not just as a category, but as a phenomenon, of consciousness and culture.

A way it is of making other Guernicas a little less inevitable.

How terrible to think that she might herself be another Kore, that she might herself be another *Femme Torero*, outcrops of buttock, breast and head in a destructive tangle of bull, woman and horse.

And yet there she is, a child with flowers in her arm or with a dove in her arm and in this, Picasso's image of her, she has in some sense harrowed our hell.

The classical world, the modern world, civilization of no matter what kind or where, is safer for what she is doing.

And yes, she has Pasiphae's calving-ground in mind, and there she will go leading the blind Bullman.

But don't be surprised if, their purpose there accomplished, they again take to the roads one morning.

Another Antigone she, she will walk with him all the way to Colonus. And if Colonus cannot cope with them, they will sit and wait for Christianity.

Their coming is crisis not just for Classical but for Christian culture.

Even when the Grove of the Erinyes has become the Garden of Olives, there will still be a question: Is the Christianity that is able for the Minotaur able for Marie Therese?

The next time she comes among us it might be the script and score of a new and purely mystical Tenebrae she will be carrying in her arm. She will in other words be challenging us to cross into Evangelanta.

Tsetsekia over ground might well replace the labyrinth under ground, but what of the Whaleman's Chapel? What of whatever in Christianity is charter myth to it? What theses, if any, might a Christian Antigone nail to its door?

Robert Lowell has prayed at that door:

> ... Hide
> Our steel, Jonas Messias, in thy side.

Going beyond what Lowell intended, we can think of that steel as the lance with which we have pierced every Presence of God that came to help us, among them Taurus Dei, Albatross Dei, Agnus Dei and Cetus Dei.

Would you nail your own book to that door?

In the last century the skin of a sperm whale's penis was chasuble and cassock to us in our Whaleman's nave.

In this century, we have softened the light of our spermaceti candle with a Nazi lampshade.

And, for centuries now, so total and so deadly has been our assault on the natural world that it wouldn't be at all fantastic to claim that we must have been drinking Ahab's grog, drinking it in a deadly *Pequod* carouse from our harpoons' sockets. We need something altogether more deeply redemptive than yet another Christian Reformation, than yet another French or Russian Revolution. We need to undergo the Great Evolutionary Egressus:

> *Et egressus est Jesus cum discipulis suis*
> *trans torrentem Cedron* (John 18:1).

And now I am in trouble. Can I tell you why?

In naming it, I have given verbal existence to the Great Transgression. As we talked about the lance with which we have pierced every Presence of God in the world, it occurred to me, to say that the socket of that lance was the chalice in Ahab's eucharist, but I pulled back, fearing the many and terrible consequences of giving something so awful a name. A sense I have is that we have transgressed greatly and the ceremony on board the *Pequod* is the image of an energy at work in our world. And I thought that by naming it we might see it, and seeing it, pray:

Save us, God, from the great transgression.

And save everything I've said from wicked misuse. May any wicked energy that I have ever named be less effective and less real for the fact that it has been named.

Is it not when it has no name that evil among us is least opposed?

Having *Moby-Dick*, we have at last a book that successfully alerts us to the peril of our condition. It alerts us not just to the peril of our cultural assumptions and axioms, they being our real harpoons. More ominously, it alerts us to inherent peril – the peril consequent in and upon the kind of beings we are:

For with little external to constrain us, the innermost necessities in our being, these still drive us on.

On and on. On and into Titanic tolma such as the singers of a stasimon on the Greek tragic stage could never have imagined, let alone foreseen.

We have crossed the Cimmerrian shadow line Greek myths stopped short at. In piety and terror stopped short. As far as this shadow line and no farther come the screams of the Caucasus eagle, come the bellowings of the Minotaur.

Somewhere within ourselves we have left the wine-dark sea for the grog-dark ocean and here we are living, and being lived by, Titanic tolma.

In Man is all whatsoever the Sun shines upon or Heaven contains, as are also Hell and all the Deeps.

And there he is now, the creature Sir Thomas Browne called that little compendium of the sixth day:

He's a queer man, Captain Ahab – so some think – but a good one. Oh, thou'lt like him well enough; no fear, no fear. He's a grand ungodly god-like man, Captain Ahab; doesn't speak much; but, when he does speak, then you may well listen. Mark ye, be forewarned; Ahab's above the common; Ahab's been in colleges, as well as 'mong the cannibals, been used to deeper wonders than the waves; fixed his fiery lance in mightier, stranger foes than whales. His lance! Aye, the keenest and the surest that, out of all our isle!

Two fiery lances, Ahab's and Black Elk's. Can't you see why the Sacred Powers of the Isle intervened? Can't you see why they took it upon themselves to replace our intentions with their intentions, our lance with their lance? Can't you see why they replaced the lance that caused the Waste Land with the lance that redeemed it? Can't you see why they replaced Ahab's diabolically baptized harpoon with Black Elk's spear, the Excalibur of a new civilization? Its correlative in Irish myth is *an tsleg boi ac Lug*, and the last person to hurl it in Ireland was Bishop Berkeley. This he did when he wrote the famous paragraph beginning, 'It is indeed an opinion strangely prevailing amongst men …' Epistemologically, Berkeley was our Vritrahan. Naive realism was the Vritra he slew. And this means that Ahab's pursuit of Moby wasn't only tragic. It was uselessly so. We had already reached safe haven. Or the way to safe haven was open.

Sad to say, the phantom laugh from the hold notwithstanding, the old doomed voyage goes on.

Look at him! There on board the *Pequod*! He is the mincer. And he is eponymous. Dressed in his black cassock, he is hectically at work, spading out 'Bible leaves' of whale blubber.

Our new Apocalypse, those 'Bible leaves', say only one thing: our New World journey from the high platform of the Pyramid of the Sun in Tenochtitlan to the not-so-high quarter-deck of the *Pequod* in the La Plata whaling ground is degradation not progression.

Little wonder that, rounding the Cape of Good Hope, sea ravens in the rigging announce our Year One Reed.

But we sail on.

Claiming Yahweh and Yojo as whalemen, we sail on.

The man in the cassock sharpens his spade.

Too momentary, both of them, to catch our attention, we don't hear the laugh from the hold or even so much as notice the sudden preternatural slackness in the sails.

But portents don't need to be preternatural. The man in the cassock, he is natural, he will do, because here – on the deck of the *Pequod* I mean – here is no sacred intention such as motivated the Aztec priest who, during the harvest liturgy, dressed himself in the skin of a young girl, she being the sacrificed surrogate of Chicomecohuatl, the Maize Goddess.

Here, Theban elders, is tolma.

Here, Prometheus, is the Great Transgression, yours and ours.

And it might well quench our galaxy.

But we have a book. And it questions us: What have ye shipped for?

Given that Western civilization is your ship, what is it ye have shipped for?

To slay Tiamat?

To break the heads of Leviathan in the waters?

To harpoon the snake we've projected into the rope?

To wound the universe?

To hear Gaia's last call?

To hear Gaia calling out, 'Bury my heart at Wounded Knee?'

Save us, God.

Tell us that our image of you isn't you.

Here in New Canaan we are still in Egypt.

Here in Salem our Egypt is what it always was:

Our Smoking Mirror.

It came in the *Mayflower* with us. It boarded the *Pequod* in us. We might have set foot on Plymouth Rock but we haven't set foot on a New World. Given the smoke in our eyes and minds, how could we? The Quest continues. The Good News is, Bright Angel is waiting. And the cradle is made.

No *vita nuova* no New World. Not here on Earth. Not elsewhere in our galaxy.

So our quest for a New World is a quest for a new way of being in the world we are already in. But given that the place of entry into that way of being in the world is no longer Plymouth Rock but the beach at Punta Alta, how likely is it that our quest can succeed?

I feel sure that Hölderlin is right when he says:

> Where the danger is, there
> Grows also what saves.

As I've already suggested, it isn't only that Bright Angel is waiting. A new face of God – Goddess and God – is emerging.

Like Simeon now is the poet who sang in the destitute time. Soon, having seen, he will sing his *Nunc Dimittis*.

According to the medieval story, it was a dolorous stroke that turned a whole kingdom into a Waste Land. Reviving the concept, which you do in your work, is surely not helpful, because whatever reality they may have as determinants in the privacy of your psyche, a speared bull, a harpooned whale or an albatross shot cannot be shown to be objective determinants in objective history. Isn't history therefore your Rorschach inkblot?

Not everyone will agree that

> We are the hollow men
> We are the stuffed men.

Not everyone will agree that

> Our dried voices, when
> We whisper together,
> Are quiet and meaningless
> As wind in dry grass
> Or rats' feet over broken glass
> In our dry cellar.

But, the stroke that turned the world into *res extensa* was indeed dolorous, and it is therefore an assumption in this book that we have come into a Cartesian desert of Zin:

Then came the children of Israel, even the whole congregation, into the desert of Zin in the first month: and the people abode in Kadesh: and Miriam died there, and was buried there. And there was no water for the congregation: and they gathered themselves together against Moses and against Aaron. And the people chode with Moses, and spake, saying, would God that we had died when our brethren died before the Lord! And why have ye brought up the congregation of the Lord into this wilderness, that we and our cattle should die there? And wherefore have ye made us to come up out of Egypt, to bring us in unto this evil place: it is no place of seed or of figs or of vines or of pomegranates; neither is there any water to drink. And Moses and Aaron went from the presence of the assembly unto the door of the tabernacle of the congregation, and they fell upon their faces: and the glory of the Lord appeared unto them. And the Lord spoke unto Moses, saying, take the rod and gather thou the assembly together, thou, and Aaron, thy brother, and speak ye unto the rock before their eyes: and it shall give forth his water, and thou shalt bring forth to them water out of the rock: so thou shalt give the congregation and their beasts drink. And Moses took the rod from before the Lord, as he commanded him. And Moses and Aaron gathered the congregation together before the rock, and he said unto them, hear ye now, ye rebels; must we fetch you water out of this rock? And Moses lifted up his hand, and with his rod he smote the rock twice: and the water came out abundantly, and the congregation drank, and their beasts also.

With a spear whose head was sharp lightning, Black Elk has released the waters in our day. An Arctic shaman has gone down to the floor of *Anima Mundi* and combed our sins against this great and sacred Earth out of Takanakapsaluk's hair. With a comb of walrus ivory he has combed them out and now again, walking through the house-high hay, you can sleep tonight in Fern Hill and when the owls and the nightjars carry the farm away and you with it, it will be good to go, and it will be good to come back into that eternal, marvellous morning when, like spellbound horses coming out of a stable, the galaxies come out, singly come out, in constellations come out, onto the fields of praise.

We have reached Ta'doiko.

What I'm saying is this: a concept you have difficulty with might have its uses – might have them even in our efforts to make sense of modern European history. To see that history as a desert journey from Descartes's dolorous stroke to Black Elk's restorative stroke is not of course to discover order but to impose it. And in doing this I am no less guilty than the Yahwist, the Elohist and the Deuteronomist. Than Vico, Hegel, Marx and Spengler. I am not, I am aware, doing anything remotely comparable in scale to what they did. I only wish to acknowledge that some of the bad habits they had, I have. And living this side of Auschwitz, I must not forget that, like the Canaanite God of Death, *heilsgeschichte* has a maw with which it has swallowed millions, among them Hivites, Jebusites, the *Pequod*, the Maidu, Tartars and Jews. But I nonetheless feel that there should still be a place for such vatic historians as Vyasa and Blake. There is a vast difference between the polymath and the bathymath – between someone who knows a lot about a lot of things and someone who knows one thing profoundly, namely human inwardness. And here I advert to something Yeats said:

There is only one history, and that is the soul's.

Draupadi, Kunti, Karna, Drona, Arjuna, Krishna and Yudishtira belong here. As do Los, Orc, Urizen, Oothoon, Vala and Thel. This book assumes that the Maymed Kynge belongs here. And if he does, so does Camelot, Chapel Perilous, Chateau Merveil, Liz de la Mervoille, the journey alone in winter through the wilderness of Wirral, Wodwo and, ever nearer as I ride, the sounds, grating and harsh, of a decapitating axe being sharpened.

> Here belong birdman and bull.
> Here belong Navajo cradle and Blue Thunder tipi.
> Here in the hush of an October evening you will
> Hear the roaring of Medicine River.

It's a long history, the history of the soul.

Think of Nietzsche's discoveries.

Think of the grace that brings us through.

Think of the night we cross from Mabinogion to mahavakya, from Gorsedd Arberth to Golgotha.

Think of God's final favours – *fana* and *baqa*.

Continuing, if that's what I'm doing, to address your question, there is one last thing I would like to say. I suggested in the first volume that Christ's wounds are wounds from within not from without. Being the wounds we inflicted on Tiamat in the beginning, and our ability to keep all memory of them out of sight and suppressed having failed, they emerged, as with a vengeance, on Good Friday, and stigmatized him.

An implication in that suggestion is that psychic determinants, be they collective or individual, are often also determinants in objective history.

Geomantically, if not geographically, Chartres is built above the pit in Lascaux.

But, in the apse above the pit, in the Charlemagne window, the lances have leafed.

And that too is an event in the history of the human soul. Could it be that Christianity itself might be ready to exchange *heilsgeschichte's* harpoon for a Tenebrae harrow?

Bringing the Tenebrae harrow with us, we might with some hope cross into the next millennium.

There are indeed rituals that create a people.

Can the apse redeem the pit?

Here we are talking not about the pit in general but about the pit in Lascaux. And about it, at this stage, there is only this that I want to say: going down into it from Cartesian Europe, and passing the lost herds of our lost Serengeti on the way, it is difficult not to conclude that, physically and philosophically, we are the species of the dolorous stroke. On the deck of the *Pequod* we are back in that pit. It matters hardly at all whether it is Taurus Dei we have speared or Cetus Dei we have harpooned. The consequences are identical. And that is why, in the third volume of this book, I give space to the Sioux and the Blackfoot to enact the remedy, this being the reinstitution among us of commonage consciousness. That done, we can, with more hope, reascend to the apse where the lances have leafed. Or efflored.

> Fragrance of flowering lances in Chartres
> Fragrance of flowering lances in Lascaux
> Fragrance of flowering lances in Esagila
> Fragrance of flowering lances in the temple of Apollo at Delphi
> Fragrance of flowering lances in the Groves of Baal
> Fragrance of flowering lances in the temple of Solomon
> Fragrance of flowering lances in the Spouter Inn
> Fragrance of flowering lances in the Whaleman's Chapel
> Fragrance of flowering lances on the quarter-deck of the *Pequod*

In the pit in Lascaux where it first started bleeding, the bleeding lance no longer bleeds.

And, though we didn't have a vision of the Grail as Grail, the whyght samyte did fall from our eyes:

It was while gliding through these latter waters that one serene and moonlight night, when all the waves rolled by like scrolls of silver; and by their soft, suffusing seethings, made what seemed a silvery silence, not a solitude: on such a silent night a silvery jet was seen far in advance of the white bubbles at the bow. Lit up by the moon, it looked celestial; seemed some plumed and glittering god uprising from the sea.

It is something we might do. We might carve this vision of Cetus Sundara Murti on the door of our Whaleman's Chapel. And, as we do it, we mustn't be surprised if, far out on the abyss where the *Pequod* went down, we hear Tiamat singing the Mandukya Om, for what else but Nada Brahma, what else but a blossoming of Nada Brahma into an oratorio, what else but that is this universe of wonders and stars we are sometimes so tragically at odds with?

First it was the Maidu, then the Maori and now the Hindu story of origins. Which of them have you settled for?

In the way that Abraham left Ur of the Chaldees, this book leaves the Middle East and, thereafter for a long while, it is culturally nomadic. Abraham's belief in the promises of the God who called him sustains him in his wanderings. The Wandering Aramaean, or the Syrian ready to perish, in this book is sustained by his belief in the Triduum Sacrum. Having this belief, he sits by many campfires, he sits in their beginnings with many peoples. And it isn't only once or twice or three times that he walks away enriched. It isn't only once or twice or three times that he walks away seeing rivers and stars, now again, for the first time.

But I don't of course expect that you will accept this as a satisfactory answer to your question. So: as will be obvious from the first few pages of this volume, I take the view that the question of origins is, ultimately and at root, an epistemological question. Consistently with this, the naive realists' question about the origin of the universe becomes a question about the nature of awareness-of-self-and-other-than-self. And this brings us back to the quarter-deck of the *Pequod* where, philosophically now, Ahab is arguing his case for the destruction of the White Whale. Central to his argument is a desire, in his case monomaniacal and intense, to break through illusion. We might say the world-illusion. But this, the deed he will stake his life on, is indeed desperate, because, in his own words:

> Sometimes, I think there's naught beyond.

Here, we are a long way down the road from Coleridge coping with his dejection or from Arnolds' tergiversation on Dover Beach. Here we have voyaged to the edge of the abyss. There is here, as indeed there is in the second of Nietzsche's discoveries, a real possibility of nihilism – of nihilism not just in a mood of passive defeat but, as with Ahab and his crew, in a covenanted will to final destruction.

Is there not some similarity between Ahab emerging from his hold and, as though he had by now become *Gotterdammerung* incarnate, Hitler emerging from his bunker?

We are, I believe, in the presence of a defining moment in the history of Western humanity. And it might well be that Pericles' funeral oration and Ahab's philosophical harangue are among the opening and closing moments of that history.

Having a saving piety, Pericles could never have said:

> I'd strike the sun if it insulted me.

Nor could he, in the mood in which Ahab asked, have asked:

> Who's over me?

I tried to picture this mood, thinking of it as a mood of Luciferian rebellion, in the first volume:

> And draped tonight
> In his nine lives
>
> The tiger prowls
> El Shaddai's heights:
>
> An ancient of days,
> An ancient of nights,
> The tiger will not tire:
>
> If it smelt of flesh
>
> The tiger would prey
> On the pillar of fire.
>
> And the Zodiac hangs
> A high beast
> Towards him too,
>
> The Great Bear's side
>
> And sirloin:
>
> Devouring his own
> Astrological sign,
>
> He will straighten,
>
> Or break,
>
> The camel's backbone,
>
> The Lord God's rod
> And plumbline.

We've harpooned our way across a shadow line – but no! We've harpooned our way across a shining line we should only ever have prayed at. We are in trouble.

Initially, the response of this book is twofold. To give epistemological import to the story of Noah and the Flood, it retells it as the story of Narada's walk with Vishnu. I'll elaborate. In the Bible, just prior to the abyssal eruptions and the rains, God as we then and there conceived him says, the end of all flesh is come before me. Here we imagine him saying, the end of naive realism is come before me.

The answer, as this book sees it, is not to build an ark but to reconstruct Tenebrae as a purely mystical ritual.

Thus reconstructed, Tenebrae will of course be our ark. And the ark that carries us to the farther shore is the ark that carries us, most surely, to the shore we are on.

The Narada initiation is the answer to your question. The Narada initiation and Tenebrae.

Fervently intent on liberating humanity from the old foeda superstitio, *French revolutionaries installed a statue of Reason in Notre Dame. Now, almost two centuries later, here you are attempting to instal Tsetsekia and Tenebrae. So are we back to opium for the people?*

I think of Tsetsekia and Tenebrae as the ritual correlatives of Gethsemane and Golgotha. I furthermore think that Gethsemane and Golgotha are the final transitions in human and earthly evolution. Indeed Golgotha is release from evolution into Turiya. So who is the dope-pusher, Jesus or Marx? A journey by night train to the Finland Station is no substitute for a journey on foot to the Kedron-Colorado. Mao's long march is not a substitute for Christ's descent and ascent of Bright Angel Trail.

Fateful for the further evolution or for the further regression of life on Earth is the choice we make between Labyrinth and Tsetsekia.

Fateful for the further evolution or for the further regression of life on Earth is the choice we make between the *Titanic* which has already foundered and the Tenebrae Temple we haven't yet built.

It must be Good News for trilobite and dinosaur that the Titan whose Titanic ways have so ravaged Gaia is undergoing re-education in a blue thunder tipi.

Erinyes such as Turbine, Meltdown, GNP, Bottom Line and Chainsaw no longer hounding and haunting him, maybe he will one day walk all the way back to Ta'doiko and sit in the lotus position. And maybe Percy Bysshe will sit with him.

The choice between Labyrinth and Tsetsekia, between Titanic and Tenebrae Temple – these aren't the only choices your book confronts us with. Implicit in your text is an equally urgent choice between two very different attitudes to animals, the attitude of the Ancient of Days and the attitude of Old Man. Do you have other or further thoughts on this?

I only need to let the two attitudes stand side by side:

And God blessed Noah and his sons, and said unto them, Be fruitful, and multiply, and replenish the earth. And the fear of you and the dread of you shall be upon every beast of the earth, and upon every fowl of the air, upon all that moveth upon the earth, and upon the fishes of the sea; into your hand are they delivered. Every living thing that liveth shall be meat for you; even as the green herb have I given you all things.

Now, if you are overcome, you may go to sleep and get power. Something will come to you in your dream, and that will help you. Whatever those animals who appear to you in your sleep tell you to do, you must obey them. Be guided by them. If you want help, are alone and travelling, and cry aloud for aid, your prayer will be answered – perhaps by the eagles, or by the buffalo, or by the bears. Whatever animal answers your prayer you must listen.

How deeply buried under Europa's 'Europe' is the voice of Old Man! How deeply buried under Europa's 'Europe' is the trail that leads to Medicine River.

This book would dig down to that voice, would uncover that trail.

Trail remembered in folktale, remembered in fairy tale.

Trail of our Altamira ancestors.

Trail on which Mouse walked under Buffalo, walked under Wolf.

So yes, another choice. A choice between Job before and Job after, between the Ancient Mariner before and the Ancient Mariner after, between Ishmael before and Ishmael after.

A choice between ways of being in the world.

If for the moment we think of your book as a search for final healing, a question poses itself: can we find that healing in a life lived immanently in the immanent world, or must we lay ourselves open to the Transcendent? Your hospitality to the Navajo cradle suggests hope in immanence, your hospitality to the Tenebrae harrow suggests despair of immanence. How successfully, if at all, have you resolved this contradiction?

A religion in which Bright Angel Trail is aisle, in which any Grand Canyon mesa is Golgotha-Borobudur – that religion is simultaneously able for the Navajo cradle and the cup of trembling, is simultaneously able for Uvavnuk's song and Christ's cry of dereliction, is simultaneously able for a total turning towards immanence and a total turning towards transcendence. The one who on Good Friday is totally turned towards the Transcendent is able on Holy Thursday to be totally turned towards the immanent. There is a sense in which Good Friday precedes Holy Thursday. Or better, Good Friday and Holy Thursday are one and the same day. On Easter morning, we know that Divine Ground is as much foreground as it is ground.

I am of course aware that this is a confessional answer to your question. But the question itself isn't immutable. After the Narada initiation it will pose itself in a very different way. Also, there is one other thing: child of nature that she is, Lucy Gray might fall asleep in a vernal wood only to wake up and find that it has become her Garden of Olives. Lucy's light might well turn out to be as wounded as the light of the paschal candle. Before she experiences herself as Lucy she might have to acknowledge and experience herself as Lyca:

> Sleeping Lyca lay
> While the beasts of prey,
> Come from caverns deep,
> View'd the maid asleep.
>
> The kingly lion stood
> And the virgin view'd
> Then he gambol'd round
> O'er the hallow'd ground.
>
> Leopards, tygers, play
> Round her as she lay,
> While the lion old
> Bow'd his mane of gold
>
> And her bosom lick
> And upon her neck
> From his eye of flame
> Ruby tears there came;
>
> While the lioness
> Loos'd her slender dress
> And naked they convey'd
> To caves the sleeping maid.

To seek to emerge from those caves, to seek to awake from that sleep, is to run the risk of provoking the opposition and wrath of leopard and tyger and lioness and lion. The only good way to emerge is through all the degrees of mystical orison. And that means laying ourselves open, totally, to transcendental assistance. In the end, more often than not, it means Tenebrae.

So, instead of bending for her, maybe the willow will be Lucy's Bodhi Tree, her *moksa pippala*, and how far is she now from an ascent of Mount Carmel, from an ascent of Golgotha-Borobudur.

> *Nada nada nada nada y en el monte nada*
>
> 'It is like being in God without being oneself.'

Could it be, continuing her imagined biography, that Lucy will one day be a sage from whom Wordsworth, still relying on impulses from the vernal wood, will have much to learn?

The Navajo cradle and the Tenebrae harrow belong to a particular estimation of our human condition and prospects. Neither singly nor together are they an endorsement of the Romantic movement in European literature. The Romantic movement in European literature hasn't walked with Lyca out of her caves. Even Blake didn't see that vision veils. Vishnu has yet to darken the door of his cleansed perceptions.

God in darkness, privation, forsakenness and insensibility, is so much God that it is, as it were, God bare and alone.

The way to the vernal wood is through the Cloud of Unknowing.

First there is a Helvellyn, then there is no Helvellyn, then again there is a Helvellyn, and now

> The floating clouds their state shall lend
> To her; for her the willow bend;
> Nor shall she fail to see
> Even in motions of the Storm
> Grace that shall mould the Maiden's form
> By silent sympathy.

We have arrived at a Navajo hogan.

As nature developed the womb, so can culture develop the cradle.

And maybe Old Man is right. Having lost none of their savagery, no Orpheus singing to them, maybe leopard and tyger and lioness and lion will breathe warmth on our second birth.

Humanity has a chance. The evolving earth might survive its collision with us.

In Job and in Nietzsche we are confronted by seismic dislocation at the foundations of traditional religion and culture. Should we yet again shore up the ruins, or shouldn't we once and for all abandon the old sites and start again? The question is though: is there any such thing as seismically unshakeable religious ground?

In Nietzsche something at once terrible and great discovered itself. It discovered itself in two phases, and although Nietzsche himself would be horrified by the ascription, I think of them as the Gethsemane and the Golgotha phases. Describing what I think of as the Gethsemane phase, he says:

I have discovered for myself that the old human and animal world, indeed the entire prehistory and past of all sentient being, works on, loves on, hates on, thinks on in me.

Describing what I think of as the Golgotha phase, he says:

I suddenly woke up in the midst of this dream, but only to the consciousness that I am dreaming, and that I must go on dreaming lest I perish – as a somnambulist must go on dreaming lest he fall.

As it stood, his religion couldn't comfort Job. He had broken through its questions and answers. Hence the new revelation. As it stood, having a ritual called Tenebrae, his religion could have helped Nietzsche with the second phase of his discovery but wanting so fiercely to be the earthquake that would finally destroy Christianity he in a sense earthquaked himself. All the more sad his final sleepwalking was when we think that he might have been our Narada.

There are, I believe, two ways in which Christianity has ritually inherited the Triduum Sacrum. One is the Mass, the other is Tenebrae. In *Turtle Was Gone a Long Time* it is assumed that the future of Christianity lies with Tenebrae. In Tenebrae, its darkness illuminating us, we come to know what the Mandukya Upanishad knows: that waking, dreaming and dreamless sleep are shakeable foundations. In them, as St Augustine might say, we have no continuing city. In separate selfhood we have no continuing city. And so it was that Al Hallaj prayed:

Between me and Thee there is an 'I am' that torments me. Ah! through thy 'I am' take away my 'I am' from between us both.

Only Divine Ground is imperturable. But since Divine Ground is in all other ground, since it grounds all perturable ground, we might as well build on the site of the old earthquakes. That way it is less likely that we will mistake religion for the Real.

Knowing its own inadequacies in this regard, and therefore forlornly, the book attempts to comfort those who have been overtaken by Nietzsche's discoveries. Yet again I'll be blamed for repeating myself, but given these discoveries, we most urgently need to naturalize two words, Gethsemane and Golgotha. We need to naturalize them in ways that Bellini and Grunewald, El Greco and Michelangelo never did. All old skills and visions inadequate, we need a Naissance not a Re-naissance.

We need a religion that can help Nietzsche when, standing three steps deep in his inner savannah, he sees the grid going up. A religion that can help him when, having woken up from waking, he comes to see that, conscious and unconscious, psyche is the blind not the window.

A Christianity that can watch with Jesus is what we need.

A Christianity that can watch with humanity is what we need, because a humanity that is transtorrentem in Jesus is transtorrentem not just in individuals, it is transtorrentem as a species.

The stupendous has happened: the grid has gone up, we have woken up from waking.

Shining with a brightness brighter than star brightness, brighter than mind brightness, our planet is a success.

Is it your belief that Nietzsche's philosophy is inadequate to Nietzsche's discoveries?

European philosophy from Thales to Heidegger is inadequate. In Jesus, however, European philosophy crossed over, as in an exodus, from metaphysics to metanoesis. Jesus is Thales, therefore, to an alternative tradition that the mystical tradition which runs from Christ himself through Gregory of Nissa to Fenelon.

Nietzsche philosophized with a hammer. Like Cortez in Mexico, he smashed what he thought of as idols.

Totally surrendered to God's good-shepherding, the Christian mystic philosophizes with a Tenebrae harrow.

Given a last opportunity to mediate this volume, what would you say of it?

I have often thought that the Book of Job is very badly served by its plot. Exposure to inner and outer immensities we will never rule over and subdue is the real story, and this is carried not by the plot but by the images and metaphors, by the language generally. Like a lapwing drawing us away from her nest by pretending to be broken-winged and therefore catchable, maybe the plot of this book is designed to distract our attention, drawing us away from too sudden a realization that the biblical world view is being subverted, not in this or that detail, but at its foundations.

Remembering this, I've allowed the plot of this volume to remain mostly subliminal. Any subversion of cultural predisposition and orientation that is going on is in full view.

Apart from this, a subliminal plot means less coercion. It certainly means less conscious coercion. And it also suggests, I think, the greater ability of the dreaming psyche to tolerate and assimilate a heterogeneity of metaphor and myth. In that sense this volume is like the primordial soup that palaeobiologists talk about. Who looking at any one sample can say which direction evolution will take? Who looking into *Anima Mundi* can say which myths will emerge to give shape to consciousness? Who looking into it can say which myths will emerge to give initial shape to an emerging culture?

This volume attempts to remain open to *Anima Mundi*: and to do this it had to be willing to forgo a pre-existing design in and through which it would evolve. Its drifts of ideas behave like plankton: they go where the currents take them. If the currents are currents in *Anima Mundi* then we can hope that there will in the end be a kind of unplanned coherence.

That said, there is a plot and, standing like Ariadne at the mouth of it, I had hoped that this introduction would help you. Now, of course, I am aware that the thread it has given you is itself as much a tangle of themes as the labyrinth of themes it is expected to bring you through. I only wish that I could take apologetic or justifying refuge in the story of the Sufi master who, before he began to formally instruct him, said to a postulant: 'Give me your certainties. Yes, all of them. In return for them, I will give you confusion.'

Tohu-bohu or *Tohu-wavohu* is the Hebrew word for the precosmic confusion above which the Spirit moved in the beginning. In a sense, it was into that confusion the *Pequod* sailed:

> Suddenly then the beasts were shod;
> The sun came up like a firing squad,
> And as if our ship was a drifting wreck,
> The Beasts of the Zodiac walked the deck –

Acknowledging no ordering Power above us, the water won, and it is therefore appropriate that this volume begins where it does, with the emergence of an idealist epistemology, with the emergence of another way of posing the question about the origin of all things. For many this question about the origin of all things becomes a question about the nature of mind. More specifically: in a ropesnake epistemology, talk about the origin of the universe becomes talk about the origin of the subjective-objective divide. It becomes talk about the experience of the subjective-objective divide. For many Hindus such experience is of the nature of dream, illusion or maya. And so it is that I sometimes imagine it: Vishnu and Berkeley walking together in a red desert.

Are you saying that Berkeley's idealist epistemology is becoming a ropesnake epistemology?

It would be better not to anticipate the outcome. It might be that it is into Tenebrae he is walking.

As indeed I hope for his own sake that it was into something like Tenebrae that Narada walked.

It isn't for me to minimize the differences between East and West.

For instance: in the East a walk with Vishnu, in the West the voyage of the *Pequod*.

And yet it is with a Tenebrae harrow that I see us emerging from our Eastern initiation and our Western voyage.

It is, I believe, in a common inheritance of the Tenebrae harrow that East and West can and will meet.

The Tenebrae harrow is *homo faber* realigned with the evolving earth.

I've interrupted you – you were responding to a final invitation to mediate this volume.

Maybe it will help if I give you a few perspectives on it.

Think of it as the log-book of Ishmael. The Ishmael I have in mind is he who, alone of all her crew, survived the wreck of the *Pequod*. An alter ego of Deucalion and therefore also of Utnapishtim and Noah, he endures the terrible transition from European tall ship to Maidu raft. Inwardly, in some of its moods it is a transition from Cosmos to Chaos, from Time to Tehom. In Yeats's terms, his is the log of the new historical cycle or gyre growing out of the old.

Appearances to the contrary, Ishmael isn't only a roughneck of the old doomed voyage. Somewhere deep within himself, he is standing in the new Tep-zepi, on the new Tai-wer, that emerged at the end of the first volume.

Like Big Mike, he is our modern Seafarer. At sea in a time of cultural disintegration, he, too, sitting alone in his boat, might sing a sea-shanty with the refrain:

> My mood 'mid the mere-flood
> Over the whale's acre, would wander wide.

How inwardly and outwardly vast the whale's acre is, we know from *Moby-Dick*:

Alone, in such remotest waters, that though you sailed a thousand miles, and passed a thousand shores, you would not come to any chiselled hearth-stone, or aught hospitable beneath that part of the sun; in such latitudes and longitudes, pursuing too such a calling as he does, the whaleman is wrapped by influences all tending to make his fancy pregnant with many a mighty birth.

Since the plot is subliminal, it follows that the shape-shift is still an active principle among its protagonists. In role if not in identity, some of them are interchangable. Ishmael enduring the wreck of the *Pequod* is Noah enduring the wreck of his ark. Ishmael going down is in a sense A'noshma going down. Ishmael coming ashore from his diluvian night of typhoons is Narada coming ashore from his diluvian night of monsoons.

The question is: what argosy of mahavakyas, myths, metaphors, what argosy of cultural possibilities, comes ashore with him?

What has the Flood washed away? And what has it washed up?

Enough for the moment to know that this most recent Deucalion comes ashore singing what for us is a new song of origins:

> Te Kore
> Te Kore-tua-tahi
> Te Kore-tua-rua ...

He hasn't a glittering eye, this most recent Utnapishtim, but he has been among the antechronical Leviathans: Zeuglodon has in some way or other dismasted him; he is the New England colt behind whom a fresh buffalo robe has been shaken; he has looked, paying the awful cost, into Polar eternities; his mind fermenting in Ahab's grog, he has stood, hands at the helm of *Pequod* culture, beneath the left wing of Judgment Day; Saturn's grey chaos has rolled over him, and if you meet him, it is likely that there will be an empty chair at the marriage of Albert and Lil in the dying cycle or gyre. You might find yourself listening not to the loud bassoon but to the Horsehead Nebula neighing, not to Lil and Lou and Lou and May talking about abortions and false teeth in a Waste Land pub, but to the roaring, still far off, of Medicine River. In a sense, therefore, this volume is a subplot to the *The Rime of the Ancient Mariner* and *Moby-Dick*. In it, Tiamat falls from our necks. In it, the new order emerges from the old.

Think of the volume as an attempt to cope with Nietzsche's discoveries, in particular with the second of them, and with its correlative in fiction: Ahab's dreadful insight and his yet more dreadful apprehension. Wherever it engages with such themes, the book is a Passion Play. Indeed, in all its three volumes that's what the book is, a Passion Play. By this I mean that it seeks to watch with the Suffering God, a theme so native to the hinterlands of the Eastern Mediterranean as to be almost a defining characteristic of religion and culture there.

Think of the volume as an attempt to integrate our Copernican revolution in epistomology. In this it gives Jesus his due. It accords to him the dignity of being Thales to an alternative, great tradition, the metanoetic tradition in philosophy.

Think of the volume as an attempt to give initial, sequential shape to the intimations of cosmos and culture which, in the age of the world's night, Turtle comes back with. As I've imagined him, Turtle didn't only dive to the floor of the Abyss, he entered the fabulous darkness out of which, according to Yeats, the Christian Aeon called:

> The Roman Empire stood appalled,
> It dropped the reins of peace and war
> When that fierce virgin and her star
> Out of the fabulous darkness called.

Think of it as a volume in which we imaginatively enter, endure and come through our Year One Reed. A year suffered and survived not by crowds but in and by an individual. I am thinking of Kierkegaard here. It is in and through the single one, it is in and through the real Job behind the fictional Job, that history finds its way.

Think of it as a volume in which the coffin texts of the Egyptians are beginning to find antiphonal response in the cradle texts of the Navajo. Think of it, yes, think of it as that. Think of it as a book of cradle texts.

Having found her, First Man and First Woman make a cradle board for Lucy – for Lucy not just in herself but for Lucy in all of her historical or mythical identities, one of whom is Europa, a Lyca or Little Girl Lost who, more than most, has declined from the Great Way.

> We have made a cradle board for you, Lucy.
> On the bow of it we have carved

Crazily, I suppose, the book would nurture a new humanity. A new humanity on an Earth newly discovered by Noah and Siduri. The Earth rediscovered as Buddh Gaia.

So there is, after all, a thesis I would nail to the door of the Whaleman's Chapel, or should I say, to the door of Western civilization:

Tehom and Tiamat are cognate words and to have converted Tehom into Tiamat or to have thought of Tehom as the habitation of a condensation of itself called Tiamat is the calamity that Western culture continues to have its origins in. To shut out Tehom is to shut out Divine Ground. And in this regard, astonishingly, Ahab's diagnosis is correct: Tiamat or, as he would have it, Moby-Dick is the mask. And he, like Marduk, will strike through that mask. The *Pequod* is Esagila at sea. It is biblical Christianity at sea. But the Maidu raft is waiting, and on it alone A'noshma Jesu calls out

Tehom is Turiya

Where you sometimes expected to find naught, Ahab, you will find Divine Ground, and of it Hindus say that it is

Shantam Shivam Advaitam

All of which means?

A new face of God in five mystical mysteries:

Jesus Grand Canyon deep in the world's karma
Jesus on the Hill of the Koshaless Skull
A'noshma Jesu
Jesu Anadyomene
Jivanmukhta Messiah preaching his first Evangelanta Sermon

Call it our Apocalypse. Call it our Exodus.

From Grand-Canyon-deep in it we've emerged not from but with the Earth.

We have come forth by day.

So I will end by imagining a deathbed dream for Einstein: he saw $E=mc^2$ spinning a cocoon for itself. It hung from a bough of the Tree of Knowledge. It emerged as

and opening its Horakhty hawk wings — over-wing green, under-wing gold — it flew, bringing news of themselves among the galaxies.

HORSEHEAD NEBULA NEIGHING

A happening but not by way of occurrence, process or event. A happening out of the Divine Ungrund. A happening in which nothing happens. A happening in which nothing takes place. Yet now it is: awareness of self and other-than-self, and at the heart of it all a Horsehead Nebula neighing: *yatra na anyat pasyati.*

A happening but not by way of occurrence, process or event. A happening out of the Divine Ungrund. A happening in which nothing happens. A happening in which nothing takes place. Yet now it is: awareness of self and other-than-self, and at the heart of it all a Horsehead Nebula neighing: *na anyat srinoti.*

A happening but not by way of occurrence, process or event. A happening out of the Divine Ungrund. A happening in which nothing happens. A happening in which nothing takes place. Yet now it is: awareness of self and other-than-self, and at the heart of it all a Horsehead Nebula neighing: *na anyad vijanati.*

A happening but not by way of occurrence, process or event. A happening out of the Divine Ungrund. A happening in which nothing happens. A happening in which nothing takes place. Yet now it is: awareness of self and other-than-self and at the heart of it all a Horsehead Nebula neighing: *sa bhuma.*

Out of that Horsehead Nebula, neighing *na na na*, our solar system evolved and here we are, heirs if we will to a healing catastrophe, heirs if we will to the Narada initiation:

Long, long ago in a wood that was over the hills and far away from the world of worldly possessions and pursuits, there lived a man whose name was Narada. He was a hermit. But that only meant that he lived remotely and alone. He wasn't jealous of his solitude. Indeed in the whole of India there wasn't a door so open and so welcoming as his was. All paths in the wood, animal paths too, were paths to his door. And people did come to see him. It was usually people who were in trouble who came. People bewildered and bruised by the first overwhelmings of Heaven, people amazed and sore, broken by the first eruptions within them of Hell. Sitting with them in his hermitage, Narada talked to them and while he talked he was as wide and wide open as a valley. And his talking to people was nearer to them than their own thinking and dreaming was. His talking to them was a reawakening in them of old pre-personal intuitions and knowings and in the end it wasn't so much the psychology of the man as the cosmology of the man that impressed them, giving them the courage, walking away, to walk on. And so it was that living alone in a wood Narada gave himself up continually and without reserve or self-interest to a growing in grace. And then one day it was Vishnu, the Great God, who was standing in human form in his clearing. He had, he said, witnessed Narada's austerities and search for the Truth throughout many lifetimes and now, wishing to reward him, he had come to grant him any favour he might choose.

You will favour me greatly, Narada replied, if you will show me the source and manner of your maya. I will be pleased if you show me the source and power over us of the world illusion. Show me how spellbound we are.

Follow me, Vishnu said, smiling strangely.

In a while, following a narrow path, they were out of the cool green twilight of the wood. And in yet another while, they were crossing a sunbaked, red desert. By noon, and it seemed to be always noon out here, they were dying of thirst. Their tongues were like boots in their mouths. Like mud drying out, their minds were cracking. And then, just as the deepest will to live in them was crumbling, they saw it, something green on the horizon, a green village in a green land.

Go and bring me water, Vishnu asked. I will sit in the shade of this rock until you come.

Narada set out crossing the last terrible salt-flats. Entering the village, he knocked on the first door and the most beautiful woman he had ever laid eyes on opened it wide to him. Instantly, he was in the spell of her. Forgetting what he had come for, he went in and sat down. No one was particularly surprised that he had come. It was as if they had lived together all their lives. In time the young woman consented to be his wife. Three children were born to them and when the old man, his father-in-law, died, he became head of the household. The rains of many years came and went. Dry seasons came and went. Their cows calved. Calves grew to be heifers and year after year his ricefields yielded a rich harvest. One year, as expected, the monsoon rains came. Never had anyone seen or heard tell of such rain. Not rain at all. This was chaos. Chaos from above, and below. Houses and trees, even rivers, were being swept away. Seeking the safety of higher ground for his wife and children, Narada walked out with them into the night, if night it was, but first one child and then another and again another was torn from him. And finally his wife, even she, he couldn't even hear her high wild crying out in the rage of swallowing waters. Then there was silence. Narada was standing in a red desert.

You've been gone for almost an hour, the voice behind him said. Did you bring the water?

Narada's great and terrible awakening. His dis-illusioning. His ragnarok.

Primarily, ragnarok is something that happens to an individual. Primarily, it is having an individual in mind that the ragnarok cocks crow. That Fjalar crows from the crossbeam of a gibbet. That Goldcomb crows in the Birdwood. That Rustred crows at the bars of Hel.

Substituting Narada's ragnarok for ragnarok as the peoples of northern Europe imagined it. Substituting Narada's apocalypse for apocalypse as Christians understand it.

What happened to Narada happened to Christ on Good Friday: the illusioning veil of his psyche was rent. But that is not the whole story. Looking down into Adam's empty skull he heard the Good News:

yatra na anyat pasyati, na anyat srinoti, na anyad vijanati, sa bhuma.

An *Argo* that brings home the Golden Fleece.

An *Argo* that brings home the Narada story.

A *Nave* that brings home Good Friday Good News: in the world the possibility of waking up from the world.

And now again Fjalar, Goldcomb and Rustred crow: There's a man walking home late one evening. Having worked all day in his rice paddies, he is weary. And he is hungry. But he hasn't far to go. Soon, seeing him coming over the brow of the hill, his children will be running to meet him. Suddenly, catching sight of a snake on the side of the road, he leaps sideways away. Again and again he leaps, putting as much distance as possible between himself and the terror. Sure that he is safe, he opens his eyes, and then there it is – fallen from a neighbour's cart, a coil of rope on the side of the road.

Projecting a snake into a rope. Projecting a world into Divine Ground. The snake we project is an illusion. So is the world. And that is the Hindu diagnosis of what ails us: we are illusioned. The remedy therefore is to be dis-illusioned. As Narada was. As, when he opened his eyes, the man walking home was.

Two parables and, neighed into the world at the origin of the world, a mahavakya.

At the birth of the world, neighed into the world, a reminder that the world isn't all of what is.

A new diagnosis of what ails us means new diagnostic words.

Viksepashakti it is called, the power by which a snake is projected into a rope, by which a world is projected into Divine Ground.

Avaranashakti it is called, the power that veils the rope by projecting a snake into it, that veils Divine Ground by projecting a world into it.

Viksepashakti and avaranashakti are forms of mayashakti, the power that projects the world-illusion. Mayashakti is thought of as female, is thought of as a goddess. Sometimes she is called not Mayashakti but Kundalashakti. When the source of maya or illusion is thought of as male it is called the Great Mayin, the Great Illusionist. In the Narada parable Vishnu is the Great Mayin, and this is not surprising because Hindus love to picture the world-illusion as having its source in Vishnu recumbent, dreaming and asleep, on the coils of Ananta, the Great Snake who, lying coiled in the primordial waters, is a condensation of Infinity. Thus recumbent, Vishnu dreams the dream which we experience as world. Thus recumbent, the Great Mayin is called Vishnu-anantasyin. Translated into Mesopotamian terms he would be Mardutiamasayin. Translated into Egyptian terms he would be Atumiru-tosayin. Translated into Greek terms he would be Zeustyphosayin. Translated into biblical terms he would be Yahwehleviathasayin.

Could it be that a famous passage in Berkeley's *Principles of Human Understanding* might bridge the gap between Vishnuanantasayin and a correlative conception of Yahweh as Yahwehleviathasayin?

It is indeed an opinion strangely prevailing amongst men that houses, mountains, rivers, and in a word all sensible objects, have an existence, natural or real, distinct from their being perceived by the understanding. But, with how great an assurance and acquiescence soever this principle may be entertained in the world, yet whoever shall find in his heart to call it in question may, if I mistake not, perceive it to involve a manifest contradiction. For, what are the forementioned objects but the things we perceive by sense? And what do we perceive besides our own ideas or sensations? And is it not plainly repugnant that any one of *these* or any combination of them, should exist unperceived?

A conclusion to be drawn from this is that we should talk not about the world as though it existed independently of our perceptions of it; rather should we talk about experience of a world, or worldly experience. And already now we are on the way to Kant's Copernican revolution in philosophy. We are on the way, who knows, to the Mandukya Upanishad, which, were we to westernize it, would suggest to us that things are indeed what Kant said they were, phenomena. And this discovery or apprehension of things as phenomena calls, not nihilistically for Ahab's harpoon, but mirumistically for the Tenebrae harrow.

The harpoon or the harrow: that's the choice.

And there is a question Schopenhauer might have posed: will the West continue to fall in with Greek *peripateia* or will it cross over into Narada's walk with Vishnu?

It is likely that no being from outer space who might one day knock on our door will be half so catastrophic to our sense of ourselves and our world as Narada knocking on it.

Nothing that might come to us from outer space will be half so enormous in its consequences for us as the consequences of a simple question already asked of us here at home: did you bring the water?

The great *Gotterdammerung* question already asked. And, neighed by the Horsehead Nebula out of which our solar system evolved, the answer already given:

> na na na sa
> *yatra na anyat pasyati, na anyat srinoti, na anyad vijanati, sa bhuma.*

Where nothing else is seen, nothing else is heard, nothing else is thought about, there's the Infinite.

In that question and in that answer we have what Wallace Stevens might call the fecund minimum. The philosophical fecund minimum. The religious fecund minimum.

Narada knocks on our door.

That single knock is like the crowing of Fjalar, Goldcomb and Rustred.

Fjalar crowing from the crossbeam of a gibbet, Goldcomb crowing from the Birdwood and Rustred crowing from the bars of Hel.

Remember now thy Creator in the days of thy youth, while the evil days come not, nor the years draw nigh, when thou shalt say I have no pleasure in them; while the sun, or the light, or the moon, or the stars, be not darkened, nor the clouds return after the rain: in the day when the keepers of the house shall tremble, and the strong men shall bow themselves, and the grinders cease because they are few and those that look out of the window be darkened. And the doors shall be shut in the streets, when the sound of grinding is low, and he shall rise up at the sound of a bird, and all the daughters of musick shall be brought low; Also when they shall be afraid of that which is high, and fears shall be in the way, and the almond tree shall flourish, and the grasshopper shall be a burden, and desire shall fail: because man goeth to his long home, and the mourners go about the streets: Or ever the silver cord be loosed, or the golden bowl be broken, or the pitcher be broken at the fountain, or the wheel broken at the cistern. Then shall the dust return to the earth as it was: and the spirit shall return to God who gave it. Vanity of vanities, saith the preacher; all is vanity.

We hear a knocking at our door. Having heard the cocks, we think it is Ecclesiastes. But no. It is Narada, and in his hands are fragments of the bowl, the pitcher and the wheel. Looking at them, and at him, we intuitively see that the ragnarok which is about to engulf us is inner not outer, is epistemological not cosmic.

Narada is a new Xerxes, and happily for us there is a philosophical Marathon and a philosophical Salamis that we will lose.

7

Narada knocks.

Narada knocks on the door of Socrates' prison cell. In imitation of Fjalar crowing he knocks the first time. In imitation of Goldcomb crowing he knocks a second time. In imitation of Rustred crowing he knocks a third time. His knocking means ragnarok at the foundations of our philosophical tradition. Heard by the man with the cup and the men in tears, it is an invitation to replace the parable of the cave with the rope-snake parable.

Narada knocks on Diotima's door. In imitation of Fjalar crowing he knocks a first time. In imitation of Goldcomb crowing he knocks a second time. In imitation of Rustred crowing he knocks a third time. Reliving a dream in which she saw the highest rung of her ladder engulfed in darkness, she listens: above as well as below the division in Plato's divided line is awareness-of. Awareness-of means dualism. Supercelestial dualism blinds us no less than does dualism in the cave.

Narada knocks on the door of our philosopher king. In imitation of Fjalar crowing he knocks a first time. In imitation of Goldcomb crowing he knocks a second time. In imitation of Rustred crowing he knocks a third time. Reliving a dream in which he saw that his sunlit palace was cave, the king listens. It is time to abandon Western metaphysics for Oriental metanoesis.

Narada is our Cortez. From now on, for a long while, what else can we do but attempt to come through our Year One Reed.

To begin with, we might rewrite Ecclesiastes: or if ever the lamp run out of oil or the mirror fall from the wall, let us accustom ourselves to the dark good-guidance of the Tenebrae harrow.

The Tenebrae harrow is our Aaron's wand. With it, Jesus opened a path through the sea of Greek and Christian metaphysics. Not countless, though, are those who have walked dryshod through. Enabled and guided and carried by grace, Eckhart walked through into what he called the still wilderness where no one is at home.

Well might Eckhart have knocked on a prison door in Athens or on a palace door in Plato's Republic or on a door in Mantineia and said: 'So long as the soul beholds forms, even though she behold an angel, or herself as something formed: so long is there imperfection in her.'

It is not dialectically while walking in a cloister or stoa that Christians practise philosophy. It is ritually, while participating in the nocturnes of Tenebrae, that they do so.

On Easter morning we won't ask Jesus, did you bring the water? Rather will we ask him, did you bring the Tenebrae harrow? Did you bring it for Narada? Did you bring it for Nietzsche?

Well might Narada say, 'we are such stuff as dreams are made on', but he will not, emerging from his initiation, go on to say, 'and our little life is rounded with a sleep'. Because now he knows: sooner or later, in one or another of our incarnations, we are shattered at our psychic foundations by a great and terrible awakening. We wake up not only from dreaming, we wake up from waking. We wake up from the dream that dreaming is, we wake up from the dream that waking is. It happened to Nietzsche:

In what a marvellous and new and at the same time terrible and ironic relationship with the totality of existence do I feel myself to stand with my knowledge! I have discovered for myself that the old human and animal world, indeed the entire prehistory and past of all sentient being, works on, loves on, hates on, thinks on in me – I have suddenly awoken in the midst of this dream but only to the consciousness that I am dreaming and that I have to go on dreaming in order not to be destroyed: as the sleepwalker has to go on dreaming in order not to fall.

Chuang Tzu, the great Taoist sage, dreamed one night that he was a butterfly, flitting from flower to flower. Next day he couldn't decide which he was, Chuang Tzu dreaming that he was a butterfly or a butterfly dreaming that he was Chuang Tzu.

Grappling with a dis-illusioning insight no less terrible in its consequences, Ahab drew our attention not to the perceiver but to the perceived:

All visible objects, man, are but as pasteboard masks

We only have to add this insight to our Psalm eight and second stasimon estimation of ourselves and here we are sailing through the Sunda Straits into a ragnarok at once nihilistic and of our own making.

Much depends on which of these two we align our civilization with: Narada walking through the pass at Thermopylae or, harpoon in hand, Ahab sailing through the Sunda Straits.

Putting this in another way: will we somnambulate into possible madness with Nietzsche or will we awaken with Narada?

A Bushman has said, there is a dream that dreams us.

The dream that dreams us is phylogenetically rooted in us, is macrocosmically rooted in us. As Nietzsche discovered, it is a very old dream. It was old already in the Devonian. Old in the trilobite. Old beyond all geological reckoning in the horseshoe crab.

Nietzsche recoiled from Narada's destiny. He refused the Narada initiation.

The Narada initiation. Call it that. Or call it Good Friday on Golgotha. On Golgotha, in the person of Jesus, we underwent our Year One Reed. Culturally and philosophically, we underwent it. On that day, everything that could walk out on Jesus walked out on him. Dreaming walked out on him. Waking walked out on him. Experience of self and other-than-self walked out on him. The veil in the temple was rent. The veiling veil, the eclipsing veil, of his psyche, unconscious and conscious, was rent. Towards the end, still experiencing the catastrophies of this great dis-illusioning, this great awakening, his head fell forward onto his chest and he looked down into Adam's skull, down into Chandogya Good News: *yatra na anyat pasyati na anyat srinoti, na anyad vijanati, sa bhuma.*

The great Chandogya saying which entitles us to call ourselves sapient.

The great Chandogya saying which since Good Friday is the rainbow in the cloud

Like Venus coming ashore, our myths came ashore wholly sea-changed on Good Friday.

Seeing him coming shorewards on Good Friday, we saw that Noah was Narada, and we knew that from now on forever we would talk not about a deluge of waters but about a deluge of awareness-of.

To attempt to naturalize Good Friday in our culture or religion is to attempt to naturalize a plant altogether more exotic than fuchsia or the potato. It isn't only that the climates and soils of our minds and hearts are unfavourable to it, they are hostile to it.

Recognizing him while he is still a long way off, our cultural immune system is ready for Narada. And yet, when he breached Jesus on Good Friday, Longinus breached our collective immunity to what until then would have been seen as a wholly alien estimation of ourselves and our prospects.

Since Good Friday, recognize it or not, Narada is Noah.

Since Good Friday, recognize it or not, Narada is indigenous.

Since Good Friday, recognize it or not, Christianity isn't just a religion that is occasionally hospitable to mysticism. Root and branch, it is itself a mystical religion. Leading us into nirvikalpasamadhi, the Tenebrae harrow is our pillar of cloud by day, our pillar of fire by night.

Habeas Corpus Christianity has blinded us to mystical Christianity.

Habeas Corpus Christianity is the new veil in the new temple.

Identified as we are with awareness-of, the deluge isn't something that happens to us, it is something we empirically became the moment we left the Divine Ungrund.

In the six hundredth year of Noah's life, in the second month, the seventeenth day of the month, the same day were all the Fountains of the Great Deep broken up and the windows of heaven were opened ... and the Flood was forty days upon the earth and the waters increased and bare up the ark and it was lift up above the earth. And the waters prevailed exceedingly upon the earth and all the high hills that were under the whole heaven were covered.

The Fountains of the Deep are inner fountains. They are Fountains of viksepashakti and avaranashakti. Fountains of awareness-of.

Nirvikalpasamadhi: our ark in the deluge of awareness-of.

And Noah sent out a raven. He sent out a dove. And the raven returning brings the Narada parable. The dove brings the Mandukya Upanishad.

Biblically, we built bars and doors against Tehom. Reading the Mandukya Upanishad, we know that it was against Turiya that we built them. It was against the Divine Ungrund that we built them. But in Jesus on Good Friday there was an immense caving in of all our bulwarks, psychological and spiritual, against the Divine, and since then we know, released from biblical terror and dread of it we know, that Tehom is Turiya.

On Good Friday the Divine revealed itself not as God but as Divine Ungrund. It revealed itself as Turiya, as Tehom.

There are Good Friday gifts, Golgotha gifts, of the Holy Spirit. Listen to Fenelon, a Christian mystic: 'God felt, God tasted and enjoyed, is indeed God, but God with those gifts that flatter the soul, God in darkness, in privation, in forsakenness, in insensibility, is so much God that He is so to speak God bare and alone.'

Darkness, privation, forsakenness, insensibility: gifts given to those who are undergoing the Golgotha initiation, the Narada initiation, into nirvikapasamadhi.

Our biblical bars and doors are a calamitous mistake. They are, so to speak, an immune system in us against the Divine, the Divine as Divine Ungrund, the Divine as Turiya, as Tehom. It is greatly to be desired that we would speak of Tehom as the Tao Te Ching speaks of Tao:

> There was something formless yet complete
> That existed before heaven and earth;
> Without sound, without substance,
> Dependent on nothing, unchanging,
> All pervading, unfailing,
> One may think of it as
> The Mother of all things under heaven.

> Great Tao is like a boat that drifts;
> It can go this way; it can go that.
> The ten thousand creatures owe their existence to it

And it does not disown them;
Yet having produced them, it does not take
Possession of them.
Tao, though it covers the ten thousand things like
A garment,
Makes no claim to be master over them,
And asks for nothing from them.
Therefore it may be called the Lowly.
The ten thousand creatures obey it,
Though they know not that they have a master;
Therefore it is called the Great.
So too the sage, just because he never at any time
Makes a show of greatness in fact achieves greatness.

Tao never does;
Yet through it all things are done.

Mo wei is a Taoist doctrine which suggests that no one or nothing makes the universe.

Out of Tao, spontaneously, the ten thousand things.

Out of Tehom, spontaneously, awareness of self and other-than-self.

Out of Tehom, spontaneously, evening and morning a first day.

We are heirs, since Good Friday, to the wisdom of the East.

Since Good Friday we can say of Tehom what the Tao Te Ching says of Tao.

Since Good Friday we can say of Tehom what the Mandukya Upanishad says of Turiya: we can say of it that it is *santam*, *sivam*, *advaitam*, which translates as, utterly quiet, peaceful-blissful, without a second.

Some of our Gods, Gods we have created, are sins, committed by us, against the Divine. They eclipse the Divine. They stand between us and the Divine.

The only good way to create a good present is to create a good past out of which it will grow.

The past can be changed. But we don't have to change it. It has been changed already. Good Friday has changed it. Good Friday changed all that came before it as much as it changed all that came after it.

Good Friday permits us, invites us, to grow again from a greatly changed past into a greatly changed present and future.

Our past has been changed all the way back to Olduvai and beyond. Everything in 'the dark backward and abysm of Time' has been changed by the victory, so awful to look at, of Good Friday on Golgotha.

Hell has been harrowed.

All our myths have been harrowed.
Our Mesopotamian myths have been harrowed.
Our Egyptian myths have been harrowed.
Our Hebrew narratives and myths harrowed.
Greek philosophy and science harrowed.
Newton's laws of gravity harrowed.
All European talk in all ages harrowed.
Earth, hell and heaven harrowed.
Our European eyes harrowed.
Our European hands harrowed.

How do we integrate it? Religiously and culturally, how do we integrate the victory of Good Friday on Golgotha?

Given our good will, given our willingness to be inspired by it, the horrible yet glorious victory of Good Friday on Golgotha would integrate itself in Upanishads and Gitas. In puranas glorious in their dark facts as in their bright. Given our willingness to be inspired by it, this awful victory on this awful Parnassus would integrate itself in splendours of architecture, in Bhuvaneshvars and Borobudurs and Mount Abus. In song and dance. In terrifying Halloweens and May mornings. It would integrate itself into the way we greet each other on a bad morning going to work.

Our myths harrowed. Our philosophies harrowed. Our cosmologies harrowed.

Christ, our Sem priest, touching the mouths of our myths with his adze or mesehtiu.

Christ, our Sem priest, opening the mouths of our myths. Opening them mythically. Opening them upanishadically.

Not now Marduk going out into the Abyss to slay and slaughter Tiamat.

Not now Atum seeking to escape from the coils of Iru-To.

Not now Yahweh breaking the heads of Leviathan in the waters. Breaking the seven, dragon-jewelled heads of Yam-Tannin-Leviathan in the waters.

Look at him now. Look at Marduk standing alone on the shore of the Abyss. He listens enraptured to Tiamat's whale song. Tiamat singing. Tiamat nursing. Tiamat giving sensuous suck, giving chakral suck, to six marvellous mornings.

Look now at Atum. Far out and far back in the Waters of Nun, Iru-To is now his protecting mandala, a garbha mandala of many stupendous coils, his high heads, which are timeless thunders, singing the *anahata shabda* mantra.

And look at Yahweh. Recumbent, like Vishnu, on the coils of Yam-Tannin-Leviathan, he has ceased from all his *yu-wei* works and days. The seven jewels of the sea-dragon's seven heads are seven mahavakyas singing themselves into the awakening worlds.

Good Friday images, Tenebrae images, of the imageless Beginning.

The supremely mysterious *mo-wei* world we live in.

Now that their mouths have been opened, the anahata sound is the only sound our cosmologies make.

He who speaks does not know

He who knows does not speak.

But we must keep talking, telling what cannot be told.

In the beginning was *anahata shabda*, the sound that isn't produced by any two things striking together. Sound beyound all syntax and all grammars. Even our resurrection grammars cannot draw near to it, cannot even point to it, cannot embody it. Unutterably mysterious sound, the first sound out of the Divine Ungrund, sound the universe is a blossoming of.

How multitudinously communicative is this sound. The multitudinous universe is what it says and it goes on saying it because, in all its multitudinousness, the universe isn't other than eternal, changeless Nirguna Brahman.

The universe is a mantraverse. Listen to the mountains. Listen to the stars. Listen to D.H. Lawrence talking about the woman who rode away:

This at length became the only state of consciousness she really recognized: this exquisite sense of bleeding out into the higher beauty and harmony of things. Then she could actually hear the great stars in heaven, which she saw through her door, speaking from their motion and brightness, saying things perfectly to the cosmos, as they trod in perfect ripples, like bells on the floor of heaven, passing one another, and grouping in the timeless dance with the spaces of dark between.

Almost all our cosmogonies and cosmologies are sins against the cosmos. And few indeed are they who don't need to ride out, bleed out, into the higher beauty and harmony of things.

Awareness-of is the deluge. And yet, in the jivanmukta, in the person who is liberated in this life, awareness-of isn't other than nirvikalpasamadhi.

An ark of nirvikalpasamadhi in the deluge of awareness-of.

And Narada-Noah sent out a raven.

And Narada-Noah sent out a dove.

And the raven returning called out:

> Tehom is Turiya
> And Time is Turiya.

And the dove returning called out:

> Emanations of awareness–of out of Brahman
> are emanations within Brahman.
> All is Brahman.

And how vast a journey is our journey to where we always already have been and are.

And how unearthly a journey it is, our journey to the earth we are already born into.

And how unworldly the world is. Even in its worldliness, how unworldly it is.

Tell Thales.

Tell Anaximenes.

Tell Democritus, especially him, tell him.

Tell all the educators of Europe that unworldliness is what the world is made of.

Pascal's *oubli du monde* is what our monde is made of.

Emanation not creation.

We sin against what is, be it universe or pluriverse, when we think of it as having come into existence as a consequence of conscious Divine Fiat.

Our sense of what is as the work of a God who consciously creates, consciously sustains and consciously brings to a foreordained conclusion – that sense of things is our sin against morning and evening the first day, against evening and morning the first night.

We believe in a God who consciously creates, consciously sustains, consciously choreographs towards a final tableau because of our dread of unconsciousness, our dread of *wu-hsin, wu wei, mo wei,* our dread of miraculousness.

Our biblical God is our bulwark against miraculousness.

In the *yu-wei* works and days which we ascribe to him, our biblical God is our sin against the Divine.

And the lily of the field invites us to ride out, it invites us into the *wu-wei* world that knows nothing of works and working days.

> Tao never does;
> Yet through it all things are done.
>
> Tao Te Ching.
> Tehom Te Ching.

Tehom never does;
Yet through it all things are done.

We must write a Tehom Te Ching.

Tehom om om om

The om in Tehom is the Mandukya Om.
Om has four quarters: vaisvanara, taijasa, susupta and Tehom. Tehom
is santam, sivam, advaitam.

Tao-Turiya-Tehom

On Good Friday, out on the Divine Deep, out of the Divine Deep,
the beginning.
On Good Friday, out on the Divine Deep, out of the Divine Deep, a
whale voice.
On Good Friday, out on the Divine Deep, out of the Divine Deep,
Tiamat.
On Good Friday, out on the Divine Deep, out of the Divine Deep,
Tiamat giving sensuous suck to six marvellous mornings.
On Good Friday, out of self loss in the Divine Deep, the moon grow-
ing big above him, he came; he, the one who was Jesus, a child now of
the Abyss, Dumuzi Abzu now, him in whom all bars and doors between
Time and Tehom have gone down.
One in whom the heavens are pleased.
One in whom all underworlds are pleased.
One in whom the Abyss is pleased.
One in whom the Earth is pleased.

Dumuzi Abzu
Jesu Ab-zu

In him are no bars and doors.

Venus Anadyomene

Venus coming shorewards on a shell.
Jesus coming shorewards on the Mandukya Upanishad.

Angels we have heard on high

The angels who sang above him lying on the straw in the stable of
Bethlehem sing above him now climbing the shingle shore. They sing
Tiamat's whale-song. The whale-song she sings giving suck to six mar-
vellous mornings.

Holiness out of Tehom.

Holiness out of the Deepest Below.

The Deepest Below is *in excelsis*.

Everything is *in excelsis*, but not everything knows it.

Hell is *in excelsis*. The deepest pit of it is *in excelsis*, but it doesn't know it.

Jesu Absu climbing the shore shingles.

Jesu Absu walking inland.

At his feet, in skylark's eggs, are summer soarings.

Caves he sleeps in are Ajantas, are Eloras.

Olduvai Ajantas. Olduvai Eloras.

Olduvai inside. Olduvai outside.

Rift Valley inside. Rift Valley outside.

Inside and outside, the Rift Valley runs north into Galilee.

Inside us the Rift Valley runs to the farthest north, the farthest south, the farthest east and the farthest west that human beings inhabit.

The Rift Valley climbs Golgotha-Borobudur with us. It walks between the windows of Chartres with us. The lights out, it closes its eyes at night in our beds with us.

There is all Africa and her prodigies in us.

In man is all whatsoever the sun shines upon or heaven contains, as also hell and all the Deeps.

I have discovered for myself that the old human and animal world, indeed the entire prehistory and past of all sentient being, works on, lives on, hates on, thinks on in me.

I have seen trunk and horn, tusk and hoof, in odd places.

How deinanthropic anthropus is.

Given that we are deinanthropic in ways that Sophocles didn't take account of, given that we are fearfully and wonderfully made, shouldn't we think again? Shouldn't we recognize that to cross from the near to the far bank of the Kedron is a journey altogether greater than any space journey we might embark on? The author of the fourth Gospel puts it very simply:

> *In illo tempore: Egressus est Jesus cum discipulis suis trans torrentem Cedron.*

Evolving life has crossed the torrent.

Evolving life is already transtorrentem, is already undergoing its final, transtorrentem transitions. The Earth therefore is the planet in space we

17

should be journeying towards. The trail to it is open. And our guardian and guide on that trail is Bright Angel.

Given our karmic condition, Bright Angel Trail is for the moment the only space journey we should set foot on.

Waiting for us here at home, Bright Angel is the Extra Terrestrial, or should we say the Intra Terrestrial, that we have most to learn from.

Guardian Angel. Guiding Angel. Bright Angel. Angel of our next, necessary initiations. Angel of our last evolutionary transitions.

If our myth says sooth, our *techne* had its source in Promethean *tolma*. We nonetheless chose and continue to choose the Titanic, Asuric way. And now it has happened. And sadly, we cannot yet see that we are ourselves the iceberg the Earth has crashed into. We are ourselves the iceberg we have crashed into.

Aeneas, Abraham, Ishmael. Aeneas leaving the burning town. Abraham walking out of a jaded age. And, his soul sea-searched but not sea-shriven, a sole survivor hands in a psalm at King David's door, hands in a stasimon at Sophocles' door, and then, standing beside Areopagus Rock, standing where Orestes stood, he tells us our story.

The voyage, he calls it. The voyage in five tall ships:

Argo, Nave, Mayflower, Beagle, Pequod

Our *polla ta deina* voyage into the Sea of Typhoons that we ourselves have become.

The voyage of deinanthropus.

Call him that, call him Deinanthropus.

The violent one, Heidegger calls him. He describes him:

The violent one, the creative man, who sets forth into the un-said, who breaks into the unthought, compels the unhappened to happen and makes the unseen appear – this violent one stands at all times in venture. In venturing to master being, he must risk the assault of the non-essent, *me kalon*, he must risk dispersion, instability, disorder, mischief. The higher the summit of historical being-there, the deeper will be the abyss, the more abrupt the fall into the unhistorical which merely thrashes around in issueless and placeless confusion.

And there he is, the violent one, the *yu-wei* one, the sole survivor, the new Deucalion, and he will not find healing as Orestes did at Areopagus Rock, nor will he find healing as Oedipus did in the Grove of the Erinyes in Colonus. The healing he needs will only be found on the far side of the Torrent, call it the Ilissus or the Kedron.

The Garden of Olives is the transtorrentem counterpart of the Grove of the Erinyes in Colonus. Golgotha is the transtorrentem counterpart of Areopagus Rock.

In the Grove of the Erinyes in Colonus and also at Areopagus Rock we are healed as Rousseau would heal us. We are healed outside ourselves, healed in our circumstances. In the Garden of Olives and on Golgotha we are healed as Christ would heal us, from within.

It is only in transtorrentem encounter with what we inwardly are that we can in any way understand Christianity – the Christianity that has its original and continuing source in the Triduum Sacrum.

Speaking, surely, from transtorrentem experience of himself, William Law reminds us that

The time of disputing and speculating upon ideas is short; it can last no longer than whilst the sun of this world can refresh your flesh and blood, and so keep the soul from knowing its own depth or what has been growing in it. But when this is over, then you must know and feel what it is to have a nature as deep and strong and large as eternity.

There is, D.H. Lawrence assures us, a form of immediate anthropology in which we know not just what we are but all that we have been:

The adventure of knowledge is not finished for us till we have got back to the very sources, discovered satisfactorily to ourselves our own sources, in sensation, as one traces back a river – it is a form of immediate anthropology, we study the origins of man in our own immediate experience, we push right back to the first, and last, sensations of procreation and death.

Not since the victories of science in the seventeenth century, not since Bruno was burned and Jacob Boehme was silenced, have we had the courage to seek in immediate anthropology for knowledge of our own and the world's origins. And yet, the risk of major error and delusion notwithstanding, there is surely no more natural place in which to look. It was, most certainly, out of immediate anthropology that the Buddha spoke when he said:

I proclaim, friend, that in this fathom-sized, feeling-afflicted, ascetic's body dwell the world and the origin of the world and the annulment of the world and the path that leads to the annulment of the world.

Within each of us is the pre-cosmic, pre-psychic silence in which can be heard the first vibration or sound out of the Divine Beyond-Being-Beyond-Nonbeing. Hindus call it *anahata shabda*, the sound that isn't the sound of any two things striking together, the sound that blossoms into the great oratorio or symphony that we call the universe.

Idealizing it, we might say: a happening but not by way of occurrence, process or event. A happening out of the Divine Ungrund. A happening in which nothing happens. A happening in which nothing takes place. Yet now it is: awareness of self and other-than-self, and at the heart of it all a Horsehead Nebula neighing: *yatra na anyat pasyati, na anyat srinoti, na anyad vijanati, sa bhuma.*

Mo wei is the corresponding Chinese concept. It suggests that no one or nothing produced or caused or created the universe.

Causation is an *a priori* category of the understanding. It has no application to eternal beginnings.

Beginnings we carry always with us.

Being within us, the beginnings of all things are always with us. It isn't only Atum who remembers his emergence from the Waters of Nun, who remembers his night, before night was or day was, in the coils of Iru-To.

In every egg, in every womb, are the Waters of Nun.

All ovum waters are the Waters of Nun.

It isn't only Venus who has come ashore. Everyone who is egg-born or womb-born has come ashore.

Venus coming ashore.

Venus Anadyomene.

Can you see her? Can you see her as Titian saw her? Hip-deep in the tide, she is wringing sea-water out of her hair. As Atum did. As you did. As I did.

Hip deep, like Venus, in the tide, we have all wrung the Waters of Nun out of our hair. Out of our hair only. Not out of our lives. Not out of our minds.

Remembered or not, our emergence from the Waters of Nun always walks with us. However far inland we walk, it walks with us.

No matter how far inland we walk, no matter how excludingly strong the city-wall we build about us, the possibility of regression walks everywhere and always with us.

But we shouldn't talk only about the possibility of regression. We should also talk about a need, now and then, for a regression.

'Everything perfect reverts to the primeval.' So says Rilke in a sonnet to Orpheus. And, in *The Books of Hours*, there is a poem of his that concludes with this stanza:

> The ore is homesick. And it yearns
> To leave the coin and leave the wheel
> That teach it to lead a life inane.
> The factories and tills it spurns;

From petty forms it will uncongeal,
Return to the open mountain's vein
And on it the mountain will close again.

And, in *Apocalypse*, D.H. Lawrence has this to say:

Man's consciousness has many layers, and the lowest layers continue to be crudely active, especially down among the common people, for centuries after the cultured consciousness of the nation has passed to higher planes. And the consciousness of man always tends to revert to the original levels; though there are two modes of reversion: by degeneration and decadence; and by deliberate return in order to get back to the roots again, for a new start.

No matter how homesick, like ore, they might be, it is difficult for Europeans to return to the primeval. The Bible has built bars and doors against it. The Bible and Greek philosophy are a kind of cultural immune system which, all too effectively, keep it at bay, which, all too efectively, keep us constrained, as ore is constrained, to civic utility.

Job was happy in his civic perfection. A man of substance, he would sit in the city gate, facing east at evening, dispensing conventional wisdom. Never once did he acknowledge or honour or make contact with the ore he had been civically minted from. Civic to his core, as he thought, he was never conscious that any residuum of ore in him yearned for the mountain. Then, suddenly, a wide breaking in of Abyssal waters. An inner hell he had never suspected was naked before him. Looking in his mirror, he saw the King of Terrors. It wasn't long until Job, hitherto so serenely civic, was confessing, to anyone who would listen, that he was a brother to dragons and a companion to owls. A spectacular and, at times, a stupendous regression was enacting itself in him. His immunities, his city wall, his bars and doors against the primeval, had been washed away.

The Gethsemane regression that Jesus consented to carried him down through all the karmic floors of the Grand Canyon. The Good Friday regression he gave himself up to carried him inwardly back through our bars and doors, carried him all the way back to the Waters of Nun.

Noah sent out a raven.

Noah sent out a dove.

The dove brought back the Narada parable.

When I wake up from the world-illusion, what, coming towards me, will Vishnu ask me?

What forgotten errand am I on?

For what forgotten reason am I here?

For what forgotten reason do I exist?

Narada I am and Noah.

Narada-Noah I am.

Narada-Noah going into a green village in a green land. Narada-Noah knocking at a door and the door opening.

And maya prevailed. Fifteen cubits everywhere upwards and down-wards did maya prevail and Narada-Noah sent out a raven and seven days later he sent out a dove, and the raven, returning, spread its world-wide wings above the ark and called out: wake up from waking.

An eclipse of dreaming and waking I am.

An eclipse of awareness-of I am.

The octopus who is, and also is in, his own eclipsing inkcloud of dreaming and waking and antarabhavic awareness-of I am.

The ostrich who is, and is in, an eclipsing sandheap of hearing, seeing, touch, taste and smell I am.

Eternal splendour transcendentally within me I eclipse.

Divine Ground transcendentally within me I eclipse.

In hearing eclipse, in seeing eclipse, in thinking eclipse, in touch, taste and smell eclipse.

And the Horsehead Nebula neighs

Na

Na

Na

yatra na anyat pasyati, na anyat srinoti, na anyad vijanati, sa bhuma.

Born with the universe a reminder that the universe isn't all of what is. Born with the universe a reminder that our life in the universe isn't all of what we are.

Born with awareness of self and other-than-self a reminder that aware-ness of self and other-than-self isn't all of what is.

On Golgotha, on Good Friday, Calvary a long way below him, Jesus underwent an epistemological ragnarok.

On Golgotha, on Good Friday, Christianity became a great Oriental religion – as such, although Berkeley and Kant have prepared the way, it has yet to come West.

It was biblical naive realism that rolled from the tomb door on Easter morning.

On the stone that rolled from the door we can write it – in Nordic runes write it – an account of Christ's epistemological ragnarok. Com-pared with that ragnarok, Kant's Copernican revolution in philosophy is miserably incomplete. Compared with Christ looking down into Adam's empty skull, and seeing himself in it, all European philosophers, includ-ing Kant, are Ptolemaic.

What was it we heard? A single cock crowing, naively, thrice? Or three cocks, each in his turn crowing, apocalyptically, once?

There are philosophical ways of being St Peter.

There are philosophical ways of being Judas.

There are ways of denying and betraying the philosophical enormity of what happened.

In the Christian tradition, ever since Good Friday on Golgotha, Tenbrae is the philosophical ur-word.

Ritually, in philosophical praxis, it is the philosophical ur-word. Its subsequent equilvalents are Cloud of Unknowing and Dark Night of the Soul.

Good Friday: the day Western metaphysics became metanoesis.

Philosophically, Narada is not at all exotic.

Philosophically, Narada is our Noah.

Rainbow in the cloud.

Mandukya Upanishad in the cloud.

And coming ashore, coming back from self-loss in the Divine Ungrund, Jesu Absu walks inland and, still within hearing of the whale-voice, he sees and he blesses the six summer soarings at his earthly feet.

In him now, seeing isn't other than samadhi. To him now the world isn't other than Nirguna Brahman.

And one day the heavens, the hells and the Earth itself will light Christmas candles to our lost and found capacity for ordinariness.

There is an Easter which is an awakening to the extraordinary. And there is an Easter, altogether greater, which is an awakening to the ordinary.

An ordinary fern in an ordinary wood.

In its presence, like Moses in the presence of the burning bush, I put off my shoes from off my feet.

In its presence I put off all passion and love from off my heart, all knowledge, all needing to know, from off my mind. All movements of passion and knowing would disturb the wonder, would eclipse the wonder, that is seeing, that is samadhi.

Actaeon, whom we read about in Greek mythology, was a mighty hunter. It had been a long winter, and an even longer spring, for he had to sit at home recovering from injuries. But now it was summer and he was out there in the wild highlands, his hounds and his instincts unleashed. A hind they sprung carried them far in a maze of goings across trackless wilderness. Breathlessly anticipating the moment when the hind would be brought down, Actaeon's attention was dangerously narrowed and so it was that, even before he was aware of it, he was drawing himself up precipitously short on the brink of an unexpected river. And he saw them, couldn't help but see them, in their nakedness, the Goddess Artemis and her nymphs bathing in a pool below him. Outraged at being so seen, Artemis turned the full power of her transforming gaze upon him, turning him into a stag. Scenting his stag-smell, his hounds howled. Actaeon pleaded, calling them by their names. He panicked. He bolted. His hounds gave chase. They ran him down and tore him asunder.

Actaeon's seeing. A seeing, sudden and terrible, into our transcendent depths. And who can see these depths and live? Who, having seen them, can live in the old ways for the old reasons? Who, having seen them, can be satisfied now with life on earth or with life in heaven? Who, having seen them, won't want heaven out of the way, earth out of the way? Who, having seen them, won't want himself or herself out of the way? Who, having seen them, won't want a path to open in the obstructing Red Sea of experience of self and other-than-self? Who, having seen them, won't want to cross the brook Kedron into Gethsemane and Good Friday?

Actaeon saw.

And Jesus saw.

As stag and lamb they crossed the Kedron.

Actaeon was hounds to himself.

Jesus was Judas to himself, was Caiaphas to himself, was Pilate to himself, was Roman soldiers to himself, was Longinus to himself.

On Good Friday the veil in the temple was rent. The veil, which the human psyche is, was rent. And, in the person of Jesus looking down into the emptiness of the empty skull at the foot of the cross, each of us at that moment was Narada undergoing the most awful of all initiations, our initiation into complete and perfect dis-illusioning. A catastrophe it is, yes. But to be engulfed in that catastrophe is our only ark.

In ancient Egypt it became customary to ritually incorporate a person who had died into the postmortem destiny of Osiris. As Osiris, having been resucitated, lived again, so, sharing his fate, would the dead person live again. So complete did they imagine the incorporation to be, that the dead person was thereafter known as the Osiris or as Osiris so-and-so, Osiris Unas, say, Osiris Ani, Osiris Tutu, Osiris Meret, Osiris Tutankhamen.

Incorporation into the revival of Osiris.

Incorporation into the dis-illusioning of Narada.

Osiris Unas. Narada Unas.

Osiris Ani. Narada Ani.

A version of the Theban recension of the Egyptian Book of the Dead, inscribed on papyrus, was interred in his tomb with Osiris Ani.

As I imagine it, it is the Mandukya Upanishad which would be interred in his tomb with Narada Ani.

The Narada initiation, the Narada knowing, in virtue of which Homo can call itself sapiens.

Emerging from his initiation, Narada will be inclined to say that, just as there is a membrane that secretes mucus, so is there a membrane that secretes maya. And mind, which can exist independently of brain, is the maya membrane. But this is just a first crude attempt to draw a conclusion from what has happened. His knowing is already more subtle than that but he hasn't words for it. He will only know it when he has the words.

Bringing the Narada parable to the Nile Valley. Bringing it to Mesopotamia and Canaan.

Replacing the Noah narrative in the Bible with the Narada narrative.

The Book of Narada, the Book of Job, the Book of Jonah.

Considering the initiations he will himself undergo, Christ's ancestors are Narada, Job and Jonah.

In medieval Christendom a person who imitated Christ to the point of being Christlike, would sometimes be called an *Alter Christus*, Another Christ.

To say Alter Christus is to say Alter Narada, Alter Job, Alter Jonah, Alter Jesus.

The initiations we undergo when we cross the Kedron.

Has Christianity learned to speak the word Gethsemane? Has it learned to speak the words Golgotha and Garden of the Sepulchre?

Gethsemane, Golgotha, Garden of the Sepulchre: a Christianity that has learned to speak these words, that has learned to speak them upanishadically, in Christian Upanishads, won't need to fear for its foundations when it hears that a new *Beagle* has set out into heavy south-westerlies. It will have earned, or re-earned, its right to think of itself as a teacher of humankind.

Three words to learn. Three words to teach.

Buddhism proposes four noble truths. Christianity proposes three.

Buddhism proposes an eightfold path. Christianity proposes the path that leads to the Kedron and crosses it.

In the century of Auschwitz, Christ must cross the Kedron again. We must learn to have confidence not only in the Heights, we must learn also to have confidence in the Depths. We must learn that the Depths are Divine.

Bars and doors aren't a good answer.

Bars and doors are trouble. Or the threat of trouble.

The breaking down of Jesus on Good Friday was the breaking down of our bars and doors. The lance pierced them and there it was:

Tao Turiya Tehom

It was our Terror of the Depths that was pierced.

And when, in our century, Jesus comes to the Kedron, he will find a well-worn path. A path walked by himself, and walked by many who have walked in his footsteps. Among them Dionysius the Areopagite, Eckhart, Tauler, Suso, Ruysbroeck, Hadewyck, the author of *The Cloud of Unknowing*, Walter Hilton, Dame Julian of Norwich, Marguerite Porete, Catherine of Genoa, Angelo of Foligno, Catherine of Siena, Teresa of Avila, St John of the Cross, Fenelon, De Caussade: legion are they who have crossed the Kedron, and their sermons, tracts, canticles, hymns to Brother Sun and Sister Moon, are our Upanishads.

The Rhine is our Ganges, Cologne our Benares.

The only Orient we are ever likely to need is here at home.

Narada, Job, Jonah are Magi who didn't only come as far as Bethlehem. They journeyed on to Good Friday, but not as spectators. They watched with him, which means they underwent with him, till the end.

Imagine them: Magi who, continuing to watch, are invited into the greatest of all journeys. A journey from Holy Thursday in the Garden of Olives to Holy Thursday in Gethsemane, from Good Friday on Calvary to Good Friday on Golgotha, from Easter morning in the Garden of the Sepulchre to Easter morning on the shore of Turiya-Tehom.

To cross the Kedron with Jesus, to watch with him, which means to undergo with him, is the Christian way of being a philosopher.

How resistant to Narada, how resistant to his story, to his initiation, is Europe's cultural immune system? How resistant to Narada and his knowing, to Job and his knowing, to Jonah and his knowing, are the city walls of Alexandria, Ephesus, Nicaea, Chalcedon, Trent, the Vatican? How resistant to their jnana, their gnosis, is Christianity's spiritual, psychological immune system?

> The Roman Empire stood appalled;
> It dropped the reins of peace and war
> When that fierce Virgin and her Star
> Out of the fabulous darkness called.

Can Christianity, as it now exists, hear the Gnostic Call, the jnana call, the arya-jnana call, that comes to it out of the fabulous darkness of Good

Friday? A call that calls it to cross over, bringing its Evangel with it, into Evangelanta. The Evangelanta that is already within it, waiting for it, with gates wide open.

Thebes was a city of seven gates. One day Dionysus, an unheard-of, tremendous new God, a God of miracles and mountain dancing, had come. A God awe-full in impulse and inspiration had come. A God of sparagmos, omophagia, enthusiasmos and ekstasis had come. He stood in the northern gate, effeminate, smiling, terrible. The question was, could the city welcome him, were the people able for him? Was the old order threatened in its most fundamental assumptions, in its most sustaining institutions? They had no choice. On the mountain that night, dressed in fawnskins, phrenzied and dancing, the women of the city were votaries, were Maenads, their heads and their hands dreaming ecstacies of havoc to young lions and old lions, to any wild animal they caught, to Pentheus the king whose reasons for climbing were sacrilegious. A terrible visitation from a terrible God who might, at any moment, stand before you, working at your loom, as boy or bull.

Imagine the modern West. Like Thebes, its cultural immune system has seven gates in it. And standing in one of them one morning is Narada and his knowing. Will we welcome him? Welcome or not, will he walk among us? Will three or four centuries of single vision and Newton's sleep be vexed to nightmare by a walking parable? Will three or four centuries of Ulro opacity and contraction be nightmared into a Great Awakening?

The nebula out of which our solar system evolved, can we hear that Horsehead Nebula neighing

Na

Na

Na

yatra na anyat pasyati, na anyat srinoti, na anyad vijanati, sa bhuma.

> Watchman, what of the Night?
> Narada, he called.
> Watchman, what of the Night?
> Monsoon clouds on all Christian horizons, he called.
> Watchman, what of the Night?
> The raven flying to and fro, he called.
> Watchman, what of the Night?
> The raven calling out, Tehom is Turiya.

Foxes have holes, birds of the air have nests, but the Son of Man has nowhere to lay his head. Outwardly, in empirical reality, nowhere.

Inwardly, on states of mind, dreaming or waking, nowhere. Mind in the elementary sense of awareness-of, mind in the sense of mental activity, isn't first and foremost, isn't foundation or ground. And so we come again to that awful, marvellous moment on Good Friday when, his head collapsed onto his chest, Jesus looks down into Adam's empty skull and the heavens, opening, were upanishadically harrowed, and hell, opening, was upanishadically harrowed, and the Earth, opening, was upanishadically harrowed, and the Angels who sang on Christmas night sang now again.

! Oh dichosa ventura

And there was round about Jesus on Golgotha all beings of all realms, round about him on Golgotha was the Pleroma of harrowed heavens, earths and hells, all of them singing

! Oh dichosa ventura
! Oh dichosa ventura
! Oh dichosa ventura

When will Christianity be big enough for Jesus? For the Jesus who has crossed the Kedron? When will it be upanishadically big enough, architecturally, ritually, religiously big enough?

Unknown to us in Christendom the Christian rosary has been blossoming with mysteries unknown to the Good News.

The sea has opened.

The sea of awareness-of has opened, is always open, and already there are many who have walked dryshod through into Turiya. And that requires of you a new song, Miriam. That requires of you a Mandukya silence at the end of your song.

There is in us all a depth that is eternally pure, eternally undefiled, eternally unharmed by the darkest of our incarnations. A depth undefiled by our vices, no radiance added to it by our virtues. A depth undefiled by our sanctity, by our sinfulness. A depth undisturbed by our sensualities and samadhis.

To believe, as Christians do, that this innermost depth of us can be defiled, polluted, darkened, corrupted, or even killed by sin is a stupendous misfortune.

It is never a question of saving one's soul. Rather is it a question of allowing the innermost depth of us to shine upon us and heal us.

Empirical seeing, viksepashakti seeing, avarana-shakti seeing, is the blindfold which prevents us from seeing the saving depths of our souls.

Empirical seeing opened and Actaeon saw.

Empirical seeing opened and Jesus saw.

Empirical seeing didn't open in Narcissus. Seeing only himself, he fell into selfhood, drowned into selfhood.

Only selfhood, Jacob Boehme says, burns in hell.

The depths of our souls aren't personal depths, hyphenated to an ego. They don't belong to us, nor are they actively involved in us, as personal identities. They are neither personal nor impersonal, antipersonal or propersonal. But anyone who looks into the silent, rich no-thing-ness of them will almost certainly become an Actaeon to his own hunger and thirst for liberating self-loss in them.

It is because of its richness that the soul at its core must be forever a no-thing-ness. In its no-thing-ness it is forever available to reabsorbption by the Divine. That is what soul in me is: it is availability in me to reab-sorbption by the Divine.

For as long as Christianity believes that the soul is defilable at its core, for so long will it have forfeited its claim to be able to administer healing to humanity.

Healing of the psyche and, in moments of mystical reabsorbption, healing from it.

The joy of heaven, the perdition of hell, the ups and downs of life on Earth, are bags we pull down over our heads to make sure we don't see, not just yet, into the depths of our soul.

It isn't with our ordinary eyes, neither is it with our third eye, that we see into the depths of our souls. Seeing is but a metaphor for what hap-pens. The Bhagavad Gita's way of saying it is: *atmani atmanam atmana*: know the atman in the atman alone through the atman.

Actaeon and Artemis. Psyche and Soul. The one cannot look upon the other and want to live in the old ways for the old reasons. And it is when there is no Artemis in it that the pool is most stupendously Divine. Vision veils. Something seen veils.

'So long as the soul beholds forms, even though she behold an angel, or herself as something formed: so long is there imperfection in her.' So says Eckhart.

The dark Good Friday seeing, which isn't seeing at all, of Actaeon.

The dark Good Friday seeing, which isn't seeing at all, of Jesus.

The seeing that isn't blinded by eyesight or by things seen.

How many times will Narcissus drown into selfhood before he is ready for the adarsana yoga and the asparsya yoga of Good Friday?

The Dark of Good Friday. The Divine Dark that shines when the eclipse of dreaming, waking and antarabhavic awareness-of is rent.

It is the so-called light of dreaming, waking and antarabhavic aware-ness-of in us that eclipses.

Depth of soul in us is Divine Deep in us.

The Divine Deep that isn't a depth.

Divine Deep. Divine Ungrund.

Divine Ungrund is ground to all that we are. It is ground to our for-getfulness of it. Ground to our blindness to it, our resistance to it. It is infi-nitely calm, safeguarding ground to our terror of it.

It would be best perhaps if we used the word 'soul' only when we wish to imply that there is something more serious about us than our empiri-cal humanity. About that in virtue of which we are more serious than our empirical humanity even ecstacy and rapture can't speak. Like ourselves, ecstacy and rapture just stand there dumbfounded.

There is no separation in the Divine. It is only in ourselves that the separation or the illusion of separation is. Think of it this way: asleep on my bed in my room at night I dream that I am in Isfahan looking up at the blue dome of a mosque. This dream experience of myself in Isfahan shuts out my experience of myself lying in my bed in my house beside the Owenmore river. I am in other words in my room, yet I am dreamingly separate from it. So also am I dreamingly and wakingly separate from the Divine I am always in.

Returning to the ark the raven spread his worldwide weary wings above it and called out: it is a deluge of dreaming and waking: wake up from dreaming. And the dove spreading her worldwide, worldforgetting wings above it called out: it is a deluge of dreaming and waking: wake up from waking.

The Great Awakening.

Narada-Noah's Great Awakening

The veil his psyche is, is rent.

How can he integrate such a stupendous event? After how many years of nights and days will he still be attempting to integrate it?

Waking has walked out on him. Dreaming has walked out on him. Desperate now, experiencing the Good Friday dereliction now, Narada-Noah might well send out a raven, might well send out a dove, in this most awful of all extremities he might well send out an eagle, a falcon, a condor, a cormorant, an albatross, an owl, a swallow, a tern, asking them to overfly all peoples, all cultures, all religions, seeking everywhere and anywhere for myths, metaphors, Upanishads, Sutras, suras, sermons, seek-ing anything anywhere that might speak to his condition. All religions are his religions now. His house now is a Musée de l'Homme.

In a late-thirteenth-century chapel in France there is a faded fresco that depicts the temptation of Eve by the Serpent. The tree about which the Serpent is entwined looks astonishingly like an *Amanita muscaria* mushroom. Whether in fact the *Amanita muscaria* mushroom was intended we cannot say. And for our purposes here it isn't necessary to decide one way or the other; it only matters that we've stumbled upon an idea. Let us suppose that the tree of knowledge of good and evil was an *Amanita muscaria* mushroom; let us also suppose that, having been ingested by them, it gave rise in Adam and Eve to the hallucinating high of dreaming and waking awareness-of; let us further suppose that, in them and in us, their descendants, this high became biologically incorporated as a permanent condition grounded and sustained in our nervous systems; and now again let us suppose that over the generations, we have become identified with this high, imagining it to be source, centre and core of us; supposing we agree that all of this is true, a true account of the Fall, it makes sense then, albeit within the parameters of these suppositions, that we would cross the Kedron and, on the far side of Gethsemane, surrender to the Great Good Friday Dis-illusioning.

Not, as in Buddhism, a twelve-fold chain, but a four-fold chain of causal co-production: *Pia mater, Maya mater, Amanita muscaria mater, Aminata muscaria mater mirageans.*

Dreaming walked out on him. Waking walked out on him.

The eclipsing, veiling high was rent. And he was derelict.

There is Yeats's poem 'The Magi':

> Now as at all times I can see in the mind's eye
> In their stiff, painted clothes, the pale unsatisfied ones
> Appear and disappear in the blue depth of the sky
> With all their ancient faces like rain-beaten stones,
> And all their helms of silver hovering side by side,
> And all their eyes still fixed, hoping to find once more,
> Being by Calvary's turbulence unsatisfied,
> The uncontrollable mystery on the bestial floor.

Any magus or pythia or sibyl or spakona or tairbfheis visionary who comes as far as Calvary and sees only the turbulence hasn't come as far as Good Friday.

Our road to Good Friday isn't a road that we walk. It is a road that walks us. And it walks us into and through the Job, the Jonah and the Narada initiations. Only then do we see beyond the turbulence. Only then are we epoptai of Chandogya Good News.

Good Friday Good News is ghora murti Good News: in appearance, in its mode of being manifest, it looks and it is terrible. Buddhist Good

News is *sundara murti* Good News; in appearance it is charming: a Buddha, vaguely smiling, sitting in the lotus position.

Ghora murti Good News. But we musn't crucify Good Friday itself to the crucifixion.

Good Friday on Calvary is synonymous with the crucifixion. Good Friday on Golgotha isn't. The darkness of Good Friday on Calvary is an absence of light. The darkness of Good Friday on Golgotha is Tenebrae.

Hindus are able for the Divine in terrible form. They are able for Bhairava and Bhairavi. They are able for Kali with her necklace of skulls, her swords and scimitars and her bloody, long, lolling tongue. They are able for Vishnu. In one of his incarnations Vishnu was a primal boar. In another he was a man-lion. And in his next incarnation, which might happen any day now, he will be a strange and terrible horse called Kalkin.

Could we think of Kalkin as a condensation of the Horsehead Nebula out of which our solar system evolved? The Horsehead Nebula that neighed Chandogya Good News into our sun and its satellites at their inception?

Universe.

Mantraverse.

Mahavakyaverse.

The mathsphysics of the Mandukya Om.

The mathsphysics of *anahata*, that first and original sound out of Nirguna Brahman, the sound that isn't the sound of any two things striking together.

It isn't with our radio telescopes that we will hear that sound. Neither will we hear it with our open heart chakra. It isn't in or with any sense of hearing, subtle or gross, that we hear it. And yet, paradoxically, there are those who have 'heard' it.

Coming ashore from the Job, the Jonah and the Narada initiations, George Gamow won't call it a Big Bang.

A scientist who, instead of putting things in a test-tube, walks into a test-tube, into a cave in Ajanta.

> Those are pearls that were his eyes,
> Those are charkras that were his callosa.

To be padmasambhava, to be lotus-born.

To be ratnasambhvava, to be jewel-born.

To stand between the windows of Chartres Cathedral and consent to be jewel-born.

Consenting to be lotus-born, to be jewel-born. Consenting to the great purification:

At midnight on the Emperor's pavement flit
Flames that no faggot feeds, nor steel has lit,
Nor storm disturbs, flames begotten of flame,
Where blood-begotten spirits come
And all complexities of fury leave,
Dying into a dance,
An agony of trance,
An agony of flame that cannot singe a sleave.

Can you hear the great antiphon of the Christmas Midnight Mass?

In splendoribus sanctorum ex utero ante luciferum genui te.

In the splendours of holiness, out of the womb, before the morning, I have begotten you.

Imagine that antiphon being sung in Chartres Cathedral. Even the notes, hanging in the air, must have seemed lotus-born, rose-born, jewel-born.

As a European, however, I'm an heir not only to Chartres. I'm an heir also to Auschwitz.

As an amoeba reshapes itself so as to incorporate a particle of food, so must Europe reshape itself, spirtually, culturally, psychologically, morally, in its efforts to come to terms with Auschwitz.

Speculum naturae, speculum historiae, speculum moralis. We look in the mirror of nature, we look in the mirror of history, we look in the mirror of morals, and like Jesus in Gethsemane we are sore amazed. By ourselves sore amazed. At ourselves sore amazed. Auschwitz points not just to regressed nature in us. It points to fallen spirit in us. To spirit become wicked. To spirit become nonchalantly demonic. Christ must cross the Kedron again.

Ancient Egyptians kept in touch, creatively and dreamingly, with Tai-wer, the most ancient land, the first land or mound that appeared above the Waters of Nun. Imagining it and reimagining it, they kept in touch, till the end of their civilization, with Tep-zepi, the first time.

On Good Friday, from the sixth to the ninth hour, darkness prevailed. Fifteen cubits upwards above the whole world it prevailed and all the high mountains and stars were covered. And Golgotha, Hill of the Koshaless Skull, was Tai-wer, lovely to behold, Golgotha was the first mound out of the Waters. There was morning and evening a first day, and this day was Tep-zepi.

First Land: Tai-wer.
First Time: Tep-zepi.

Seals must keep breathing-holes open in the ice. So must we keep breathing-holes open into Tep-zepi, onto Tai-wer. Like seals hauling themselves out onto the ice, so must we haul ourselves out onto and into the Beginning. And to begin with, it will do to haul ourselves out onto and into the beginning as ancient Egyptians have imagined it, as Chinese have imagined it, or as Hindus have imagined it, or as Navajo, Maidu, or Maoris and Australian Aborigines have imagined it, as people everywhere and anywhere have imagined it. We must breathe the Beginning. We must walk with the very first stirrings of the human and universal imagination in Tep-zepi and Tai-wer.

The beginning, Heidegger says, is the strangest and mightiest. What comes afterwards is not development but the flattening that comes from mere spreading out; it is inability to retain the beginning ...

The Navajo have songs which they call hozhonji songs. Hozhonji songs are holy songs given to them by the Gods. These songs don't only describe a journey to the sacred land beyond the mountains, they are that journey and anyone who, as it were, boards a hozhonji song, goes on its journey with it.

Imagine a hozhonji song taking us to the pure Beginning, to the pure time and the pure land, to Tep-zepi and Tai-wer:

> Swift and far I journey,
> Swift upon the rainbow,
> Swift and far I journey,
> Lo, yonder, the Holy Place.
> Yea, swift and far I journey
> To Sisnajinni and beyond it,
> Yea, swift and far I journey,
> The Chief of Mountains and beyond it.
> Yea, swift and far I journey
> To Life Unending and beyond it.
> Yea, swift and far I journey
> To Joy Unchanging and beyond it,
> Yea, swift and far I journey.
>
> Homeward now shall I journey,
> Homeward upon the rainbow.
>
> Homeward behold me starting,
> Homeward upon the rainbow.
>
> Homeward behold me faring,
> Homeward upon the rainbow.

Now arrived home behold me,
Now arrived on the rainbow,
Now arrived home behold me,
Lo, here, the Holy Place.

Yea, now arrived home behold me
At Sisnajinni, and beyond it,
Yea, now arrived home behold me
The Chief of Mountains, and beyond it,
Yea, now arrived home behold me,
In Life Unending and beyond it,
Yea, now arrived home behold me
In Joy Unchanging, and beyond it,
Yea, now arrived home behold me.

Seated at home behold me
Seated amid the Rainbow,
Seated at home behold me
Lo, here, the Holy Place!

Yea, seated at home behold me
At Sisnajinni and beyond it,
Yea, seated at home behold me
The Chief of Mountains and beyond it,
Yea, seated at home behold me
In Life Unending and beyond it,
Yea, seated at home behold me
In Joy Unending and beyond it,
Yea, seated at home behold me.

The Navajo way, the way of the hozhonji song. The hozhonji songs
that take us to Tep-zepi

Yea, walking in Tep-Zepi behold me
Cutting turf for my fire behold me,
Feeding my hens behold me,
Turning out my cows after milking behold me,
Thatching my house in Tep-zepi behold me
Yea, living with my wife and my child in Tai-wer behold me.

Tep-zepi always is. Tai-wer always is.
Tep-Zepi is where we are.
Only the greatest of hozhonji songs can take us to where we are.
Arriving where I always have been I listen to Lao-Tzu talking about
the Taoist sage:

Without leaving his door
He knows everything under heaven.
Without looking out of his window
He knows all the ways of heaven.
For the farther one travels (from Tao)
The less he knows.
Therefore the sage arrives without going,
Sees all without looking,
Does nothing, yet achieves everything.

I listen to him talking about the ideal community:

The neighbouring settlements may be so close that one can hear the cocks crow
and the dogs bark, but the people may grow old and die without going back and
forth.

In Bacon's terms, people who have given themselves to movement
essential aren't much interested in movement local. And again, people
who have given themselves to movement essential will choose to journey
by a hozhonji song to Tep-zepi or Tai-wer not by a locomotive engine to
the Moon or Mars.

In Tao, the Tao Te Ching tells us, the only motion is returning. And
The Secret of the Golden Flower is emphatic: whoever seeks eternal life must
seek for the place whence human nature and life began.

As Rilke has it: coerced to civic utility, the ore seeks the mountain:

The ore is homesick. And it yearns
To leave the coin and leave the wheel
That teach it to lead a life inane.
The factories and tills it spurns;
From petty forms it will uncongeal,
Return to the open mountain's vein
And on it the mountain will chose again.

But, heirs as we are to the Promethean theft of fire, we have made a
cultural choice: ours is the way of the movement-local locomotive engine
not the way of the hozhonji song; ours is the way of the revs-per-second
wheel not the way of the bodhimandala.

And yet, although less coerced to civic utility or to civic perfection
than most of us, Wordsworth, like the ore, has yearnings:

The world is too much with us; late and soon,
Getting and spending, we lay waste our powers:
Little we see in Nature that is ours;
We have given our hearts away, a sordid boon!

This sea that bears her bosom to the moon;
The winds that will be howling at all hours,
And are up-gathered now like sleeping flowers;
For this, for everything, we are out of tune;
It moves us not. – Great God! I'd rather be
A Pagan suckled in a creed outworn;
So might I, standing on this pleasant lea,
Have glimpses that would make me less forlorn;
Have sight of Proteus rising from the sea;
Or hear old Triton blow his wreathèd horn.

A humanity that is out of tune with nature will continue yet awhile to build the Willie Loman Land of its own exile, but nothing that is out of tune survives. To be out of tune is the great sickness.

There is, however, a creed, not yet outworn, that might give us suck. It comes not from Willie Loman Land but from the land submerged beneath it, the Land called Turtle Island. Nunataks of this Land are few and far between. And few are they who remember and return to its Tepzepis and its Tai-wers. Few are they who hear the voice of Old Man:

Now, if you are overcome, you may go to sleep and get power. Something will come to you in your dream, and that will help you. Whatever those animals who appear to you in your sleep tell you to do, you must obey them. Be guided by them. If you want help, are alone and travelling, and cry aloud for aid, your prayer will be answered – perhaps by the eagles, or by the buffalo, or by the bears. Whatever animal answers your prayers you must listen.

Is this the primeval way back into which, according to Rilke, everything perfect returns?

Returning to the primeval, whether within or without, is not, as Job found out, without its great and stupendous perils.

Confronted by enormities within himself, none of which he could rule over and subdue, Job cried out: When I say my bed shall comfort me, my couch shall ease my complaint, then thou scarest me with dreams and terrifiest me through visions so that my soul chooseth strangling and death rather than my life.

In Job our biblical mandate to rule over and subdue was seen for what it was, a pathetic arrogance.

A blessing indeed it is that here, as elsewhere, the Bible has called its own bluff.

In Job is our cultural enantiodromia, and that means that after the voice in the whirlwind the voice of Old Man:

Whatever animal answers your prayer you must listen.

Could it be that Behemoth will answer our prayer? Could it be that Leviathan will answer it? that Unicorn will answer it? Could it be that there is a depth of our psyches, a musical depth, an Orphic depth, a depth at which we are indeed in league with the stones of the field, a depth at which the beasts of the field and the savannah are at peace with us?

Could it be that in the Book of Job we have crossed from one to another age, from the age in which Yahweh slays Leviathan to the age in which Yahweh lies recumbent on the coils of Leviathan?

The Book of Job is the real Book of Exodus. It is the biblical book in which we biblically walked away from biblically induced ecological calamity.

Saying the same thing in terms of Greek mythology: the age of Herakles and his club has been replaced by the age of Orpheus and his lyre.

Beating our dragon-slaying swords into a necklace for Tiamat, into a flukelace for Leviathan.

Turning our clubs into lyres.

Replacing our wheels with bodhimandalas.

Our bodhimandalas will carry us to destinations our locally locomoting wheels will never reach.

The rainbow road that takes us to where we are.

The hozhonji song that takes us to where we are.

Where we are is pristine time, is pristine ground.

The star at my window, here where we are, is like the biography of a jivanmukta, biography dissolved into a pure and simple shining in the eternal now. It isn't out of any universe that we have imagined, it isn't out of any cosmology that we have corralled the stars into, that it shines. Look at it. Open your opened eyes and look at it. It isn't out of a universe that it shines. Out of the Divine Ungrund it shines.

The hozhonji song that brings Timaeus to Tep-zepi.

The hozhonji song that brings Timaeus to Tai-wer.

Sitting in the lotus position on Tai-wer, Timaeus can hear the *anahata* sound, the sound that spontaneously elaborates itself, no demiurge interfering, into a universe.

Timaeus on Tai-wer.

Timaeus listening to Tiamat. Listening in the world's first silence to her whale song. Her medicine song. The song that heals us in our cultural, in our religious, beginnings.

In Tao the only motion is returning.

Not all returns go all the way back to Tep-zepi, all the way back to Tai-wer.

Huichol Indians live in the Sierra Occidental mountains in Mexico. Like Moslems who go on pilgrimage to Mecca, Huichols go on pilgrimage to Wirikuta, the Sacred Land of Peyote. Here they harvest the sacred plant and they bring it home and throughout the year, in religious rites of great fervour, they eat it, yielding themselves up to it, to the visions, the openings, the nierikayas it gives them access to. This is their way of communing eucharistically with their Gods. This is their way of remaining in touch with Divine inspirations and guidance.

The Bodhi Tree and the peyote bush.

Within us all is a peyote bush whose hallucinogens and mescalins give rise to dreaming and waking awareness-of.

The dark night of the soul is the dark night of our inner peyote bush. It is an extinguishing, a quenching, a nirvana of it.

In the course of this dark night we come down from our peyote high of dreaming and waking awareness-of.

Climbing Mount Carmel, or Calvary, or Golgotha, is coming down from our high.

The Mara'akame or Huichol medicine man who leads us to Wirikuta. The guru who leads us out of it.

The Sidpa Bardo during which we yearn for and journey into yet another realm of Wirikuta awareness-of. The dark night of the soul during which we journey out of it.

In Wirikuta Mount Carmel, Golgotha and Borobudur are nunataks.

And the mystical journey isn't a nierikaya, it isn't a journey through extraordinary portals into extraordinary realms in which we have extraordinary experiences. All such extraordinary realms are realms of awareness-of. The mystical journey is a journey away from awareness-of.

A membrane or gland that releases adrenalin.

A membrane or gland that releases mescalin.

A membrane that releases maya.

Pia mater mirageans.

Pia mater mayans.

The mystical journey isn't a gift or grace of peyote.

Peyote bush isn't bodhi bush.

It is likely that, in the course of the mystical journey, nierikas will open, and it is further likely that, because of karmic propensities, we will walk through them.

Peyote bush, maya bush. Mucous membrane. Maya membrane.

There is Good Friday on Calvary and Good Friday on Golgotha.

To surrender to the calamities of pupation in the expectation of a life of *imago* marvellousness: that is Good Friday on Calvary. To surrender to calamities of growings no less immense while having no desire to rediscover oneself in one's selfhood: that is Good Friday on Golgotha.

Good Friday on Calvary happens to us. Good Friday on Golgotha is a going beyond happenings.

The Darkness of Good Friday on Golgotha is a Dark too divinely deep for happenings.

On Calvary, even in the dark, we have existential sight of ourselves. On Golgotha such existential sight is in abeyance.

On his way into the Darkness of Good Friday on Golgotha Jesus left an impression of his face in Veronica's napkin. In this, he was signifying his willingness to lose his empirical identity.

On Calvary, happenings. On Golgotha, release from happenings.

On Calvary form undergoes transformative change. On Golgotha form is out of the way.

In the healing calamities of Good Friday on Calvary there is a nature which is the subject and object of a change taking place. On Golgotha we are in a Divine Deep which is beyond all doing and being done unto.

In dreamless sleep all sense of self and other-than-self has been reabsorbed unconsciously. In the Darkness of Good Friday on Golgotha all sense of self and other-than-self has been reabsorbed, yearningly, willingly, consciously.

Not even me standing between me and God.

The existence of a me between me and God becomes intolerable.

An experiencer experiencing God, standing between me and God, becomes intolerable.

Setting foot on Golgotha, we pray the great prayer of Al Hallaj: Between me and thee there is an 'I am' that torments me. Ah! Through thy 'I am' take away my 'I am' from between us both.

Wirikuta or the Still Wilderness where no phenomenalizing is. Buddhists call it Nirabhasagocara, this still wilderness.

Calvary is a hill in Wirikuta. Golgotha is the same hill in the Still Wilderness.

On Calvary I die with an obol or peyote button in my mouth. On Golgotha I die with a Chandogya mahavakya in my mouth: *yatra na anyat pasyati, na anyat srinoti, na anyad vijanati, sa bhuma.*

Holy Thursday night in the Garden of Olives is portal to Good Friday on Calvary. Holy Thursday night in Gethsemane is portal to Good Friday on Golgotha.

In the gulf between Calvary and Golgotha our rock of faith becomes an abyss of faith.

Abyss of faith. Turiya of faith. Tao Turiya Tehom of faith.

On Calvary the Way is still a way, on Golgotha it is wayless.

Evangel on Calvary. Evangelanta on Golgotha.

In the tomb on Easter morning after Good Friday on Calvary there were two bright angels announcing that Jesus had risen. In the tomb on Easter morning after Good Friday on Golgotha, there was silence. The silence that follows the sounding of the Mandukya om, the A, U, and M of it, the waking, dreaming and dreamless sleep of it. The silence that was before the world was or psyche was. The silence that signifies and is Turiya.

> Easter Morning
> Mandukya Morning
>
> Easter Morning
> Advaitaevangelanta Morning

Towards the end of Christmas week three wise men came, bringing gifts of gold, frankincense and myrrh. At the beginning of Holy Week they came, bringing the stories of Job, Jonah and Narada.

Holy Week. Holy originally. Holy subsequently, in ritual re-enactment.

Of all the rituals of Holy Week there is none so dreadfully holy as Tenebrae.

In the course of the Christian centuries Tenebrae has undergone changes, none of them affecting its essential import. At its simplest it might be enacted as follows: it being Holy Week, there are, everywhere in the church, signs of a most deadly sorrow. All its altars, main altar, side altars, aisle altars, the altar in the lady chapel, all altars are stripped of their glories. All tabernacles are empty, their doors wide open, the vivible, tangible presence of God gone, leaving the world derelict. Their garments of heavenly light, emblazoned and embroidered, have been removed from all statues and now they are appalled in purple, the colour of mourning. A candle rack, triangular in shape, stands in the sanctuary. It is known as the harrow or hearse. On each of its ascending sides are seven candles. A candle at the apex completes their number, fifteen in all, all of them lighted. It is night in the church and the only light is the lighted hearse, the lighted harrow. The scene is set. Liturgically now, in liturgically re-enacted time, it is Good Friday, at the sixth hour, and everyone participating in the rite knows the awful words:

Erat autem fere hora sexta, et tenebrae factae sunt in universam terram usque in horam nonam. Et obscuratus est sol: et velum templi scissum est medium.

In the King James translation it reads:

And it was about the sixth hour, and there was a darkness over all the earth until the ninth hour. And the sun was darkened, and the veil in the temple was rent in the midst.

It is the darkness of Good Friday we are in, and now the nocturnes begin, nocturnes of tragic psalms and lamentations. Chanted antiphonally back and forth, they continue into the deepening dark because every now and then, at appropriate breaks in the chanting, a candle is extinguished. In the end only the candle at the apex of the harrow or hearse is lighted, and now that last light of the world is removed and taken around behind the high altar and interred in a cave there. The church is engulfed in the darkness of Good Friday.

Having Tenebrae, Christianity is a great religion.

Having Tenebrae, Christianity is a light in the world.

Having Tenebrae, Christianity can have a great future.

Having Tenebrae, Christianity has a ritual in which the religious mysticisms of the world can ecumenically meet.

Having Tenebrae, Christianity can see how far short of its own innate possibilities for growth it has fallen.

Imagine it: a Tenebrae that includes readings from the Christian mystics.

Imagine it: a Tenebrae that includes not only readings from the Christian mystics but readings also, where appropriate, from the mystical texts of other religions.

Imagine it: an ecumenical Tenebrae.

Magi bringing gifts of gold, frankincense and myrrh to the baby in Bethlehem.

Magi bringing mahavakyas to the man undergoing Tenebrae on Golgotha.

Surely the mahavakyas are welcome. As welcome as were the gold, the frankincense and the myrrh.

A new Tenebrae.

New nocturnes for a new Tenebrae.

Evangelanta nocturnes for an Evangelanta Tenebrae.

Texts we have, texts from the writings of the Christian mystics, but who will shape a selection of them, shape them and score them, into a suite of fourteen nocturnes, so that, at the end of each, it will seem appropriate to extinguish a candle?

Candles extinguished. Senses or faculties extinguished, or suspended, or rapt, or held in abeyance, or reabsorbed, while the soul, thus denuded and stripped, goes forward in darkness.

Plotinus talks about procession and return. Procession out of the One and return to it. Tenebrae and the dark night of the soul are a stage, one and the same stage, on our return journey. And St John of the Cross insists that, while we are on this return journey, our senses and faculties, operating naturally, are a hindrance not a help. This is what he has to say:

O wretched condition of this life wherein it is so dangerous to live and so difficult to find the truth! That which is most clear and true, is to us most obscure and doubtful, and we therefore avoid it though it is most necessary for us. That which shines the most, and dazzles our eyes, that we embrace and follow after, though it is most hurtful to us, and makes us stumble at every step. In what fear and danger then must man be living, seeing that the very light of his natural eyes, by which he directs his steps, is the very first to bewilder and deceive him when he would draw near unto God. If he wishes to be sure of the road he travels on, he must close his eyes and walk in the dark, if he is to journey in safety from his domestic foes, which are his own senses and faculties.

Closing our eyes, the natural light of which bewilders and deceives us.

Closing our senses and faculties. Quenching candles on the Tenebrae hearse.

Closing our senses and faculties, consenting to their being suspended or reabsorbed as they are in dreamless sleep, so that we can walk on, all the more safely, in a darkness in which there aren't lighted candles lighting our way.

Mucus membrane. Maya membrane. Membranes that secrete mucus. Membranes that secrete maya.

Pia mater. Pia mater mirageans. Pia peyote mater mirageans. Pia mescala mater mirageans. Pia amanita muscaria mater mirageans. Pia maya mater mayans.

Mayashakti. Piashakti.

Piapeyoteshakti: that in us which projects the world-illusion.

Imagine it this way: a man who is ill goes in turn to three different doctors. All three of them agree that his trouble isn't imaginary. Each of them gives him a different diagnosis, however. And this means that each of them offers a different remedy. As with these doctors, so with the world's religions. The religions of the world agree on one thing, and that is that something ails humanity. In their diagnosis of what ails us, however, many of them disagree, sometimes quite radically. The Christian diagnosis has it that all the evils, spiritual and physical, that afflict humanity derive from an original and continuing disobedience to the will of the one true God. Unlike Christianity and Islam, Hinduism doesn't demand assent to a single, explicitly articulated creed. It would therefore be unwise to assume that there is any such thing as a single, universally accepted Hindu diagnosis, and yet it wouldn't be altogether wide of the mark to suggest that the Narada parable is a diagnosis most Hindus assent to. The Narada parable and the parable of the man who projected a snake into a rope, and who, by analogical extension, projects a world into Divine Ground.

I noticed it one night: crossing my kitchen to the light switch by the far door, I could see the moonlit sea through the picture window. Having switched on the light, I returned to the table and sat down, but now, to my great disappointment, I couldn't see the sea. The light I had switched on was eclipsing it.

O wretched condition of this life wherein the light of my senses and faculties with which I would seek the truth eclipses the truth.

Quenching the eclipsing light of my eyes and mind. Quenching the candles on the Tenebrae harrow.

Switching off the light I had switched on, I went back to the table and sat down and I looked for hours at the moonlit sea.

Sitting in Tenebrae, my senses and faculties suspended, I see.

Sitting in Tenebrae, the eclipsing light of my mind reabsorbed, I see.

Having Tenebrae, Christianity is a great religion.

Having a ritual that quenches the light, Christianity is a light in the world.

Can you see it, that wriggling? It is the Ropesnake coming through the pass at Thermopylae.

The Ropesnake and Narada.

Narada quenching the candles on our Tenebrae harrow.

O noche amable mas que el alborado

O night more lovely than the dawn

The process of individuation as Jung describes it. The process of tenebration as St John of the Cross describes it:

It is therefore very expedient and necessary, if the soul is to advance to these heights, that the dark night of contemplation should first bring it to nothing, and undo it in all its meannesses, bringing it into darkness, aridities, loneliness and emptiness; for the light that is to be given it is a certain divine light of the highest nature, surpassing all natural light, and not naturally cognizable by the understanding. If the understanding is to be united with that light, and become divine in the state of perfection, it must first of all be purified and annihilated as to its natural light, which must be brought actually into darkness by means of this dim contemplation. This darkness must continue so long as it is necessary to destroy the habit, long ago contracted, of understanding things in a natural way, and until the divine enlightening shall have taken its place. And therefore inasmuch as the power of understanding, previously exerted, is natural, the result is that the darkness now endured is awful, and most afflictive, as it were solid, because it reaches to, and is felt in, the innermost depths of the spirit.

The Gethsemane phase and the Good-Friday-on-Golgotha phase of contemplative tenebration. Very often, the Gethsemane phase is precipitated by the Golgotha phase, and runs concurrently with it.

It is likely that most people who have been through it would consider it a great loss not to have undergone puberty and the intense experiences that become possible as a consequence of it. An altogether greater loss would it be not to have undergone the dark night of the soul.

A great loss to a dragonfly nymph not to have undergone metamorphosis. A great loss to a person not to have undergone the Triduum Sacrum.

As life itself is, so to speak, a genetic keeper of puberty so must Christianity be a cultural keeper of the Triduum Sacrum, democratizing it as ancient Egyptians democratized the Osiris destiny.

In what way or ways can Christianity be more hospitable to the Triduum Sacrum? In what way or ways can it integrate it more creatively into its origins? A first requirement surely is that it should integrate its own mystical tradition into those origins, that it should, in other words, Evangelantize the Evangel.

A Christianity that opens its origins to the Hindu diagnosis of what ails us.

A Christianity that opens its Ephiphany door to Narada, Job and Jonah.

A Christianity that opens its Ash Wednesday door to the ropesnake parable.

A Christianity that opens its Holy Week door to an interpretation of the Fall that pictures Adam and Eve approaching a hallucinogenic mushroom about whose stem a serpent is entwined.

A Christianity that opens its Pentecost door to a Tenebrae harrow whose tongues of fire and light are mystical mahavakyas.

A Christianity that opens its Alexandrian, Ephesian, Nicean and Chalcedonian doors to Evangelanta.

Thesis: Greco-Romanized Christianity; antithesis: Hinduized Christianity; synthesis: Evangelantized Christianity.

The Rhine of the Rhineland mystics is our Ganges.

Imagine it: a Christianity that isn't afraid of the New Testament, that isn't afraid of its own Evangelanta greatness.

Wirikuta and Golgotha. The place of awareness-of, ordinary and extraordinary, and the no place at all of nirvikalpasamadhi.

Golgotha is a nunatak rising serenely above our Wirikuta world of pia-peyote-awareness-of.

The mystical life is a journey out of Wirikuta towards Golgotha. It is a waiting in the Tenebrae of Good Friday on Golgotha. It is a waiting in nirvikalpasamadhi.

Golgotha, the place of the skull, place of our mystical coming down from the veiling high of dreaming-waking-and-chonyid-awareness-of.

The veil in the temple was rent. The veiling psyche, conscious and unconscious, was rent. The eclipse of dreaming-waking-and-antarabhavic-awareness-of was rent.

It is like waking up in dreamless sleep and finding that dreaming-waking-and-antarabhavic-awareness-of has walked out on us.

The fountains of the Deep, which are now seen to be fountains of maya, have dried up.

The asravas, or outflows, of kama, bhava and avidya have dried up.

The haemorrhage of klesa-and-jneya-avaranas has dried up.

The nunatak or Ararat on which Christ looked down into Adam's empty skull.

The night we come down from the pia-peyote-high with which we have identified ourselves is a night of stupendous desolation, dereliction and woe.

Fear not. Fear not. Fear not, the Tibetan Book of the Dead keeps saying. And how good it is that it keeps on saying it: Fear not. Fear not. Fear not. And yet how aware, how compassionately aware, the Tibetan Book of the Dead is that now, as a consequence of karmic propensity, it is likely that our addiction to awareness-of won't die, not at its root, outright. And so it is that, in life as in death, the chonyid bardo dawns: we have begun to people the void with wonders and terrors. We are devils and tormentors to ourselves now. We are Marasena to ourselves. The rope blooms with our projections.

A Mahayana Buddhist would perhaps go all the way, would perhaps say: since it is in and through our genetic high that we are empirical persons, it follows that any coming down from this high is also in some sense a coming down from ourselves as persons. And in this regard he would perhaps remind us of the udana the Buddha uttered on the morning of his enlightenment:

> Housebuilder! I behold thee now.
> Again a house thou shalt not build.
> All thy rafters are broken now,
> The ridgepole also is destroyed.
> My mind, its elements dissolved,
> The end of craving has attained.

'I proclaim, friend', says the Buddha, 'that in this fathomsized, feeling-afflicted, ascetic's body dwell the world and the origin of the world and the annulment of the world and the path that leads to the annulment of the world.'

When our time comes to come down, God, may we be as out of your way awake as we are in dreamless sleep.

When our time comes to come down, God, may we be as out of your way awake as we are in dreamless sleep.

When our time comes to come down, God, may we be as out of your way awake as we are in dreamless sleep.

In dreamless sleep I am absent from myself. It is in and with what remains during this absence that I speak the word God, that I seek God. At this depth there is of course no I that speaks. And there is no speaking. The God that can be spoken isn't God. And yet before falling asleep at night I ask that speechless deep to speak the unspeakable God. My absence from myself is my way to you, God.

In my nothingness, God, is my supreme hope.

In my nothingness, God, is my supreme hope.

In my nothingness, God, is my supreme hope.

How infinitely more alive to Divine possibility my no-thing-ness is than my some-thing-ness is.

There is something more serious about me than my somethingness.

There is something more serious about me than my empirical biography. That something more serious Hindus call Atman-Brahman.

Hindus also say that all is Brahman. There isn't anything that isn't Brahman. It follows therefore that there aren't things that are more and things that are less serious. The snake we project into it is as serious as the rope. What eclipses Brahman is also Brahman. And yet we won't find rest until we absorb our projections, until we reabsorb the projected scenery of dreaming and waking, until, all reabsorbed, we wait in asparasa yoga

47

and adarsana yoga upon the mystical moment when we ourselves are divinely reabsorbed. As Eckhart has it:

Comes then the soul into the unclouded light of God. It is transported so far from creaturehood into nothingness that, of its own powers, it can never return to its agents or its former creaturehood. Once there, God shelters the soul's nothingness with his uncreated essence, safeguarding its creaturely existence. The soul has dared to become nothing and cannot pass from its own being into nothingness and back again, losing its own identity in the process, except God safeguarded it. This must needs be so.

> Yatha nadyah syandananah samudre
> Astam gacchanti namarupe vihaya
> Tatha vidvan namarupad vimuktah
> Paratparam purusam upaiti divyam.

Which, translated into English, reads: 'As flowing rivers go to rest in the ocean and there leave behind them name and form, so likewise the Knower, released from name and form, goes to that divine Being beyond the beyond.'

The pia-peyote high during which we see a snake in the rope. The pia-peyote high during which we see a world of space and time in spaceless, timeless Nirguna Brahman.

Were he to speak the language of Haight-Ashbury in the nineteen-sixties, the Buddha would say that this high of ours, this life of ours, is a bum-trip.

The bum-trip we are identified with and addicted to.

The bum-trip of everyday, hallucinogened hearing and seeing walks out on us on Good Friday.

The veil is rent. And by veil we mean *pia amanita muscaria mater mirageans.*

The Hindu word for veil, in the sense in which we are using it, is kosha. That body might be a veil is an idea Europeans have been familiar with since Plato. That mind might be a veil is an idea we haven't seriously engaged with. We haven't engaged, that is, with Adam's empty skull, his koshaless skull, at the foot of the cross.

Koshaless skull.
Hill of the koshaless skull.
Nunatak of the koshaless skull.
Nunatak that shines so serenely above our Wirikuta world of awareness-of.

Thinking of Golgotha as Golgotha-Borobudur. Thinking of Golgotha-Borobudur as Tai-wer, the first mound to appear out of the inundation of awareness-of.

Let us build a temple called Golgotha-Borobudur, the beautiful Nunatak, our beautiful new Esagila.

A muezzin calling to us from the summit of Esagila. Calling us to
come out of the deluge of maya, a deluge of awareness-of.

Gnostics believed in such a call from on high. A call called down into
the stupefaction and turmoil that constitute our world. A call that would
rouse us from our worldly drunkenness and forgetfulness. A call that
would awaken Nietzsche from his sleepwalking, his sleepwalking asleep,
his sleepwalking awake.

The Horsehead Nebula calling a Gnostic call into our world. Calling
it from the beginning. Calling it always. Once called, it goes on calling.

Our ascent into Tenebrae on the hill of the koshaless skull.

Speaking of the blessed Bartholomew in his book called *Mystical Theology*, Dionysius the Areopagite has this to say:

Methinks he has shown by these his words how marvellously he has understood
that the Good Cause of all things is eloquent yet speaks few words, or rather
none; possessing neither speech nor understanding because it exceedeth all things
in a super-celestial manner, and is revealed in its naked truth to those alone who
pass right through the opposition of fair and foul, and pass beyond the topmost
altitudes of the holy ascent and leave behind them all divine enlightenment and
voices and heavenly utterances and plunge into the Darkness where truly dwells,
as saith the Scriptures, that One which is beyond all things.

When the soul, forgetting itself, dwells in that radiant darkness (says Suso), it loses
all its faculties and all its qualities, as St Bernard has said. And this, more or less
completely, according to whether the soul – whether in the body or out of the
body – is more or less united to God. This forgetfulness of self is, in a measure,
a transformation in God; who then becomes, in a certain manner, all things for
the soul, as Scripture saith. In this rapture the soul disappears, but not yet entirely.
It acquires, it is true, certain qualities of Divinity, but does not naturally become
divine ... To speak in the common language, the soul is rapt, by the divine
power of resplendent Being, above its natural faculties, into the nakedness of the
Nothing.

The nothing that isn't nihil. The Divine no-thing-ness that heals us
forever of nihilism.

Being a thing, however supernal, would mean that the Divine has
boundaries, has limits.

Na ita, na ita, or *neti neti,* is an Upanishadic mahavakya. Literally, it
means not this, not that. The Divine is beyond every this and that. This
idea we also encounter in Eckhart:

So long as the soul beholds forms, even though she behold an angel, or herself as something formed, so long is there imperfection in her. Yes, indeed, should she even behold God, in so far as he is with form and number in the Trinity, so long is there imperfection in her. Only when all that is formed is cast off from the soul, and she sees the Eternal One alone, then the pure essence of the soul feels the naked, unformed essence of the divine Unity – more still, a Beyond Being. O wonder of wonders, what a noble endurance is that where the essence of the soul suffers no suggestion or shadow of difference even in thought or in name. There she entrusts herself alone to the One, free from all multiplicity and difference, in which all limitation and quality is lost and is one. This One makes us blessed.

A Beyond-Being.

The Divine Beyond-Being.

The Divine: as far beyond being as it is beyond non-being. As far beyond non-being as it is beyond being. Neither being nor non-being. Neti neti.

Again Eckhart is forthright:

Everything which has being, hangs in the Naught. And that same Naught is such an incomprehensible Aught that all the spirits in Heaven and Earth cannot comprehend it or sound it.

Had I a God whom I could understand, I would no longer hold him for God.

God is our sin against the Divine.

The Divine Beyond-Being-Beyond-Nonbeing. The very thought of it brings us, rapturously, to the Kedron.

Jesus didn't cross the Kedron alone. The biblical tradition, as it then existed, crossed it with him. Watching with him, it underwent an alchemical purification, a passion, a death and a resurrection. Still recognizable in their risen splendour, the Book of Job, the Book of Jonah, the Book of Daniel, Psalm twenty-three, the Song of Songs and Ecclesiastes had become Upanishads.

A new Old Testament.

An Old Testament of six Upanishads.

Six Old Testament Upanishads preparing the way for a still unwritten Evangelanta Gospel called the Triduum Sacrum.

> The Roman Empire stood appalled,
> It dropped the reins of peace and war,
> When that fierce Virgin and her Star
> Out of the fabulous darkness called.

There is a Darkness yet more strange than the fabulous darkness. Tenebrae it is called. Out of Tenebrae he comes, and Christianity, catching sight of him, is appalled. In its gospels appalled. In its sacraments appalled. In its candles appalled. In its sanctuary lamp appalled.

Actaeon catching sight of Artemis.

Christianity catching sight of the Christ who walks out of Tenebrae.

How, catching sight of the Christ who walks out of Tenebrae, can Christianity live within its traditional limits, doctrinal and liturgical?

No room in the inn for the woman with child.

Is there room in Christianity for the Christ who walks out of Tenebrae?

Are there two Palm Sundays, one at the beginning and one at the end of Holy Week?

Imagine the second Palm Sunday: the mystical writings of the world are the palms we wave, welcoming the Christ who walks out of Tenebrae.

A wandering Jew.

A wandering Christian.

Lets imagine the Wandering Christian: he committed what for him was a terrible sacrilege: catching sight of the Christ who walks out of Tenebrae, he blessed himself and said, the Christ of our Christian creed isn't the whole story. Sprinkling holy water on himself he said, the Christ who walks out of Tenebrae is a Christ who, this time round, wasn't sidetracked into a resurrection, an ascension and a return in judgment and glory.

Can sacrilege be holy?

Although terrible in its consequences for the person who commits it, is it ever the case that sacrilege is religiously necessary?

Can sacrilege be at once objectively terrible and yet innocent, giving a particular religion at a particular time the scope that it needs?

From Veda to Vedanta. Or more specifically: from the asva-medha to the Mandukya Upanishad.

From Hinayana Buddhism to Mahayana Buddhism. Or more specifically: from the Dhammapada to the Lotus of the Good Law.

From Evengel to Evangelanta. Or more specifically: from Holy Thursday in the Garden of Olives to Holy Thursday in Gethsemane, from Good Friday on Calvary to Good Friday on Golgotha, from a Christ coming in judgment and glory to Jivanmukta Messiah walking out of Tenebrae.

> Kyrie eleison
> Kyrie eleison
> Kyrie eleison
>
> Christe eleison
> Christe eleison
> Christe eleison

> Have mercy on Actaeon
> Have mercy on the Wandering Jew
> Have mercy on the Wandering Christian

The Wandering Christian who, knowing the sacrilege, would yet have harrowed our Christian creed with the Tenebrae harrow.

Piers Plowman.

Piers Harrowman, harrowing foundations in Alexandria, Ephesus, Nicea and Chalcedon.

Christianity touching the hem of Christ's Evangelanta garment and being healed of its issue of blood.

From asva-medha to Mandukya Upanishad.

From agnu-medha to samadhi.

From the Mass to Tenebrae.

And yet, given the world of carnivores and raptors we live in, and given our phylogenetic rootedness in that world and its instincts, Geoffrey Hill has claimed that 'there is no bloodless myth will hold'. He claims it in a poem called 'Genesis':

I

> Against the burly air I strode,
> Where the tight ocean heaves its load,
> Crying the miracles of God.

> And first I brought the sea to bear
> Upon the dead weight of the land;
> And the waves flourished at my prayer,
> The rivers spawned their sand.

> And where the streams were salt and full
> The tough pig-headed salmon strove,
> Curbing the ebb and the tide's pull,
> To reach the steady hills above.

II

> The second day I stood and saw
> The osprey plunge with triggered claw,
> Feathering blood along the shore,
> To lay the living sinew bare.

> And the third day I cried: 'Beware
> The soft-voiced owl, the ferret's smile,
> The hawk's deliberate stoop in air,
> Cold eyes, and bodies hooped in steel,
> Forever bent upon the kill.'

III

And I renounced, on the fourth day,
This fierce and unregenerate clay,

Building as a huge myth for man
The watery Leviathan,
And made the glove-winged albatross
Scour the ashes of the sea
Where Capricorn and Zero cross
A brooding immortality –
Such as the charmèd phoenix has
In the unwithering tree.

IV

The phoenix burns as cold as frost;
And like a legendary ghost,
The phantom-bird goes wild and lost,
Upon a pointless ocean tossed.

So, the fifth day, I turned again
To flesh and blood and the blood's pain.

V

On the sixth day, as I rode
In haste about the works of God,
With spurs I plucked the horse's blood.

By blood we live, the hot, the cold,
To ravage and redeem the world:
There is no bloodless myth will hold.

And by Christ's blood are men made free
Though in close shrouds their bodies lie
Under the rough pelt of the sea;

Though earth has rolled beneath her weight
The bones that cannot bear the light.

Yes, we need a myth that can look osprey in the face, can look crocodile in the face, can look the wholesale extinction of species during the
Triassic and the Permian in the face, can stand on the beach at Punta Alta,
can go ashore on Galapagos, can open one of its seven gates to Coatlicue,
the Aztec Earth Mother, she of the hissing, ungulate head, she who wears
a skirt of serpents.

Jesus having left his Good Friday face in it, Christianity doesn't readily throw in the towel.

In Christianity, ghora murti Good News.
In Buddhism, sundara murti Good News.
In Christianity, Golgotha.
In Buddhism, Borobudur.
Golgotha is the ghora murti of Borobudur.
Borobudur is the sundara murti of Golgotha.
So long as it is understood to posit the existence of Divine Ground, surely we can think ecumenically of a hypostatic union of the two:

GolgothaBorobudur

And standing there by itself, Golgotha isn't all ghora murti. It is, when we think of it as the Hill of the Koshaless Skull, indescribably beautiful. More beautiful than anything Rublev could iconically hint at.

The Triduum Sacrum isn't only atonement in the sense of expiation or appeasement. It is the mystical journey and in that sense it is the redemptive at-one-ment of all things with the Divine Ground out of which they emerged.

Calvary is Evangel.
Golgotha is Evangelanta.
Magi who journey from Evangel to Evangelanta will need well-watered camels. Will need to bring Upanishads, Christian and Hindu, with them. Will need to bring mahavakys with them:

> Nothing nothing nothing nothing and on
> the mountain nothing, only God alone

> God felt, God tasted, God enjoyed is indeed
> God but God with those gifts that flatter the
> soul. God in darkness, privation, forsakenness
> and insensibility is so much God that He is
> so to speak God bare and alone.

Between me and thee there is an 'I am' that torments me. Ah! Through thy 'I am' take away my 'I am' from between us both.

The cleansing of the body is water and the cleansing of the heart is the cleansing of the eyes to otherness.

It is like being in God without being oneself.

A Triduum Sacrum exodus. An exodus, within Christianity, from Evangel to Evangelanta.

An exodus within the Roman Empire from the rule of Caesar to the rule of Christ.

The Roman Empire stood appalled,
It dropped the reins of peace and war,
When that fierce Virgin and her Star
Out of the fabulous darkness called.

The Christianity of

Chalcedon
Skellig
Chartres
Mount Athos
The Ardagh Chalice
Missa in Nocte
Handel's *Messiah*

That Christianity standing appalled, delighted and appalled, by its new
Evangelanta understanding of itself.

Traditionally, reaching his early adulthood, a Sioux Indian would leave
his people and go into the wilderness to cry for a vision. He would cry
not just for a vision for himself. He would cry to the Sacred Powers for a
vision for his people, for a vision that would enable his people to live. No
Christian needs to go into the wilderness to cry for an Evangelanta ritual.
We already have such a ritual. We have Tenebrae.

A Christianity, the sacred origin of which is Jesus of Nazareth crossing
the Kedron, is Jivanmukhta Messiah walking out of Tenebrae.

Palms we wave, welcoming him.

The Mystical Theology of Dionysius we wave.

The Sermons of Eckhart we wave.

The Sparkling Stone by Ruysbroeck we wave.

The Mirror of Simple Souls by Marguerite Porete we wave.

The Ascent of Mount Carmel by St John of the Cross we wave.

The Mandukya Upanishad we wave.

The Chandogya Upanishad we wave.

The Brihadaranyaka Upanishad we wave.

The Svetasvetara Upanishad we wave.

The Diamond Sutra we wave.

The Heart Sutra we wave.

The Lotus of the Good Law we wave.

The Tao Te Ching we wave.

The Tibetan Book of the Dead we wave.

The Tibetan Book of the Great Liberation we wave.

Atma Bodha we wave.

The Crest Jewel of Wisdom we wave.

The writings of Farid Al-Din Attar we wave.
The writings of Niffari we wave.
The writings of Al Junayd we wave.
The Mathnawi we wave.
A Zohar of great sayings we wave.
Mystical texts not yet written we wave.
The mystical sayings and doings of all peoples we say and do.
A Sun dance we dance.
An Eland dance we dance.
A tsurunga we raise welcoming Messiah into his Kingdom.
Seeking to understand you is what we are up to, Jesus.
Seeking to understand you in your growing out of and away from our traditional understanding of you.
To go to your tomb bringing spices.
To go to Nicea bringing spices.
To go to Chalcedon bringing spices.
To go to these towns and find, yet again, that you have left angels behind you announcing that you are gone. Gone from our first attempts to understand you. Gone from our first attempts to limit and fix you, saying to you: thus far shall you grow and no farther. Here in Chalcedon is your growing stayed.

The cloud that Jesus ascended into on Ascension Thursday – it didn't offer him peaceful passage. It didn't open for him as the Red Sea opened for the Children of Israel. It closed over him and in it, waiting, was Leviathan. It was into the maw of Leviathan he ascended. Closing it upon him, she turned flukes and sounded, carrying him down into the void below the roots of his psyche, into the void below the roots of the universe. Initially terrified, fearing that he was forever lost, Jesus came gradually to see that he was never so at home as he was now. The Void was Divine. The Divine-Without-Form-and-Void. Compared with it, the Heaven he had been ascending into is but a distraction of eclipsing ecstacies and raptures. Recovering from a moment of mystical reabsorbption, he saw that Heaven also must be harrowed.

The Void is Divine. The Void is Pleroma. In its dream of itself as an Abyss, the Void is Divine. As Abyss, it is Divine.

Divine also is Jesu Leviathasayin

Divine is Jesu Anadyomene

A first emanation out of the Abyss:

Jesu Leviathasayin

A first coming ashore:

Jesu Anadyomene

All of these tranformations and more Jesus walked into when he walked into the Triduum Sacrum.

Is all of this, all that I am saying, not saying it now by proxy in a Wandering Christian, is it all sacrilege, Jesus?

Why, reading what I have written, do I not, like Caiaphas, rend my garments?

Can the sacrilege, if sacrilege it is, be forgiven me? Will you think of it as a sacrilege of honour and praise? Will you think of it as a crying for a vision by which Christians can live?

I will tell you a story, Jesus:

John Welsh lived in a world of wide horizons. His house was high on the side of a hill and from the fields he farmed he looked down, looking south-west, on the Shannon losing its identity in the ocean. It was, if you like, a world of wide questions that called for wide answers. Questions and answers that made sense on the shores of the Sea of Galilee didn't always make the same kind of sense on the shore of the ocean. Like a boat, John's religion had opened at the seams. It was drawing abyssal water. John was lonely, not because there were no people in his life, but because of his unshareable intuitions about things. Sometimes, having milked them, John would drive out his cows and go down to the village and drink all day. And so it was on Christmas Eve: John was more alone than ever when, coming up to eleven o' clock, Eileen the barwoman called on everyone to finish their drink and go to midnight Mass. When the pub was almost empty, John went up to the counter and asked Eileen for a couple of bottles of Guinness to take with him. He paid for them and taking them by their necks he dropped them into the great patch pockets of his Crombie overcoat and walked out following the others. As usual, he didn't go through the inner doors into the great blaze of the church. John felt uncomfortable in places from which the dark was excluded. The porch with its shadows was more hospitable to him and that's where he stayed. Within the body of the church everything was proceeding as everyone expected it would. Angels had been heard on high. Three Orient Kings had mounted their camels and set out westwards following a star. Shepherds above whom the heavens had opened were already, in reverence, extinguishing the worldly light of their lanterns at a stable door. Then the choir fell silent. The people were hushed; aware that they had crossed into the sacrificial sanctum of the Mass, they bowed their heads, averting their senses and faculties from the glorious arcana conducted with such solemnity on the altar. This was the moment when the frightful cry of Good Friday would erupt inaudibly into the silence but now tonight there were sounds in the silence, sounds of someone walking in wellington boots, sounds of John Welsh walking, very unsurely, up the aisle. In row after row as he walked people emerged from their bowed introversion and looked in alarm at John. Oblivious of the consternation he was causing, John continued walking, recovering, less than triumphantly sometimes, from an odd very serious stagger. Reaching the altar, or the altar rails, I don't know which, there being two versions of the story, reaching the altar, John drew a bottle of Guinness out of his pocket and, giving it to the priest as his offering, he said that he wanted to stand a drink to Jesus for Christmas. Resolutely in his mind, unsurely in his walk, the aisle shepherding him into a bearable straightness of gait and going, John found his way to the porch. That's it. That's the story I wanted to tell you, Jesus.

'I thirst', you cried, crying out in agony on Good Friday. On Christmas Eve, two thousand years later, John Welsh reached up a drink to you.

That thirst still is. Only now it's the Christian story that thirsts. It thirsts to be relived and retold. It thirsts with a Good Friday thirst for temples and rituals in which to live. For myths and metaphors in which to live. For melodies in which to live. For an eland dance in which to live. For a raised tsurunga in which to live.

Into a Golgotha avalanche he climbed. Up under it, resignedly, and it carried him down into our inner Hell. By being harrowed in it, he harrowed.

Into the maw of Leviathan he ascended. Leviathan carried him down out of all worlds, all worlds above, all worlds here, all worlds below. Into unutterable unworldliness she yawned him. Into the Divine Ungrund all worlds derive their existence from.

John of Patmos invited us to behold a great wonder in heaven. And a great wonder it surely was and is: a woman clothed in the sun, having the moon under her feet, and on her head a crown of twelve stars.

It is time, now maybe, to behold a great wonder in the Abyss: Jesus recumbent on the coils of the Piercing Serpent, even she the Crooked Serpent, she who has seven heads, each head in turn splaying and displaying its crest jewel of wisdom, each head in turn singing its medicine song.

Since he crossed the Kedron, seeking among other things to give us a better past from which to grow, Jesus recumbent on the coils of Leviathan is prototype to all Middle Eastern and East Mediterranean beginnings:

> Jesus recumbent on the coils of Leviathan
> Atum recumbent on the coils of Iru-To
> Marduk recumbent on the coils of Tiamat
> Baal recumbent on the coils of Yam
> Zeus recumbent on the coils of Typhon

Apollo recumbent on the coils of Python
Herakles recumbent on the coils of Hydra.

Jesus Leviathasayin
Atum Iru-Tosayin
Marduk Tiamasayin
Baal Yamsayin
Zeus Typhosayin
Appolo Pythosayin
Herakles Hydrasayin

Leviathasayi Jesu
Iru-Tosayi Atum
Tiamasayi Marduk
Yamsayi Baal
Typhosayi Zeus
Pythosayi Apollo
Hydrasayi Herakles

Leviathashaya
Iru-Toshaya
Tiamashaya
Yamshaya
Typhoshaya
Pythoshaya
Hydrashaya

Leviathashaya: Jesus recumbent on the coils of Leviathan.
Olympians replacing Titans.
Leviathashaya replacing Olympians.
Leviathashaya redeeming Olympians and Titans:

Zeus recumbent on the coils of Typhon
Apollo recumbent on the coils of Python

In that one lance thrust on Good Friday, Jesus became scabbard to all dragon-slayer's weapons. And so, instead of Marduk lobotomizing the Abyss, we have Marduk recumbent on the coils of Tiamat. And instead of Herakles lobotomizing the Earth, we have Herakles recumbent on the coils of Hydra, each of her nine heads singing a medicine song into the depths of her psyche.

Jesus crossed the Kedron and an exodus of many strands enacted itself in him. In one of its strands it was an exodus from dragon and dragon-slayer to Dracoshaya. In another of its strands it was, as we have imagined it, an exodus from Hebrew to Hindu beginnings: in the beginning was the recumbent Dreamer. And in yet another of its strands, it was an exodus from *yu wei* to *wu wei*.

In Leviathashaya *yu wei* has been replaced by *wu wei*.

In Leviathashaya *wu wei* is from the Beginning.

Jesus crossed the Kedron and now we have a healed and a healing past from which to grow.

Jesus crossed the Kedron. He became as nothing, so the Beginning re-enacted itself in him. In him we are healed in our beginnings, healed back into and therefore from the first inaudible stirrings in the Waters of Nun. In him we are healed from before Tep zepi, the First Time, from before Tai wer, the first or most ancient land.

Behold a great wonder in Heaven: a woman clothed in the sun, having the moon under her feet, and on her head a crown of twelve stars.

Behold a great wonder in the Abyss: Jesus recumbent on the coils of Leviathan, her seven heads singing a medicine song into his regressed but re-evolving human psyche.

But Jesus isn't a recumbent Dreamer. He is also fully awakened. He comes ashore.

Venus coming ashore is called Venus Anadyomene, Venus rising from or coming in from the sea.

Jesus coming ashore. Jesus Anadyomene

As Titian pictures her, Venus Anadyomene stands hip-deep in the tide wringing her hair out. This Jesus doesn't do, happy that the Abyss should always be in him, should always walk with him.

How beautiful upon the shingle shore are the feet of him who brings good tidings. Speaking in a sea-soft voice he says to a fisherman, Tehom is Turiya, and walks on, neither Testament, neither the Old nor the New, having any claim on him now.

Jivanmukhta Messiah walking inland: in him, on Good Friday, the bars and doors between Time and Tehom were broken down, and now, as he walks on, his biography has no claim to him. His biography he might leave behind him, as he leaves it behind him in dreamless sleep, but he wouldn't notice. Neither would he feel any the poorer for having lost it. In inner depths beyond and before his biography, he is grounded in God. And yet, how beautiful he is biographically. Few indeed are they who will look upon him and not swoon.

> Stay me with flagons
> Comfort me with apples
> For I have seen Messiah.

And what, walking inland, will you find, Jivanmukhta Messiah? Will you find we have welcome for you? Will you find we understand you?

It might be that, as you walk inland, you will yourself have to sow the seeds of the religion that can welcome you, and understand you.

Would it help if, meeting you on the shore, we read the sermons of Eckhart and Tauler to you?

'Everything depends on a fathomless sinking in a fathomless nothingness,' Tauler says. And he continues:

If a man were to say, 'Lord, who art thou that I must follow thee, through such deep, gloomy and miserable paths?', the Lord would reply, 'I am God and man and far more God.' If a man could answer then, really and consciously from the bottom of his heart, 'then I am nothing and less than nothing', all would be accomplished, for the Godhead has really no place to work in but ground where all has been annihilated. As the Schoolmen say, when a new form is to come into existence the old must of necessity be destroyed. And so I say, If a man is to be thus clothed upon with this Being, all the forms must be done away that were ever received by him in all his powers of perception, knowledge, will, work, of subjection, sensibility and self-seeking! When St Paul saw nothing, he saw God. So also when Elias wrapped his face in his mantle, God came. All strong rocks are broken here, all on which the spirit can rest must be done away. Then when all forms have ceased to exist, in the twinkling of an eye the man is transformed. Therefore, thou must make an entrance. Thereupon speaks the Heavenly Father to him: 'Thou shalt call me Father, and shalt never cease to enter in; entering ever further in, ever nearer, so as to sink the deeper in an unknown and unnamed Abyss; and above all ways, images and forms, and above all powers, to lose thyself, deny thyself, and even unform thyself.' In this last condition nothing is to be seen but a ground which rests upon itself, everywhere one Being, one Life. It is thus, man may say, that he becomes unknowing, unloving and senseless.

Elsewhere, Tauler has this to say:

The great wastes to be found in this divine ground have neither image nor form nor condition, for they are neither here nor there. They are like unto a fathomless Abyss, bottomless and floating in itself. Even as water ebbs and flows, up and down, now sinking into a hollow, so that it looks as if there were no water there, and then again in a little while rushing forth as if it would engulf everything, so does it come to pass in this Abyss. This, truly, is much more God's dwelling place than heaven or man. A man who verily desires to enter will surely find God here, and himself simply in God; for God never separates himself from this ground. God will be present with him, and he will find and enjoy eternity here. There is no past nor present here, and no created light can reach unto or shine into this divine ground; for here only is the dwelling place of God and his sanctuary. Now this Divine Abyss can be fathomed by no creatures; it can be filled by none, and it satisfies none; God only can fill it in his infinity. For this Abyss belongs only to the Divine Abyss, of which it is written: *Abyssus abyssum invocat.* He who is truly conscious of this ground, which shone into the powers of his soul, and lighted and inclined its lowest and highest powers to turn to their pure Source and true Origin, must diligently examine himself, and remain alone, listening to the voice which cries in the wilderness of this ground. This ground is so desert and bare, that no thought has ever entered there. None of all the thoughts of man which, with the help of reason, have been devoted to meditation on the Holy Trinity (and some men have occupied themselves much with these thoughts) have ever entered this ground. For it is so close and yet so far off, and so far beyond all things, that it has neither time nor place. It is a simple and unchanging condition. A man who really and truly enters, feels as though he has been here throughout eternity, and as though he were one therewith.

The Divine Abyss.

The Divine Abyss the Bible would shut out, building bars and doors against it.

The Divine Abyss you came ashore from, Jesus. Little to be wondered at that you didn't wring your hair out.

'All strong rocks are broken here, all on which the spirit can rest must be done away.'

Our rock of faith has become an abyss of faith.

Abyss of faith. Tehom of faith. Turiya of faith.

It was out of Turyia you came, coming ashore, Jesus.

According to the Mandukya Upanishad, Turyia is *santam*, meaning utterly quiet; it is *sivam*, meaning peaceful-blissful; and it is *advaitam*, meaning without a second.

> Santam
> Sivam
> Advaitam

The snake we project into the rope. The Tohu-Wavohu we project into the divine Deep, the divine Ground, the divine Ungrund, that is *santam, sivam, advaitam.*

The great swallowing that swallowed Jonah. That great swallowing waiting for Jesus in the Ascension Thursday cloud.

Enantiodromia in the Ascension Thursday cloud. Enantiodromia not only for Christ. Enantiodromia also for Christianity.

Ascension Thursday turned out to be a stupendous Good Friday.

A Good Friday without a Calvary or a Golgotha. The Good Friday that is all Divine Ungrund. The Good Friday in which Ungrund is Ground.

The Good Friday in which we learn that the Abyss 'is much more God's dwelling-place than heaven or man'.

That's the new rainbow, isn't it? That's the new rainbow in the cloud: the Abyss is much more God's dwelling-place than heaven or man.

Had he been able for it, that is the news the raven would have brought back to Noah: the Abyss is much more God's dwelling-place than heaven or man.

The Abyss that has nothing of Tohu-Wavohu in it. The Abyss that is Turiya, that is *santam, sivam, advaitam*.

Beach-combing the shores of Turiya. Beach-combing for words with which to understand the terrible but marvellous thing that happened to you, Jesus.

Ransacking the religions, seeking for upanishadic clarities with which to greet you, in which to clothe you, as Venus was clothed when she stepped off her shell onto the shore.

The old Titanic testicles carried out by the waves. The old generative powers of a brutal, old world seeding the sea-foam, impregnating the primordial waters and here she comes nude from the nude sea.

> Full fathom five thy father lies;
> Of his bones are coral made;
> Those are pearls that were his eyes:
> Nothing of him that doth fade,
> But doth suffer a sea-change
> Into something rich and strange.
> Sea-nymphs hourly ring his knell.
> Ding-dong
> Ding-dong, bell.

A nude new order of Love and Grace setting foot on the hurt Earth.

Venus Anadyomene.

Jesus Anadyomene.

Thanks be to God for the Swallowing in the cloud.

The enantiodromia Jesus himself, as in a dream, set up in advance in the cloud.

His blessed downfall. His blessed undoing.

Resurrection, Ascension and Return, as Lord in Judgment and Glory were the final temptations.

Here we go again. Sacrilege again.

Forgive the sacrilege, Jesus. Bless the sacrilege. Let the sacrilege be somehow sacred. Heal the sacrilege of its issue of religious hurt. Transform the sacrilege into a sacrament, Jesus. Make the heresy holy.

The Wandering Jew knocking on the door of the temple of Solomon.

The Wandering Christian knocking on the door of St Peter's.

Scandalized by what he hears himself saying, the Wandering Jew has rent his garments.

And the Wandering Christian also. He, too, scandalized, stands there in rags.

Gyrans gyrando spiritus vadit: Holy Thursday in the Garden of Olives, Good Friday on Calvary, Easter morning in the Garden of the Sepulchre. Holy Thursday in Gethsemane, Good Friday on Golgotha, Easter morning on the shingle shore of Turiya-Tehom. Holy Thursday at the end below of Bright Angel Trail, Good Friday in a fathomless sinking in a fathomless nothingness, Easter morning on the shore of Tao-Turiya-Tehom.

Jivanmukhta Messiah.

What better way to greet you than to give thanks – thanks that you gave yourself to the Triduum Sacrum, thanks that the Triduum Sacrum realized all of its latent grandeurs in you.

Ancient Egyptians democratized the destiny of Osiris.

Christians democratizing the destiny of Jesus. Democratizing the mystical journey.

Biologically, each of us is heir to puberty. Spiritually, and biologically also perhaps, each of us heir to the Triduum Sacrum.

Persons in whom the Triduum Sacrum is genetically encoded. A religion in which it is ritually encoded.

Holy Thursday, Good Friday and Easter morning in our DNA.

In Chalcedon, Christians were concerned to define who Jesus was. Our concern now should be to know what the Triduum Sacrum is.

Architecturally, none of our churches or cathedrals knows what the Triduum Sacrum is.

A Tenebrae Temple. The Triduum Sacrum architecturally expressed.

A Tenebrae Temple in which a section of floor is a shingle shore of Tao-Turiya-Tehom.

Beach-combing on the shore of Tao-Turiya-Tehom.

How sea-changed, washed back up to us, are our myths.

How sea-changed the Bible. Those are nirvikalpasamadhis that were its eyes. Those are Upanishads that were its folktales. That is Triduum Sacrum talk that was talk of *heilsgeschichte*. Those are a Tenebrae harrow of lighted mahavakyas that were Jeremiah's lamentations. Those are the songs of a bhakta that were the songs of the Shulamite.

And yet, given the Triduum Sacrum source and core of it, Christianity can never become a *sundara murti* myth, a myth lovely in all its 'shewings', charming in all its epiphanies. Christ isn't Krishna. And, whatever else it also is, the Hill of the Koshaless Skull will always be a place of abandonment and dereliction. Grand Canyon mesa that it is, it can never be wholly assimilated to Borobudur. Golgotha isn't triumph above and beyond the earthly condition. It is triumph from within it. It is triumph at the roots of it. Little wonder that it isn't always, in all its aspects, pleasant to look at. And yet, at the end of it, Bright Angel Trail is aisle. Ascending and descending, it is aisle. Ascending and descending, it is ascent. So yes, in spite of the horror, Golgotha has a *sundara murti*. It is *sundara murti* mesa. A mesa which, like Borobudur, is terraced for mystical *peripateia*.

How glad we were on Easter morning, how like Noah catching sight of Ararat we were, when we saw that Golgotha had become Tai-wer, that Tai-wer itself had become a temple, the Tenebrae Temple we journey through back into Divine Ground.

Born with the world is the possibility of entering it, is the possibility of leaving it. They who totally leave it are best able to totally enter it.

Borobudur is terraced outwardly. Golgotha-Tai-wer is as it were terraced inwardly.

The five outer ascents and terraces of Borobudur. The four inner journeys through Tai-wer.

We have good news: Bright Angel Trail is aisle.

Tai-wer is temple.

Who will be our Suger? Who our Sinan?

Could it be that Vishvakarman, the architect of the Gods, will show up?

Could it be that the Samildanach will show up?

Could it be that even now the Goban Saor and his son are walking our roads?

In medieval Ireland it would sometimes happen that closing his door at evening a man would see cattle grazing in the green field across the river and yet when he opened the door in the morning, there where the cattle were it would be, a monastery of cut stone, its bell already tolling, no coign or pinnacle needing to be completed.

Chartres Cathedral didn't rise overnight, but given the faith and dedication of the people who built it, it did rise glory by glory:

Who has ever seen! − Who has ever heard tell, in times past, that powerful princes of the world, that men brought up in honour and in wealth, that nobles, men and women, have bent their proud and haughty necks to the harness of carts, and that, like beasts of burden, they have dragged to the abode of Christ these waggons, loaded with wines, grains, oil, stone, wood and all that is necessary for the wants of life, or for the construction of the church? But while they draw these burdens, there is one thing admirable to observers; it is that often when a thousand persons and more are attached to the chariots, – so great is the difficulty – yet they march in such silence that not a murmur is heard, and truly if one did not see the thing with one's eyes, one might believe that among such a multitude there was hardly a person present. When they halt on the road, nothing is heard but the confession of sins, and pure and suppliant prayer to God to obtain pardon. At the voice of the priests who exhort their hearts to peace, they forget all hatred, discord is thrown far aside, debts are remitted, the unity of hearts is established. But if any one is so far advanced in evil as to be unwilling to pardon an offender, or if he rejects the counsel of the priest who has piously advised him, his offering is instantly thrown from the wagon as impure, and he himself ignominiously and shamefully excluded from the company of the holy. There one sees the priests who preside over each chariot exhort everyone to penitence, to confession of faults, to the resolution of better life. There one sees old people, young people, little children, calling on the Lord with a suppliant voice, and uttering to Him from the depth of the heart, sobs and sighs with words of glory and praise! After the people, warned by the sound of trumpets and the sight of banners, have resumed their road, the march is made with such ease that no obstacle can retard it … When they have reached the church they arrange the waggons about it like a spiritual camp and during the whole night they celebrate the watch by hymns and canticles. On each wagon they light tapers and lamps; they place there the infirm and sick, and bring them the precious relics of the Saints for their relief. Afterwards the priests and clerics close the ceremony by processions which the people follow with devout heart, imploring the clemency of the Lord and of his blessed Mother for the recovery of the sick.

It was above all when Jesus crossed the Kedron that we became heirs to the promise addressed, as it were, to Anthropus in the Book of Job:

For thou shalt be in league with the stones of the field, and the beasts of the field shall be at peace with thee.

The promise realized in us, we will build our temple, be it Chartres or Tai-wer, knowing that the stones we build it with are working with us.

When the stones are in league with us laying the plinth, when they are still in league with us completing the first pinnacle, then we can surely assume that our temple isn't just on the Earth but is up out of it and, like an outcrop, is still geomantically one with it. Looking at it, we will see that for all its architectural splendours it is as native to its place as a Grand Canyon mesa, or, should it rise out of a plain, as native to it as Uluru.

It isn't from but with the Earth that we must go forward. And forward with it we can go, because even the magma of the Grand Canyon floor isn't other than samadhi. We could indeed call it *sa-magma-madhi*.

Even now in the West, forgetting that Jesus crossed the Kedron, it is from the Earth and away from the Earth that we would go forward.

To go forward in grace with the Earth. Or to go forward technologically from it.

Any anodos that isn't a coming forward from a kathodos will only bring us to places not worth going to.

To be a spectator in another galaxy is no better than being a spectator in the galaxy we were born into.

In no other galaxy is there a frontier greater than the Kedron-Colorado.

It would be altogether better for humanity to cross the Kedron-Colorado than to cross into another galaxy.

Spiritually and morally, Bright Angel Trail is our trail to the heart of the universe.

Bright Angel Trail is our space journey to the Earth. It is a journey in three phases: Gethsemane, Golgotha, Garden of the Sepulchre.

The Triduum Sacrum is the only space journey worth embarking on. At the end of it, opening our eyes, we will see the Earth as Buddh Gaia and the universe as a Bodhi tree. At the end of it we might with justice call ourselves *homo sapiens sapiens*. At the end of it our sapience won't be knowledge, it will be a way of being in the world.

What a shame it would be if, evolution having brought us to the Kedron-Colorado, we refused to cross it, yet again placing all our evolutionary hopes on advancement local, not on, not in, advancement essential.

To cross from a planet to its satellite or to cross from Wirikuta to Golgotha, from pia-peyote-mater mirageans to nirvikalpasamadhi.

To cross from the ropesnake to the rope and then, knowing that the snake is as much the rope as the rope itself is, crossing back again.

A vehicle called Apollo on its way to the moon, or, laying his sword aside, the god Apollo walking into his Triduum Sacrum in the gorge in Delphi.

Jesus walking into the Triduum Sacrum.

On his way in, seeking to distract him from his purpose, the powers of Maya come to meet him.

First comes Tatei Hikuri, our Great Grandmother Peyote. She shows him the stupendous nierika or opening into her world. In reverence, Jesus says no, and walks on.

Then comes Great Grandfather Teonanacatl. He shows him something of the world of visions and wonders he knows the way to, is the way to. You only need to eat my flesh and drink my blood, he says, and five most glorious mysteries, not known to your rosary, will come to escort you. In reverence, Jesus says no, and walks on.

Wearing his own face, signifying her identity with him, Yaje Woman comes. She offers him, he being thirsty, a bowl of ayahuasca. And look, she says, the vine whose roots are in heaven, the vine growing downwards from heaven, the life-line to wonder let down by the Gods from their heaven, the vine through which heaven would, once again, be umbilical with Earth, the vine into which, most tragically, Adam and Eve projected a snake. Lord of the Yaje vine, not victim with the grape vine, you shall be, she says. Eye hasn't seen, she says, and ear hasn't heard. And tonight, you will walk with me in Paradise. In reverence, Jesus says no, and walks on.

Ka'uyumari, spirit deer to all great openings into non-ordinary worlds, crosses his path, and looks back, lingering, wishing him to follow. Acknowledging him, Jesus walks on.

Veronica comes, offering him a napkin to wipe his face with. Leaving the imprint of his features in it, leaving his ego-identity in it, he hands it back to her and walks on.

And now again, lifting nierikas, Tatei Hikuri is there, and Jesus, turning, but not turning aside, says to her: *yatra na anyat pasyati, na anyat srinoti, na anyad vijanati, sa bhuma.*

And now again, offering the mycelia of mind awake to divine wonder, Teonanacatl is there and Jesus turning, but not turning aside, says to him: *yatra na anyat pasyati, na anyat srinoti, na anyad vijanati, sa bhuma.*

And now again, like a sushumna blossoming chakrally, the vine growing downwards from heaven, is there, and Yaje Woman pointing to it is there, and Jesus turning, but not turning aside, says to her: *yatra na anyat pasyati, na anyat srinoti, na anyad vijanati, sa bhuma.*

And now again Ka'uyumari comes. Looking up, his eyes dazed, he says: behold a great wonder in Heaven. Jesus says to him: *yatra na anyat pasyati na anyat srinoti, na anyad vijanati, sa bhuma.*

Tempted, tempted, and yet again tempted. Tempted in the desert by the Great Adversary. Tempted on your way into the Triduum Sacrum by Mayashkti in unfamiliar disguises and guises. Tempted within the Triduum Sacrum into a compassionate conformity with the expectations and hopes, of your followers, with the religious limitations of your followers. But how like a withered cactus, how like a withered peyote bush your head was on Good Friday, Jesus.

The withered cactus and the koshaless skull.

The withered cactus looking down into the koshaless skull.

Wirikuta overcome, Wirikuta with all its nierikas overcome is the world overcome.

Wirikuta overcome is pia peyote mater overcome.

In his way and in his terms St John the Evangelist apprehended the enormity of what happened:

For all that is in the world, the lust of the flesh and the lust of the eyes, and the pride of life, is not of the Father but is of the world. And the world passeth away, and the lust thereof, but he that doeth the will of God abideth forever.

Tatei Hikuri offers us the peyote bush.

Jesus offers us the Tenebrae harrow.

The bush or the harrow, addiction or liberation from addiction, it's a harsh choice. Jesus chose. And could it be that there is a sense in which Good Friday on Golgotha precedes Holy Thursday in Gethsemane? This precedence of Good Friday suggests that it was only because he had overcome the world or his addictions to it that Jesus could go down into the depths of the world and drink the karmic cup.

Depths of the earth. Depths of the psyche.

Grand Canyon in the Earth. Grand Canyon in the psyche.

Palaeozoic strata in the earth's Grand Canyon. Palaeozoic strata in the psyche's Grand Canyon.

> O the mind, mind has mountains, cliffs of fall
> Frightful, sheer, no-man-fathomed. Hold them cheap
> May who ne'er hung there.

Mountains and mesas.

All inner and outer Grand Canyon mesas are temples.

Did you, descending, visit Buddha in his temple, Jesus? Did you, descending, visit Shiva in his temple, visit Vishnu in his temple?

Did Buddha invite you into his temple? Did he offer you night-shelter in the grand mahayana hospitalities, in the grand philosophical and epistemological hospitalities, of his religion?

Did Shiva invite you into his temple? Did he, inviting you in, offer his abhaya-mudra hand to you?

In which of his avatars did Vishnu show himself to you? Did he stand in his temple door as Adi Varaha, the Primal Boar?

Or as Kalkin neighing the three neighings neighed so long ago by the Horsehead Nebula, neighings now again echoing and re-echoing, between the rock-walls of our karma? Or did he stand in his temple door as Krishna? Sitting in his temple with you, did he play Krishna flute-music to you?

Did you ask Vishnu, Shiva and Buddha to come down with you and watch with you?

Vishnu in one or another of his animal incarnations. Vishnu as Kurma, a turtle.

Shiva as Bhairava. Shiva in his terror form, his form in which our most terrible impulses and energies have come snarlingly to the surface.

Mucalinda Buddha, the Buddha about whom a seven-headed serpent has protectively entwined himself.

Kurma, Bhairava and Mucalinda Buddha going down to watch with Jesus, on the dark, igneous floor of our karmic canyon.

Hundreds of millions of years above them life is beginning to colonize the land.

In a rock-wall disappearing from view trilobites are becoming extinct.

The scree of sea-floors laid down before hearing and seeing had evolved are set audibly in motion by a startled bighorn who climbs and climbs, clattering upwards, until, out of danger at last, he turns and stands looking down at them from a Precambrian pinnacle.

Down into the inner gorge they go.

Emerging onto the canyon's floor, the floor that is called Gethsemane, Jesus begins to be sorrowful and very heavy. Kurma, Bhairava and Mucalinda Buddha watching with him, he prays: O my Father, if it be possible, let this cup pass from me; nevertheless not as I will, but as thou wilt.

Beside them, beside the river, there is a rock-pool. It mirrors the canyon's rock walls, and the rock walls also of far-off Olduvai. They stand, making a mirrored circle, on the rim of it. Kneeling, Jesus cups his hands, hands that were feet, that were fins, at a depth before hands or feet or fins existed, and he fills his cupped hands with the mirroring water and drinks it, taking the Earth's karma into him, taking it upon him, and now, heavy, and turgid, and terrible as the Aztec Earth Mother, he begins to climb, Kurma, Bhairava and Mucalinda Buddha climbing with him. Late the next day, having reached a summit called Golgotha, he looks down, dying, into Adam's empty skull, and it is accomplished, and Buddha knows he must compose another Sutra, and Shiva knows he must compose another Upanishad and karika, and Vishnu knows he must compose another Gita.

Our Grand Canyon Sutra.
Our Olduvai Upanishad and Karika.
Our Golgotha Gita.

Sutra Ananda. Upanishad Ananda. Gita Ananda.

Lamb of God looking down on a bighorn sheep looking down from a Precambrian pinnacle.

> O the mind, mind has mountains, cliffs of fall
> Frightful, sheer, no-man-fathomed. Hold them cheap
> May who ne'er hung there.

Jesus hung there. Like a fossilized archaeornis he hung there, soared there. And, sharing in his victory, all the old sea-floors beneath him hung there, soared there. For one brief moment only did all things hang with him, soar with him, there. In that brief moment an immensity of redemption was accomplished.

And who knows! Maybe our planet shines with a new, enlightened light now. And maybe there are beings in another galaxy who see in this light, and they are glad, seeing a new star in their night sky.

Healing the past.

All the way down to the floor of Grand Canyon our past has been healed.

All the way down to the floor of the Grand Canyon there is now a healed past out of which a healed present and future can grow.

> *Te Deum laudamus*
> *Te Deum laudamus*
> *Te Deum laudamus*

Christ has crossed the Kedron and a first vast consequence for religion and culture, indeed for the Earth itself, is that the mirroring rockpool has taken over from the smoking mirror and nirvikalpasamadhi has taken over from viksepashakti.

Viksepashakti: the power by which we project a snake into a rope.

Innumerable are they whom we have fed, sometimes with holocaustic zeal, to that snake.

Is that snake the first and continuing mover of history?

How much of what we call history proceeds from the smoking mirror? Are we, in our enlightened present, caught up in historical motives and goals that proceed from our smoking mirror?

Is every historical year a Year One Reed in which history fails? Fails as much for Cortez as it does for Montezuma?

> or ever the silver cord be loosed, or the golden bowl
> be broken, or the pitcher be broken at the fountain.

The historical, whole bowl with which Cortez draws from the fountain has as little in it as has Montezuma's broken pitcher:

> I met a traveller from an antique land
> Who said: Two vast and trunkless legs of stone
> Stand in the desert. Near them, on the sand,
> Half sunk, a shattered visage lies, whose frown,
> And wrinkled lip, and sneer of cold command,
> Tell that its sculptor well those passions read
> Which yet survive, stamped on these lifeless things,
> The hand that mocked them, and the heart that fed:
> And on the pedestal these words appear:
> 'My name is Ozymandias, king of kings:
> Look on my works, ye Mighty, and despair!'
> Nothing beside remains. Round the decay
> Of that colossal wreck, boundless and bare
> The lone and level sands stretch far away.

The trunkless legs of Ozymandias and beyond them waving his wand above it, Aaron opening a path through the Red Sea.

Is history's path through the sea a path through the trunkless legs of Ozymandias?

It might be good for us, if only now and then, to despair of history and politics:

> Then he asked why the serpent's head
> Was fanged,
> White meat or dark
> He was still the law.
>
> He hung the earth in its place
> And was hanged,
> And the scythe
> Reappeared in his Father's jaw.

It is well known that there are peoples who, unlike us, locate themselves not in sacred time but in sacred space.

A buffalo skull at his feet and a sacred pipe with which he offers them smoke, an Oglala medicine man prays to the Sacred-Powers in the East, the Sacred-Powers in the West, the Sacred-Powers in the North, the Sacred-Powers in the South, the Sacred-Powers in the Great Above and the Great Beneath.

Given the permanence of these places and these powers, it has been concluded that peoples who locate themselves in sacred space are altogether more psychically secure than peoples who locate themselves in sacred time, as mutable in the present, and also perhaps in the future, as it has been in the past.

Always it seems, above Areopagus Rock wherever it outcrops, in Athens, Paris or St Petersburg, the scythe reappears in *heilsgeschichte*'s jaw. Guillotine appears in it and Gulag. And looking at himself in the smoking mirror of his Thousand-Year Reich, our most recent pharaoh, become Führer, sees not a uraeus but a ropesnake hissing at him from his high, *uber alles*, Aryan brow.

But Plato imagined the Philosopher King.

When he emerges from his cave of smoking mirrors, will we see that uraeus on his brow has been replaced by a mahavakya on his brow? Or, as though a universal redemption has occurred, will uraeus on his brow speak a mahavakya from his brow?

> *Yatra*, she says,
> *Yatra na anyat pasyati, na anyat srinoti,*
> *na anyad vijanati, sa bhuma.*

To the people who built Chartres Cathedral, Christ was King, and at vespers on Passion Sunday they sang the great hymn:

> *Vexilla Regis prodeunt.*

And Jesus returned in the power of the Spirit into Galilee; and there went out a fame of him through all the region round about. And he taught in their synagogues, being glorified of all. And he came to Nazareth, where he had been brought up: and as his custom was, he went into the synagogue on the sabbath day, and stood up for to read. And there was delivered unto him the book of the prophet Esaias. And when he had opened the book, he found the place where it was written: The Spirit of the Lord is upon me, because he hath anointed me to preach the gospel to the poor; he hath sent me to heal the broken-hearted, to preach deliverance to the captives, and recovering of sight to the blind, to set at liberty them that are bruised.

To set at liberty them that are philosophically bruised, and nowhere more effectively did he do this, in word if not yet in deed, than in the Sermon on the Mount. Long before he came to the Kedron, Jesus was a Taoist:

Therefore I say unto you, take no thought for your life, what ye shall eat, or what ye shall drink; nor yet for your body, what ye shall put on. Is not the life more than the meat, and the body than raiment? Behold the fowls of the air: for they sow not, neither do they reap, nor gather into barns; yet your heavenly father feedeth them. Are ye not much more than they? Which of you by taking thought can add one cubit to his stature? and why take ye thought for raiment? Consider the lilies of the field, how they grow: they toil not, neither do they spin: and yet I say unto you, that even Solomon in all his glory was not arrayed like any of these.

All of which sounds like the Tao Te Ching:

> Heaven is eternal, the Earth everlasting.
> How come they be so? It is because they do not foster their own lives;
> That is why they live so long.
> Therefore the Sage
> Puts himself in the background, but is always to the fore.
> Remains outside; but is always there.
> Is it not just because he does not strive for any personal end,
> That all his personal ends are fulfilled?
>
> What is of all things most yielding
> Can overwhelm that which of all things is most hard.
> Being substanceless it can enter even where there is no space;
> That is how I know the value of action that is actionless.
> But that there can be teaching without words,
> Value in action that is actionless,
> Few indeed can understand.

Imagine it: Jesus reading from the Tao Te Ching in the synagogue in Nazareth:

> Learning consists in adding to one's stock day by day;
> The practice of Tao consists in subtracting day by day,
> Subtracting and yet again subtracting
> Till one has reached inactivity.
> But by this very inactivity
> Everything can be activated.

Consider the lilies of the field, how they grow; they toil not, neither do they spin; and yet I say unto you, that even Solomon in all his glory was not arrayed like one of these.

In the Sermon on the Mount, Jesus challenges us to join him in an exodus from *yu wei* to *wu wei*.

Christianity building an ark that will take us from *yu wei* to *wu wei*.

As the Bible mirrors him in its smoking mirror, Yahweh is pure *yu wei* and it is from this *yu wei* image of him that our *yu wei* world derives its legitimacy.

Historically, the Christian Ark became *Nave, Mayflower* and *Pequod*.

Modern culture is *Pequod* culture. Carrying our biblical mandate to rule over the Earth and subdue it, we have already sailed into the Sea of Typhoons.

> Full fathom five thy father lies;
> Of his bones are corals made;
> Those are pearls that were his eyes:
> Nothing of him that doth fade,
> But doth suffer a sea-change
> Into something rich and strange,
> Sea-nymphs hourly ring his knell.
> Ding-dong.
> Ding-dong, bell.

Full fathom one thousand and five the *Pequod* lies, and of its ribs an ashram is made.

Sweeping the temple floor in that ashram, Ishmael remembers the biblical God talking to Noah, remembers him giving all things earthly into his hand:

And God blessed Noah and his sons and said unto them, Be fruitful and multiply and replenish the earth. And the fear of you and the dread of you will be upon every beast of the earth, and upon every fowl of the air, upon all that moveth upon the earth, and upon all the fishes of the sea; into your hand are they delivered. Every moving thing that liveth shall be meat for you, even as the green herb have I given you all this.

But the deluge of human dominion is altogether more awful than the deluge of waters. And it will only subside if we heed Old Man:

Now, if you are overcome, you may go to sleep and get power. Something will come to you in your dream, and that will help you. Whatever those animals who appear to you in your sleep tell you to do, you must obey them. If you want help, are alone and travelling, and cry aloud for aid, your prayer will be answered – perhaps by the eagles, or by the buffalo, or by the bears. Whatever animal answers your prayer you must listen.

Yahweh talking to Noah and his sons. Old Man talking to Ishmael, sole survivor of the *Pequod*, our most recent Deucalion.

Keeping watch before the mast one night, long before they entered the Sea of Typhoons, Ishmael remembered the Book of Job:

Canst thou draw out Leviathan with an hook? Or his tongue with a cord which thou lettest down? Canst thou put an hook into his nose? Or bore his jaw through with a thorn? Will he make many supplications unto thee? Will he speak soft words unto thee? Will he make a covenant with thee? Wilt thou take him for a servant forever? Wilt thou play with him as with a bird? Or wilt thou bind

him for thy maidens? Shall the companions make a banquet of him? Shall they
part him among the merchants? Canst thou fill his skin with barbed irons? Or his
head with fish-spears? Lay thine hand upon him, remember the battle, do no
more. Behold, the hope of him is in vain.

Seemingly in vain also, sometimes, is the hope of our own unconsciousness. Seemingly in vain for someone who, like Nietzsche, discovers
that 'the old human and animal world, indeed the entire prehistory and
past of all sentient being, works on, loves on, hates on, thinks on in me'.

Did the biblical God give you dominion over your own unconscious,
Adam? Will your unconscious speak soft words to you, Adam? Will it
make many supplications unto you? Will it make a covenant with you?
Will you take it for a servant for ever? Will it dream your dreams for you?
Or will it dream its own dreams?

Job didn't only lose all outer dominion, he lost all inner dominion too:

When I say my bed shall comfort me, my couch shall ease my complaint, then
thou scarest me with dreams and terrifiest me through visions, so that my soul
chooseth strangling and death rather than my life.

Yes indeed. In Job was our biblical bluff called. It was also called in the
voyage of the *Pequod*. Long before the *Pequod* sailed into the Sea of
Typhoons it was called:

Tell me, Ishmael asks, why this strong, young colt, foaled in some peaceful valley
in Vermont, far removed from all beasts of prey – why is it that upon the sunniest day, if you but shake a fresh buffalo robe behind him, so that he cannot even
see it, but only smells its wild animal muskiness – why will he start, snort, and
with bursting eyes paw the ground in phrensies of affright? There is no remembrance in him of any gorings of wild creatures in his green northern home, so
that the strange muskiness he smells cannot recall to him anything associated with
the experience of former perils; for what knows he, this New England colt, of
the black bisons of distant Oregon? No: but here thou beholdest even in a dumb
brute, the instinct of the knowledge of the demonism in the world. Though
thousands of miles from Oregon, still when he smells that savage musk, the rending, goring bison herds are as present as to the deserted wild foal of the prairies,
which this instant they may be trampling into dust.

Though thousands of miles from Oregon, still when he smells that
savage musk ...

Though thousands of miles from Olduvai ...

Though thousands of miles from the floor of the Grand Canyon ...

Tell me, Noah, Ishmael might ask: the God who gave all things earthly
into your hand, did he also give you your own unconscious into your

hand? Did he give you dominion over the entire prehistory and past of all sentient life in you? Did he give you dominion over your reflex reactions to ancient savannah scents? Did he give you dominion over the Vermont colt in you? Over the Vermont colt's response to bison musk?

A colt grazing peacefully in a valley in Vermont.

Noah planting a vineyard in a valley in Ararat.

A fresh buffalo robe shaken behind the colt.

The buffalo robe of all our latent terrors, Cainozoic, Mesozoic and Palaeozoic, shaken behind Noah.

It was shaken behind Job. Asleep on his couch it was shaken behind him. The King of Terrors shook it behind him.

Hell is sometimes naked before us. It was naked before Job.

Undergoing his crisis, undergoing a biblical enantiodramia on behalf of us all, Job was some nights a brother to dragons and a companion to owls.

We must reimagine you, Noah. We must somehow release you from biblical hard bondage. As it is told in the Bible, the story you live in is your Land of Goshen.

An exodus is possible.

It would help you, wouldn't it, Noah, if we told you the Narada story. Having listened to it, we could call you Narada-Noah.

It would help you, wouldn't it, and it would also help us, to imagine you asking Vishnu to show you the secret of his maya.

It would help you and us to imagine you walking with Vishnu in Wirikuta.

The Deluge of awareness-of having opened, we imagine you walking dryshod through.

We imagine you sitting forlorn and alone in the desert of Zin.

All seems lost. But then you hear the great god's voice: you've been gone for a hundred or more incarnations, did you bring the water?

It will help you to tell you, won't it Noah, that throughout the biblical generations the Triduum Sacrum has been waiting for someone who would walk into its terrible and great initiations, and finally there was someone: Jesus of Nazareth dropped his tools and, finding that he had walked into it, he surrendered to it and now we have a healed past to emerge with.

Having lived itself to the lees in Jesus, the Triduum Sacrum sheds its light backwards and forwards, backwards upon all old stories, changing them, recreating them, releasing any Gethsemane, Good Friday, or Garden of the Sepulchre intuitions that are latent in them.

Subliminal in your story, Noah, are the Job and the Jonah initiations.

There being all Africa and its prodigies in us, you might, sitting in it, have imagined the ark to be an archetype of you. Sitting in it, drifting with it, you might have discovered what Jesus discovered, what Nietzsche discovered, that all of ancient life lives on, loves on, hates on, thinks on, dreams on in you.

You didn't need to build an ark, Noah. You already were an ark.

In one of his self-revelations, Vishnu is Vishvarupa. Literally, Vishvarupa means Omniform, the Form that contains all other forms, the life that contains all lives.

In Gethsemane, Jesus was Vishvarupa, he was Vishvajuga, and in him all the ancient life that dreamed itself in Nietzsche, that dreamed itself in Noah, all that ancient life was redeemed.

And so, we imagine an anodos for you, Noah. An anodos all generations since Adam and Eve can participate in. An anodos all animals, living and extinct, can participate in. An anodos the earth can participate in, for the earth has yet to come ashore, has yet to awake to its own transcendent self, has yet to have a precognitive dream of itself as Gaia Anadyomene.

They had drifted already six days and six nights on the waters when Noah dreamed. The ark he dreamed had begun to breathe, had begun to roll, had become a whale. Turning flukes, she sounded, carrying him down and yawning him out into the void below his psyche. He wasn't appeased when he woke up. He was cross that his mind would do this kind of thing to him. Being in his mind wasn't a safe place to be.

After forty days in the ark, Noah climbs to the upper deck, and there it is, the great and sacred Earth. After seven days he hasn't reached it. Remaining in sight it remains afar off, as if it was saying, not yet, not yet.

In a dream one night Owl told him why: for as long as you retain a biblical image of it as a thing to be ruled over and subdued the Earth will remain distant. Even if you go ashore and live on it, it will remain distant. Your attitude to the Earth separates you from the Earth. Your eyes and mind need the medicine of a great story. It is only when a great story of origins originates great seeing in you, originates great dreaming and great waking in you, that the Earth, itself so great, will come co-creatively close.

In his dream, Noah saw what to do.

Asking her to find a story of origins that medulla and mountain could flourish in, he sent out Cormorant.

Cormorant was gone a long time. She came back with this story:

There was only water and over it a fog. On the water was foam. The foam whirled round and round continually and from it came a voice. After a time there issued from the foam a person in human form. He had wing feathers of the eagle on his head. This was Solitude Walker. He floated on the water and sang. He stood on the foam. There was no light. He walked on the water. He made a rope and laid it from north to south, and he walked along it revolving his hands one about the other, and behind him the earth was heaped up along the rope. But the water overwhelmed it. Again he did this, and again the water prevailed. Four times he did this. Solitude Walker was constantly talking to himself: I think we had better do it this way. I think we had better try it that way. He imagined another way. He made four lilkae and planted them, one in the north, and the others in the south, west and east. Then he stretched them out until they were continuous lines crossing the world in the centre. He spoke a word and the earth appeared. Then he walked along the edge and lined it with whale-hide so that the ocean could not wash it away. He shook the earth to see if it was solid, and sometimes, even now, he shakes it, causing earthquakes.

The Earth remains afar off. Noah sends out Otter.
The story Otter brings home dreams itself in his dream before Noah:

Was it not an illusion? The Father touched an illusory image. He touched a mystery. Nothing was there. The Father, Who-Has-an-Illusion, seized it and, dreaming, began to think. Had he no staff? Then with a dream thread he held the illusion. Breathing he held it, the void, the illusion, and felt for its earth. There was nothing to feel. I shall gather the void, he thought. He felt, but there was nothing. Now the Father, Who-Has-an-Illusion, thought the word 'Earth'. He felt the void, the illusion, and took it into his hands. Who-Has-an-Illusion then gathered the void with dream thread and pressed it together with gum. With the dream-gum iseike he held it fast. He seized the illusion, the illusory earth, and he trampled it and trampled it, seizing it, flattening it. Then as he seized it and held it, he stood on it, on this that he had dreamed, on this that he had flattened. As he held the illusion he salivated, salivated, salivated, and the water flowed from his mouth. Upon this, the illusion, this, as he held it, he settled the sky roof. This, the illusion, he seized, entirely, and peeled off the blue sky, the white sky. Now in the under world, thinking and thinking, the maker of myths permitted this story to come into being. This is the story we brought with us when we emerged.

The earth remains afar off. Noah sends out Seal.
The story that Seal brings back dreams itself in his dream before Noah:

In the beginning this universe was the Self alone, in the likeness of a great person. Looking around he saw nothing other than himself. First of all he said, this is I. He was afraid. He thought to himself and said: Since nothing exists other than I, of whom, or of what, am I afraid? And this fear departed from him. He found no pleasure in being alone. He longed for a second. Now he was of the size of a man and a woman in close embrace. He split this self in two and from it arose husband and wife. He copulated with her and human beings were born. She thought to herself and said: how is it that he copulates with me although he generated me from his very self? Very well, I will disappear. She became a cow, he a bull, they copulated and cattle were born. She became a mare, he a stallion, she a she-ass, he a he-ass. They copulated and single-hoofed animals were born. She became a she-goat, he a he-goat, she became a ewe, he a ram. They copulated and goats and sheep were born. So did they bring forth all the couples that exist, even ants. So did they bring forth the whole universe.

The Earth remains afar off. Noah sends out Eagle.
The story Eagle brings back speaks itself to Noah in his dream:

> Then, even nothingness was not, nor existence.
> There was no air then, nor the heavens beyond it.
> What covered it? Where was it? In whose keeping?
> Was there the cosmic water, in depths unfathomed?
> Then there were neither death nor immortality,
> Nor was there then the torch of night and day.
> The One breathed windlessly and self-sustaining.
> There was that One then, and there was no other.
> At first there was only darkness wrapped in darkness.
> All this was only unillumined water.
> The One which came to be, enclosed in nothing,
> Arose at last, born of the power of heat.
> In the beginning desire descended on it –
> That was the primal seed, born of the mind.
> The sages who have searched their hearts with wisdom
> Know that which is, is kin to that which is not.
> And they have stretched their cord across the void
> And know what was above, and what below.
> Seminal powers made fertile mighty forces.
> Below was strength and over it was impulse.
> But, after all, who knows, and who can say
> Whence it all came, and how creation happened?
>
> The Gods themselves are later than creation,
> So who knows truly whence it has arisen?
> Whence all creation had its origin?
> He, whether he fashioned it or whether he did not,
> He, who surveys it all from highest heaven,
> He knows – or maybe even he does not know.

All night long the animals come, each of them bringing a story. Loon comes. Mantis comes. Alligator comes. And the ark, which was an ark of animals only, is now also an ark of creation stories floating on the Abyss. And, in its turn, every story opens its door to the Earth, but the Earth, not yet imagined as it would be imagined, stands afar off.

Noah wakes from his dream.
And then he hears it.
The Earth coming closer sings it:

> Te Kore
> Te Kore-tua-tahi
> Te Kore-tua-rua
> Te Kore-nui
> Te Kore-roa
> Te Kore-para
> Te Kore-whiwhia
> Te Kore-rawea
> Te Kore-te-tamaua
> Te Po
> Te Po-teki
> Te Po-terea
> Te Po-whawha
> Hine-Make-moe
> Te Ata
> Te Au-tu-roa
> Te Ao-marama
> Whai-tua
>
> Maku
> Mahora-nui-a rangi
>
> Rangi-potiki
> Papa
>
> The Void
> The First Void
> The Second Void
> The Vast Void
> The Far-Extending Void
> The Sere Void
> The Unpossessing Void
> The Delightful Void
> The Void Fast Bound
> The Night
> The Hanging Night
> The Drifting Night
> The Moaning Night
> The Daughter of Troubled Sleep
> The Dawn
> The Abiding Day

The Bright Day
Space
Moisture
Great Expanse of Heaven
The Heavens
Earth

Now at last the Earth looked hospitable and reachable, and as it drifted onto it, Noah opened the doors of the ark.

Six nights later, in bed in their tent, Siduri explained her recent reticence to Noah: 'It worries me that, setting foot on the Earth, you said nothing. You just stood there barefoot under the stars. We thought you were pondering what you would say. But then, saying nothing, you walked inland. It is six nights later now and you haven't yet said anything.'

'Can you guess why I didn't say anything?' Noah asked

'Was it that no good words came to you?'

'No. I deliberately didn't say anything. Standing there on the wet shingle, I wanted my mind to be as barefoot as my feet. I didn't want my mind to be shod in any of the old cosmologies, or in any new cosmology either. Nor did I want the Earth to be shod in them. I wanted to give the Earth a break, however brief, from all our efforts to appropriate it into our intentions and desires. For the few minutes that I stood there, the Earth was unconscripted. So, as for saying something as I set foot on it – I leave that to the generations who will come after us. It is for them to imagine what I might have said. By whatever they think I should have said, by that shall they know themselves, by that shall they define themselves and order themselves before God and the stars.'

A liberation for earth and stars it was that the demiurgic metaphor didn't go ashore with Siduri and Noah.

Nothing so damages the universe and our relationship to it as our image of it as something made, as handiwork. But, even though Jesus was a carpenter, even though he was, in the most literal sense, a demiurge by trade, the demiurgic metaphor never lived in him. In him we find metaphors of seed sowing and growing:

And he said, so is the kingdom of God, as if a man should cast seed into the ground, and should sleep, and rise night and day, and the seed should spring and grow up, he knoweth not how.

As if Jesus was saying: God isn't a maker, the universe isn't handiwork as a chair is, it isn't something made. Yet, tragically for us as perceivers, there the old debilitating metaphor is, alive and perniciously well, not just in everyday language but in the Christian Creed:

I believe in one God, Father Almighty, maker of heaven and earth ...

In one very profound way the Fall was and is a fall into bad cosmological metaphors.

Metaphors that survive the flood as the Bible understands it. Metaphors that survive the life of Christ. That survive the Gospels.

The Fall was something that happened to us as perceivers. It was a fall into bad cosmologies not into a bad cosmos.

The deluge will come to an end only when our minds and eyes are cleansed. Only when, seeing it, we know that the Earth is Buddh Gaia. Only when, seeing it and living in it, we know that, overhanging us above and below, the universe is a Bodhi Tree.

Walking ashore, Siduri and Noah know, setting foot on it, that the universe overhangs them in heavens above, overhangs them in heavens below.

Setting foot on a Maori shore of Buddh Gaia, Siduri and Noah sing a Song of Origins. Emerging from Nirvikalpasamadhi with it they sing it:

> Te Kore
> Te Kore-tua-tahi
> Te Kore-tua-rua ...

The emergence of the universe is the emergence of consciousness-of out of Nirvikalpasamadhi. It is the emergence of awareness of self and other-than-self out of Nirvikalpasamadhi.

Let us emerge with it:

> Te Kore
> Te Kore-tua-tahi
> Te Kore-tua-rua
> Te Kore-nui
> Te Kore-roa
> Te Kore-para
> Te Kore-whiwhia
> Te Kore-rawea
> Te Kore-te-tamaua
> Te Po
> Te Po-teki
> Te Po-terea
> Te Po-whawha
> Hine-Make-moe
> Te Ata
> Te Au-tu-roa
> Te Ao-marama

Whai-tua
Maku
Mahora-nui-a rangi
Rangi-potiki
Papa

Sapient under the sapient soles of our feet is Buddh Gaia.

Happy are we who have survived the Flood. Happy are we who have survived our Narada initiation.

Even if our *Pequod* culture should founder, having a story of origins we have a raft, and our goal from now on must be to come ashore. Time and time and time again, long after we have gone ashore, we must come ashore.

Hine-make-moe, the Daughter of Troubled Sleep, coming ashore.

Daughter of Troubled Sleep, Daughter of Troubled Waking, coming forth by day.

Day when Anadyomene is epithet to all things.

Day when Akhty is epithet to all things.

Day when *pert em hru*, the three greatest words that Egyptians could speak, are spoken by all things.

Daughter of Troubled Sleep. Daughter of Troubled Waking. Call her Lyca as Blake did. Call her Lucy as anthropologists do. Think of her as Little Girl Lost. Think of her as Little Girl Found.

Lyca who is akhty, who is of the morning horizon, as Horus is.

Lucy who is anadyomene, who rises from troubled sleep and troubled waking as Venus rose from the troubled sea.

Pert em hru: Lucy's first three words. The first three words of the new humanity.

Pert em hru: let us imagine them to be the words that Noah spoke as he set foot, the first human being to do so, on Buddh Gaia.

Coming forth philosophically. Coming forth culturally.

Coming forth from our Psalm eight estimation of ourselves. Coming forth from our second stasimon estimation of ourselves.

Coming forth from our demiurged world of works and days. Coming forth from our demiurgic perceptions of all things.

Horus of the horizon.

Venus anadyomene.

Siduri and Noah coming forth from hard bondage in their biblical story. Coming forth from hard bondage in our biblical perceptions of them.

According to Hindus the ideal life falls into four stages. The first stage is that of being a pupil. The second, that of being a householder, being married, rearing a family. The third is the stage of meditative retirement in the forest. And the fourth is the stage of being a wandering ascetic.

Imagine it: their lives as householders, as parents, having come to an end, Siduri and Noah retire to the forest. Imagine them having spent ten years there. Imagine them talking to each other in much the same way as the great Upanishadic sage, Yajnavalkya, and his wife, Maitreyi, talk to each other.

NOAH: You dreamed of the hind again last night, didn't you, Siduri? You fol-lowed her into that marvellous world again, didn't you?

SIDURI: What makes you think so?

NOAH: I only have to look at you. I only have to listen to the river.

SIDURI: What's so different about me? And the river, what's so different about the river?

NOAH: I've been waiting all day for you to tell me.

SIDURI: Never once looking behind her to see if I was following her, the hind led me into the Ark. It was empty. Even the hind left no scent of herself in it. No wind blowing it, the Ark moved out into the Great Deep. Even if they were still there, sitting on their perches, I knew it would be a waste of time to send out the raven and the dove. And then, as it happened to you in your dream, the Ark became Leviathan, it turned flukes and sounded, carrying me down, down, down – down below all deeps and all depths – and she yawned me out, me screaming in terror – but no! It wasn't into the perdition I had anticipated that she yawned me. It was into myself walking back from the well she yawned me. We have come ashore, Noah. There is no eternity of God deeper than the eternity of God we are in, than you gathering firewood in the hills, than me coming back from the well.

Imagine Abraham talking to his son Isaac in much the same way, or to similar effect, as Aruni, another great Upanishadic sage, talks to Svetaketu, his son.

ISAAC: It's the knife you would have sacrificed me with, isn't it?

ABRAHAM: It's the knife that mirrored the Intervening Angel. To save my life, I looked at him only in his reflection.

ISAAC: You didn't strike me, but a wound did open in me. It hasn't closed.

ABRAHAM: It will close.

ISAAC: When?

ABRAHAM: When you recognize it for what it is. It wasn't when I held the knife above you that it opened. That wound came into existence with you. The one side of it is you seeing, the other is the objects that you see. On our way back to God who is one and undivided it closes.

ISAAC: And then?

ABRAHAM: Then we must wait until it pleases God to carry us across the final threshold.

ISAAC: And then?

ABRAHAM: Then who we are, where we are, pitching and breaking camp, eating with Hagar and Ishmael in their wadi.

ISAAC: And the knife? Does the knife go with us?

ABRAHAM: Always during my prayers I pray to the Intervening Angel. He hasn't intervened for the last time, or the second last time. We mustn't pretend prematurely to universal protection. The knife that we carry, praying to the Angel, is altogether less dangerous than the knife that pursues us, and, sure that we needn't look back, possesses us.

Upanishadic conversations in our Holy Book. Conversations that amount to a mystical Magna Carta such as Pico della Mirandola would later elaborate:

O supreme generosity of God the Father, O highest and most marvellous felicity of man! To him is granted whatever he chooses, to be whatever he wills. Beasts as soon as they are born (so says Lucilius) bring with them from their mother's womb all they will ever possess. Spiritual beings, either from the beginning or soon thereafter, become what they are to be for ever and ever. On man when he came into life the Father conferred the seeds of all kinds, and the germs of every way of life. Whatever seeds each man cultivates will grow to maturity and bear in him their own fruit. If they be vegetative, he will be like a plant. If sensitive, he will become brutish. If rational, he will grow into a heavenly being. If intellectual, he will be an angel and the son of God. And if, happy in the lot of no created thing, he withdraws into the centre of his own unity, his spirit, made one with God, in the solitary darkness of God, who is set above all things, shall surpass them all.

The rainbow in the cloud condensing into a mystical Magna Carta in the cloud, condensing into a Mandukya Magna Carta in the cloud.

An exodus within the biblical tradition. An exodus from life defined by the rainbow in the cloud to life defined by the Mandukya Upanishad in the cloud.

An exodus within the Christian tradition. An exodus from Evangel to Evangelanta. An exodus, bringing the Evangel with us, from Evangel to Evangelanta.

And it shall be when thou art come in unto the land which the Lord thy God giveth thee for an inheritance and possessest it, and dwellest therein, that thou shalt take of the first of all the fruit of the earth, which thou shall bring of thy land that the Lord thy God giveth thee, and shalt put it in a basket, and shalt go unto the place which the Lord thy God shall choose to place his home there. And thou shalt go unto the priest that shalt be in those days and say unto him, I profess this day unto the Lord thy God that I am come unto the country which the Lord swore unto our fathers for to give us. And the priest shall take the basket out of thine hand, and set it down before the altar of the Lord thy God. And thou shalt speak and say before the Lord thy God, a Syrian ready to perish was my father and he went down into Egypt, and sojourned there with a few, and became there a nation, great, mighty and populous. And the Egyptians evil entreated us, and afflicted us, and laid upon us hard bondage. And when we cried unto the Lord God of our fathers, the Lord heard our voice, and looked on our affliction, and our labour, and our oppression. And the Lord brought us forth out of Egypt with a mighty hand, and with an outstretched arm and with great terribleness, and with signs, and with wonders. And he hath brought us in unto this place and hath given us this land, even a land that floweth with milk and honey.

An exodus from philosophical hard bondage.

An exodus from epistemological hard bondage.

An exodus from the hard bondage of biblical naive realism to Kantian idealism.

An exodus in which we walk dryshod through the Red Sea of con-sciousness-of.

An exodus in which we walk through the Narada initiation.

And Jesus returned in the power of the Spirit into Galilee, and there went out a fame of him throughout all the region round about. And he taught in their syn-agogues, being glorified of all. And he came to Nazareth where he had been brought up, and, as his custom was, he went into the synagogue on the Sabbath day and stood up for to read. And there was delivered unto him the book of the prophet Esaias. And when he had opened the book, he found the place where it was written; the Spirit of the Lord is upon one, because he hath anointed me to preach the gospel to the poor; he hath sent me to heal the broken-hearted, to preach deliverance to captives, and recovering of sight to the blind, to set at lib-erty them that are bruised.

To set at liberty them that are philosophically bruised.

Philosophically, almost all of us are broken-hearted.

Philosophically, almost all of us are captives.

And there was delivered unto him the book of the prophet Esaias.

And there was delivered unto him the Mandukya Upanishad.

And there was delivered unto him the Chandogya Upanishad.

And Jesus who speaks comfortably, who speaks Upanishads and Gitas, speaks to us who are epistemologically bruised.

In philosophy, Christ, not Kant, is Copernicus. In him, looking down on Good Friday into Adam's empty skull, metaphysics yielded ground to metanoesis.

Golgotha is the Christian Ionia. It is home to a great succession of mystical philosophers, among them such luminaries as Dionysius the Areopagite, Eckhart, Marguerite Porete, Catherine of Genoa, the author of *The Cloud of Unknowing*, Teresa of Avila and St John of the Cross.

It is ritually, in Tenebrae, that Christian philosophy finds its final dignity. Its mystical dignity.

On Good Friday, Greek dialectics yielded ground to the nocturnes of Tenebrae.

On Good Friday, Greek *peripateia* in a stoa became Christian ambulation in a Tenebrae Temple.

Good Friday is Philosophy's Great Day.

Why then are we philosophically bruised?

Why then are we culturally bruised?

Why then are we civically bruised?

Civically bruised in Isaiah's Zion. Civically bruised in Blake's London:

> I wander throu' each chartered street,
> Near where the chartered Thames does flow,
> And mark in every face I meet,
> Marks of weakness, marks of woe.
>
> In every cry of every man,
> In every infant's cry of fear,
> In every voice; in every ban,
> The mind-forged manacles I hear.
>
> How the chimney-sweeper's cry,
> Every blackening Church appalls,
> And the hapless soldier's sigh,
> Runs in blood down palace walls.
>
> But most thro' midnight streets I hear,
> How the youthful harlot's curse,
> Blasts the new-born infant's tear,
> And blights with plaques the marriage hearse.

'Mind-forged manacles.'

But the mind that forges our socio-political manacles, that institutes the socio-political, socio-economic hard bondage we are hewers of wood and drawers of water in, isn't that very mind itself forged, biologically forged, biologically chartered, biologically manacled? Isn't it, mostly, an instrument of a more or less blind will to live? Itself biologically manacled, it manacles us to the snake we project into the rope. And how greatly will it improve things, William, if we cleanse the doors of perception, if we open them more widely? If we cleanse them with mescalin, if we open them more widely with ayahuasca? There are Hindus and Buddhists who talk not about cleansing our senses and minds, but about going beyond them. And, guiding us to the summit of Mount Carmel, St John of the Cross says: 'On this road, therefore, to have our faculties in darkness is to see the light.'

An appalled church.

A church whose Christian conscience is appalled.

A church appalled for Tenebrae.

'*Erat autem fere sexta hora, et tenebrae factae sunt in universam terram usque in horam nonam. Et obscuratus est sol, et velum templi scissum est medium.*'

The veil in the temple was rent.

The veil of biologically manacled mind in us rent.

The Red Sea of consciousness-of opened.

Three hours of Good Friday Darkness, three hours of Tenebrae, in which our planet becomes a success.

Jesus coming ashore out of Tenebrae.

Jesus Anadyomene.

Gaia Anadyomene. Gaia coming home to her awakened self.

Buddhists have built a temple on the spot where the Buddha won enlightenment. It is called Buddh Gaya.

Buddh Gaya. Buddh Gaia. Calling our Earth Buddh Gaia.

Our awakened Earth. Our enlightened Earth.

> Hear the voice of the Bard!
> Who present past and future sees,
> Whose ears have heard,
> The Holy Word,
> That walked among the ancient trees.
>
> Calling the lapsed soul,
> And weeping in the evening dew,
> That might control,
> The starry pole,
> And fallen, fallen light renew.
>
> O Earth, O Earth, return!
> Arise from out the dewy grass;
> Night is worn,
> And the morn,
> Rises from the slumberous mass.

> Turn away no more:
> Why wilt thou turn away?
> The starry floor,
> The watery shore,
> Is given thee till the break of day.

Speak not now of the slumberous mass. Speak now of the awakened Goddess. Speak now of Bhu Devi. Speak now of Buddh Gaia.

Gaia Anadyomene.

Jesus Anadyomene.

Vishvarupa Anadyomene.

Vishvayuga Anadyomene.

Vishvayuga setting foot on Buddh Gaia.

Vishvayuga setting foot on all the Grand Canyon floors of Buddh Gaia.

Vishvayuga setting foot on all the Grand Canyon floors of Buddh Gaia, knowing that in doing so, he is setting foot also on all the Grand Canyon floors of the psyche.

Bright Angel Trial in the Earth. Bright Angel Trail in the psyche.

Geological sediments in the Earth. Psychological sediments in the psyche.

Geological strata in the Earth. Karmic strata in the psyche.

Precambrian era in the Earth. Precambrian era in the psyche.

Vishnu formation in the Earth. Vishnu formation in the psyche.

Mesa-temples in the Earth. Mesa-temples in the psyche.

Will we ever find our way to the Earth we were born into? Will we ever, following Jesus, set sacred anodyomene foot on it? Will we ever, following Jesus whose sign is the fish, set fin-become-foot on it?

A space journey to the moon. A space journey to the Earth we are already on.

There are other giant steps, Neil.

There are three giant steps, Neil. Steps gigantic in their humility. Steps gigantic in their daring. The step that carries us across its threshold into Gethsemane. The step that carries us across its threshold into Good Friday. The step that carries us across its threshold onto the great and sacred Earth.

An Earth so sacred that all our Ascension Thursdays out of it are Christmas nights that carry us back down into it.

It is on Christmas night that our Ascension Thursday longings find fulfilment.

And there were in the same country shepherds abiding in the fields keeping watch over their flocks by night, and, lo, the Angel of the Lord came upon them,

90

and the glory of the Lord shone round about them and they were sore afraid. And the Angel said unto them, fear not, for behold, I bring you tidings of great joy, which shall be to all people, for tonight there is opened unto you a Bright Angel Trail to the Earth, a Bright Angel Trail to the psyche. And unto you is born this night a child who will stand on all the old floors of the earth, on all the old floors of the psyche. On an igneous floor he will kneel, and the chalice won't pass. He will drink the wine of astonishment. He will drink the dregs of the cup of trembling and wring them out.

Trail to the karmic depths of the psyche.

Tell Freud, tell Jung, tell them that the Trail to the karmic depths of the psyche is presided over by a Bright Angel who says fear not.

Fear not, the Tibetan Book of the Dead says to us when, in the Chonyid Bardo, we encounter our Karmic propensities objectified now as peaceful and wrathful Deities.

> Bhu Devi in wrathful form,
> Bhu Devi as Bhairavi,
> Bhu Devi as Coatlicue,
> Bhu Devi as wrathful Deity of the chonyid bardo.

He will drink the wine of astonishment. He will see hard things. He will drink the dregs of the cup of trembling and wring them out.

> Stay with him, Bright Angel
> Pray with him, Bright Angel

It isn't by taking up revolutionary arms against it, it isn't by assaulting its Bastilles, nor is it by legislative fiat, that we will successfully deal with our inner psychological ancient regime. The regime of cravings, hungers, impulses, energies, which, for the most part, were biologically instituted in the Palaeozoic. The ancient regime we innately are.

Ordinarily, our awareness of this ancient regime in us isn't a problem. But, on the purifying igneous floors of Gethsemane, our awareness of it is agony. In the inwardly illuminating light of purgatory, our awareness of it is agony.

Some there are who do not sanely survive the discovery of this ancient regime in them. Was Nietzsche one of them?

'I have discovered for myself', Nietzsche says, 'that the old human and animal world, indeed the entire prehistory and past of all sentient being, works on, loves on, hates on, thinks on in me.'

If, having made this discovery, Nietzsche had crossed the Kedron with Jesus, if he had knelt on the igneous floor with him, if, despairing of his own abilities, he had surrendered to the terrible Good Shepherding which, even in the belly of the whale, offers its *abhaya mudra* hand to us, he might have come through, as so many Christian mystics came through.

In biblical times Hebrews believed, exceptions notwithstanding, that you couldn't see God and live. How much of itself can the human psyche see and live? Can the ego see the whole psyche and live?

In Gethsemane, Jesus saw his whole psyche. The whole human psyche became conscious in him. It lived itself consciously in him. It lived itself consciously through him. And he was sore amazed. But he didn't turn back:

> Our heart is not turned back, neither have our
> steps declined from thy way, though thou hast sore
> broken us in the place of dragons, and covered us
> with the shadow of death.

There is Gethsemane Good News: the human psyche can look into its own deepest depths and live. We can live from the depths of our psyches, we can be lived by the depths of our psyches, and not harm a hair of another person's head.

A city of seven gates,

A psyche of seven gates,

Thebes in trouble,

Troy in trouble,

The civilized psyche of Europeans in trouble.

Our Trojan horse is a colt from Vermont, and Melville has opened the western gate of our secular city to him. He has, in other words, opened it to some of the most terrible anamnesias of the human psyche.

The *Argo* coming home with a Golden Fleece. The sea-slimed, wrecked *Pequod* coming home, the fresh buffalo robe of all our terrors its only sail.

As Heidegger reminds us: 'The menace which assails man's nature arises from that nature itself.' But Heidegger doesn't sit in despair, help-lessly awaiting assault from within. He quotes Hölderlin's lines:

> But where the danger is, there grows
> Also what saves.

And he comments:

It may be that any other salvation than that which comes from where the danger is, is still within the unholy. Any salvation by makeshift, however well-inten-tioned, remains for the duration of his destiny an insubstantial illusion for man, who is endangered in his nature. The salvation must come from where there is a turn with mortals in their nature.

Rilke is talking about a turn in our nature when, speaking of poetry and poets, he says:

All that the rest forget in order to make their life possible, we are always bent on discovering, or magnifying even; it is we who are the real awakeners of our monsters, to which we are not hostile enough to become their conquerors; for in a certain sense we are at one with them; it is they, the monsters, that hold the surplus strength which is indispensible to those that must surpass themselves. Unless one assigns to the act of victory a mysterious and far deeper meaning, it is not for us to consider ourselves the tamers of our internal lions. But suddenly we find ourselves walking beside them, as in a Triumph, without being able to remember the exact moment when the inconceivable reconciliaton took place.

Marduk reconciled with Tiamat. Baal reconciled with Yam. Yahweh reconciled with Leviathan. Apollo reconciled with Python. Zeus reconciled with Typhon. Hercules reconciled with Hydra. Andromeda reconciled with Ketos. Mary reconciled with Kundalini.

The buffalo of distant Oregon and the New England colt reconciled.
Moby-Dick and Ahab reconciled.
Phylogeny in us and ontogeny in us reconciled.
Id and ego reconciled.
A marriage in us of Heaven and Hell.
Thinking of Mucalinda Buddha as the enlightened exemplar and archetype of all such reconciliations and conjunctions.
One of his comforters assures Job that if he can bring himself to not despise his correction and chastening at the hand of the Almighty, then a most marvellous transformation in his relations with the world will occur:

At destruction and famine thou shalt laugh; neither shalt thou be afraid of the beasts of the earth. For thou shalt be in league with the stones of the field, and the beasts of the field shall be at peace with thee.

In league with the stones of the field.
The stones of the field in league with humanity. They must have been in league with the builders of Gothic cathedrals. They must have been in league with the builders of Bhuvaneshvar.
What has been can be again.
We can break into song as Uvavnuk our Inuit medicine woman broke into it:

> The great sea has set me in motion,
> Set me adrift,
> Moving me as the weed moves in a river.
> The arch of sky and mightiness of storms,

Have moved the spirit within me
Till I am carried away
Trembling with joy.

There is, maybe, an Orphic music in all things. And if, sinking into it within ourselves, we give it leave to score new growing in us, then indeed will we be in league with the stones of the fields, then will the beasts of the field be at peace with us. Living shamanically, we will walk, as Rilke says, with our inner lions. And we will be bear dreamers, we will be bison dreamers, otter dreamers, eagle dreamers, horse dreamers, thunder dreamers, the bear, the bison, the otter, the eagle, the horse, the thunder giving us, now again, the medicines and the myths they gave us in the Pleistocene.

Thunder dreamers.

Wolf Collar and Black Elk: two Pleistocene thunder dreamers of our time. Thunder dreamers who brought thunder medicines to us, degenerate beyond remedy perhaps, at the end of our Promethean day.

Kali yuga. Prometheus yuga. *Yu wei* yuga.

Nave. Mayflower. Pequod.

Imagine it: Ishmael, sole survivor, leading Europa and Prometheus into a Grove of Erinyes, not in Attica, but in Turtle Island. No. It is not a Grove. Nightingales don't sing here. And there are no trees. It is into a scrapyard they are walking. And there they are. An Erinys called Turbine. An Erinys called GNP. An Erinys called Slag. An Erinys called Mushroom. An Erinys called Meltdown. An Erinys called Bottom Line. An Erinys called *Pequod* Culture. An Erinys called Sea of Typhoons. An Erinys called Bubbles. They have angle-grinder voices. Sometimes they sing in unison, sometimes singly. A metallic motet of nine soliloquies can outlive our metallic ages, our age of El Dorado gold, our ages of silver, bronze and iron. Now, however, as Prometheus and Europa walk in, they fall silent. but not for long. Rising to greet them, Turbine, GNP and Bottom Line sing a song called Revs Per Second. They mean well. Erinyes always mean well. They mean their songs to be the couple's epithalamion.

Oedipus and Antigone at Colonus.

Prometheus, Europa and Ishmael in Detroit.

Dialogue between Oedipus and a stranger in the Grove of the Erinyes in Colonus.

Dialogue between Prometheus and a stranger in the scrapyard of the Erinyes in Detroit:

STRANGER: By your size I see that you are a Titan. And since you are here, these Erinyes hounding you, you must be he who stole fire from heaven and founded Titanic culture.

PROMETHEUS: I am who I am, a lover of humankind.

STRANGER: And now you know, standing under a hole in the ozone layer you know, that Titanic humanity is the iceberg the Earth has crashed into.

Thunder above the Grove of the Erinyes in Colonus.

Wakinyan Tanka, the thunderbird of native North America, above the scrapyard of the Erinyes in Detroit.

Theseus, its king, welcoming Oedipus and Antigone to Attica.

Wolf Collar, a Thunder dreamer, welcoming Europa and Prometheus to Native North America. Having pity for them, he invites them to come with him to the far West, land of savage bear and buffalo musks. Sitting with them one night in his Blue Thunder tipi he tells them a story:

Once upon a time there was a community of mice. They were very busy mice. Morning, noon and night they were busy. Busy harvesting the grass seeds. And after the grass seeds, they'd be busy again collecting the ripened rosehips. And the choke-cherries – they were the worst. No one looked forward to bringing them home, the bushes being so far away and the paths to them so uneven and rough. And that wasn't all. Their nests must be tidied and cleaned. Litters must be suckled and licked. Dead mice must be hauled away. And there were disputes. There were wrongs that had to be righted. They were very busy mice. But, as you'd expect, there were among them a few mice who weren't as devoted to their work as they should be. Recently, there was a lot of talk about one particular mouse. He was not so reliable any more, and sometimes he'd do a very strange thing: breaking off from what he was doing, he would stand on his hind legs, stretch himself to his full height and, flaring his ears, he would continue in that unnatural posture, seeming to listen.

Can you hear it? he would ask a neighbouring mouse, when he had dropped back down to all fours.

Hear what? the neighbouring mouse would ask.

Can you hear the roaring?

Roaring! What roaring? his neighbour would scornfully ask. Roaring indeed! There is no roaring. You're imagining things. And you'd better behave. Already, behind your back, they are taking you off. And they are calling you Standing Mouse.

And it happened to his face one day.

How are you, Standing Mouse? a little mouse asked, and then she giggled, and all the little mice giggled with her.

It wasn't easy for Standing Mouse. Sometimes when there was silence he would hear the roaring and then, without thinking, he'd be on this hind legs again, his ears would be flared, and he would be listening, oblivious to the wise-

95

cracks and the hilarity. One day the roaring seemed like a calling and when he dropped down on all fours he didn't resume his work. To his great surprise and delight, he felt he had the courage now and he started to run, and he kept running, and nothing would stop him, and it never occurred to him, not once, that he should turn back and finish what he was doing, all thought of what he had been doing and had yet to do were far behind him now, and he was running, already he had run farther into the unknown than any mouse before him had ever done. Breathless, he stopped, but only to catch his breath, not to reconsider. There was no need to reconsider. Whatever it was, the roaring was real and, unless a great giant wielding a club should kill him and eat him, he would keep going. Breathing more easily, he looked up. And there they were, spots in the sky, and he knew what they were, they were eagles, and eagles, his grandmother had told him, have big eyes, and from whatever heights they choose to circle and soar in, they can, looking down, see the smallest movements in the grass, mouse movements in the grass they can see.

Remembering all the old stories about mice who didn't come home, Standing Mouse was suddenly terrified. In spite of himself, he was reconsidering. Could it be that he was imagining things? And what would he be doing now if he hadn't left home? And what were they saying about him? And why didn't others whose hearing was as good as his, why didn't they also hear it? Had he ever heard it? Desperate to find out, and in spite of the eagles circling above him, he raised himself up on his hind legs, stretched himself up to his full height and listened, and there it was, the roaring. Now again he was running. If anything, he was running faster and more confidently than before. In and out of hoof tracks he was running. And some of them had water in them. But he didn't mind. Getting wet wasn't the worst thing in the world. And it didn't matter now what he looked like. There were no other mice to make fun of him. Maybe someday, when all this was over, he'd have time to lick his coat, to groom his face and whiskers. For the moment, he must give all his energy to one thing and that was to keep running towards the roaring. He'd have doubts if he stopped.

But then, suddenly, he had to stop, because right there in front of him there was a heaving something, something very big, heaving hoarsely. He turned and ran back a little way and then, turning again, he looked, and now he could see what it was, it was a buffalo. He hadn't ever seen a buffalo, he had only heard about them, about the beard, about the horns, about the head hung low. This surely was a buffalo. And bigger and grander he appeared to him to be than the beings who live only in fables.

What a great being! he said.

What a great being!

But I am blind, Buffalo said.

Blind! A being as great as you are, blind! Do you mean you can't see, do you mean you can't even see me? Standing Mouse asked.

I know it's daytime, Buffalo said, for I feel the heat, but I'm in the dark, and

I've fallen behind the herd. I'm five or six days behind them already, so I've given up, unable on my own to find the way to the winter grazing grounds.

But you're such a great being, Standing Mouse said. Never in my whole life have I seen so great a being. And I am only a little being, and I have two eyes, I will give you one of them.

Instantly, his right eye flew out of Standing Mouse's head and went into the head of Buffalo. And now Buffalo could see. He looked down at Standing Mouse.

Hello, Little Brother, Buffalo said. How wet you look. How famished you look. What are you doing on your own out here?

I'm almost ashamed to tell you. You'll probably laugh at me. But I'm used to being laughed at, so I will tell you. I sometimes hear a roaring, a great roaring, a roaring that tells me that the busy world we live in isn't the world at all. It tells me that waiting for us beyond our busy world there is a great world, so I left our busy world and I'm out here searching for the great world, and now that I've met you I know that it exists, even if you were only your beard and nothing else I would know looking at it that the great world exists, and I won't stop now. I will keep going, I am travelling in the direction of the roaring, but sometimes I'm very frightened. The great world is a dangerous world, look up and you'll see, those spots up there, circling up there, they are eagles and eagles have big eyes and big clutching claws, I'm afraid of them, but my fear of them hasn't stopped me. That's how great the roaring is, it draws me into my fear, it draws me through my fear, my fear gives me strength, I'm travelling under eagles to find it. Do you think I'm foolish?

No, no, no, Buffalo said. No, Little Brother, you aren't foolish, you are on a journey and I can help you. I am a big animal. Eagles don't bother me. Come in under me and when I start walking you start running, that way the eagles won't see you, and maybe we'll reach the roaring together.

Off they went together, Buffalo and Mouse – Mouse more afraid of the hooves than he was of the eagles. The eagles were high in the sky, but the hooves were coming down, constantly coming down, all around him. If I run too fast, he thought, or if I fall behind, one of them will surely crush me. In a very short while, however, he had found the rhythm, he was in the rhythm of Buffalo's walking. Somehow or other his running was absorbed into the easygoing, calm gait of Buffalo's walking. His running and Buffalo's walking were one wonderful going. And so it continued until they came to the mountains and there they stopped.

How are you, Little Brother? Buffalo asked.

I'm fine, I'm fine, can't you see I'm fine, but at first I was terrified. I was sure I'd be crushed by one of your hooves.

You had no reason to worry, Little Brother, because I am a Buffalo, I don't hurt the Earth, I walk the Earth in the sundance way. You gave me your eye, Little Brother, and I have given you the way I walk, the way that my people walk when we walk between grazing grounds. But now we have reached the mountains. I'm not a mountain person. I'm a person of the prairies and now with your eye I can once again find my way in them.

Goodbye, Little Brother.

Goodbye, Great Being.

Standing Mouse looked up at the mountains. They were great beings too. They didn't need to be kind to him. They didn't even need to be recognized by him.

If that was me now, Standing Mouse thought, looking up at them, if I was a mountain like one of them, I'd have made some attempt to soften my savageries. I need to be liked. But then, I'm only a little being, and they are great beings, and they won't even ask me why I'm here. Their beards are glaciers. Buffalo's beard blows in the wind.

Mouse had no ground cover now and he couldn't hear the roaring. Even when he stood on his hind legs and listened he couldn't hear it. But he wasn't deterred. Relying on his old conviction, he started climbing, across the bare pavements and up the rock walls. In a ravine sitting there, seemingly unaware of him, was Wolf.

Wolf didn't look happy, he didn't look good.

But what a great being! Mouse thought. What a great being!

Hello, Great Being, Mouse said.

Who's there? Who's there? Wolf asked.

It's me, it's Mouse. It's Standing Mouse. Can't you see me?

No, Wolf said, no, I'm blind, I'm sitting here waiting to die.

But you are a great being, Mouse said, and I am only a little being and I have an eye and I'll give it to you.

Instantly, his eye reopened in Wolf's head. I can see! I can see! I can see! Wolf shouted. I can see! I can see! I can see! And he ran to the edge of the precipice and ran back. He sat on his thin tail-end, he threw back his head and he howled, howled, howled, and all the rock-walls of the mountain howled. And all of them echoed, I can see! I can see! I can see! And the rock-walls could see!

Mouse almost died of fright. His little heart was pounding and again now, his whiskers having nothing familiar to touch, he was having to ask himself was he able at all for the great world. He could well understand why all his friends had turned their backs on it, had closed their doors on it. And good doors you'd need to keep out what he'd heard, a mountain of six rock-walls howling his howls with Wolf.

Wolf loped towards him.

Hello, Little Brother. What are you doing here?

I'm crossing the mountains.

Have you heard of owls and hawks?

I have: And I've heard of eagles.

And you still want to go?

I want to go.

Even though you're blind?

Even though I'm blind. But the mountains can see, I think. Maybe the mountains will see me through.

Maybe there is some way I can help you, Wolf said. Let me think, he said. Wolf was a long time thinking. Nothing came to him. So he went to the edge of the precipice and started again. I have it, he said suddenly and all excited, he somersaulted twice coming back to Mouse.

I've a great plan, he said. Not many would think of it. Maybe no one else would think of it, but I've thought of it. This is it: I'm great on mountains and now again, thanks to you, I can see where I'm going. Here's what we'll do. Stand in under me here and when I start walking you start running, that way you'll be protected, that way the eagles, the owls and the hawks won't get you.

Three days later they walked into a prairie on the other side. Sniffing the wind, Wolf stopped. Mouse emerged from beneath him. This is the end of my range, said Wolf. I must turn back.

Goodbye, Wolf.

Goodbye, Mouse.

From a long way off Wolf called back, Goodbye, Little Brother.

Mouse was alone but he wasn't afraid because now, even without standing on his hind legs, he could hear the roaring. Struggling through thick grass, he broke into a beaver path and now he could run, and he ran and he ran and he ran, over its bank into Medicine River.

A current was carrying him downstream. Frog, who was sitting on a wet rock, saw him. Frog was a strong swimmer, so Frog dived in and retrieved Mouse, hauling him to the nearest bank.

Frog didn't wait to the thanked. Within moments he was back on his rock.

And now the wind came and a voice called out, Go with it Mouse, go with the wind, hang on to the wind, and the wind was taking him up, up and up, up above the foothills, up above the hawks and the owls, up above the summits of the mountains, only the eagles were above him now, but not for long, it wasn't long till Mouse was among the eagles, till Mouse was above the eagles, and, looking up, he saw the Sun door opening, it was opening for him, and he could go through or not go through, the choice was his. He chose to return.

And that's the story of Standing Mouse.

The story that tells how Standing Mouse, having become a Great Being, came back to his people. It's the story with which I welcome you both, you Europa and you Prometheus, to my Blue Thunder Tipi. Here we can live remote from the world ye come from. We can wait for what next the Thunders will do.

Standing Mouse. A culture-hero altogether greater than Prometheus, altogether greater than Herakles.

Let us give Rilke leave to say it again:

All that the rest forget in order to make their life possible, we are always bent on discovering, or magnifying even; it is we who are not the real awakeners of our monsters, to which we are hostile enough to become their conquerors; for in a certain sense we are at one with them; it is they, the monsters, that hold the surplus strength which is indispensable for those who must surpass themselves. Unless one assigns to the act of victory a mysterious and far deeper meaning, it is not for us to consider ourselves the tamers of our internal lions. But suddenly we find ourselves walking beside them, as in a Triumph, without being able to remember the exact moment when the inconceivable reconciliation took place.

What Rilke has to say can, without violence we hope, be appropriated to serve as a commentary, not only on the story of Standing Mouse. It can serve as a commentary also on the story of Job. Job lived from the biblical mandate to rule over the earth and subdue it. He had vast herds and flocks and gaggles and coops of tamed and domesticated animals and fowls. One day Behemoth walked through the front gate. Ostrich walked through it. In a dream that night, Leviathan laughed at his fishhooks; with all of her seven proud heads raised high above the proud waters, she laughed at his fishspears. Job was in trouble. Job's biblical bluff had been called.

Speak comfortably to Job, Rainer Maria. Advise him to let go of his culturally acquired need to rule over the earth and subdue it. Tell him that, if only he will let go, an inconceivable reconciliation with Behemoth, Ostrich and Leviathan is possible. Tell him the story of Standing Mouse. Tell him to listen for the roaring of the great, wild world. Tell him to leave his busy world. Tell him to go to Siberia. Tell him to live in a yurt there. Tell him to apprentice himself to a Yakut Shaman. Rowing himself across the Bering Straits, tell him to listen in her igloo in the tundra to Uvavnuk singing:

> The great sea has set me in motion,
> Set me adrift,
> Moving me as a weed moves in a river.
> The arch of sky and mightiness of storms,
> Have moved the spirit within me,
> Till I am carried away,
> Trembling with joy.

Job on his way to Siberia. On his way, representing us all, he exchanges our biblical mandate for an Orpheus lyre.

Job in a Yakut yurt whose pole is the *axis mundi*. Prometheus and Europa in a Blue Thunder tipi.

Healing ourselves through healing our myths, ancient and modern. Healing ourselves through healing our cosmologies, ancient and modern.

Myths and cosmologies aren't daydreams that never engage with reality. They are, very often, damaging actions, damaging ways of being in the world.

Aztecs weren't the only people to ritually and liturgically elaborate a religion of the Smoking Mirror.

Smoking Mirror. Smoking Lamp.

A mirror that only mirrors its own smoke. The smoke of its own bad dreams. The smoke of its own delusions.

Bacon talked about four kinds of delusions that will tend to blind us in our quest for a true understanding of the world about us. He called them *idola: idola specus, idola tribus, idola fori, idola theatri* — delusions of the cave, of the tribe, of the marketplace, of the theatre.

Has Christianity, in some of its moods, been a religion of the smoking mirror, a religion of the smoking lamp?

Even Hui Neng, maybe, would agree that the smoking mirror and the smoking lamp we have always with us.

Let us listen again to St John of the Cross:

O wretched condition of this life wherein it is so dangerous to live and so difficult to find the truth! That which is most clear and true, is to us most obscure and doubtful and we therefore avoid it, though it is most necessary for us. That which shines the most and dazzles our eyes, that we embrace and follow after, though it is most hurtful to us, and makes us stumble at every step. In what fear and danger then must man be living, seeing that the very light of his natural eyes, by which he directs his steps, is the very first to bewilder and deceive him when he would draw near unto God. If he wishes to be sure of the road he travels on, he must close his eyes and walk in the dark, if he is to journey in safety from his domestic foes, which are his own senses and faculties.

Our senses and faculties: our smoking mirrors, our smoking lamps.

The dark night of our smoking mirrors and smoking lamps, our viksepashakti mirrors, our avaranashakti lamps.

The Tenebrae of our smoking mirrors, our smoking lamps.

All Middle and Near Eastern religious traditions crossed the Kedron with Jesus.

Healed in the person of Jesus, our surrogate walking into the Triduum Sacrum. Religiously healed. Culturally healed.

Dare we imagine it, therefore: a Risen Bible!

The kathodos and anodos of our Holy Book.

The kathodos and anodos of our Smoking Mirror.

The kathodos and anodos of our Smoking Lamp.

The lamp that illumines our Guernica *Gotterdammerung*.

The smoking lamp that illumines its own projected delusions, its own projected *idola – idola specus, idola tribus, idola fori, idola theatri.*

A religion that, if only for three days a year, leads its people into the healing dark beyond the mirror and the lamp.

A religion that takes the dark night of the soul seriously. A religion that enacts it.

> Full fathom five our lamp lies
> And of its lights are Upanishads made.

Time to go beachcombing on the shore of Turiya-Tehom.

Our lamp washed up.

Our mirror washed up.

Jivanmukhta Jesus coming ashore.

'What are poets for in a destitute time?' It's a question Hölderlin and Heidegger asked. And in the course of addressing the question, Heidegger quotes from a poem by Hölderlin:

> ... the heavenly powers,
> Cannot do all things. It is mortals
> who reach sooner into the abyss, so the turn is
> with these. Long is
> The time. But the true comes into
> Its own.

This he quotes having somberly said:

The era is defined by the God's failure to arrive, by the 'default of God'. But the default of God which Hölderlin experienced does not deny that the Christian relationship with God lives on in individuals and in the churches; still less does it assess the relationship negatively. The default of God means that no God any longer gathers persons and things unto himself, visibly and unequivocally, and by such gathering disposes the world's history and our sojourn in it. The default of God forebodes something even grimmer, however. Not only have the Gods and the God fled, but the divine radiance has become extinguished in the world's history. The time of the world's night is the destitute time, because it becomes even more destitute. It has already grown so destitute, it can no longer discern the default of God as a default. Because of this default, there fails to appear for the world the ground that grounds it. The word for abyss – Abgrund – originally means the soil and ground toward which, because it is undermost, a thing tends downward. But in what follows we shall think of the Ab – as the complete absence of the ground. The ground is the soil in which to strike root and to stand. The age for which the ground fails to come hangs in the abyss. Assuming that a turn still remains open for the destitute time at all, it can come some day only if the world turns about fundamentally – and that now means, unequivocally: if it turns away from the abyss. In the age of the world's night, the abyss of the world must be experienced and endured. But for this it is necessary that there be those who reach into the abyss. The turning of the age does not take place by some new God, or the old one renewed, bursting into the world from ambush at some time or another. Where would he turn, on his return, if men had not first prepared an abode for him? How could there ever be for the God an abode fit for a God, if a divine radiance did not first begin to shine in everything that is? The Gods who 'were once there' 'return' only at the 'right time' – that is when there has been a turn among persons in the right place, in the right way.

The turn, the conversion, the metanoia of our age involving us in an encounter with the Abyss. But not only with the Abyss. With the Beast also.

Beast and Abyss.

Job encountered the Beast. Jonah encountered the Abyss. Jesus encountered both. Within himself he encountered them.

For forty days in the desert Jesus 'was with beasts'. He was with what is beastly in our humanity. And this was but a prelude to his encounter with it, to his endurance of it, Grand Canyon deep in Gethsemane.

In Gethsemane, Jesus was sore amazed, seeing from within himself, knowing from within himself, how wonderfully and fearfully we are made. In the darkness of Good Friday he saw, not seeing with his eyes or mind, that the Divine Ungrund is Ground. In Eckhart's words he saw that 'Everything which has being hangs in the Naught. And that same Naught is such an incomprehensible Aught that all the spirits in Heaven and upon earth cannot comprehend it or sound it.'

To return to the language of Heidegger: the Abyss has been endured. The Beast has been endured. Jesus has endured them. His endurance of them is, and yet isn't, an unfinished symphony. Rather should we say, perhaps, that it is a continuing endurance and in every generation there are those who are called to participate in it with him. It is they, in Heidegger's phrase, who prepare an abode for his return. But since his return is not from the grave but from the Abyss we should call it his anodos.

Jesus Anadyomene.

We watch him coming ashore and now we know that reaching into the Abyss is reaching into the Divine because, as Tauler has told us, the Abyss is much more God's dwelling-place than heaven or man. And than that there can be, within our tradition, no greater transvaluation of mythic and religious values.

The snake we project into the rope, the Abyss we project into Turiya, into Tao-Turiya-Tehom.

The Tao-Turiya-Tehom out of which Jivanmuhkta Messiah comes ashore. Seeing him, we ask the questions Heidegger asked: Where will he turn on his return? Have we prepared an abode for him? Are we willing, bringing the Risen Bible with us, to walk with him into Evangelanta? Are we willing to be heirs to everything the Triduum Sacrum has made us heirs to? Are we willing to be heirs to the Mandukya Upanishad and the Tao Te Ching? Are we willing to be heirs to our own Evangelanta Upanishads and Mahavakyas? Are we willing to build a Tenebrae Temple, a temple out of which we would walk, able at last to set sensitive, anadyomene foot on the great and sacred Earth?

Palm Sunday before the Triduum Sacrum. Mahavakya Sunday after it.

Calling Easter Sunday Anodos Sunday,

Anodos Day,

Anoday.

Day when, not wringing his hair out, Jivanmukhta Messiah comes ashore.

On that day we are all poets. On that day each of us is 'the kind of poet who answers to the coming world era'.

But the coming world era won't be a heilsgeschichte era, inaugurated by scimitar or sword. It will know nothing, will want to know nothing, about the march of history. People who invent a thing called history, who script an apocalyptic goal for it and then set it marching, sword in hand, towards that goal, have always caused havoc to Jebusites, Perizzisites, Amalakites deemed to be standing in its way. Let us recall the biblical Book of Numbers, chapter 31:

And the Lord spoke unto Moses saying, Avenge the children of Israel of the Midianites: afterward shalt thou be gathered unto thy people. And Moses spoke unto the people saying, Arm some of yourselves unto the war, and let them go against the Midianites, and avenge the Lord of Midian. Of every tribe a thousand throughout all the tribes of Israel, shall ye send to the war. So there were delivered out of the thousands of Israel a thousand of every tribe, twelve thousand and armed for war. And Moses sent them to the war, a thousand of every tribe, them and Phineas the son of Eleazar the priest, to the war, with the holy instruments and the trumpets to blow in his hand. And they warred against the Midianites, as the Lord commanded Moses, and they slew all the males. And they slew the kings of Midian beside the rest of them that were slain: namely, Evi and Rakem and Zur and Hier and Reba, five kings of Midian: Balaam also the son of Beor they slew with the sword. And the children of Israel took all the women of

Midian captives, and their little ones, and took the spoil of all their cattle, and all their flocks, and all their goods. And they burnt all the cities wherein they dwelt, and all their goodly castles, with fire. And they took all the spoil, and all the prey, both of men and of beasts. And they brought the captives and the prey and the spoil unto Moses, and Eleazer the priest, and unto the congregation of the children of Israel, unto the camp at the plains of Moab, which are by Jordan, near Jericho. And Moses was wroth with the officers of the host, with the captains over thousands, and captains over hundreds, which came from the battle. And Moses said unto them, Have ye saved all the women alive? Behold, these caused the children of Israel, through the counsel of Balaam, to commit trespass against the Lord in the matter of Peor, and there was a plague among the congregations of the Lord. Now therefore, kill every male among the little ones, and kill every woman that hath known man by lying with him. But all the women children, that have not known a man by lying with him, keep alive for yourselves ...

Can you hear her, a Midianite Anne Frank sitting on the Holocaust ashes of her people?

Bury my *heilsgeschichte*-ravaged heart at Wounded Knee.

It isn't out of *heilgeschichte* that Jesus walks on Anodos morning. And it isn't into it, walking inland, that he walks. Coming ashore out of the Divine Ungrund, neither the history of a particular people, nor world history, has any claim to him. His coming ashore isn't an event in history. In his presence, history becomes trans-historical.

It isn't with the smoke of our smoking mirror, nor is it with the smoke of our smoking lamp, and it isn't with the smoke of a smoking city, whether Jericho or Somnath, that we welcome you, Jesus. It is with the transhistorical mahavakyas that we are now heirs to we welcome you.

'In the age of the world's night', Heidegger says, 'the abgrund of the world must be endured.' A Christian correlative but not equivalent of this would be: in an age when our seals' breathing-holes into the Transcendent have closed over, someone must cross the Kedron. Jesus has crossed the Kedron, the Triduum Sacrum has lived itself out completely in him, he has come ashore and now again we have sacraments, now again we have Tenebrae rituals, at which, as at seals' breathing-holes, we can breathe transcendently.

Seven Evangelanta sacraments, seven seals' breathing-holes into the Transcendent.

Locating the Transcendent not only outside ourselves but also inside ourselves, as did Boehme and Blake.

'In man lies all whatsoever the sun shines upon, or heaven contains, as also hell and all the deeps.'

' … in your own bosom you bear your heaven and earth and all you behold, tho it appears without it is within in your imagination of which this world of mortality is but a shadow.'

In us transcendently is Divine Ground.

Keeping an inner seal's breathing-hole open into inner Divine Ground.

An ice-cap without a seal's breathing-hole. A psyche without a seal's breathing-hole.

In relation to the Transcendent, psyche is an eclipse. In relation to Divine Ground transcendently within us, it is the blind not the window.

Hölderlin and Heidegger seem to talk lightly about reaching into the Abyss. It is likely that Jonah wouldn't talk lightly about it. Neither, almost certainly, would Jesus.

Reaching into the Abyss isn't like walking into a neighbour's yard. Actually, it is nothing less than the Narada initiation. Carried to the terrible denouement of Good Friday, it means the rending of the psychic veil. As the Red Sea opened so does the psyche open and we walk through into a vast emptiness, a vast no-thing-ness, which we cannot as yet recognize to be Divine, and this being so, we will tend to see only the threatening Abyss we project into it.

It wasn't mind in Jesus, or psyche in Jesus, or heart in Jesus, it wasn't anything empirical in him, that endured the Abgrund. It was Divine Ungrund in him that endured the Divine Ungrund. And that means there was no endurance. There weren't, in other words, two realities, one small and one great, the small enduring the great. At this depth, there is only the Divine Unity, the Divine One.

Habakkuk, the biblical prophet, has this to say:

… Tehom uttered his voice, and lifted up his hands on high.

A mistranslation of the original this might be, but how fortunate, how providential, we might even say how necessary a mistranslation it is. Indeed, we could with some justice insist that whatever error there is resides not in the translation but in the original.

Ancient Egyptians believed that the Abyss of dark, primordial waters was either a god or the home of a god called Nun and they sometimes pictured him lifting up the Sun, high up over his head, into our world.

Nun and Tehom.

And what, we might ask, what when he utters his voice does Tehom say? And what when he lifts them up does he have in his hands? It matters not so much that we should know these things. What matters, and it matters hugely, is that for one brief moment in the Bible Tehom is more like Turiya than it is like a chaos of raging waters.

Here again, it is appropriate to remember one of Tauler's most startling assertions: 'The Abyss', he says, 'is much more God's Dwelling-place than heaven or man.' In this, Tauler has rescued the Abyss from its Mesopotamian and biblical bad name. What we thought of as the dwelling-place of Tiamat, a monster irredeemably hostile to the cosmos, turns out to be the dwelling-place of God, the source and sustaining ground of the cosmos. So when, in the course of the mystical journey, our rock of faith dissolves into an abyss of faith, that is not so great a calamity as it will at first sight seem. The Abyss of faith is the Tao of faith, it is the Turiya of faith, it is the Tao-Turiya-Tehom of faith. It is the Divine Ungrund of faith. And it goes without saying of course that there is no Ground so grounding and so sustaining as the Divine Ungrund. Our calamity is not that we have collapsed into this Ungrund, it is that we should for so long have relied on other ground, other so called ground, empiral or universal.

Tehom uttered his voice, and lifted up his hands on high.

In the way that a first Bible condensed around the revelation on Mount Sinai, so might a second, more mystical Bible condense around this single sentence. And in the writings of the Christian mystics maybe we already have such a Bible, a holy book of Christian Upanishads in which we think of God not anthropomorphically as King and Lord but as Divine Ground that is santam, sivam, advaitam.

The om of Tehom is the Mandukya om.

When Hindus listen to Tehom, when in deeps within themselves they hear the om, then they cross from Veda to Vedanta.

When Christians listen to Tehom, when in deeps within themselves they hear the om, then they cross from Evangel to Evangelanta.

> Tehom
> Tehom om
> Tehom om om om

What a transvaluation of religious values! The second syllable of a two-syllable word that named our greatest fear is now, most marvellously, our mantra:

> Tehom om
> Tehom om om om om

Biblically, we built bars and doors against Tehom but when, like a dream we had dreamed, all memory of them vanished on Good Friday, then there was silence, and in that silence it happened again. Exactly as it happened in the beginning it happened:

Tehom uttered his voice, and lifted up his hands on high.

Hindus call it the *anahata shabda*, the sound that isn't the sound of any two things striking together:

> Tehom uttering om
> Tehom uttering the Mandukya om.

And, wonderful to relate, someone in our tradition has been silent enough for long enough to hear it, and that is Good News:

> Out of Tehom Om
> Out of Tehom the Mandukya Om.

The Mandukya Om or Aum is four, it is the three sounds A, U, M and the silence that follows them, this silence being called Turiya, the fourth.

A is vaisvanara or waking awareness, U is taijasa or dreaming awareness, M is susupta or dreamless sleep. Turiya is the Divine Ungrund or Ground out of which these states emerge and back into which, back into the bliss of which, they are reabsorbed.

It could be the new first page of our Bible.

Out of Tehom Om.

Out of Tehom the Mandukya Om.

Out of Om all that we experience and see.

Out of Om the more than marvellous Mandukya morning that is breaking over us.

Out of Om, out of it with worldly experience a reminder that worldly experience isn't all of what is.

Out of it, out with it, a neighing and a knowing:

> *Yatra na anyat pasyati, na anyat*
> *srinoti, na anyad vijanati, sa bhuma.*

In the beginning was the word:

Tehom uttered his voice, and he lifted up his hands on high.

Hearing that word, that *anahata shabda* word, we cross from Evangel to Evangelanta.

And again now maybe we can go back to what Heidegger has to say:

The turning of the age does not take place by some new god, or the old one renewed, bursting into the world from ambush at some time or other. Where would he turn to on his return if men had not first prepared an abode for him? How could there ever be for the god an abode fit for the god, if a divine radiance did not first begin to shine in everything that is?

Now that our biblical bars and doors between Time and Tehom have gone down,

Now that Tehom has uttered his voice,

Now that, hearing Tehom, we know that Tehom is Turiya,

Now that Narada is our Noah,

Now that, walking with him in Ararat, we have listened to Old Man and are beginning to live his advice,

Now that we know that, crossing the Kedron, Jesus is our Narada, our Job, and our Jonah,

Now that we know that, far from being a negative dark, the darkness of Good Friday is Tenebrae,

Now that we know that there is a lesser and a greater Easter, a lesser Easter in which we awaken to the extraordinary and an altogether greater Easter in which we awaken to the ordinary,

Now that we know that the universe is as stupendous in a daisy as it is in a galaxy,

Now that we know that everything is *in excelsis*,

Now that looking at it we see, not magma, but sa-magma-madhi,

Now that, looking around us, we know that for all our experience of exile we have never left home,

Now that all this is so, can we assume that we are undergoing the necessary turning, the turning or conversion that will enable the God to come back among us?

It is time, is it not, to harness ourselves to the wagons.

> The heavenly powers
> Cannot do all things. It is mortals
> Who reach sooner into the abyss. So the turn is
> With these. Long is
> The time, but the true comes into
> Its own.

Harnessed to the wagons, can we, without sacrilege, imagine the God's return?

> As Venus came ashore on a shell, so might
> He, coming out of Tehom, come shorewards
> Towards us on the Mandukya Upanishad.

It is *sundara murti* morning that is breaking over us.

The turn that must take place among mortals before the God can return.

The turn that enacted itself in Narada.

Welcoming Narada into the biblical tradition. Giving him, within it, a stature equal to that of Job, equal to that of Jonah.

Welcoming Narada into the Greek tradition. Imagine it: the sea god Glaucus and Narada walking in Periclean Athens. Late by three or four days for the Banquet, it could nevertheless be that it is towards Agathon's house they are walking. And Glaucus! God bless his soul! How wholly without civic sophistication he is. And the noise of him walking. Poor old Glaucus. He does indeed look very much as Plato has described him: his limbs are broken and worn and deformed, and hardly a part of him that isn't covered with shells and seaweed and rocks. And yet, although Plato couldn't see this, in him is the innocence of immersion – of immersion in body, of immersion sea-floor, deep in worldly experience. And not only that. This innocence of immersion is altogether richer than the innocence of those unembodied beings who, unimmersed, ride in the heavenly cavalcade of Zeus. And with him as he walks, Narada. Narada is the true Deucalion. In his case, the wide breaking in of diluvian waters was epistemological and philosophical, not physical. It wasn't so much the world as his philosophical estimation of it that was washed away. At the reconvened Banquet in Agathon's house, neither Glaucus nor Narada has much to say. And like the oracle at Delphi they argue not at all for what it is they have to say. And yet, looking at Narada, Socrates knows that souls who are immersed in the sensible world are not more eclipsed than souls who are immersed in the intelligible world. It is as if, telepathically across the centuries, he was listening to Eckhart:

So long as the soul beholds forms, even though she behold an angel, or herself as something formed: so long is there imperfection in her. Yes, indeed, should she even behold God (as separate), in so far as He is with form and number in the Trinity: so long is there imperfection in her. Only when all that is formed is cast off from the soul, and she sees the Eternal One alone, then the pure essence of the soul feels the naked, unformed essence of the Divine Unity – more still, a Beyond-Being. O wonder of wonders, what a noble endurance is that where the essence of the soul suffers no suggestion or shadow of difference even in thought or in name. There she entrusts herself alone to the One, free from all multiplicity and difference, in which all limitation and quality is lost and is one. This One makes us blessed.

And the marvel is that, ignoring Eckhart, we still listen to Socrates. A marvel it also is that, ignoring Narada, we still listen to Aristotle, even though from the sixth to the ninth hour on Good Friday we learned that, conscious and unconscious, psyche is the blind not the window.

Erat autem fere hora sexta, et tenebrae factae sunt in universam terram usque in horam nonan. Et obscuratus est sol: et velum templi scissum est medium.

The rending of the outer veil was but a sign of the rending of an inner veil. This inner veil Narada would call the veil of all our koshas. And, philosophically, to what else but this rending is Christianity the heir? In Tenebrae, the most tremendous, the most mystical, of rituals, it is heir to it.

There is an exodus we mostly refuse: the philosophical exodus from a banqueting house in Athens to Tenebrae in a Tenebrae temple.

Their souls drying out in the desert of Zin, the Children of Israel yearned for the fleshpots of Egypt.

Refusing the derelictions and deprivations of Tenebrae, Christians have many times regressed to the philosophical banquets of Greece.

A Christianity that was schooled in Tenebrae wouldn't need, seeking admission, to linger at Agathon's door or at the door of Plato's academy. If it did so linger it would be to invite the participating guests and also their host, even if their host was Plato, to walk with it in an exodus whose pillar of fire by night and whose pillar of cloud by day is the Tenebrae harrow, the light that best lights our way not when its candles are lighted but when they are extinguished.

Plato participating in Tenebrae. Plato taking the only candle still not extinguished from the harrow and placing it in the cave behind the altar. That, ritually, would be the consummation not just of Greek philosophy but of philosophy wherever and howsoever it has been or will be practised.

A Christianity that has the courage to grow from its Triduum Sacrum origins, that has the courage to grow from them because it has the courage to grow into them, that Christianity will be adequate to any religious crisis, individual or collective. It will not be afraid to look through Galileo's telescope. Drawing its life from a source inaccessible to thinking, it will not be perturbed by changes of paradigm in our thinking. Such changes as will accrue from a voyage to Galapagos or as might accrue from a voyage to a galaxy whose light hasn't yet reached us.

The quenched Tenebrae harrow might give light to a still-bewildered galaxy, to a still-bewildered Bethlehem star.

The quenched Tenebrae harrow has nothing to fear from microscope or telescope. It remains to be seen whether, reverently in the presence of the quenched Tenebrae harrow, microscope and telescope are willing to close their narrowly seeking hunter's eyes, their nakedly staring Actaeon's eyes.

> The Way is like an empty vessel
> That yet may be drawn from
> Without ever needing to be filled.
> It is bottomless; the very progenitor of all things in the world.
> In it all sharpness is blunted,
> All tangles untied,
> All glare tempered,
> All dust smoothed.
> It is like a deep pool that never dries.
> Was it too the child of something else? We cannot tell.
> But as a subtanceless image it existed before the Ancestor.

It is not in spite of but because of its Good Friday Darkness that Golgotha is the 'seeing' summit of Mount Palomar.

A harrow of quenched candles is a harrow of darkly lighted, darkly guiding mahavakyas.

The advent of the Tenebrae harrow is a stupendous evolutionary event. Indeed, looking at it, evolution is looking at its own consummation. Or putting it in another way: in Jesus, having crossed the Kedron, evolution has come to where, a cup in one hand, a Tenebrae harrow in the other, Bright Angel is waiting for it. And so, search as we may, we will find no evolutionary transition of comparable importance in the orogenized seafloors, high or low, of the Grand Canyon. Going further: search as we may, we will find no evolutionary transition of comparable consequence in the whole of the archaeozoic, in the whole of the Mesozoic, in the whole, thus far, of the Cainozoic.

The possibility of release from evolution or, in other words, Christ looking down into Adam's empty skull, is what we are talking about, so we should, perhaps, put this event in initial perspective. Geologists now believe that the earth is about 4600 million years old. If we scale this down to 46, then we have to confess that about the first seven years of its existence we know nothing at all, and about how things were during the next 35 years our knowledge is sketchy. This brings us to 42 at which time biological life appeared. At 45, which by our scale is just a year ago, the dinosaurs appeared. Mammals arrived eight months ago. In the middle of last week human-like apes evolved into ape-like humans. Modern humans have been around for four hours. It was during the last hour that we discovered agriculture. And the industrial revolution began just one minute ago. In a lonely moment between the discovery of agriculture and the industrial revolution, Jesus crossed the Kedron and now, whatever else we might say of it, we can say of our planet that it is a success.

Looked at historically it was a simple *egressus*:

> *Egressus est Jesus cum discipulis suis trans torrentem Cedron.*
> Jesus went forth with his disciples over the brook Cedron.

Looked at through the rent veil, it was in that simple *egressus trans torrentem* that we sequentially acquired evolutionary legitimacy and release from evolution. Here belongs Christ's sore amazedness and his cry of dereliction:

My God, my God, why hast Thou forsaken me?

Here belongs the Buddha's udana:

> Housebuilder! I behold thee now.
> Again a house thou shalt not build.
> All thy rafters are broken now,
> The ridgepole also is destroyed.
> My mind, its elements dissolved,
> The end of craving has attained.

Here belongs the Horsehead Nebula neighing

> na   na   na   sa
> *Yatra na anyat pasyati na anyat srinoti*
> *na anyad vijanati, sa bhuma.*

Here belongs our trans torrentem answer to some of our cis torrentem questions:

> ! Oh Dichosa ventura

Jesus Trans Torrentem: Jesu beyond, gone beyond, the Torrent is evolution beyond, gone beyond, the Torrent. Gone beyond it into and through three initiations, the Job, the Jonah and the Narada initiations. And, looking down with him tomorrow into Adam's empty skull, we will make the greatest of all discoveries: conscious and unconscious, psyche is the blind not the window.

The egressus and the anodos.

Venus Anadyomene,

Jesus Anadyomene.

Venus coming ashore on an empty shell.

Jesus coming ashore on an empty skull.

But, no skull we will ever encounter will be so unlike a death's head as this one is.

This skull, this koshaless skull, is Good News. Mandukya Good News. Evangelanta Good News. Good News that speaks itself in mahavakyas.

The emptiness of the empty skull is pleroma. So there is a mahavakya that can speak itself in two ways:

> *Yatra na nayat pasyati, na anyat srinoti,*
> *na anyad vijanati, sa bhuma.*

> or

> *Yatra na anyat pasyati, na anyat srinoti,*
> *na anyad vijanati, sa pleroma.*

Zephyrs, themselves divine, blow Venus ashore, and she being who she is, roses of a most heavenly fragrance and colour come shorewards with her. Mahavakyas no less fragrant, although apophatically so, come shorewards with Jesus.

It is a mandukya morning that is breaking over us.

With Jesus, if we would, we can come up out of any and every Land of Goshen. With him we can come up out of any and every religion that is a Religion of the Smoking Mirror. The Smoking Mirror will of course come with us. But, unlike Moses on a famous occassion, we mustn't be angry at that. A religion that had no room in it for the Smoking Mirror would be a calamity. And even though there are many who will go beyond it into the dark night of the soul, it is nonetheless true that not everything we see in the Smoking Mirror is a delusion. And yet welcoming Narada into Christendom is welcoming a religious vocabulary that will include such words as *viksepashakti, avaranashakti, mayashakti, adhyaropa, apavada, samadhi, nirvikalpasamdhi* and coming with him as gifts from Mahayana Buddhism words such as *avidya, moha, asrava, cittamatra, acittatva, asraya-paravritti, nirabhasagocara, animitta, apranihita, sunyata.*

Among our religious words, among them most crucially in the literal sense of the word, are words that have an epistemological reference.

In spite of Good Friday most Christians continue to be epistemologically naive, epistemologically Ptolemaic. We refuse to go with the Copernican revolution in religion. We refuse the exodus from metaphysics to metanoesis.

Golgotha is always the next Galapagos, the next total re-estimation of ourselves and our world.

The crisis of Good Friday on Golgotha is in part an epistemological crisis.

A Mahayana Buddhist might be inclined to think of the Darkness of Good Friday on Golgotha as the most critical, most perilous, hours of an asraya-paravritti.

Outwardly the crux is physical, inwardly it is epistemological. Not that that of course is the whole story.

Coming to us in our Year One Reed, Narada is our Cortez. Epistemologically, he is our Cortez.

It isn't from outside our religion that Narada comes. It is from Golgotha he comes.

Bringing the Tenebrae harrow, he comes.

Bringing our Christian mahavakyas and Upanishads, he comes.

How willing are we to be conquered by a parable?

How willing were the people of Thebes to open a gate of their city to Dionysus?

How willing are we to open a gate of our religion to Narada?

Dionysus standing in a gate of Thebes. Narada standing in a gate of Christendom.

Christians electing Pascal to welcome Narada into Christendom. Electing him because he had this to say:

If we dreamed the same dream every night, it would affect us as much as the objects that we see every day. And if a workman were to be sure of dreaming for twelve hours every night that he was king, I think he would be almost as happy as a king who dreamed for twelve hours every night that he was a workman. If we dreamed every night that we were pursued by enemies and harassed by these fearful phantoms, or that we spent all our days in different occupations, as one does on a journey, we should suffer almost as much as if this were true; and we should be afraid to sleep, as we are afraid of waking when we in fact dread to meet with just these misfortunes. Dream, indeed, would cause more or less the same distress as reality. But because dreams are all different and each one takes diverse forms, what we see in them affects us much less than what we see when awake. For waking is continuous, though it is not so continuous and unvarying as not to change too. But it changes less abruptly, except occasionally when we are travelling; and then we say, 'I seem to be dreaming'. For life, though less changeable, is only a dream.

As the Kalahari Bushman said to Laurens van der Post, there is a dream dreaming us.

The dream of Vishnu Anantasayin, of Vishnu Recumbent on the coils of Ananta in the primordial waters.

The Uitoto are a forest-dwelling people of south-eastern Colombia. Quoted already, their story of origins bears repetition:

Was it an Illusion? The Father touched an illusory image. He touched a mystery. Nothing was there. The Father, Who-Has-An-Illusion, seized it and dreaming, began to think. Had he no staff? Then with a dream-thread he held the illusion. Breathing, he held it, the void, the illusion, and felt for its earth. There was nothing to feel: 'I shall gather the void.' He felt, but there was nothing. Now the Father thought the word 'Earth'. He felt for the void, the illusion, and took it into his hands. The Father then gathered the void with dream-thread and pressed it together with gum. With the dream gum iseike he held it fast. He seized the illusion, the illusory earth, and he trampled and trampled it, seizing it, flattening it. Then as he seized it, held it, he stood on it, on this that he had dreamed, on this that he had flattened. As he held the illusion, he salivated, salivated, and salivated, and the water flowed from his mouth. Upon this, the illusion, this, as he held it, he settled the sky roof. This, the illusion, he seized, entirely, and peeled off the blue sky, the white sky. Now in the underworld, thinking and thinking, the maker of myths permitted this story to come into being. This is the story we brought with us when we emerged.

There are Hindus who, hearing these opening questions, would say to the Uitoto, yes, it was an illusion and it is an illusion and we are junkies to it, seeking incarnation after incarnation after incarnation, seeking fix after fix after fix.

From the East himself, Chuang Tzu might also predispose us to let our cultural immune system go down a little:

Once upon a time, I, Chuang Tzu, dreamt that I was a butterfly, flitting around and enjoying myself. I had no idea I was Chuang Tzu. Then suddenly I woke up and was Chuang Tzu again. But I could not tell, had I been Chuang Tzu dreaming I was a butterfly, or a butterfly dreaming I was now Chuang Tzu?

Even Hindus, however, haven't gone so far as to call the Father and author of all things, Who-Has-An-Illusion. Although, come to think of it, they do sometimes call the author of it all the Great Mayin, the Great Creator, that is, of illusion, the great creator of illusory effects.

Who-Has-An-Illusion in us all.

The Great Mayin in us all.

Let us watch him again. Let us watch Who-Has-An-Illusion at work:

> He touches an illusory image
> He touches a mystery
>
> There is nothing

He holds the illusion with a dream-thread
Breathing, he holds the illusion, he feels for its earth.

Seizing it, he tramples and tramples the illusory earth
He stands on the earth, the illusory earth, he has flattened.

Well indeed might it serve as an introductory masque to a play by Calderon called *La Vida es Sueno*, Life is a Dream. Or serving as a masque within *The Tempest* by Shakespeare, it might conclude with:

> Our revels now are ended. These our actors,
> As I foretold you, were all spirits and
> Are melted into air, into thin air:
> And like the baseless fabric of this vision,
> The cloud-capped towers, the gorgeous palaces,
> The solemn temples, the great globe itself,
> Yea, all which it inherit, shall dissolve,
> And, like this insubstantial pageant faded,
> Leave not a rack behind. We are such stuff
> As dreams are made on; and our little life
> Is rounded with a sleep.

The Good News is: there is a waking up from dreaming, there is a waking up from waking, the dark night of contemplation ensues and singing of this night St John of the Cross exults:

> *O noche amable mas que el alborado.*
> O night more lovely than the dawn.

The story the Uitoto emerged with.

A story Christians might re-emerge with. A simple story, simple in incident, but vast in its spiritual implications. Our Eden was our Wirikuta, the place of our first fix. Dreaming and waking awareness-of is the high this fix gave rise to. Becoming biologically established, this high elaborated senses and a psyche in and through which it would continue, greedily, to maintain and promote itself, intensify itself. Organically, therefore, we are junkies. The high we organically are and are addicted to eclipses the Divine. It exiles us from the Divine. Following Jesus into the Triduum Sacrum, undergoing with him what he underwent, is a Christian way of being at the disposal of the Divine, is a Christian way of being yearningly available to the possibility of gracious re-absorption back into the Divine.

Organically and psychologically, we are an immunity to the Divine. Even when we are praying to the Divine we are, very often, barricaded within our immunity to the Divine. There are few of us who aren't a Krak des Chevaliers built to withstand the Divine. Fiercely sometimes, during our Triduum Sacrum, our immunity to the Divine is broken down. This isn't a pleasant experience. In the case of Jesus, it isn't even pleasant to look at. Our ideas of it should, however, be glorious, the glory of the end shining back on every stage of the process. It is in the highest degree religiously unfortunate that, traditionally, Christians concerned themselves, almost exclusively, with a forensically exact account of what happened physically. Habeas Corpus Christianity is itself a veil and some Good Friday or other it might be rent.

Now in the underworld, thinking and thinking, the maker of myths permitted this story to come into being. It is the story we brought with us when we emerged.

The story that emerged with Jesus, the story that came ashore with him, is the story of what he did and of what happened to him after he had crossed the Kedron:

> Jesus Grand-Canyon-deep in the world's karma
> Jesus on the hill of the Koshaless Skull
> Jesus reabsorbed into the Divine Unity
> Jesus Apsusayin
> Jesus Anadyomene
> Jivanmukhta Messiah preaching his first Evangelanta sermon.

Our transtorrentem destiny we might call it. But, bound up with our very identity and defending that identity, there is in us a psychological immune system that all too successfully resists it. All too successfully across all too many incarnations, it resists it.

As individuals we aren't only a psychological immunity to the Divine. We are a spiritual immunity to it. As often as not, we are in our acts of worship and prayer a religious immunity to it.

Selfhood is as successful at surviving religiously as it is at surviving irreligiously. It survives as successfully on a foundation of theistic belief as it does on a foundation of atheistic belief. Of this William Law is quite sure:

Would you know, Academicus, whence it is that so many false spirits have appeared in the world, who have deceived themselves and others with false fire and false light; laying claim to inspirations, illuminations, and openings of the Divine Life, pretending to do wonders under extraordinary calls from God? It is this: they have turned to God without turning from themselves; would be alive in God before they were dead to their own nature; a thing as impossible in itself as for a grain of wheat to be alive before it dies. Now religion in the hands of self, or corrupt nature, serves only to discover vices of a worse kind than in nature left to itself. Hence, are all the disorderly passions of religious men, which burn in a worse flame than passions only employed about worldly matters: pride, self-exaltation, hatred and persecution, under a cloak of religious zeal, will sanctify actions which nature left to itself would be ashamed to own.

Elsewhere he says: We are without God, because we are in the life of self.

And Jacob Boehme has said that selfhood is the only thing that burns in hell.

Little wonder that so many mystics talk not only about self-denial but about self-loss.

Madame Guyon was not afraid to overpass the limits laid down by dogma: the soul which is reduced to the nothing, ought to dwell therein, without wishing, since she is now but dust, to issue from this state, nor, as before, desiring to live again. She must remain as something which no longer exists and this, in order that the Torrent may drown itself and lose itself in the sea, never to find itself in its selfhood again: that it may become one and the same thing with the Sea.

This is how Eckhart describes our crossing into the Divine:

Comes then the soul into the unclouded light of God. It is transported so far from creaturehood into the nothingness that, of its own powers, it can never return to its agents or its former creaturehood. Once there, God shelters the soul's nothingness with his uncreated essence, safeguarding its creaturely existence. The soul has dared to become nothing, and cannot pass from its own being into nothingness and then back again, losing its own identity in the process, except God safeguarded it. This must needs be so.

Christianity isn't founded on a myth. It doesn't emerge from a myth. Emerging from the Triduum Sacrum means that it emerges from a process as inevitably natural as puberty in humans, as metamorphosis in insects. The Triduum Sacrum is, however, wholly incommensurate with either puberty or metamorphosis. And it isn't, of course, inevitable in any one incarnation.

Metamorphosis in insects is a crossing over from one to another morphic condition, from a morphic condition that is larval to a morphic condition that is imaginal. There are mystics who talk rather about going beyond any and every morphic condition. Some there are who openly talk about being unformed:

> My spirit has grown out of all separateness
> So I stand unformed in my own being.

Of not altogether dissimilar import are the following:

119

Form is a veil to you, and your heart is a veil.
When the veil vanishes you will become all light.

Between me and thee there is an 'I am' that
torments me. Ah! Through thy 'I am' take away my
'I am' from between us both.

Between me and thee is thy self-experience:
cast it away and I will veil thee from thyself.

I have passed away, 'I' and 'Thou' no more
exist. We have become one and I have become
altogether Thou.

It is like being in God without being oneself.

Jesus Transtorrentem.

Our transtorrentem destiny.

So concerned is each of us, nowadays, for our individual uniqueness,
that all thought of baptismal incorporation into a trans-individual destiny
has become wholly repugnant to us. Even when we are assured that our
individual uniqueness will be gloriously restored to us, we still recoil from
it:

Know ye not, that so many of us as were baptized into Jesus Christ were baptized into his death? Therefore, we are buried with him by baptism into death:
that like as Christ was raised up from the dead by the glory of the Father, even
so we also should walk in newness of life.

Seventeen hundred years later, William Law is still thinking along similar lines:

Now, here is opened to us the true reason of the whole process of the Saviour's
incarnation, passion, death, resurrection and ascension into heaven: it was
because fallen man was to go through all these stages as necessary parts of his
return to God; and therefore if man was to go out of his fallen state, there must
be a son of this fallen man, who as the head and fountain of the whole race, could
do all this, could go back through all these gates, and so make it possible for all
the individuals of human nature, as being born of him, to inherit his conquering
nature, and follow him through all these passages to Eternal Life.

A temple which, being a sacrament in architectural form, would good-
shepherd us through these passages and gates.

The passages and gates of a Tenebrae Temple.

Passages and gates in the gate of Paradise.

There are Buddhists who say it is a gateless gate.

On the way out, it might indeed be a gateless gate. On our way back in, it might, however, not always be so. Not so even if the passages and gates are but the creation of our own terror.

The passages are of course rites of passage, inevitable as puberty. And the gates we can think of as initiations. Initiations not unlike those Job, Jonah and Narada walked into. Easier it altogether is to walk into them then to walk through them, or to walk out of them.

We only need to look at Jesus in Gethsemane and we know that in him our inner, collective hell is being harrowed.

The only good way to harrow is to consent to be harrowed. And this is why Jesus is so different from Marduk, so different from Herakles, so different even from Orpheus. This is why the redemption that occurred in Agnus Dei is so different from the redemption achieved by Adi Varaha. In the first, in Bacon's terms, we have advancement essential, in the second advancement local.

Passages and gates in the Gateless Gate.

Good it is that there are passages and gates in the Gateless Gate. Else might our fate be like that of Actaeon.

Terrible it is to prematurely open a protecting gate, to prematurely open a protecting veil.

There are Hindus who talk about the lie of otherness. And while he doesn't go so far, it is obvious that for Niffari, the great Muslim mystic, awareness of otherness is a veil:

> The cleansing of the body is water, and the cleansing
> of the heart is the closing of the eye to otherness.

Can we therefore think of the Fall as a declension into awareness of self and other-than-self?

Should we talk at all about the world as though it had an independent, objective existence? Should we talk rather about awareness of self and other-than-self in its dreaming and waking modes? If so, then surely we are on the threshold of singing the Mandukya Om.

Jneyavarana is yet another astonishing word that will come with Narada into our culture.

It was with soldiers, some of them mounted, that Cortez came into Mexico. It is with words that are carriers not just of a new kind of gnosis but of a new kind of diagnosis that Narada will come into Christendom.

Mexico's Year One Reed.

Europe's Year One Reed.

Christendom's Year One Reed. Year of Jesus anadyomene. Year of Jivanmukta Messiah preaching his first Evangelanta sermon.

Who knows what form or forms the Paraclete might yet take? Might he not take the form of Narada walking towards us?

One thing is sure: Christianity has a long, long way to go before it can say of itself that it has caught up with the Triduum Sacrum.

Could it be that Hinduism has engaged altogether more nearly with the philosophical consequences of the Golgotha phase of the Triduum Sacrum than has Christianity?

Could it be that, long before the advent of Christianity, Hinduism had already domesticated the philosophical consequences of the Triduum Sacrum?

A Christianity, indeed any religion, that is beginning to catch up with the Triduum Sacrum is most gloriously to be desired.

Ritually we catch up with it when we light and one by one extinguish the candles of the Tenebrae harrow.

A temple that, being a sacrament in architectural form, would good-shepherd us through the Triduum Sacrum.

'A serious house on serious earth' we always need. And who knows! What has been might be again. Again maybe, grace abounding, we will harness ourselves to the wagons.

Having its source in the Triduum Sacrum, Christianity cannot but have newness of life in it. Newness of architectural life. Newness of ritual life. Newness of religious life. Newness of ordinary life. Newness of life lived in a world that is never an everyday world.

Seen through those pure and virgin apprehensions that Traherne talks about, the corn is Orient and immortal wheat.

A Christianity that focuses not on who Jesus was but on what he did and underwent after he had crossed the Kedron.

The glory of Christianity is this: the Triduum Sacrum lived itself out completely in its founder.

Before Jesus was the Triduum Sacrum is.

We have a story to emerge with.

We have a story that will house us in the splendours of its truth.

A story that tells itself ritually, that tells itself architecturally. That needs to tell itself and ground itself ritually and architecturally. We don't need, like Poor Tom on the heath, to be acold. We don't have to be unaccommodated. There is a story that begins: 'Then cometh Jesus with them unto a place called Gethsemane and saith unto the disciples, sit ye here while I go and pray yonder.'

The 'yonder' he went to pray in was as far away as the Palaeozoic at the end below of Bright Angel Trail.

Angel of the Jabbok. Angel of the Colorado. Rilke has begun to assess the significance of an encounter with the Angel of the Jabbok:

I can tell by the way the trees are bent, after
so many dull days, on my worried windowpanes,
that a storm is coming,
and I hear the far-off fields say things
I can't bear without a friend,
I can't love without a sister.

The storm, the shifter of shapes, drives on
across the woods and across time,
and the world looks as if it had no age:
the landscape, like a line in a psalm book,
is seriousness and weight and eternity.

What we choose to fight is so tiny!
What fights with us is so great!
If only we would let ourselves be dominated
As things do by some immense storm,
We would become strong too, and not need names.

When we win it's with small things,
And the triumph itself makes us small.
What is extraordinary and eternal
Does not want to be bent by us.
I mean the Angel who appeared
To the wrestlers' of the Old Testament:
When the wrestlers' sinews grew long like metal strings
He felt them under his fingers
Like chords of deep music.

Whoever was beaten by this Angel
(who often simply declined the fight)
Went away proud and strengthened
and great from the harsh hand,
That kneaded him as if to change his shape.
Winning does not tempt that man.
This is how he grows: by being defeated decisively
By constantly greater beings.

Angel of the Colorado. What does he look like? Like Coatlicue? Like the wizard of Les Trois Frères? Like Vishvarupa? Like Vishvayuga? Is it in defeat at his hands that the new great age will be born? Is in defeat at his hands that Bright Angel Trail will become aisle?

Extant or eroded, every stratum of the Grand Canyon is housed in the Christian story. Correlatively, every stratum of the psyche is housed in it.

Pascal distinguished between 'a book accepted by a people, and a book that creates a people'.

Having the story of the Triduum Sacrum as it lived itself in Jesus, we have a story that can create us, individually and as a people.

A story whose images and metaphors are the rods and cones of our retinas.

A story whose images and metaphors are the forms of our sensibility and the categories of our understanding.

A story whose seeing subsumes biological sight.

A story that is our third eye.

Our third eye isn't a separate eye. It is a way of seeing things that informs the eyes we already have.

Eyes informed by great myths. Eyes informed by great metaphors. Eyes informed by Upanishads, Gitas and mahavakyas. Eyes informed by morals informed by the truth, by lives informed by the truth.

'Our whole age', Mallarmé has said, 'is seeking to bring forth a holy book.'

A Risen Bible. A Bible that guides us through, that speaks comfortably to us as we go through, the Triduum Sacrum.

We've already heard Heidegger say that 'the era is defined by the god's failure to arrive, by the 'default of God'. But is it? Is the default God's or is it ours? Any God who invites us to walk with him into and through the Triduum Sacrum is unlikely to be given a serious hearing. Unlikely because, just as there is in us an immune system that fights sickness so also is there in us an immune system that fights final health, the health of being reabsorbed into the Divine.

Listening again to Hölderlin:

> ... the heavenly powers
> Cannot do all things. It is mortals
> Who reach sooner into the abyss. So the true is
> With these. Long is
> The time, but the true comes into
> Its own.

Listening again to Heidegger:

The age for which the ground fails to come hangs in the abyss. In the age of the world's night, the abyss of the world must be experienced and endured. But for this it is necessary that there be those who reach into the abyss.

It is time perhaps to invite Hölderlin and Heidegger to listen to the creation story of the Maidu:

In the beginning there was no sun, no moon, no stars. All was dark and everywhere there was only water. A raft came floating on the water. It came from the
north and in it were two persons – Turtle (A'noshma) and Father-of-the-Secret-
Society (Pehe'ipe). The stream flowed very rapidly. Then from the sky a rope of
feathers, called Po'kelma, was let down, and down it came Earth-Initiate. When
he reached the end of the rope, he tied it to the bow of the raft and stepped in.
His face was covered and was never seen, but his body shone like the sun. He sat
down, and for a long time said nothing. At last A'noshma said, 'where do you
come from?' and Earth-Initiate answered, 'I come from above'. Then Turtle
(A'noshma) said, 'Brother, can you not make for me some good dry land, so that
I may sometimes come up out of the water?' Then he asked another time, 'Are
there going to be any people in the world?' Earth-Initiate thought a while, then
said 'yes'. Turtle asked, 'How long before you are going to make people?' Earth-
Initiate said, 'I don't know. You want to have some dry land; well how am I
going to get any earth to make it of?' Turtle answered, 'If you will tie a rock
around my left arm, I'll dive for some.' Earth-Initiate did as Turtle asked, and
then reaching round, took the end of a rope from somewhere and tied it to
Turtle. When Earth-Initiate came to the raft, there was no rope there; he just
reached out and found one. Turtle said, 'If the rope is not long enough, I'll jerk
it once, and you must haul me up; if it is long enough, I'll give two jerks, and
then you must pull me up quickly, as I shall have all the earth that I can carry.'
Just as Turtle went over the side of the raft, Father-of-the-Secret-Society began
to shout loudly.

Turtle was gone a long time. He was gone six years; and when he came up
he was covered with green slime, he had been down so long. When he reached
the top of the water, the only earth he had was a very little under his nails; the
rest had all washed away. Earth-Initiate took with his right hand a stone knife
from under his left armpit and carefully scraped the earth out from under his
nails. He put the earth in the palm of his hand, and rolled it about till it was
round; it was as large as a small pebble. He laid it on the stern of the raft. By and
by he went to look at it; it had not grown at all. The third time he went to look
at it, it had grown so that it could be spanned by the arms. The fourth time he
looked, it was as big as the world, the raft was aground, and all around were
mountains as far as he could see.

When the raft had come to land, Turtle said, 'I can't stay in the dark all the
time. Can't you make a light so that I can see?' Earth-Initiate replied, 'Let us get
out of the raft, and then we will see what we can do.' So all three got out. Then
Earth-Initiate said, 'Look that way, to the east; I am going to tell my sister to
come up.' Then it began to grow light and day began to break; then Father-of-
the-Secret-Society began to shout loudly and the sun came up. Turtle said,
'Which way is the sun going to travel?' Earth-Initiate answered, 'I'll tell her to
go this way and go down there.' After the sun went down, Father-of-the-Secret-
Society began to cry and shout again and it grew very dark. Earth-Initiate asked

Turtle and Father-of-the-Secret-Society, 'How do you like it?' And they both answered, 'It is very good.' Then Earth-Initiate answered, 'No, I am going to do more yet.' Then he called the stars each by its name, and they came out. When this was done, Turtle asked, 'Now what shall we do?' Earth-Initiate replied, 'Wait, and I'll show you!' Then he made a tree grow at Ta'doiko, the tree called Hu'kimtsa, and Earth-Initiate and Turtle and Father-of-the-Secret-Society sat in its shade for two days. The tree was very large and it had twelve different kinds of acorns growing on it ...

'The age for which the ground fails to come hangs in the Abyss.' But this isn't something Eckhart would be frightened of. Being a mystic he knows that 'Everything which has being hangs (is suspended) in the Naught and that same Naught is such an incomprehensible Aught that all the spirits in heaven and upon earth cannot comprehend it or sound it.'

Hanging in the Naught, having only the Divine Ungrund for ground wasn't a state of affairs A'noshma was happy with. He needed solid ground. Ground he could come ashore on. Long primordial beaches he could leave his tracks on. He needed to experience himself as a real being in a real world and if this meant forsaking the Divine Ungrund as ground so be it. Weighted with a rock, he slipped over the side of his only support and he sank down, down, down. He was gone a long time, so long the green slimes of the Abyss had time to colonize him. But A'noshma came back and with him came experience of empirical ground, with him came experience of real life in a real world.

A'noshma and a long time later Narada undergoing his awful initiation.

A'noshma and a long time later Chuang Tzu having questions about his empirical identity.

In A'noshma we emerge from Divine Ungrund to empirical ground. In Narada we return from empirical ground to Divine Ungrund. A day comes when for both A'noshma and Narada empirical ground and the Divine Ungrund are one and the same sustaining blessedness.

A'noshma and Narada. Narada and A'noshma. In them we can discover a just estimation of who and what we are?

A'noshma, in Heidegger's understanding of these things, had endured the Abyss and through him ground that would ground a good age came up from below.

Jesus is our A'noshma. He went down into those depths that Jonah went down into but didn't endure. Jesus endured. And as with A'noshma, a new experience of the world came ashore with him.

Jesus isn't only Agnus Dei, he is A'noshma Dei, and this has consequences we haven't even begun to imagine, let alone realize, architecturally and ritually.

A'noshma anadyomene. Drying out, the green slime becomes Good News:

Abyssal or solid, Divine Ungrund is ground.
A'noshma anadyomene. Narada anadyomene.
Opening our Christian gates to Narada.
Opening our Christian gates to A'noshma.
Opening our Christian gates to the Diver myth.

We have a new myth by which to understand you, Jesus. We have a new name by which to call you, the name by which the Maidu might call you, A'noshma Jesu.

Its the great biography, isn't it? The Evangelanta biography of Jesus:

> Jesus Grand-Canyon-deep in the world's karma
> Jesus on the hill of the Koshaless skull
> A'noshma Jesu
> Jesu Apsusayin
> Jesu Anadyomene

The Triduum Sacrum has become a Quinduum Sacrum.

'Every man', Sir Thomas Browne says, 'hath a double horoscope, one of his humanity, his birth, another of his Christianity, his baptism ... '

Great life. Wasteland life.

In his vision of Waste Land life, Eliot could only see birth, copulation and death.

> Unreal city,
> Under the brown fog of a winter dawn,
> A crowd flowed over London Bridge, so many,
> I had not thought death had undone so many.
> Sighs, short and infrequent, were exhaled,
> And each man fixed his eyes before his feet,
> Flowed up the hill and down King William Street,
> To where St Mary Woolnot kept the hours
> With a dead sound on the final stroke of nine.
> There I saw one I knew, and stopped him, crying, Stetson!
> You who were with me in the ships of Mylae!
> That corpse you planted last year in your garden,
> Has it begun to sprout? Will it bloom this year?
> Or has the sudden frost disturbed its bed?

Oh keep the dog far hence that's friend to men,
Or with his nails he'll dig it up again!
You, hypocrite lecteur, man symblable, mon frère!

Does our culture nourish us or does it vampire us? A womb that vampires us instead of nourishing us wouldn't be good for us. How good for us is our built world? Our chartered world? World of the tabloid horoscope?

Standing in Ta'doiko, calling each of them by its name, Earth-Initiate called the stars into existence. And now again, calling them by their names, he calls five new constellations into our night sky. As he calls them they come:

A constellation called
Christ Grand-Canyon-deep in the world's karma

A constellation called
Christ on the hill of the koshaless skull

A constellation called
A'noshma Jesu

A constellation called
Jesu Apsusayin

A Constellation called
Jesu Anadyomene.

The age of the world's night is coming to an end.

The world's great age begins anew,
The Golden years return,
The earth doth like a snake renew
Her winter weeds outworn:
Heaven smiles, and faiths and empires gleam,
Like wrecks of a dissolving dream.

A brighter Hellas rears its mountains
From waves serener far;
A new Peneus rolls his fountains
Against the morning star.
Where fairer Temples bloom, there sleep
Young Cyclads on a sunnier deep.

A loftier Argo cleaves the main,
Fraught with a later prize;
Another Orpheus sings again,
And loves and weeps and dies;

A new Ulysses leaves once more
Calypso for his native shore.

O, write no more the tale of Troy,
If earth deaths scroll must be!
Nor mix with Laian rage the joy
Which dawns upon the free;
Although a subtler Sphinx renew
Riddles of death Thebes never knew.

Another Athens shall arise,
And to remoter time
Bequeath, like sunset to the skies,
The splendour of its prime;
And leave, if nought so bright may live,
All earth can take or Heaven can give.

Saturn and Love their long repose
Shall burst, more bright and good
Than all who fell, than one who rose,
Than many unsubdued;
Not gold, not blood, their after dowers,
But votive tears and symbol flowers.

O cease! Must hate and death return?
Cease! Must men kill and die?
Cease! Drain not to its dregs the urn
Of bitter prophecy.
The world is weary of the past,
O might it die or rest at last!

God bless Percy Bysshe. Believing that Greek experience, archaic and classical, is paradigm, the best he could imagine for humanity is a repetition, revival or renaissance of it. Not for him an *Argo* coming home with a golden fleece of Upanishads and Sutras. Not for him the Celtic Dreamtime. Not for him the marvellous, dangerous depths of earth and psyche from which Merlin and Morgan Le Fay lives. Not for him to say, I am of the realme of Logrys. For him the Athenian Acropolis not Gorsedd Arberth. For him the Ilissus not the ryver at Camelot.

At Camelot, it was a custom that on Whit Sunday, King Arthur and his knights would not sit down to supper at the round table until a great adventure had been achieved. These being the marvellous times they were, an adventure did always present itself. One Whit Sunday a squire announced that below in the river there was a stone with a sword stuck to its hilt in it. The king and his knights proceeded to the river. Many famous knights attempted to draw out the sword but it was a knight newly dubbed called Sir Galahad who at last succeeded. And now, the adventure that presented itself having been achieved, the king and his knights returned and sat down to supper at the round table. Then a great thing happened, happens now to everyone who reads it in Sir Thomas Malory's words:

Than anone they harde crakynge and cryynge of thundir, that hem thought the palyse sholde all to-dryve. So in the myddys of the blast entyrde a sonnebeame, more clerer by seven tymys than ever they saw day, and all they were alyghted of the grace of the Holy Goste. Than began every knyght to beholde other, and eyther saw other, by their semynge, fayrer than ever they were before. Nat-forthan there was no knyght that myght speke one worde a grete whyle, and so they loked every man on other as they had bene doome.

Than entird into the halle the Holy Grayle coverde with whyght samyte, but there was none that myght se hit nother whom that bare hit. And there was all the halle fulfylled with good odoures, and every knyght had such metis and drynkes as he beste loved in thys worlde. And whan the Holy Grayle had bene borne thorow the hall, than the holy vessell departed suddeynly, that they wyst nat where hit becam. Than had they all breth to speke, and than the kyng yelded thankynges to God of Hys good grace that He had sente them.

'Sertes,' seyde the kynge, 'we ought to thanke oure Lorde Jesu Cryste gretly that he hath shewed us thys day at the reverence of thys hyghe feste of Pente-cost.'

'Now', seyde Sir Gawayne, 'we have bene servyd thys day of what metys and drynkes we thought on. But one thyng begyled us, that we myght nat se the Holy Grayle: hit was so preciously coverde. Wherefore I woll make here a vow that to-morne, withoute longer abydynge, I shall laboure in the queste of the Sankgreall, and that I shall holde me oute a twelve-month and a day or more if nede be, and never shall I returne unto the courte agayne tylle I have sene hit more opynly than hit hath bene shewed here. And iff I may nat spede I shall returne agayne as he that may nat be ayenst the wylle of God.'

Other knights vowed the same vow that Sir Gawain had vowed and on the morrow they were ready to depart, and reading Malory's account of their departure we do in a sense depart with them:

Ryght so departed Sir Launcelot and founde hys felyship that abode hys com-mynge, and than they toke their horsys and rode thorow the strete of Camelot. And there was wepyng of ryche and poore, and the kynge turned away and mygth not speke for wepyng.

Although it occurs in a fiction, surely this moment when Sir Gawain comes to his feet, stands humbly and courteously at his full height and vows to ride out for a year and a day or more if need be in quest of the vision, surely this is one of the great moments in the European soul.

Wherefore I woll make here a vow that to-morne, withoute longer abydynge, I shall laboure in the queste of the Sankgreall ...

The whyght samyte that covers the grail is our European consensus about reality which, like a scum, covers our retinas.

One night, however, towards the end of our European voyage in five tall ships, this veil of whyght samyte opened and we saw:

Days, weeks passed, and under easy sail, the ivory *Pequod* had slowly swept across four several cruising-grounds: that off the Azores; off the Cape de Verdes; on the Plate (so called), being off the mouth of the Rio de la Plata; and the Carrol Ground, an unstaked, watery locality, southerly from St Helena.

It was while gliding through these latter waters that one serene and moon-light night, when all the waves rolled by like scrolls of silver; and by their soft, suffusing seethings, made what seemed a silvery silence, not a solitude: on such a silent night a silvery jet was seen far in advance of the white bubbles at the bow. Lit up by the moon, it looked celestial; seemed some plumed and glittering god uprising from the sea.

I think of Moby-Dick as a later incarnation of Tiamat. And I think of Ishmael as a later incarnation of Sir Gawain. This of course means that his vision-quest didn't come to an end at the end of a twelve-month and a day. But now at last, on board the *Pequod*, the veil of whyght samyte opens and he sees him, Cetus Psychopompos, plumed and glittering, uprising as Tiamat originally uprose from the sea. Could he but come closer, he would see how deeply embedded in his side is Marduk's harpoon. It was indeed a dolorous stroke. And it isn't only the Maymed Kynge who is an afflicted heir to it. All who are heirs to Mesopotamian, Hebrew and Greek beginnings are heirs to it. All who belong in a civilization to which Lascaux is Labyrinth are heirs to it.

Cetus Dei
Taurus Dei
Agnus Dei
Albatross Dei

Little wonder that, taking the form of sea-ravens, Erinyes have so imperturbably settled on our rigging. But, Christianity having shrivelled to a Whaleman's Chapel in New Bedford, we with its blessings sail on into a last re-enactment of the calamities of our Mesopotamian beginnings.

Other beginnings or healed beginnings we most desperately need.

Having examined the varieties of religious experience, William James concluded that 'there should be no premature closing of our account with reality'.

It isn't only organisms that have immune systems. Cultures have them also. Religions have them and sometimes they work so well that all foreign estimations of ourselves and our world are kept at bay.

Christianity keeping the ropesnake parable at bay.

Christianity keeping the Narada parable at bay.

Once upon a time there was a community of mice. They had closed their account with reality. In one of them one day a strange thing happened. In him, their cultural immune system, long ago interiorized, wasn't working so well. He could hear a roaring. In the days and weeks that followed he wouldn't only hear it, he would break off work in order to listen to it. One day, wanting to be near it, he left home. It turned out to be the roaring of Medicine River.

The Horsehead Nebula neighing.

The roaring of Medicine River.

And at Pentecost in Camelot, a crakynge and a cryynge of thundir.

Here am I, Lord. Is it I, Lord? I have heard you calling in the night. I will go, Lord, if you lead me. I will hold your people in my heart.

Standing Mouse left home.

Gautama left home.

Jesus left home.

Galahad left home.

As Indo-European mythology imagines it, there are in the world restrainers and releasers, Danavas and Adityas. Coming up out of nature itself, coming up out of its woods and lakes, Galahad is a releaser. He releases the stone. The stone blossoms into a shrine in which there is a linga and a yoni, and within a few centuries, Europeans, themselves released, will be building gothically.

Unless and until Sir Galahad had drawn the sword out of the stone, neither Chartres nor Rheims nor York nor Cologne cathedrals could have been built.

Galahad drew the sword from the stone and there they are: Chartres, Rheims, York and Cologne.

Releasing the Gothic transcendence that is in stone. Releasing the mystical, architectural geometry that is in stone. Releasing the rose window wonder that is in stone.

Sir Galahad releasing the Celtic-Christian linga in the inhibited stone.

Now we can build one in Christendom. In Christendom now we can build a Lingaraja Temple.

Sir Galahad, Sir Gawain, Sir Launcelot, Sir Bors, and other great and famous knights setting out in quest of the Grail. Setting out to release the Rich Fisher King, its keeper, from his sexual wound. Setting out to release the Waste Land from its barrenness.

The night before he rode out, Sir Galahad dreamed: he was lying, shackled to its floor and sides, in the oubliette of the Grail Castle. A bleeding lance passed before him. He knew he must ask: Why is it bleeding? But instead, by a slip of the tongue, he asked: Why is it menstruating? He blushed. And the sexually wounded king who had been waiting for so long for that question to be asked, he also blushed. What connection could there be, he wondered awake, between the bleeding lance and sexuality?

After years riding sixteen hands high in the world, Galahad hadn't found his way. He dismounted one evening at a hermitage. In complete steel, shining coldly, he walked down to a big-bouldered, clear stream. Laying his sword on a rock, he bent, like a spear breaking, and drank from a pool too disturbed to mirror him. Rising, he saw a great marvel. His sword was sinking into the rock point downwards. Taking hold of it, he sought with all his strength to retrieve it. He couldn't, and had he not let go, he too would have been pulled without trace into sure obliteration. He stood there dumbfounded and bereft.

It is ore now, the hermit said.

Galahad raised his visor.

Like my anvils and hammers, the hermit said.

Courteously, not enquiring, Galahad waited for further disclosures.

I was a swordsmith, the hermit said. The swords I made had yearnings in them for a hero's hand. For the hand of Michael the Archangel they yearned. They yearned for the last battle. There are those who say, and they say sooth, that the sounds of me making swords were like church bells summoning them to matins and lauds. My swords thirsted for dragon blood.

And now? enquired Galahad.

As you see, the hermit said, pointing to a blackbird digging woodlice out of his thatched roof.

Galahad waited.

On Good Friday night, nineteen years ago, I saw – or a seeing that opened in me saw – that all the world's weapons were in the lance of Longinus, every spear and sword and dagger and scimitar that was ever forged was in that lance and in it went, in, in, in, like breath going in, and in it could go, because Christ at that moment was as deep as a mountain, in a way that I can't explain he was a mountain, and within it all the world's weapons returned to their seams, they reverted to ore.

I didn't go back to my forge, he said, looking hard at Galahad. I didn't even go back to open its door for my apprentices. You can only use a weapon well, as well as you do, when you've turned your mind into a weapon, or worse, you use a weapon as well as you do only when you've become a weapon. But someone who has become a weapon, who is weapon-hard, weapon-bright, he won't find the Grail, because for all its brightness when it first appears to you, the Grail is a stone, a humble stone, Lapis Exillis it is called. As stone, the Grail is a way of being in the world, it is a way of life. We will go indoors. I have stories to tell you.

Inside, the house was simple. Like the shoes he was wearing, it looked as though over the years it had taken on the shape of his living.

It's about a man from the land of Uz that I would talk to you. His name was Job. He feared God and he did no evil. His wife was a good woman. Whenever the occasion demanded it, she stood her ground, graciously. They had seven sons and seven daughters. Job's grazing grounds reached as far as the mountains, a whole day's walk away. He had herds of asses and camels, flocks of goats, flocks of sheep, each flock and herd having keepers who kept with them day and night. Inwardly and outwardly, Job was a man of substance. He would sit in the city gates in the evenings and there even men who were older than him deferred to him.

One evening, coming it would seem from afar, a stranger came towards them. Like a man he was who had taken risks with a summit, and suffered. He hadn't come back from where the avalanche had left him.

Even before they had time to greet him, he cried out: I am sore broken in the place of dragons! I am sore broken in the place of dragons! I am sore broken in the place of dragons! Something snapped in Job, the man of substance. Startling the elders he was sitting with, he rose to his feet and raged:

> There are no dragons!
> There are no dragons!
> There are no dragons!

Troubled by the outburst he had provoked, the stranger went his ways and in a while Job was again an elder in the city gate, giving good counsel.

It chanced that, going his ways, the stranger called at Job's house hoping for food.

Thanking Job's wife for her great generosity, he took to the road again, not looking back.

Little more than an hour had elapsed and Job's wife was herself on that road, walking after him. It wasn't to catch up with him that she was walking after him. It was something in herself, something that hadn't awakened in her, that she was seeking. She was seeking the precipice her religion had protected her from.

Closing his door behind him that night, Job called out a greeting to his wife.

Getting no answer, he went from room to room calling her. Only his eldest son was at home.

Where is everyone, where is your mother? Job asked.

Gone after the stranger, his son said.

Gone what?

Gone after the stranger. Your wife and your seven daughters and six of your sons, all of them gone, gone after the stranger. Only I stayed behind. I stayed to tell you: your perfection, your kind of perfection, has blighted us, it has been a blight in this house, withering us. Deep inside us, it has denied us. Deep inside us, it has slain us.

Like the others, Job's oldest son, taking nothing, took to the road. In his house alone that night, in the empty, echoing rooms of it, Job, roaring it now, denied the dragon:

> There is no dragon!
> There is no dragon!
> There is no dragon!

Every room in his house echoed, and re-echoed it:

> There is no dragon!
> There is no dragon!
> There is no dragon!

All night long, in every room of it, his house echoed and re-echoed it:

> There is no dragon!
> There is no dragon!
> There is no dragon!

By daybreak, Job was in the wilds.

By nightfall, sitting on the ashes of his finery, he was challenging the stars and the God who created them to answer him. In the night a chalice came to him. He prayed that it might pass and yet, as if spellbound, even while he was still praying, he reached for it; it was from somewhere deeper within himself than conscious intention and purpose that he reached for it.

He drank the wine of astonishment.

And the cup of trembling came. And he prayed that it might pass and again, from an inner depth he had no conscious access to, he reached for it.

The very dregs of it he drank.

Ostrich came. He threatened to claw him. He clawed him and yet in some strange way he didn't.

Behemoth came. He threatened to trample him. He trampled him and yet, like waking from a dream, he had no broken bones, no bruises.

Unicorn came. He threatened to run him through. He did run him through. And yet he didn't.

Leviathan surfaced. She swallowed him. Waking, he walked ashore.

At the edge of the world, among mountains there, Job sat down.

Lifting his head, he saw them coming. The elders who used to sit with him in the city gates were coming and while they were still afar off, frightened for them, frightened for what they would see in him, Job cried out:

I'm a brother to dragons and a companion to owls!

And the rock walls echoed it. Three times they echoed it:

I'm a brother to dragons and a companion to owls!
I'm a brother to dragons and a companion to owls!
I'm a brother to dragons and a companion to owls!

Involuntarily, at a depth within himself altogether deeper and older than his sense of civic dignity and gravity, Job had acknowledged the dragon.

And out of the mountains behind him, big as the morning, the green dragon came and with a tongue as vast as the starry night she licked his civically compromised head, she linked his civically complacent heart. She licked his groin. She licked his hands. She licked his feet.

And Job was well.

And Job walked home.

And within a year his wife came home.

And his daughters and his sons came home.

And at matins every morning, and every evening at compline, they thanked the Lord their God that they were brothers and sisters to dragons and companions to owls.

From then on, during all the days of his life, Job was a shaman in the city. Job was in league with the stones of the field and the beasts of the field were at peace with him.

There is another story I would like to tell you, the hermit said. I'll tell you why. You have ambitions to be a hero, a great European hero, the hero of the Grail Quest. In telling you this last and this next story, I'm trying to prepare you, trying to re-educate you. Old heroics are not sufficient for the times we live in.

The story I will tell you now, I've told so often to so many seekers of the Grail that the blackbirds who dig for grubs in my thatch must know it.

It is the story of Theseus and the Minotaur.

A dreadful story. It might perhaps be better if I didn't tell it at all. But sooner or later in our lives, either inside ourselves or outside ourselves, the dreadful will confront us. So maybe we should anticipate that moment now. Maybe we should rehearse it. With God's help maybe we can, without harm, rehearse it.

It is dangerous, even in a story about them, to summon the Bull, to invite the Beast, to call the Dragon. They might indeed come when we call them but they might not go when we wish to send them away.

With God's help, asking God for his protection, I will tell you the story, keeping it short.

In far-off times when dreaming not waking was the norm, early one morning in those far-off times, a white bull came up out of the sea and walked inland
into Crete, ruled at that time by King Minos. Watching the bull as he walked,
or stood, Poseidon-potent among his cows, King Minos was happy. And
Pasiphae, who was queen, she was happy. Not only happy. She was enchanted.
Her enchantment deepened, it darkened. An unassuageable desire to mate with
the bull took possession of her and one day, contriving to look like a cow, she
felt the surge, at the bewildered roots of her bewildered life she felt it, and nine
months later a child was born. He was bull from the heart up, human from the
heart down. Like a mind attempting to suppress an unacceptable impulse, civilization suppressed the unacceptable child. He was deposited against the back
wall of a very deep labyrinth of caverns and caves under the island. That didn't
solve the problem, however. Not completely. Like the human mind itself, civilizations pay the price for their suppressions.

The monster turned carnivorous, turned cannibal, hungering for humans. He
had to be fed. Else, in his rage, he would shake foundations.

And so it was, year after year, in ships they came coming to Crete, boys and
girls coming to destruction in the labyrinth. One day, on one of the ships, Theseus came. Theseus was a hero. He had a hero's sword. Hearing of his arrival at
port, Ariadne, the daughter of Pasiphae, was at the mouth of the labyrinth, waiting for him. She had come to help him. Holding the loose end of it, she gave
him a ball of thread and as he journeyed through the maze of caverns and caves
he unwound it. Reaching the final cave, he slew the Minotaur and then, rewind-
ing the thread, he retraced his steps, emerging at last into the light of day.

That is the story. It's an old story. The final scene is always the same. The hero
triumphant, the monster slain. But a slain monster isn't a totally dead monster. A
seed of him, a root of him, a hallucination of him, will always survive, a memory
of him will survive, a memory of him, if only in a lost legend, is enough. Out of
that memory of him he will come to life, to a purer intensity of violent life.

I therefore imagine a twist in the story. I will tell it as a dream might tell it,
as a dream dreamed by Theseus long after the event might tell it:

Unwinding the ball of thread, Theseus journeys, sword in hand, through the
labyrinth. Approaching the final cave he hears the hungry, carnivorous roaring.
Or is it the hollow cave echoings of his own terror that he hears? He cannot say.
Against the back wall he sees it, the bull shape, waiting. For a while he cannot
comprehend what has happened. But then, his terror subsiding, he sees: it was
his own bull-shaped shadow he had lunged at.

Can you imagine it? the hermit asked. Can you imagine that final scene? The
hero's heroic sense of himself lying shattered at his own hoofed feet?

There is another way, though, the hermit said. There is another way of
approaching the Minotaur.

Embarking on a voyage as marvellous and terrible as the voyage of Odysseus,
Theseus sails west to Mount Etna. Standing on the rim of the crater, he prayed

to the Gods, prayed in particular to Hephaistus, their smith, asking them and him to think benevolently of what he was doing. His prayers ended, he did what he long ago imagined he would one day do, he heaved his sword into the smoking maw of the mountain asking it to swallow it down into its liquefying intensities. Not swallowed himself, as he expected he might be, not struck by lightning, he returned to his ship and sailed for home.

Heeding the promptings of a dream at sea, he changed course and made landfall in Crete.

A great day it was, a day of great rejoicing, the day he and Ariadne were married.

As the end of his dream at sea, dreamed again, demanded, it was in the outermost cave of the labyrinth that Theseus and Ariadne set up house. A daughter and a son were born to them there. For all four of them, from wool shorn from their own sheep, Ariadne made tunics. And whenever any one of them dreamed a big dream, a dream dreamed by the theriomorphic depths of the psyche, that dream she embroidered on that person's tunic. One day all four tunics that all four of them were wearing were covered in dreams. No lizard skin or snake skin was as colourful as theirs were.

What they were in their theriomorphic depths they were epidermally. Now they were ready. And so it was that one night, praying to the powers above and to the powers below, sending love not only to the powers that might help them, but also to the powers that might destroy them, they set out inwards and downwards to the Minotaur depths of the labyrinth. It was a long journey. Even in the telling of it, there is vast danger. And maybe someday someone will tell it. Someone who has all the protection of a great religion all around him. Incarnate again in such a religion, maybe Ariadne herself will tell it.

Foundations quaked and intentions quaked when, hearing them approach, the Minotaur roared. It was a rummaged roaring. In it there was ancient, awful sorrow. In that ancient, awful head, now thrown back because it didn't wish to see what it had to devour, in it somewhere, helpless and unable, was its own inchoate opposite. In it somewhere, maybe among the roots of its murderous molars, there was pity for the shiploads. But the mind and the heart and the molars salivated. And the Beast roared and the roaring now wasn't rummaged by conscience, wasn't rummaged by sorrow. Big as his shadow above her, he smelled Ariadne. Under her arms and under her mind he smelled her. He smelled her dreams. Her dreams had the smell of his own theriomorphic imaginings. He smelled Theseus, and his smell, too, it wasn't an alien smell, it was the smell of his kind, of minotaur kind. He smelled the children, at armpit and crotch he smelled them. In them, in Ariadne also and in Theseus, it was the healing depths of his own psyche he had smelled.

Turning, transformed, towards the end wall of the labyrinth, he beckoned to them to follow and four human beings who had integrated what was dreadful in them walked behind him into Paradise. The Paradise we were born into.

The great and terrible Paradise in which the wolf will not lie down with the lamb.

These are stories I wanted to tell you, Galahad. You listened to them as innocent ancient sailors listened to the sirens singing. Looking at you as you listened to them, I could see that you have but recently come up out of nature into culture, and now already you have set out on a perilous, spiritual quest, and you have come this far, and here in a hermit's cell you have listened to the siren's song in nature, to the siren's song in culture, to the siren's song in religion, and you haven't like Odysseus tied yourself to a mast in order that, listening to them, you might sail past them. No. Lacking the spiritual discernment of the old Homeric hero, you jumped overboard and swam ashore. As I did myself the first time I heard them. As I did myself the first few times I told them. I was myself a siren luring myself ashore with my own songs. And the songs lured you. You didn't come through your first test. I must therefore warn you. You must think of the stories I told you as temptations. You must think of them as tempting you to believe that we can, by our own efforts, find final healing in nature, that we can, by our own efforts, find final healing without contact with the Transcendent. It is only when you have resisted and rejected these stories as temptations, it is only when you have sailed past them, as Odysseus sailed past the songs of the Sirens, that they will have something worthwhile to say to you.

And now the story of a hunter, Actaeon his name. Born into a savage land, he could himself be savage, and when he set out, the gulf between him and his hounds, never very wide, would slowly close. Somewhere within him, and he knew it, he belonged to the pride, was accepted by the pride. Two valleys from his own door, he was one with the pack. And so it was one day when, unexpectedly, the stag broke cover. Six hours later the great antlered head was looking down at him, not from his chimney breast but from a precipice. They had come into country in which other hunters had seen Centaurs. In their dreams, always pursuing this very stag, they had seen them. Seeing them, even in their dreams, they would always call off their hounds and turn back. So like his own hounds, his attention so narrowed, Actaeon couldn't. Couldn't hear how smothered in foamings the echoed and re-echoed howlings were. On and on it went. On and on, all howling ceased, it went. And then the brink. Then the vision. Then the change. Howling behind him, one of them already within his antlered shadow, his hounds were closing him down.

And now, yet another mirror for you to look in.

Human inwardness being what it is, our road to civilization is precipitous. Time was when not only was it precipitous, it was Sphinx-infested. Monstrously and antagonistically alive in the Sphinx was all that stands between human hopes and their realization in culture. Confident in himself as he came along that road from his savage outback, Oedipus didn't quake, in neither body nor mind did he quake, at her challenge. He defeated her. And then, well pleased with himself, he went on, knowing that by nightfall he would be welcomed as a hero in the city. Within days, having married Jocasta, the widowed queen, he was king. And right royal he was when, presenting himself to his people, he presided, liturgically accoutred and robed, on his acropolis. In him even the night-watchmen could see that an age of reason had emerged from a violent and brutal past. Wasn't it after all by an exercise of confident, calm reason that he had defeated that pestilent hybrid, that wholly horrid amalgamation of woman and lion. What a revelation it was! Reason could reign! And wherever reason reigned, it wasn't only the Sphinx who would now have no choice but to hurl herself over her precipice. All that was monstrous inside them and outside them would have to do so too.

In vain, seeking out Hydra, would Hercules come to their country.

In vain, seeking out Bullman, would Theseus come to their city.

They hadn't yet seen, these people, how irrational it is to expect so much from reason.

Only Tiresias, the old, blind seer, had misgivings. His divinations in the livers of slaughtered sheep and in the flight of birds were clouded.

And then, there it was. The smell of moral pollution in the city. And plague in the city.

In the end, not having found the cause elsewhere, Oedipus looked within, and there, waiting for him beneath his civilized self, it stared him in the face. Not knowing who he was, he had murdered his father at a crossroads. Not knowing that she was his mother, he had married Jocasta. Children of incest, his daughters by his mother, Ismere and Antigone were his sisters.

Too polluted ever again to look upon the sun, he lanced his eyes as though they were boils and walked away, Antigone leading him, out of his city.

Years later, they came to Colonus and now again, innocently but in sacrilege, they walked in the Grove of the Erinyes.

They were not destroyed.

Instead, out of the midst of low, muttering thunder, an unknown God called on Oedipus to come forward.

Coming to his feet, this innocent yet guilty man walked on alone.

Holes where his eyes were, still called by the God, he walked out of our world.

That's it.

That's the story of the abandoned child who, becoming a man, took upon himself the task of re-opening the road to civilization and culture.

And now, regressing to the first ages of the world, I will tell you a story that, for all its brutality, nurtures the hope of a universl anodos.

At the instigation of Gaia his mother and using a saw-toothed sickle she had made for the purpose, Cronus harvested the monstrous, monster-begetting genitals of Ouranus, his father, and threw them, the still tumesent, bleeding heap of them, into the sea.

The waves carried them out, all the way out and back, into the Abyss of primal potencies. The foam caressed them and from them, or from between them, Venus was born. Wind and wave wafted her shorewards and, barren till then, the earth she set foot on bloomed to her touch, bloomed in a bright sur-prise of Spring spreading inland.

Walking swards that morning, the Daughters of Ocean gave a name to the first open flower they had ever seen. They called it the primrose. And the bird who sang those first few notes, him with the yellow bill, him they called the blackbird.

Further inland than they had intended to go, they saw a stooping hawk.

In a glen coming home they saw the half-eaten carcass of the doe who, but a few hours earlier, had so curiously observed them.

Seeing it, the last of them to lift her lovely eyes from it said, more terrible than the terror of the world is the hope of the world. The terror I can take. The hope, I don't know.

There is one last mirror I would have you look in.

Though it dreamed itself in me, it has you as well as me in mind.

It is King Herod's birthday and to entertain him and his dignitaries, Salome is dancing before them. Strangely, there is in her dance no provocation to blood-shed or lust. And yet, there is breathless expectation. A dungeon door opens and, led by a headless John the Baptist, I walk in. In simple mime-movements, the Baptist watching, Salome removes seven veils from my eyes. I wake up to a naked vision of things and, within a few hours, you, a knight of the Grail quest, ride into my yard.

It is, Sir Knight, a precipitous road you have set out on. All that is still uncon-scious in you is your Sphinx. But you mustn't do what Oedipus did, you must-n't attempt to defeat her with reason. Reason needs grace as much as unreason does. Intending as you do to re-open the road to vision, you must win her friendship.

Six stories, six mirrors, we all might look in because terribly now, there is need in our culture for a turning. The question is: Are you the kind of man in whom turning can take place? Are you the kind of man savage animals will help, or are you the kind of man they will destroy? So much depends, doesn't it, on how you stand in relation to animal nature in yourself. Go the civic way of Job or the savage way of Actaeon and you mightn't survive. So before you resume your quest, there is something I'd like to know. You are able, I know, to sit in Siege Perilous, but are you also able to sit in an ordinary chair? Are you able to sit in the chair you are sitting in? But you know it, don't you? These questions are feints. Not of course the terrible playful feints of a cat with an already cap-tured mouse. They are necessary feints, protecting me as well as you. This much, though, I know for a truth: the whyght samyte that veils the Grail is an inner veil and it shields us against too sudden sight of what we inwardly are. What we inwardly are below our dreaming and waking experience of ourselves is the pool that Actaeon, long before he was ready for it, looked down into. It is as dangerous to steal vision from heaven as it is to steal fire from it. And there is room on his Caucasus rockwall for more than Prometheus. The Grail quest is serious. It might indeed mean that you will have to become incarnate in many religions and cultures. The Grail itself will draw you into them, will draw you through them. And depending on your readiness, the Grail will change and it isn't in Chapel Perilous, or in Chateau Merveil or in the Grail Castle itself that you will realize that vision veils. Vision of the Grail veils the Grail. And it might be that at the end of your seeking, Christianity will help you because Christianity will have grown with you.

There is one last thing I would like to say to you. I sometimes think that I am an Island of Sirens to knights of the Grail Quest. Suggesting as two of them do that nature can heal nature, the stories I tell are Siren songs and I am myself very often the first victim of them. But no. Nature cannot heal nature. Nature's efforts to heal nature leave nature bogged down in nature. We must open our lives to the Transcendent. And, tying himself like Odysseus to the mast, the knight of the Grail Quest must sail past any and every religion, sail past any and every culture, that cannot walk with him into Tenebrae. A religion that can watch with you, that can stay awake with you, during your Tenebrae, is what to begin with you are in quest of. So you see, the quest we set out in isn't always the quest we continue in. The question therefore is: Can you change with the quest as it changes, can you grow with the quest as it grows? Compassion is the greatest of virtues but it might well be that there is a quest that compels us, killingly, to ride past the maymed kynge in his castle.

However wide open to the marvellous and the terrible it might be, the Grail Quest is something altogether more than a journey from Camelot to Corbenic. Both Camelot and Corbenic are states of fascination with the marvellous and the terrible. Both Camelot and Corbenic are mirages of Chateau Merveil and in them every bed is a *liz de la mervoille*. If he is to succeed, the hero of the Grail Quest must first overcome in himself   this wholly unsuspected addiction of an entire people throughout an entire age to the terrible and the marvellous. The Grail Quest is a journey backward and therefore also forward to Good Friday. It is a journey backward and therefore also forward to ordinary sunlight on Easter Morning. It is a journey to a Pentecost of ordinary rain, or, putting it another way, it is a journey to the Pentecost of the five senses we were born with. A capacity for ordinariness is the most sanctifying gift the Holy Ghost can send down upon us. What a crakynge and cryynge of thundir there will be when, the whyght samyte of long familiarity fallen from his eyes, the new Christian hero will more openly see, not the Grail, but a daisy.

In complete steel, sitting sixteen hands high in the world, his horse caparisoned, Sir Galahad resumed his quest. Standing in his door, watching him go, the hermit wondered how far he would ride. Would he ride beyond nature, would he ride beyond culture, would he ride beyond any religion that couldn't lead him through the labyrinth into the darkness of Good Friday?

The hero of the labyrinth isn't Theseus, isn't Ariadne, nor is it either of their children. The hero of the labyrinth is the ability of the psyche to heal itself.

The healed psyche isn't the end of the journey. It is a more or less inevitable by-product of the journey.

There is healing of the psyche and healing from it.

Conscious and unconscious, the healed psyche is the blind not the window.

The House of Minos journeying through the labyrinth. The House of Laius journeying through it. The House of Atreus journeying through it. The House of David journeying through it.

Thinking of the stable in Bethlehem as the outermost cave of a Holy Land labyrinth.

Mary stitching the theranthropic dreams of Jesus into his Holy Thursday tunic.

To suppress the theranthropic in ourselves, in the way that Minos and Pasiphae did, is to look for trouble.

Eliminating the theranthropic as a category of psychological understanding, as Christians have done, is catastrophically unwise.

We have most desperate need for a theranthropic Goddess or God in our religion.

The suppression of Cernunnos was and is one of Europe's greatest psychological calamities. Had we continued to be religiously hospitable to him, he might have evolved into a gracious, theranthropic, divine Patron of integration.

A Hathor or a Cernunnos who would help us to integrate the phylogenetic, the therogenetic, in us.

A Prometheus who would help humanity not by stealing fire from heaven but by writing and staging a Pasiphae Passion-Play at the end of which Pasiphae is able to accept her theranthropic child with as much delight and love as the Hindu Goddess Parvati, divine daughter of the divine mountain, was able, with love and delight, to accept hers.

Having not only the head of an elephant, having also the strength of an elephant, Ganesha, Parvati's son, is worshipped and loved by Hindus as the God who removes obstacles, as the God who opens ways.

Parvati and Pasiphae accepting their children. And we ourselves, living this side of the voyage of the *Beagle*, accepting and integrating the phylogenetic in ourselves.

A Hathor or a Cernunnos who would help someone who, like Nietzsche, has discovered that 'the old human and animal world, indeed the entire prehistory and past of all sentient being, works on, loves on, hates on, thinks on in me'.

Inviting the Minotaur into our religion. Asking him to be our Ganesha. Asking him to be, for us, a remover of obstacles, an opener of ways.

An opener of ways, a remover of obstacles, in the labyrinth under our civilization.

A psychopompos in the underworld of our psyches, in the underworld of our religion.

About this underworld D.H. Lawrence says:

The abyss, like the underworld, is full of malefic powers injurious to man. The abyss, like the underworld, represents the superseded powers of creation. The old nature of man must yield and give way to new nature. In yielding, it passes away down into Hades, and there lives on, undying and malefic, superseded, yet malevolent-potent in the underworld. This very profound truth was embodied in all old religions, and lies at the root of the worship of the underworld powers. The worship of the underworld powers, the chthonioi, was perhaps the very basis of the most ancient Greek religion. When man has neither the strength to subdue his underworld powers – which are really the ancient powers of his old superseded self; nor the wit to placate them with sacrifice and the burnt holocaust; then they come back at him, and destroy him again. Hence every new conquest of life means a 'harrowing of hell'.

The ancient Egyptian underworld, or Duat, as it was called, was certainly a place of malefic, malevolent-potent powers, the most terrible of which was a serpent called Apep or Apophis. Through this underworld every night, the Sun God, sitting amidships in his night barque, must journey. Through it also must journey the dead who would reach the other world. Little to be wondered at that ancient Egyptians sought to equip themselves physically and spiritually – some would say magically – for this journey. Mortuary practice saw to it that they would be buried, sometimes quite literally, in layer after layer of spells and prayers, of hekau, meaning mighty words of power, all of which would enable the deceased to supply themselves with whatever they needed in the Duat, which would also enable them to proceed, overcoming all enemies, to the realm of Osiris. Think of the four shrines that enclosed Tutankhamen's sarcophagus, this sarcophagus itself enclosing three coffins, each of them – – shrines, sarcophagus and coffins – a membrane of magical efficacy.

As spell 124 of the Book of the Dead has it: 'My spirit comes equipped, for I am an equipped spirit and I have equipped all the spirits.'

How equipped are we? What hieroglyphs have we? What hekau, or mighty words of power, have we? Have we words or deeds that are effective against inner insurgency? Are we, echoing Yeats, helpless before the contents of our own minds?

Knowing how ill equipped we are, D.H. Lawrence pleads with us:

> Build then thy ship of death, for you must take
> the longest journey, to oblivion.
> And die the death, the long and painful death
> that lies between the old self and the new.

The Sun God, sitting amidships in his night barque, journeying through the terrors and enmities of the Duat.

How wonderful it is, the thought that the Duat can be harrowed; the thought, as Christians have it, that hell can be harrowed.

Time was when the cooks and innkeepers of Chester staged this harrowing, and it might be no harm, setting psychoanalysis aside for a while, to look at a certain scene of it:

Then shall come Jesus and a clamour shall be made, or a loud sound of things striking together and let Jesus say: 'Lift up your heads, O ye gates; and be ye lift up, ye everlasting doors; and the King of Glory shall come in.'

JESUS: Open hell gates anon,
You princes of pain, every one,
That God's Son may in gone,
And the King of bliss!

2ND DEMON: Go hence, poplard, from this place,
Or thou shalt have a sorry grace!
For all thy boast and thy menace,
These men thou shall miss.

SATAN: Out, alas! What is this?
Saw I never so much bliss
Toward hell come, iwis,
Since I was prince here.
My masterdom now fares amiss,
For yonder a stubborn fellow is,
Right as wholly hell were his,
To reave me of my power.

3RD DEMON: Yea, Satanas, thy sovereignty
Fails clean; therefore flee,
For no longer in this see
Here shalt thou not sit.
Go forth! Fight for thy degree,
Or else our prince shalt thou not be;

For now passeth thy postie,
And hence thou must flit.

Then let them hurl Satan from his throne

SATAN: Out, alas! I am shent;
My might fails, verament;
This prince that is now present
Will spoil from me my prey.
Adam, by my enticement,
And all his blood, through me were blent;
Now hence they shall all be hent,
And I in hell for ay.

JESUS: Open up hell gates, yet I say,
You princes of pine that be present,
And let the King of bliss this way,
That he may fulfil his intent.

He enters the gates of hell

SATAN: Say what is he, that King of bliss?

JESUS: That Lord, the which almighty is.
There is no power like to his;
Of all joy he is king,
And to him is none like, iwis.
As is soothly seen by this,
For man that sometime did amiss,
To his bliss he will bring.

Then Jesus shall take Adam by the hand

Peace to thee Adam, my darling,
And to all thine offspring
That righteous were in earth living;
From me you shall not sever.
To bliss now I will you bring;
There you shall be without ending.
Michael, lead these men singing
To joy that lasteth ever.

MICHAEL: Lord, your will done shall be.
Come forth, Adam, come with me!
My Lord upon the rood-tree
Your sins hath forbought.
Now shall you have liking and lee,
And be restored to your degree,

That Satan with his subtlety
From bliss to bale hath brought.

Then Michael shall lead Adam and the saints to Paradise ...

The cooks and the innkeepers of Mycenae harrowing the House of Atreus.

The cooks and the innkeepers of Thebes harrowing the House of Laius.

The cooks and the innkeepers of Dublin harrowing the House of Here Cometh Everyman.

If Haechel is right, Everyman is a recapitulation of evolution. Embryonically, in other words, each of us is a single-celled zoa, is fish, is amphibian, is reptile, is mammal, is man-like ape, is ape-like man, is human. It is the psychological correlative of all these stages and ages in us that needs to be harrowed. And just as there is a physical appendix in us, so also, after a week of bad dreams, will we sometimes conclude that there is a karmic appendix which, becoming inflamed, can also burst. And is that what happened to Jesus in Gethsemane? Did our karmic poisons come to the boil in him? Did they boil themselves away, sweat themselves away, in him? And if they didn't, the process once begun, what would have happened? Would he have simmered down, or condensed, into another Coatlicue?

To be human is a stupendous risk. We need only think of Nebuchadnezzar:

The same hour was the thing fulfilled upon Nebuchadnezzar: and he was driven from men, and did eat grass as oxen, and his body was wet with the dew of heaven, till his hairs were grown like eagle's feathers, and his nails like bird's claws.

In other words, here cometh Nebuchadnezzar, not as King of Kings and Lord of Lords, but as Enkidu. As something altogether more degraded than Enkidu.

Not doubting that the Fall occurred, William Law is acutely, if not also overzealously, aware of its consequences for us and in us:

Now, though the light and comfort of this outward world keeps even the worst of men from any constant, strong sensibility of that wrathful, fiery, dark and self-tormenting nature that is the very essence of every fallen, unregenerate soul, yet every man in the world has, more or less, frequent and strong intimations given him, that so it is with him in the inmost ground of his soil. How many inventions are some people forced to have recourse to in order to keep off a certain inward uneasiness which they are afraid of, and know not whence it comes? Alas, 'tis because there is a fallen spirit, a dark, acting fire within them, which has never had its proper relief, and is trying to discover itself and calling out for help at every cessation of wordly joy.

Why are some people, when under heavy disappointments or some great worldly shame, at the very brink of distraction, unable to bear themselves, and desirous of death of any kind? 'Tis because worldly light and comforts no longer acting sweetly upon the blood, the soul is left to its own dark, fiery, raging nature, and would destroy the body at any rate, rather than continue under the sensibility of its own wrathful, self-tormenting fire. Who has not at one time or other felt a sourness, a wrath, a selfishness, an envy and a pride, which he could not tell what to do with or how to bear, rising up in him without his consent, casting a blackness over all his thoughts, and then as suddenly going off again, either by the cheerfulness of the sun or air, or some agreeable accident and again at times as suddenly returning upon him? Sufficient indication are these to every man that there is a dark guest within him, concealed under the cover of flesh and blood, often lulled asleep by worldly light and amusements, yet such as will, in spite of everything, show itself, and which, if it has not its proper relief in this life, must be his torment in eternity. And it was for the sake of this hidden hell within us that our blessed Lord said when on earth, and says now to every soul, 'come unto me, all ye that labour and are heavy laden, and I will give you rest'.

Elsewhere he says:

Repentance is but a kind of table-talk till we see so much of the deformity of our inward nature as to be in some degree frightened and terrified at the sight of it. There must be some kind of an earthquake within us, something that must rend and shake us to the bottom, before we can be enough sensible, either of the state of death we are in, or enough desirous of that Saviour who alone can save us from it. A plausible form of an outward life, that has only learned rules and modes of religion by use and custom, often keeps the soul for some time at ease, though all its inward root and ground of sin has never been shaken or molested, though it has never tasted of the bitter waters of repentance, and has only known the want of a Saviour by hearsay. But things cannot pass thus: sooner or later repentance must have a broken and a contrite heart. We must with our Blessed Lord go over the brook Cedron, and with Him sweat great drops of sorrow, before he can say for us, as He said for Himself, It is finished.

There are Hindus who insist that at its core every soul is as pure as a drop of water on a lotus leaf. And Sir Thomas Browne has declared that 'there is surely a piece of Divinity in us, something that was before the elements, and that owes no homage unto the sun'. And yet, although all of this be so, it is nonetheless simultaneously true that when we are inwardly earthquaked we do indeed to our great terror see that 'hell is naked before us, and destruction hath no covering'.

There is something more serious about us than the accumulations in us of organic evolution.

And so it is that the innkeepers and cooks of Chester have a play to put on and less than a quarter of an hour into it Jesus will come to the monstrous, gaping hell-mouth and when the racket of clashed pots and pans dies down he will call out:

Lift up your heads, O ye gates; and be ye lift up, ye everlasting doors; and the King of Glory shall come in.

It was an ancient socio-political regime that the insurgent citizens of France took torch and sword to. It was our inner phylogenetic ancient regime, the one that Nietzsche discovered, that Jesus harrowed, and it was in Gethsemane, consenting to be himself harrowed, that he harrowed it.

To take torch and sword to an external ancient regime, to do so before our inner collective hell has been harrowed, is to run the risk of opening the door to guillotine and Gulag.

> Could great men thunder
> As Jove himself does, Jove would ne'er be quiet,
> For every pelting, petty officer
> Would use his heaven for thunder,
> Nothing but thunder. Merciful heaven,
> Thou rather with thy sharp and sulphurous bolt
> Splits the unwedgeable and gnarled oak
> Than the soft myrtle; but man, proud man,
> Dressed in a little brief authority,
> Most ignorant of what he's most assured,
> His glassy essence, like an angry ape
> Plays such fantastic tricks before high heaven
> As makes the angels weep …

Walking not towards but away from the Kedron, we build and build and build a civilization of fantastic but trite technological tricks. Tricks and more tricks. In the meantime, walking in the opposite direction, evolution has crossed the Kedron into Gethsemane and Good Friday.

Christ walking into the hell-mouth.

Not wielding a club like Herakles, not playing a lyre like Orpheus, speaking no hekau, he walks in.

It was with hard, hallucinating eyes, not with Christian eyes, that Dante read:

> Abandon hope all who enter here.

Although medieval Christians didn't imagine it, maybe we should: hell harrowed so deeply that even Satan and all his demons cross over into Paradise.

Saying the same thing in an ancient Egyptian way: going down into Manu, the Western Mountain, the Sun, aged at his setting, was called Atum. Coming up, young and triumphant, over Bakhu, the Eastern Mountain, he was called Horakhty, which means Horus of the Horizon.

Although ancient Egyptians didn't imagine it, maybe we should: all the inhabitants of the Duat, all, that is, who live at and from the limits of opacity and contraction, all of them, even Apep, coming over the horizon one morning with Horus.

The morning when 'Akhty', meaning 'of the horizon', is suffix to every name. Horakhty, Apepakhty, Ammitakhty, Satanakhty, Evakhty, Adamakhty, Cainakhty, Gogakhty, Magogakhty ...

Of the horizon are all things.

Seeding reality with an event seen only in fancy in the hope that one day we will see it in fact.

As the Zohar so repeatedly has it: 'The impulse from below calls forth that from above.' Glossing this statement, Scholem says:

The earthly reality mysteriously reacts upon the heavenly, for everything, including human activity, has its 'upper roots' in the realm of the Sefiroth. The impulse which originates from a good deed guides the flow of blessing which springs from the superabundance of life in the Sefiroth into the secret channels leading into the lower and the outer world.

Awaiting the impulse from above, we sing:

> All shall be well
> And all shall be well
> And all manner of thing shall be well

Hell shall be harrowed and all that we subliminally are shall be of the morning horizon.

Of the horizon our inner ancient regime, of the horizon the old animal and human life.

Of the horizon the entire prehistory and past of all sentient being.

Of the horizon all that is uninventoried in myth and mask.

Of the horizon the fresh buffalo robe.

Of the horizon the savage musks of Oregon.

Of the horizon Erebus.

Of the horizon all cliffs of fall frightful.

Of the horizon all caverns of our Book of Caverns.

Of the horizon all gates of our Book of Gates.
Of the horizon all karmic gates, all Grand Canyon gates:

Lift up your heads, O ye gates; and be ye lift up, ye everlasting doors; and the King of Glory shall come in.

Of the horizon all the gates of our geological Duat:

> Kaibab Gate
> Toroweap Gate
> Coconino Gate
> Hermit Gate
> Supai Gate
> Redwall Gate
> Muav Gate
> Bright Angel Gate
> Tapeats Gate
> Shinumo Gate
> Hakatai Gate
> Bass-Rock Gate
> Vishnu-Formation Gate

No more say, where id is ego shall be. Say something that has the effulgence of morning in it. Say something that has the effulgence of a new world order in it. Say – Akhty. Say idakhty.

No more say Duat, no more say Erebus. Say Erebus and Duat have haloes now. Say Duatakhty, Erebusakhty. Talk from now on about downward as well as upward transcendence.

And here he comes, rising he comes, his falcon's head and shoulders showing between the double lion of the horizon. Here he comes, Erebus rising with him, Horus-Christ of the horizon.

Compared with the innkeepers and cooks of Chester dashing in and out of the hell-mouth, banging their pots and pans in it, Coleridge is imperially severe:

All things that surround us, and all things that happen to us, have but one common final cause, namely the increase of consciousness in such wise that whatever part of the *terra incognita* of our nature the increased consciousness discovers our will may conquer and bring into subjection to itself under the sovereignity of reason.

Reading this, we can only conclude that the stupendous cultural enantiodromia that enacted itself in Job did so in vain. Reading it, we conclude that it was in vain that a mariner, not so ancient then, dropped below kirk and hill and lighthouse. We are back to Genesis chapter 1, verses 26 and

28. Not only must we rule over and subdue all that is outward, we must also rule over and subdue all that is inward. Little wonder that, catching fright like Daphne, the muse fled from him. Little wonder that the God of the Book of Job died in our kirk, that the nymphs departed from our hill, that the humanist light of our humanist lighthouses went out all over Europe.

Yet again, in our day, Christ must walk into the hell-mouth. Its newest name is Auschwitz.

Our inner, collective hell harrowed, it will then, once again, be safe to bring in Carnival, to give Erebus its sacred outing, to give the Duat its festival. It might be that it would help Coleridge in his dejection, it might even revive his genial powers, were he to join the innkeepers and the cooks in their masked merrymaking. Indeed, the very dead albatross of Genesis 1 verses 26 and 28, might once and for all fall from his neck.

Dead albatross by day. Eagle with unappeasable appetite for innards by night.

Minotaur bellowing in his caverns. Eagle screaming between Caucasus rockwalls.

The eagle screaming above him, the Minotaur bellowing beneath him, Jesus walked into Gethsemane.

Co-operating with Christ in his efforts to harrow our hell. Co-operating with ancient Egyptians in their efforts to guide us through, to see us through, to help us come through, to help us to come forth by day, because that's what they called their pyramid texts, their coffin texts, that's what they called the collections of spells and hymns and prayers in which they buried their dead, they called them *Pert em hru*, the generally accepted translation of which is 'coming forth by day', and the hieroglyphic rendering of which is

Pert em hru, three small sounds from which a culture might draw its characteristic life.

Five hieroglyphs which, pointing the way, might give a culture its direction.

Hieroglyphs the Christ child learned, learning them as his a, b, c, during his stay in Egypt.

Hieroglyphs an ancient Egyptian nurse stitched into the beginnings of Christian consciousness.

Hieroglyphs which culture, taking over from nature, might stitch into our genes.

Pert em hru as genetically encoded in humanity as metamorphosis is in insects.

The hieroglyphs Ariadne gives us when we come to the mouth of the labyrinth. The labyrinth isn't a deadend. The labyrinth is a way through.

Hieroglyphs Ariadne gives to Dante.

Hieroglyphs inscribed above the door of our Christian hell.

Ariadne meeting us at the mouth of the labyrinth, at the mouth of the Duat. Ariadne meeting us at the beginning of Bright Angel Trail.

Karmically, Bright Angel Trail is the labyrinth, it is the Duat. It is where we meet the Minotaur in ourselves.

The labyrinth, the Duat and the Grand Canyon: the Christian name for all three is Gethsemane. In Gethsemane, in the person of Jesus, the labyrinth, the Duat and the Grand Canyon came forth by day. But Jesus didn't himself come forth. In a moment of awful consent, he walked into Tenebrae.

The Precambrian coming forth by day. The Devonian and the Silurian coming forth by day. Gaia in all her ages and eras coming forth by day.

Gaia's *pert em hru*.

Gaia's *egrediendi in lucem*.

Gaia coming forth into the light of enlightenment.

Buddh Gaia.

> All shall be well
> And all shall be well
> And all manner of thing shall be well

Even as Aztecs imagined her, even as Coatlicue, the Earth Mother, shall come forth by bodhisattvic night and day.

Anticipating that day, William Blake invites us to

> Hear the voice of the Bard!
> Who present, past and future sees;
> Whose ears have heard
> The Holy Word
> That walk'd among the ancient trees.
>
> Calling the lapsed soul,
> And weeping in the evening dew,
> That might control
> The starry pole,
> And fallen fallen light renew!
>
> O Earth, O Earth, return!
> Arise from out the dewy grass;

Night is worn,
And the morn
Rises from the slumberous mass.

Turn away no more;
Why wilt thou turn away?
The starry floor
The wat'ry shore
Is giv'n thee till the break of day.

Hear the voice of the Bard! Hear the Roaring of Medicine River! Hear Upanishads, hear Sutras! Hear the Tao Te Ching! Hear the Sermon on the Mount! Hear the Ropesnake Parable! Hear Vishnu's question: Did you bring the water? Hear the Horsehead Nebula neighing

Na
Na
Na

*Yatra na anyat pasyati, na anyat srinoti
na anyad vijanati, sa bhuma.*

Hearing the roaring of Medicine River, Standing Mouse walked out. Who, hearing the Horsehead Nebula neighing, will also walk out?

'What shall I do to be saved?' a rich young man asked Jesus. Jesus replied: 'Sell all you have, give the proceeds to the poor, take up your cross and follow me.' Translated into the Hindu diagnosis of what ails us his reply would be: 'Hear the Ropesnake parable and follow me. Hear the Narada story and follow me. Hear Vishnu's question and follow me.'

Our religion, taking over from nature, stitching five hieroglyphs into our genes, stitching Vishnu's question into our genes.

The roaring of Medicine River.

The roaring of the Kedron.

For those who have ears to hear it, the roaring of the Kedron is the roaring of the Colorado in the Grand Canyon. And if, like Standing Mouse, someone were to set out, intending to draw near it, who knows! Maybe tyrannosaurus would come out of his mountain so that the endangered pilgrim might walk, protected, under him, for as Jesus said, 'Seek ye first the Kingdom of God and all things else shall be added unto you,' and as Hölderlin said, 'Where the danger is, there grows also what saves.'

Narada and Nietzsche. Narada intent on waking up. Nietzsche intent on remaining asleep.

Narada prevailing upon Vishnu to show him the secret of his maya, Nietzsche taking refuge with Somnus:

I suddenly woke up in the midst of this dream but only to the consciousness that I am dreaming and that I must go on dreaming lest I perish – as a somnambulist must go on dreaming lest he fall.

Do we go for a walk with Vishnu or do we stay in his house with Somnus?

Dare we ask Chuang Tzu's question: Am I Chuang Tzu dreaming that I am a butterfly or am I a butterfly dreaming that I am Chuang Tzu?

Narada's request and Chuang Tzu's question might well have Good Friday on Golgotha for consequence.

Too frightened to look down, as Jesus did, into Adam's empty skull, Nietzsche chose the thyrsus not the Tenebrae harrow. Given his discoveries, he chose neither wisely nor well.

As Jesus crossed the Kedron so must Dionysus cross the Ilissus. Seen from the far side of the Ilissus, Tmolus looks like Calvary, Kithairon looks like Golgotha.

For those who have woken up from waking there is no 'slumberous mass', there is only Buddh Gaia. So to hear the voice of the bard is to hear the roaring of Medicine River, is to hear Upanishads and Sutras, is to hear the Tao Te Ching, is to hear the Sermon on the Mount, is to hear the ropesnake parable, it is to hear Vishnu asking, did you bring the water?

It is to hear Christ's cry of dereliction, it is to hear the Horsehead Nebula neighing.

'And they came to a place which was named Gethsemane, and he said to his disciples, sit ye here, while I shall pray. And he taketh with him Peter and James and John, and began to be sore amazed, and to be very heavy.'

Karmically heavy, scapegoat heavy, heavy as Coatlicue.

As it had in Coatlicue, his inner ancient regime had come to the surface, if not morphically then as a nightsweat, and looking back at it from here we wonder was the flight into Egypt a flight? Or was it a regression? A deliberate regression?

In his last book, called *Apocalypse*, D.H. Lawrence says:

Man's consciousness has many layers, and the lowest layers continue to be crudely active, especially down among the common people, for centuries after the cultured consciousness of the nation has passed to higher planes. And the consciousness of man always tends to revert to the original levels; though there are two modes of reversion: by degeneration and decadence; and by deliberate return in order to get back to the roots again, for a new start.

The regression under Mount Sinai:

And when the people saw that Moses delayed to come down out of the mount, the people gathered themselves together unto Aaron and said unto him, up, Make us Gods which shall go before us, for as for this Moses, the man that brought us up out of the land of Egypt, we wot not what is become of him. And Aaron said unto them, Break off the golden earrings which are in the ears of your wives, of your sons and of your daughters and bring them unto me. And all the people brake off the golden earrings which were in their ears and brought them unto Aaron. And he received them at their hand and fashioned it with a graving tool after he had made it a molten calf. And they said, these be thy Gods, O Israel, which brought thee up out of the land of Egypt. And when Aaron saw it, he built an altar before it, and Aaron made a proclamation and said, Tomorrow is a feast to the Lord. And they rose up early on the morrow and offered burnt offerings, and the people sat down to eat and to drink and rose up to play.

Think of the stupendous regression that enacted itself, staged itself, in Job. A regression from field to savannah, from the tamed to the wild, from the milch goat and shorn ewe to Behemoth and ostrich, from wiseman sitting in the city gate to outcast crying out, 'I'm a brother to dragons and a companion to owls.'

In spite of savage assaults, from within and without, Job continued to be human, continued to be a person, throughout his regression. Nebuchadnezzar didn't: 'The same hour was the thing fulfilled upon Nebuchadnezzar; and he was driven from men, and did eat grass as oxen, and his body was wet with the dews of heaven, till his hairs were grown like eagles' feathers and his nails like birds' claws.'

Nebuchadnezzar is portent. We ought never to forget that we are fearfully and wonderfully made. Nor ought we to forget that to open the door wide enough to let in God is to open the door wide enough to let in the King of Terrors, to open the door wide enough to let in the light is to open the door wide enough to let in the dark, to open the door wide enough to let in unearthly sanity is to open the door wide enough to let in insanity, to open the door wide enough to let in heaven is to open the door wide enough to let in hell.

It might be of a disintegrated psyche that Isaiah speaks when he speaks of Idumea:

The cormorant and the bittern shall possess it; the owl also and the raven shall dwell in it ... and thorns shall come up in her palaces, nettles and brambles in the fortresses thereof; and it shall be an habitation of dragons, and a court for owls. The wild beasts of the desert shall also meet the wild beasts of the island, and the satyr shall cry to his fellow; the screech owl also shall rest there, and find for herself a place of rest. There shall the great owl make her nest and lay and hatch and gather under her shadow; there shall the vultures also be gathered, every one with her mate.

Little wonder, knowing what was possible, that Jesus prayed that the chalice might pass from him.

'Save me from the lion's mouth: for thou hast heard me from the horns of the unicorns.'

'Let not the waterflood overflow me, neither let the deep swallow me up, and let not the pit shut her mouth upon me.'

It is perilous and very foolish to set out the spiritual journey without ritually acknowledging all that is subliminal in us, all that is phylogenetic in us. In this regard, the Auspices are good for Christians. Jesus was born in a stable. An ox and an ass breathed warmth upon him.

A stable. A cave. The outermost cave of a labyrinth running Bright Angel Trail deep into the Earth.

And maybe that's why Jesus went down into Egypt. He went down, maybe, to acknowledge and honour the theranthropic Goddesses and Gods. He went down, maybe, to win the good will of the theranthropic in himself.

During his forty days in the wilderness, Jesus was with beasts. And shouldn't we imagine that it wasn't biblically, seeking dominion over them, that he was with them. Shouldn't we imagine that he was with them as a Lakota elk dreamer or eagle dreamer or bear dreamer or thunder dreamer would be with them, with them in commonage consciousness, with them as givers of medicines, givers of power.

Jesus in the Wilderness. Job in the savannah. Europeans in their Pleistocene Serengeti.

A European, a Lakota European, a Blackfoot European, who would go down into the pit in Lascaux and win the good will of the speared bison; who, having won the good will of the bull would ask the woolly rhinoceros not to walk away.

Born in the stable a modern French farmer had set up in the Palaeolithic cave of Combarelles.

A Pleistocene antelope breathing warmth on the Christ child. A mammoth breathing warmth on him. All the lost animals of our lost Serengeti breathing warmth on him. The woolly rhinoceros breathing warmth on him. The speared bison breathing warmth on him. All of our instincts breathing warmth on him. His own phylogenetic depths breathing warmth on him.

Jesus in the Wilderness. Job in the savannah. A Lakota European in the Pleistocene Serengeti Europa's Europe has obliterated.

Ariadne's way, not Europa's way, of dealing with the Bull.

Ariadne, not Europa, giving her name to the lands we inhabit.

Rewriting the story of Job as the kathodos of a man whose anodos was partial and premature.

Following an ibis-headed God by day and a jackal-headed God by night, Job returns to the subliminal land of Goshen.

The reversal of Exodus in Job.

Lamb of God. Wolf, who will not lie down with the lamb, of God.

Lamb of God. Lion, who will not eat straw like an ox, of God.

Lamb of God. Tyger Tyger burning bright in the forests of the night of God.

'The roaring of lions, the howling of wolves, the raging of a stormy sea and the destructive sword are portions of eternity too great for the mind of man.' Too great, to begin with, for Job. But were they too great for the author of the Book of Job? Were they too great for the Hindu who wrote chapter eleven of the Bhagvad Gita? Were they too great for the Kwakiutl who, in their Tsetsekia ceremonies, invited them into their fire-light?

Job in the subliminal land of Goshen.

Job in Frazer Canyon. The door of his house is a totem pole. Carved on it, in Kwakiutl splendour, from the top down, are Unicorn, Ostrich, Raven, Hawk, Horse, Behemoth and Leviathan. The open mouth of Leviathan is his doorway.

Job's Tsetsekia.

In Job, vicariously, our Tsetsekia:

Then the Lord answered Job out of the whirlwind and said: Who is this that darkeneth counsel by words without knowledge? Gird up thy loins now like a man, for I will demand of thee and answer thou me ... Canst thou bind the sweet influences of the Pleiades, or loose the bands of Orion? Canst thou bring forth Mazzaroth in his season? Or canst thou guide Arcturus with his sons? Knowest thou the ordinances of heaven? Canst thou set the dominion thereof in the earth? Canst thou lift up thy voice to the clouds, that abundance of water may cover thee? Canst thou send lightnings, that they may go and say into thee, here are we? ... Behold now Behemoth which I made with thee. He eateth grass as an ox. Lo now, his strength is in his loins and his force is in the navel of his belly. He moveth his tail like a cedar, the sinews of his stones are wrapped together. His bones are as strong pieces of brass, his bones are like bars of iron. He is the chief of the ways of God. He that made him can make his sword to approach unto him. Surely the mountains bring him forth food where all the beasts of the field play. He lieth under the shady trees, the willows of the brook compass him about. Behold, he drinketh up a river and hasteth not, he trusteth that he can draw up Jordan into his mouth. He taketh it with his eyes, his nose pierceth through snares. Canst thou draw out Leviathan with an hook? Or his tongue with a cord which thou lettest down? Canst thou put an hook into his nose? Or bore his jaw through with a thorn? Will he make many supplications unto thee? Will he speak soft words unto thee? Will he make a covenant with thee? Wilt thou take him for a servant forever? Wilt thou play with him as with a bird? Or wilt thou bind him for thy maidens? Shall the companions make a banquet of him? Shall they part him among the merchants? Canst thou fill his skin with barbed irons? Or his head with fishspears? Lay thine hand upon him, remember the battle, do no more. Behold, the hope of him is in vain. Shall not one be cast down even at the sight of him? None is so fierce that dare stir him up: who then is able to stand before him? .... Who can discover the face of his garment? Or who can come to him with his double bridle? Who can open the doors of his face? His teeth are terrible round about. His scales are his pride, shut up together as with a close seal. One is so near to another that no air can come between them. They are joined one to another, they stick together that they cannot be sundered. By his neesings a light doth shine and his eyes are like the eyelids of the morning. Out of his mouth go burning lamps, and sparks of fire leap out. Out of his nostrils goeth smoke as out of a seething pot or cauldron. His breath kindleth coals and a flame goeth out of his mouth. In his neck remaineth strength, and sorrow is turned into joy before him. The flakes of his flesh are joined together. They are firm in themselves, they cannot be moved. His heart is as firm as a stone, yea, as hard as a piece of the nether millstone. When he raiseth up himself, the mighty are afraid: by reason of breakings they purify themselves. The sword of him that layeth at him cannot hold: the spear, the dart nor the harbergeon. He esteemeth iron as straw and brass as rotten wood. The arrow cannot make him flee, slingstones are turned with him into stubble. Darts are counted as stubble: he laugheth at the shaking of a spear. Sharp stones are under him: he spreadeth sharp pointed things upon the mire. He maketh the deep to boil like a pot: he maketh the sea like a pot of ointment. He maketh a path to shine after him: one would think the deep to be hoary. Upon earth there is not his like, who is made without fear. He beholdeth all high things. He is a king over all the children of pride.

Behemoth in our tradition. Numxilexiu in the tradition of the Kwakiutl.

Yam-Tannin-Leviathan in our tradition. The Great Iakim in the tradition of the Kwakiutl.

The monomaniacal voyage of the *Pequod* in our tradition. Tsetsekia, or Red Cedar Bark ceremonies, in the tradition of the Kwakiutl.

Time for our *Pequod* culture to change course. Time, top gallants and royals set, to tack and again tack in the hope of a landfall on a Kwakiutl shore.

It would be altogether to misunderstand the voice in the whirlwind demanding of us that we 'Behold', were we to zoologically identify Leviathan as whale and Behemoth as hippopotamus. We won't even understand, let alone accept, the challenge to us in the person of Job until we realize that it is the Great Ther that we are being invited or commanded to behold. Before whale was or hippopotamus was, the Great Ther is. Before stegosaurus was or mastodon was, the Great Ther is. Great Ther doesn't need to exist zoologically in order to exist in the world outside us, nor does he need to exist psychologically in order to inwardly haunt and assault us. Delighted that we have slain it outside us as whale it erupts within us as Shalyat, his seven heads singing a new first page to our Holy Book.

In the first year of Belshazzar, King of Babylon, Daniel had a dream and visions of his head upon his bed. And he wrote the dream and told the sum of his visions. Daniel spoke and said, I saw in my vision by night, and behold, the four winds of heaven strove upon the great sea. And four great beasts came up from the sea, diverse one from another. The first was like a lion and had eagle's wings: I beheld till the wings thereof were plucked and it was lifted up from the earth and made stand upon its feet as a man, and a man's heart was given to it. And behold another beast, a second, like a bear, and it raised up itself upon one side and it had three ribs in the mouth of it between the teeth of it: and they said thus unto it: arise, devour much flesh. After this I beheld, and lo another like a leopard, which had upon the back of it four wings of a fowl; the beast had also four heads and dominion was given unto it. After this I saw in the night visions, and behold, a fourth beast, dreadful and terrible, and strong exceedingly; and it had great iron teeth: it devoured and brake in pieces, and stamped the residue with the feet of it: and it was diverse from all the beasts that were before it and it had ten horns. I considered the horns and behold, there come up among them another little horn, before whom there were three of the first horns plucked up by the roots: and, behold, in this horn were eyes like the eyes of a man, and a mouth speaking Great Things.

And Daniel

Would know the truth of the fourth beast which was diverse from all the others, exceedingly dreadful, whose teeth were of iron, and his nails of brass, which devoured, brake in pieces, and stamped the residue with his feet. And of the ten horns that were in his head, and of the other which came up, and before whom three fell; even of that horn that had eyes, and a mouth that spoke very great things, whose look was more stout than his fellows. I beheld, and the same horn made war with the saints, and prevailed against them, until the Ancient of Days came, and judgement was given to the saints of the most high and the time came that the saints possessed the Kingdom.

Andromeda and Ketos.
Daniel and the Fourth Beast.

Job and Behemoth.

Nietzsche and his inner Ancient Regime.

Lawrence and our inner, unharrowed hell of superseded life.

As for me, Daniel, my cogitation's much troubled me, and my countenance changed in me, but I kept the matter in my heart ... and I, Daniel fainted, and was sick certain days. Afterward I rose up and did the king's business, and I was astonished at the vision, but none understood it ... therefore, I was left alone and saw this great vision and there remained no strength in me, for my comeliness was turned in me into corruption, and I retained no strength.

During Tsetsekia, the Kwakiutl singers sing:

> The Great Iakim will rise from below,
> He makes the sea boil, the Great Iakim,
> And we are afraid.

Encountering the Great Ther. On land encountering it. Encountering it at sea.

It was as Moby-Dick that Ahab encountered him. But he didn't approach him as the Kwakiutl approach the Great Iakim. Nor did he approach him as Ariadne and her family approached the Minotaur.

Ahab will attempt to do what Marduk did, what Baal did, what Yahweh intends to do:

Aye, aye! And I'll chase him round Good Hope, and round the Horn, and round the Norway Maelstrom, and round perdition's flames before I give him up. And this is what ye have shipped for, men! To chase that white whale on both sides of land, and over all sides of earth, till he spouts black blood and rolls fin out.

To this end he prevails upon the blacksmith on board the *Pequod* to make a harpoon from the hardest steel they know of – the studs of horseshoes. And when it is made Ahab himself baptizes it – in nomine diaboli he baptizes it in the blood of his three savage harpooners, Queequeg, Tashtego and Dagoo.

In Ahab, we are still possessed by our Mesopotamian beginnings, beginnings that compel us to repeat the *protarchos ate*, the primal act of madness. In him, we are still possessed by the pit in Lascaux. The *Pequod* is that pit carried down in an Eastern Maelstrom of our own making.

From Esagila in ancient Babylon to the Whaleman's Chapel in New Bedford, what progress? None.

From the pit in Lascaux to the *Pequod*, what progress? None.

Cetus Dei
Taurus Dei

Agnus Dei
Albatross Dei

The Plymouth Rock that hangs from our collective, New World neck
has all four of them carved on it.

No. Plymouth Rock is not a new Areopagus Rock. Our Erinyes
boarded the *Mayflower* with us.

They that go down to the sea in ships, that do business in great waters, they see
the works of the Lord and his wonders in the deep.

In Spenser's *The Faerie Queene*, Guyon goes to sea and sees:

> Most ugly shapes, and horrible aspects,
> Such as Dame Nature selfe mote feare to see,
> Or shame, that ever should so fowle defects
> From her most cunning hand escaped bee:
> All dreadful pourtraicts of deformitee:
> Spring-headed Hydraes, and sea–shouldering whales,
> Great whirlpooles, which all fishes make to flee,
> Bright Scolopendraes, armed with silver scales,
> Mighty Monoceroses, with immeasured tayles.
>
> The Dreadful Fish, that hath deserved the name
> Of Death, and like him lookes in dreadful hew,
> The Griesly Wassermann, that makes his game
> The flying ships with swiftnesse to pursew,
> The horrible sea–satyre, that doth shew
> His fearefull face in time of greatest storme,
> Huge Ziffius, whom mariners eschew
> No lesse than rockes (as travellers informe)
> And greedy Rosmarines with visages deforme.
>
> All these and thousand thousands many more,
> And more deformed monsters thousand fold,
> With dreadful noise and hollow rombling rore,
> Came rushing in the foamy waves enrold,
> Which seemed to fly for feare, them to behold;
> Ne wonder, if these did the kight appall;
> For all that here on earth we dreadfull hold,
> Be but as bugs to fearen babes withall,
> Compared to creatures in the sea's entrall.

Creatures in the sea's entrall.
A tangle of beastly energies in the mind's entrall:

I am walking in Soho. I am walking, that is, in the red-light area of my own psyche. I cross into Old Compton Street. I have only walked a little way when I see, on the other side, a striptease house I used to go into in my young days. I cross over and walk in. Immediately I cross the threshold I see, I am amazed to see, that a great transformation has taken place. In the old days, on every floor of it, this house had a feeling of crypts about it. Crypts in a sad underground. Crypts hiding from themselves in their own chiaroscuro. A labyrinth of obscure seeing. But a great transformation had occurred. The house had come over ground, the light of day had come in scattering the dark corners luridly lit up, scattering the chiaroscuro and the peepshows. It was as if the seven veils in my eyes were being removed. I have crossed a threshold, and with eyes stripped down to their naked seeing I see that this, the ground floor, has rack after rack after rack of bright summer clothes in it. The clothes are happy. They glow with the heavenly light everyday light eclipses. In the wonder of what it is I am seeing, I see that all the garments are unisexual. Breaking free from the wonder as Odysseus broke free from Calypso, I walk out.

Walking down the street I realize I have a farm fork in my hand. It has four prongs and there are scales of dry cow dung on them.

I turn into Wardour Street.

I am walking in an eighteenth-century park. It is in the European Age of Reason I am walking. It is very civilized, very domesticated, not a leaf out of place, not a wild corner in it. As if a magic wand had been waved over it, this park is suddenly a savannah. It is earlier than the appearance of the first human beings. There might be hominids about. Maybe Lucy is watching me from the bushes, but I can't see her.

Lucy looking at her future.

I disappoint her. I am ashamed.

Walking to no apparent purpose, I come to a place where the ground looks subtly different. I begin to dig, using the farm fork. I uncover three granite steps. I climb down.

Standing on the lowest step, I see a vast oceanarium below me. Far, far away, in space and time, below me. On the far embankment, far below, there is a man. Bending over the edge, he reaches with both hands down into the water. As if the gesture or make-believe of lifting were in itself sufficient, a submerged iron grid begins to rise, breaching the surface. Rising of its own accord, it swings, as it were on hinges upwards and backwards towards me, merging vertically with the high embankment I am standing on.

Now that this repressing grid is lifted, an immense tangle of living creatures rise from the depths. Draped across them all is an undulating snake-form. I call it a dogfish. And yet, so vast is it in its undulations above and below the water that I cannot but wonder whether it contains the universe or the universe contains it. But it is inwardly, above all, that it is tremendous. There are tundras and taigas under its thunderously blooming, lucent skin. Evenings Archaeornis saw and waterfalls Stegosaurus heard are under it. Auroras older than eyesight are under it.

I am walking on the far embankment. So far away, even Lucy looking down from the steps couldn't see me now. An otter walks past and I recoil, withdrawing my foot, fearing it will bite my small toe. I remembered seeing a corral snake biting the small toe of a boy in a forest between Mexico and Guatemala.

I am sitting far out on the surface of the oceanarium. Behind me there is an immense Mesozoic monster. I can see it without looking around me.

Opening its mouth, big as a canyon, it comes at me, veering at the last moment to the left of me. Playing with me, intensifying its appetite for me, it comes at me again, veering this time to the right of me. His rehearsals over, he manoeuvres himself into better position behind me.

His canyon agape, he comes at me a third time. This is it, I think, already overshadowed, expecting engulfment. To my great relief and surprise, it doesn't happen. I am sitting there, still surrendered, but the terrible gaping thing has become a shy, timid little animal swimming away to safety.

Our minds stripteased, stripped, until we see the union of opposites, until we see we have no reason to fear 'the entire prehistory and past of all sentient being' that 'works on, loves on, hates on, thinks on' in us. The suppressing grid goes up and we aren't engulfed. Manure fork in hand, we can cross the shadow-line between our eighteenth-century park and Lucy's savannah and survive. We can walk the red-lit, lurid street or ascend the primeval river into the heart of our darkness and not become a demon of the place. But how many times must we cross the shadow-line? Before he can say he is safe, how many times must Kurtz ascend the river?

Pasiphae's external labyrinth. Our internal suppressing grid.

Does our inner suppressing grid turn what it suppresses into a Duat of hostile, angry Zoas, Zoas as angry and terrible as Apep, Ammit, Sobk? Does it turn what it suppresses into a Marasena, the Marasena which, on the right of his enlightenment, assaulted the Buddha?

The sea's entrall.

The mind's entrall.

Samskarahs, or karmic formations, in the mind's entrall.

What happened to Job? What happened to Daniel?

'Am I a sea or a whale?' Job cries out, 'Am I a sea or a whale that thou settest a watch over me? When I say my bed shall comfort me, my couch shall ease my complaint, then thou scarest me with dreams and terrifiest me through visions, so that my soul chooseth strangling and death rather than my life.'

Job's chonyid bardo bed.

The Liz de la Mervoille in Chateau Merveil that Sir Gawain, in quest of a clearer vision of the Grail, will lie on.

Chateau Merveil. Chapel Perilous.

Chapel Perilous, Chateau Merveil and Liz de la Mervoille are states of his own psyche or mind into which, usually at nightfall, the questing knight is likely to ride.

Liz de la Mervoille isn't a particular bed. It is a state of subliminal effusion I can experience on any bed. I can experience its terrors and its wonders on the ordinary bed in the ordinary house I live in.

Nights there are and times there are when the mind is King of Terrors to itself. While this is so, any chapel we take refuge in is likely to be our Chapel Perilous, any castle we are made welcome in is likely to be our Chateau Merveil and any bed we lie on is likely to be our Liz de la Mervoille.

Japanese Zen Buddhists talk of a realm or state called makyo. It is as if the King of Terrors is also King of most alluring wonders. As both, he is the Great Adversary seeking to weaken our resolve to single-mindedly walk the path to enlightenment.

The human mind in makyo mood.

Nights when every lobe of consciousness seems to be a makyo lobe.

The mesektet boat, or night boat, in which the Egyptian Sun God journeyed through the Egyptian underworld.

Job's mesektet bed. Bed of the Divine Cow in Tutankamen's tomb. At what phylogenetic depths of itself, at what telepathic, clairvoyant and visionary depths of itself, does our psyche become active when we lie on that bed.

Descending sixteen stone steps within himself, did Job lie on that bed:

A Spirit passed before my face and the hair of my flesh stood up.

Descending sixteen stone steps within himself, did Daniel lie on it:

Daniel spake and said, I saw in my vision by night, and, behold, the four winds of heaven strove upon the great sea. And four great beasts came up from the sea, diverse one from another –

Up from the mind's entrall they came, the mythic four Zoas:

> Ne wonder if these did the knight appall;
> For all that here on earth we dreadfull hold,
> Be but as bugs to fearen babes withall,
> Compared to creatures in the sea's entrall.

Little wonder that in mind as well as in body Daniel was sometimes prostrate:

And I Daniel fainted and was sick certain days –

Therefore I was left alone and saw this great vision and there remained no strength in me, for my comeliness was turned in me into corruption, and I retained no strength.

In Europe we give voluble attention to persons through whom, in our view, history either deepened its old way or found a new way. But what about people through whom *Anima Mundi* emerges!

Emerges and ebbs, leaving behind it on the shore the symbols and myths that invite people and enable people to live in ways, and for reasons, hitherto unimagined.

When *Anima Mundi* is no longer with a particular historical epoch or age the sooner it throws in the towel the better.

Is *Anima Mundi* with the modern West? Some there are who would say no, and with good reason would say, for this let us give thanks, because myth can mean moha. Moha is a Sanskrit word meaning delusion. The very sound of it suggests fantastic delusion. So there we have it: myth can mean moha and in our century moha has cast a very nasty, nationalist-socialist shadow called, for short, *Mein Kampf*. And yet we do need to be nourished by the deeper levels of our psyches. We do need to be nourished by what Australians call the Dreaming. A people who aren't nourished by sacred, sacramental contact with the Dreaming can become very poisonous indeed. Poisonous not only to themselves. Poisonous to the very sources of life, as we ourselves most assuredly are. The truth is, there can be and often is an irrational misuse of the rational, and so it is that our *aufklarungs* aren't all of them always benign. At every level of the individual psyche, even when it is most reasonable, at every level of the collective psyche, and at every level of *Anima Mundi*, we need the gift of discernment and it is said that discernment is a heavenly gift, grace from a source from beyond the psyche. We don't have to climb the pyramids of the sun and the moon at Teotihuacan to learn that in no matter what mood, secular or sacred, and at no matter what height or depth of itself, the psyche can be a Smoking Mirror. A great risk it is, seeking nourishment, to lie *Anima-Mundi*-deep in our psyches. A great risk it is to get up out of Freud's secular chaise longue and, descending the sixteen stone steps, to lie on the bed of the Divine Cow. Could it be that there is in the end no alternative to Tenebrae, no alternative to the quenching of candles, however high or low on the harrow they might be? 'Reach me a gentian', D.H. Lawrence called. But maybe we have to imagine it: a harrow of quenched gentians, a harrow of quenched candles.

> In darkness and secure ...
> O night more lovely than the dawn ...

The Tenebrae harrow is the next most important event in evolution since the origin of biological life.

An angel called Gabriel announced Christianity. An angel called Bright Angel asks Christianity to adjust, in profundities of growing, in exaltations of growing, to Gethsemane and Golgotha.

It is time we acknowledged Bright Angel. It is time we invoked Bright Angel. It is time we prayed to Bright Angel:

> Go before us going down, Bright Angel.
> Stay with us, pray with us, watch with us, below, Bright Angel.

It is time that we honoured Bright Angel. It is time that Bright Angel had his Mont or Mesa-Saint-Michel.

There is, we know, an adrenalin gland. Is there also, undiscovered within us somewhere, a mescalin gland? A gland that secretes the wine of astonishment? Is there a karmic gland, a gland which, over many lifetimes, fills our cup of trembling?

Is there a Lord of Karma? A Lord who comes to us bringing the Wine of Astonishment, the Cup of Trembling?

For in the hand of the Lord there is a cup, and the wine is red; it is full of mixture; and he poureth out of the same; but the dregs thereof, all the wicked of the earth shall wring them out and drink them.

O God thou hast cast us off, thou hast scattered us, thou hast been displeased; O turn thyself to us again. Thou hast made the earth to tremble; thou hast broken it; heal the breaches thereof, for it shaketh. Thou hast shewed thy people hard things, thou hast made us to drink the wine of astonishment.

Thus saith the Lord, the Lord and thy God, that pleadeth the cause of his people, Behold I have taken out of thy hand the cup of trembling, even the dregs of the cup of my fury; thou shalt no more drink it again.

And they come to a place which was named Gethsemane, and he saith to his disciples, sit ye here, while I shall pray. And he taketh with him Peter and James and John and began to be sore amazed, and to be very heavy. And saith unto them, my soul is exceeding sorrowful even unto death, tarry ye here, and watch. And he went forward a little, and fell on the ground, and prayed that, if it were possible, the hour might pass from him. And he said, Abba, Father, all things are possible unto thee; take away this cup from me; nevertheless not what I will, but what thou wilt.

Do we, over lifetimes, create our own karmic King of Terrors?
Do we, over lifetimes, create our own Kama Mara, our own Marasena?
What happened to Job? What happened to Daniel?
What happened to Goya?
Did Goya, farm fork in hand, walk down an Old Compton Street in his psyche? Did he uncover stone steps in an inner savannah? Did the grid go up? Did the hallucinating samskarahs, or karmic formations, come to the surface? Did the walls of his mind become the walls of his house, the walls of his Duat? Karmically possessed, did Goya become his own King of Terrors? Or was it transpersonal? Was it Europe's Inner Demons that dreamed their dreams in him?

Chapel Perilous, Chateau Merveil, Liz De La Mervoille, Chonyid Bardo bed, Karmic King of Terrors, Marasena, Wine of Astonishment, Cup of Trembling, the Sun God's night journey through the Duat, Pert em hru, Horakhty, all of these should be concepts, image-concepts, in psychoanalysis.

Karmically, the sea's entrall and the mind's entrall are one entrall. An entrall of Palaeozoic, Mesozoic and Cainozoic depths. But we don't need to be afraid of those depths. That was the dream's Good News. The grid goes up, yet we aren't swallowed.

The striptease house in my psyche's Soho. The house in which I, the perceiver, was stripped of old ways of seeing things. A house that should be called

PERT EM HRU.

A house in which I began to come forth by day.
A house whose sign should be

A Christianity that would help people to come forth by day, to come forth into night and day, to come forth into healed seeing by day and by night.

Meeting Blake in Old Compton Street. Detaining me, he shows me how philosophically and epistemologically chartered my eyes are, how philosophically and epistemologically chartered my mind is. 'Come forth', he says, pointing to the five hieroglyphs under which we have met, 'Come forth by day'.

Under the sign of the five hieroglyphs in my psyche's Soho, Blake tells me that Tyger has left a medicine bundle behind in his house in South Molton Street.

I quote the advice of Old Man:

Now, if you are overcome, you may go to sleep and get power. Something will come to you in your dream and that will help you. Whatever those animals who appear to you in your sleep tell you to do, you must obey them. If you want help, are alone and travelling, and cry aloud for aid, your prayer will be answered – perhaps by the eagles, or by the buffalo, or by the bears. Whatever animal answers your prayer, you must listen.

That I said is the *Mayflower* that will bring us to the New World.

Once there we will lie Lyca-Europa in the Navajo cradle her Navajo foster-parents are already making for her:

> We make a cradle board for you, Europa,
> May you grow to a great old age,
> Of the sun's rays we make the back,
> Of dawn clouds we make the blanket,
> Of rainbow we make the bow,
> Of river mirrorings we make the side loops,
> Of lighting we make the lacings,
> Of evenings on high horizons we make the footboard,
> Of canyon shadows we make the covering,
> Of Earth's welcome for you we make the bed.

As we rock her cradle, singing it for our own sake as much as for hers, we will sing Uvavnuk's song:

> The great sea has set me in motion,
> Set me adrift,
> Moving me as the weed moves in a river.
> The arch of sky and mightiness of storms
> Have moved the spirit within me
> Till I am carried away
> Trembling with joy.

And when she asks us how things came to be, how rivers and mountains and stars, how coyote and bear and people came to be, we will give her the answer a Maori would give:

> Te Kore
> Te Kore-tua-tahi
> Te Kore-tua-rua
> Te Kore-nui
> Te Kore-roa
> Te Kore-para
> Te Kore-whiwhia
> Te Kore-rawea
> Te Kore-te-tamaua
> Te Po
> Te Po-teki
> Te Po-terea
> Te Po-whawha
> Hine-Make-moe
> Te Ata
> Te Au-tu-roa
> Te Ao-marama

And when she is a young woman we will tell her this Navajo story:

In the early days of the world First Man and First Woman lived in a hogan. White Bead Girl lived in it with them. White Bead Girl yearned for a mate. Going out into the canyon she would lie towards the sun. She would lie under ledges of rock.

One day, coming into the hogan, First Man said to First Woman and to White Bead Girl, It is time to harvest the grass seeds at the eastern end of Black Mesa. Next morning, at sunrise, First Woman and White Bead Girl were filling their baskets with dry, ripe seeds. By noon, First Woman was afraid. The eastern foothill of the Black Mesa was a long, long way from home. Surely there are monsters here, she thought. Surely they are looking at us from the clumps of sage brush and from the crevices. Losing courage, she broke off from her work and set out for home, White Bead Girl reluctantly following her. Three days later, White Bead Girl returned alone to the Mesa. Her basket almost half full, she was aware of something beside her.

Not daring at first to look up, she saw the hooves and the white legs of a horse. Hearing her name called, she looked up. It was the Sun God, gloriously mounted on his glorious horse. I have seen you lie towards me, the Sun God said. Many times I have seen you do it. Your yearnings for me have called me down. Don't be afraid. This you must do. Ask First Man to build a brush hogan. Make a meal of the seeds you have, put it in the basket and cross it with pollen so that it is divided into four sections. Every night for four nights you and First Man must come to the brush hogan. Bring the basket of meal with you. At midnight every night, First Man will go back to First Woman and you will stay on alone.

First Man and White Bead Girl came to the brush hogan. At midnight First Man went home and White Bead Girl remained on alone.

What happened, they asked her next morning. Nothing, White Bead Girl said.

Nothing that I was aware of while I slept. But when I awoke I saw a horse track on the floor and I also saw that one section of the meal in the basket had been taken.

A second time, late in the evening, First Man and White Bead Girl came to the brush hogan. At midnight First Man returned home and White Bead Girl stayed on alone.

What happened, they asked her next morning.

Nothing, she said. Nothing that I was aware of. But when I awoke I saw two horse tracks on the floor and I also saw that a second section of the meal in the basket had been taken.

A third time, late in the evening, First Man and White Bead Girl came to the brush hogan. At midnight First Man went home and White Bead Girl stayed on alone. Did anything happen? they asked her when she returned the next morning. No, she replied. But when I awoke there were three horse tracks on the floor and a third section of the meal had been taken.

At midnight on the fourth night First Man went home and White Bead Girl, lying down to sleep, prayed that she would be worthy of this great thing that was happening to her. In the night, while she slept, she felt that someone touched her and when she awoke she saw four horse tracks on the floor and the last section of meal had been taken. Four days later, tidying her home hogan, White Bead Girl felt something move inside her. She told First Woman. The Sun has been husband to you, First Woman said. Sons who will one day seek their Father will be born to you.

A Navajo upbringing for Lyca, Lyca-Europa, the lapsed soul.

And if Lyca should fall ill, physically ill or philosophically ill, the Navajo will do a Sing for her, reintegrating her, through sand paintings and song, into the sacred origins, the sacred dispositions and ways of all Kings.

Songs such as this they will sing for Lyca-Europa:

> Swift and far I journey
> Swift upon the rainbow
> Swift and far I journey
> Lo, yonder, the Holy Place
> Yea, swift and far I journey

To Sisnajinni, and beyond it,
Yea, swift and far I journey
The Chief of Mountains and beyond it,
Yea, swift and far I journey,
To life unending and beyond it,
Yea, swift and far I journey
To Joy unchanging, and beyond it,
Yea, swift and far I journey.

Homeward now shall I journey
Homeward upon the rainbow

Homeward, behold me starting,
Homeward, upon the rainbow

Homeward, behold me faring
Homeward, upon the rainbow
Now arrived home behold me
Now arrived on the rainbow
Now arrived home behold me,
Lo, here, the Holy Place.

Yea, now arrived home behold me
At Sisnajinni, and beyond it,
Yea, now arrived home behold me;
The Chief of Mountains, and beyond it,
Yea, now arrived home behold me;
In Life Unending, and beyond it,
Yea, now arrived home behold me
In Joy Unchanging and beyond it,
Yea, now arrived home behold me.

Seated at home behold me
Seated amid the rainbow,
Seated at home behold me
Low, here, the Holy Place.

Yea, seated at home behold me
At Sisnajinni and beyond it,
Yea, seated at home behold me,
The Chief of Mountains and beyond it.
Yea, seated at home behold me
In Life Unending, and beyond it,
Yea, seated at home behold me

In Joy Unending and beyond it
Yea, seated at home behold me.

The Navajo cradle, Uvavauk's song, 'Sings' or Kleje Hataals, hozhonji songs: having these, we already have as much as Aeneas had walking out of the burning town, as Abraham had walking out of a jaded age, as Ishmael had drifting away on a raft from a foundered civilization.

A culture that can help a lapsing soul, help it to not lapse all the way down into 'single vision and Newton's sleep', into what Heidegger calls an 'age of the world's night', into what Blake calls the limits of opacity and contraction.

This is how Macrobius describes the lapse of the soul:

Looking down from the highest summit and perpetual light, and having with secret desire contemplated the appetence of the body and its 'life', so called on earth, the soul by the very weight of this its earthly thought gradually sinks down into the nether world ... In each sphere [that it passes] it is clothed with an ethereal envelopment, so that by these it is in stages reconciled to the company of this earthen garment. And thus it comes through as many deaths as it passes spheres to what here on earth is called 'life'.

A culture that would stay Europa's descent.

The Navajo cradle that might stay Europa's descent.

First Man and First Woman finding and fostering Lucy, finding and fostering Lyca-Europa.

First Man and First Woman singing Uvavnuk's song to Lucy, to Lyca-Europa.

Having the cradle, the song and the hogan we are already rich in cultural beginnings. Having them, we have the beginnings of an alternative to Europa's Europe as we have known it for the last two thousand years.

A civilization now of fantastic tricks before high heaven, Europa's Europe has run its course. Not all doors to present, past and future are closed against us, however. The Book of Job is our doorway back into the Aurignacian, the doorway through which we can come forward again, the Bison Bull, the Birdman and the Woolly Rhinoceros of Lascaux walking with us.

In Lascaux the animals have turned their angry, horned front ends and their even more angry defecating rear ends towards us.

The mural in Lascaux and Picasso's *Guernica* are the alpha and omega of Europa's Europe. But the Book of Job could yet become, among the Navajo it could yet become, our hozhonji song to the primal world. Turning it, over nine nights, into a succession of medicine circles on a hogan floor, they might reappropriate it for us as a kleje hataal.

The kleje hataal that would sacramentally good shepherd us across the threshold from economic earth to Buddh Gaia.

Simultaneous with ordinary day and in the same place as it is the Great Day. Among Christians, the threshold between them is the Triduum Sacrum.

Buddh Gaia isn't another Earth. It is the Earth we are already living in. How lamentable it is that so few of us ever find our way to where we are.

The wolf will not lie down with the lamb in Buddh Gaia. It is not at all safe for a child to sit and play by the hole of an asp in Buddh Gaia. Behemoth is alive and very dangerously well in Buddh Gaia.

Sometimes though, in Buddh Gaia, we will find ourselves saying that the empirical mind is the third eye's blindspot.

Sometimes, after sitting all day by a waterfall in Buddh Gaia, we will find ourselves saying there's a quiet state of mind that makes the head obsolete.

Mostly, however, in Buddh Gaia, is the seeing of the prajnacaksus or wisdom-eye that Buddhists talk about.

Buddh Gaia regained. Paradise regained.

Little Girl Lost.

Little Girl Found.

Europa Found.

Europa, now our White Bead Girl, living in their hogan with First Man and First Woman.

Looking out through their hogan door she can see the 'jaguar-splashed, puma-yellow, leopard-livid' mountainsides of the new world she has awakened to. She knows, should she walk too heedlessly there, that angels won't save her from the 'rush dreadful'. And yet this to her is indeed a new world. This to her is Paradise. And it is so because, some-how or other, she has awakened to the innocence of experience, to the innocence of hoof marks on her hogan floor.

First Man and First Woman teaching Europa the hozhonji songs that will guide her, maybe bring her, across the tremendous threshold to where she already always has been.

Between us and where we are is a threshold as tremendous as waking up from sleep, as tremendous as waking up from waking.

The day might yet come when, her re-education complete, Europa will, without shame, come home and meet Buddh Gaia in the once-won-derful world where she has been most violated.

It was into a Hades below ground that Persephone was rapt, was raped. It was into a Hades over ground, a Hades built and maintained by us, that Buddh Gaia was rapt, was raped.

To give a helping hand to modern civilization is to give a helping hand to Hades.

Who will be Orpheus to Little Girl Lost? Who will be Demeter to Europa? Living in a hogan between the four sacred mountains of the Navajo, will First Man and First Woman be Orpheus to her, Demeter to her?

Who will be Orpheus, who will be Demeter, to Buddh Gaia? Or in Heidegger's phrase, who will be the kind of poet who answers to the coming world era?

The anodos of Persephone.

The anodos of Europa. The anodos of Buddh Gaia.

Demeter meeting Persephone Anadyomne. Buddh Gaia Anadyomne meeting Europa Anadyomne. And the first thing Prometheus unbound might do is script that meeting as a modern miracle play.

Dreadful though it was, what Zeus, as aroused bull, did to Europa is not at all comparable to what Prometheus, her supposed benefactor, did to her. Did to Buddh Gaia.

> This is the end of the whaleroad and the whale
> Who spewed Nantucket bones on the thrashed swell
> And stirred the troubled waters to whirlpools
> To send the *Pequod* packing off to hell ...

The question is: Have we as a species lost evolutionary legitimacy? In exactly the way that a socio-political regime might lose it, have we lost it? Did we ever acquire it? Recoiling from us, will evolution seek for both legitimacy and credibility in the dolphin? Or, crossing the Kedron with Jesus, will it need to go all the way back and come forward again? Is it only in Jesus Anadyomne, in Gaia Anadyomne, that it will find the justifying, teleological cause of all that has been and will be? Or do all such questions issue only in this: we have yet to learn what Job learned. Tyrannosaurus is as much Telos, as much Final Cause, as is Jesus Anadyomne. It is out of the same Divine Ground that tyger and lamb, tyrannosaurus and dove, have emerged. And yet on his way to work on a wet morning a man will get off his bike and lift an earthworm off the road, believing, in spite of all that so obviously contradicts it, that this unknown little thing he is doing is for the moment the meaning of the universe. Meanwhile the wake of western history is the wake of the *Pequod* which, as we know, took a spectacularly different direction, not altogether circumnavigational, in the Sea of Typhoons.

Could it be that, rising from ship and whale, Old Man's words will bubble to the surface:

Now if you are overcome you may go to sleep and get power. Something will come to you in your dream, and to you in your sleep tell you to do, you must obey them. If you want help, are alone and travelling, and cry aloud for aid, your prayer will be answered – perhaps by the eagles, or by the buffalo, or by the bears. Whatever animal answers your prayer, you must listen.

Coming to us from behind the calamity to commonage consciousness in Lascaux, these words, were we to heed them, might guide us into evolutionary legitimacy. They are at once *Mayflower* and Plymouth Rock to the Great World we were born into but haven't reached, mostly because it hasn't occurred to us that it exists.

Compared with this Plymouth Rock, the other is 'a delusion of Ulro'. It could only ever give us foothold on Willie Loman Land.

A mandate to rule over and subdue from the heights. Advice to surrender and listen from the depths.

The depths, the Deep below all depths, the Tao-Turiya-Tehom, from which, on Easter morning, Jivaamukhta Messiah came ashore.

A religion that opens its door to this anodos will have a future whose roots reach back, praying with it, growing with it, into the deepest past.

In Jesus not just in Gethsemane but also coming ashore the whole of evolution is psychologically synchronous, and this means that the religion that opens its door to him will never be tempted to cut its moorings to things as they have been, things as they are, or things as they will be.

Since Jesus left his Good Friday face in it, the religion that opens its door to him will not be tempted to throw in the towel. Not on the beach at Punta Alta. Not in Galapagos. Not in the Coliseum. Not in Auschwitz.

The anodos of Jivanmukhta Messiah.

The anodos of Buddh Gaia.

Ancient Egyptians called it Tai-wer, the first mound out of the waters.

Evenings there are when the world is wholly unworldly. Evenings there are when 'Life here, with the things of earth' isn't 'a sinking, a defeat, a failing of the wing'.

Evenings there are when it isn't true to say, as Sir Thomas Browne says: 'Thus is Man that great and true Amphibian whose nature is disposed to live, not onely like other creatures in divers elements, but in divided and distinguished worlds: for though there be but one to sense, there are two to reason, the one visible, the other invisible …'

Evenings there are when we aren't amphibians living in divided and distinguished worlds.

Evenings there are when all is Brahman, an experience Emerson jingled and cheapened not a little in a poem he called 'Brahma':

If the red slayer thinks he slays,
Or if the slain thinks he is slain
They know not well the subtle ways
I keep, and pass, and turn again.

Far and forgot to me is near;
Shadow and sunlight are the same;
The vanished Gods to me appear;
And one to me are shame and fame.

They reckon ill who leave me out;
When me they fly I am the wings;
I am the doubter and the doubt,
And I am the hymn the Brahmin sings.

The strong gods pine for my abode,
And pine in vain the sacred seven;
But thou, meet lover of the good!
Find me, and turn thy back on heaven.

What Emerson says might well be true, but the way he says it makes it untrue. Putting jingles into the mouth of Ultimate Reality isn't religiously helpful. It isn't a poem we would sing beside a Navajo cradle. Nor is it a poem that White Bead Girl will teach her sons when the time has come for them to set out and seek their Father. Better altogether to teach them an Upanishad or two.

Europa our Lucy, Europa our White Bead Girl.

Europa yearning for a mate.

Europa lying towards the sun.

Europa asleep on a brush hogan floor.

Europa telling the story of Standing Mouse to her first child.

In Europe a great thing has happened. We have followed a fox we were hunting into Altamira. We have followed a dog who strayed from us into Lascaux.

The Aurignacian has opened its caves to us.

Following a fox and a dog, we have returned, not by way of a decadent regression, to the commonage consciousness of the Pleistocene.

And a Pleistocene medicine man has come among us.

A Pleistocene Thunder Dreamer.

An Aditya he was.

A Vritrahan of a sort he was.

A Vajrin he was.

His name was Black Elk. He speaks:

Maybe it was not this summer when I first heard the voices, but I think it was, because I know it was before I played with bows and arrows or rode a horse, and I was out playing alone when I heard them. It was like somebody calling me and I thought it was my mother, but there was nobody there. This happened more than once, and always made me afraid, so that I ran home. It was when I was five years old that my Grandfather made me a bow and some arrows. The grass was young and I was on horseback. A thunderstorm was coming from where the sun goes down and just as I was riding into the woods along a creek there was a kingbird sitting on a limb. This was not a dream, it happened. And I was going to shoot at the kingbird with the bow my Grandfather made when the bird spoke and said: 'The clouds all over are one-sided.' Perhaps it meant that the clouds were looking at me. And then it said, 'Listen! A voice is calling you.' Then I looked up at the clouds and two men were coming there, headfirst, like arrows slanting down, and as they came they sang a sacred song and the thunder was like drumming. I will sing it for you. The song and the drumming were like this:

> Behold, a Sacred Voice is calling you,
> All over the sky a Sacred Voice is calling.

I sat there gazing at them and they were coming from the north, where the White Giant lives. But when they were very close to me, they wheeled about to where the sun goes down and suddenly they were geese. Then they were gone and the rain came with a big wind and a roaring. I did not tell this vision to anyone. I liked to think about it, but I was afraid to tell it.

Calling all over the sky.

Are we all being called? Are the foxes we would hunt and kill calling us? Are the pet dogs that stray from us calling us, luring us, guiding us?

It is an ordinary day in modern Europe and we follow the fox we are hunting into the Pleistocene. We follow a dog that has strayed from us back into a wood, back into the Aurignacian. And in modern times also, an Aurignacian boy, out hunting alone with his first bow and arrows, takes aim at a bird sitting in a tree and the bird speaks to him.

Speak to us, Bird. Call to us, Fox. Find for us, Dog, a wild wood we can wait in till our souls catch up. Find us a story we can live in till the res extensa we see is again a world, till the res inextensa with which we see is again a psyche. We have come up into a Cartesian desert of Zin.

In Eanna high and low there is weeping.

Wailing for the house of the Lord they raise.

The wailing is for the plants; the first lament is 'they grow not'.

The wailing is for the barley; the ears grow not.

For the habitations and the flocks it is; they produce not.

For the perishing wedded ones, for perishing children it is; the dark-headed people create not.

178

The wailing is for the great river; it brings the food no more.

The wailing is for the fields of men; the gunu grows no more.

The wailing is for the fish-ponds; the dasuhur fish spawn not.

The wailing is for the cane-brake; the fallen stalks grow not.

The wailing is for the forests; the tamarisks grow not.

The wailing is for the highlands; the masgam trees grow not.

The wailing is for the garden store-house; honey and wine are produced not.

The wailing is for the meadows; the bounty of the garden, the sihta plants grow not.

The wailing is for the palace; life unto distant days is not.

Black Elk speaks:

It was the summer when I was nine years old and our people were moving slowly towards the Rocky Mountains. We camped one evening in a valley beside a little creek just before it ran into the Greasy Grass and there was a man by the name of Man Hip who liked me and asked me to eat with him in his tepee. While I was eating a voice came and said: 'It is time, now they are calling you.' The voice was so loud and clear that I believed it and I thought I would just go where it wanted me to go. So I got right up and started. As I came out of the tepee both my thighs began to hurt me and suddenly it was like waking from a dream and there wasn't any voice. So I went back into the tepee, but I didn't want to eat. Man Hip looked at me in a strange way and asked me what was wrong. I told him that my thighs were hurting me. The next morning the camp moved again and I was riding with some boys. We stopped to get a drink from a creek and when I got off my horse my legs crumpled under me and I couldn't walk. So the boys helped me up and put me on my horse and when we camped again that evening I was sick. The next day the camp moved on to where the different bands of people were coming together and I rode in a pony drag for I was very sick. My legs and my arms were swollen badly and my face was all puffed up. When we had camped again I was lying in our tepee and my mother and my father were sitting beside me. I could see out through the opening and there two men were coming from the clouds headfirst, like arrows, slanting down, and I knew they were the same I had seen before. Each now carried a long spear and from the points of these a jagged lightning flashed. They came clear down to the ground this time and stood a little way off and looked at me and said: 'Hurry! Come! Your Grandfathers are calling you!'

Then they turned and left the ground like arrows slanting upward from the bow. When I got up to follow, my legs did not hurt anymore and I was very light. I went outside the tepee and yonder where the men with flaming spears were going a little cloud was coming very fast. It came and stopped and took me and turned back to where it came from, flying fast. And when I looked down I could see my mother and my father and I was sorry to be leaving them. Then there was nothing but the air and the swiftness of the little cloud that bore me and those two men still leading up to where white clouds were piled like mountains on a wide blue plain and in them thunder beings lived and leaped and flashed.

Now suddenly there was nothing but a world of cloud and we three were there alone in the middle of a great white plain with snowy hills and mountains staring at us, and it was very still, but there were whispers.

Then the two men spoke together and they said: 'Behold him, the being with four legs.'

I looked and saw a bay horse standing there and he began to speak: 'Behold me,' he said. 'My life history you shall see.' Then he wheeled about to where the sun goes down and said: 'Behold them! Their history you shall know.' I looked and there were twelve black horses all abreast with necklaces of bison hooves and they were beautiful, but I was frightened, because their manes were lightning and there was thunder in their nostrils.

Then the bay horse wheeled to where, in the north, the Great White Giant lives and said: 'Behold.' And yonder there were twelve white horses all abreast. Their manes were flowing like a blizzard wind and from their noses came a roaring and all about them white geese soared and circled.

Then the bay horse wheeled round to the east where the sun shines continually and bade me look, and there twelve sorrel horses, with necklaces of elk's teeth, stood abreast with eyes that glimmered like the daybreak star and manes of morning light. Then the bay horse wheeled once again to look towards the south and yonder stood twelve buckskins all abreast with horns upon their heads and manes that lived and grew like trees and grasses and when I had seen all these the bay horse said: 'Your Grandfathers are having a council. These horses shall take you, so have courage.'

Then all the horses went into formation, four abreast, the blacks, the whites, the sorrels and the buckskins, and they stood behind the bay who turned now to the west and neighed and, yonder, suddenly, the sky was terrible with a storm of plunging horses in all colours that shook the world with thunder, neighing back. Now turning to the north the bay horse whinnied and yonder, all the sky roared with a mighty wind of running horses in all colours, neighing back.

And when he whinnied to the east, there too the sky was filled with glowing clouds of manes and tails of horses in all colours, singing back.

Then to the south he called and it was crowded with many-coloured, happy horses, nickering. Then the bay horse spoke to me and said: 'See how your horses all come dancing.' I looked and there were horses, horses everywhere, a whole skyful of horses dancing around me.

'Make haste,' the bay horse said, and we walked together side by side, while the blacks, the whites, the sorrels and the buckskins followed, marching four by four. I looked about me once again and suddenly the dancing horses without number changed into animals of every kind and into all the fowls that are and these fled back to the four quarters of the world from whence the horses came and vanished.

Then as we walked there was a heaped-up cloud ahead that changed into a tepee and the open door of it was a rainbow and through it I saw six old men sitting in a row.

The two men with the spears now stood beside me, one on either hand, and the horses took their places in their quarters, looking inward, four by four. And the oldest of the Grandfathers spoke with a kind voice and said: 'Come right in and do not fear'. And as he spoke, all the horses of the four quarters neighed to cheer me. So I went in and stood before the six, and they looked older than men can ever be, old like hills, like stars.

The oldest spoke again: 'Your Grandfathers all over the world are having a council and they have called you here to teach you.' His voice was very kind, but I shook all over with fear now, for I knew that these were not old men, but the Powers of the World. And the first was the Power of the West; the second, of the North; the third, of the East; the fourth, of the South; the fifth, of the Sky; the sixth, of the Earth. I knew this and I was afraid until the First Grandfather spoke again: 'Behold them yonder where the sun goes down, the Thunder Beings! You shall see and have from them my power and they shall take you to the high and lonely centre of the earth that you may see, even to the place where the sun continually shines, they shall take you there to understand.'

And as he spoke of understanding, I looked up and saw the rainbow leap with flames of many colours over me. Now there was a wooden cup in his hand and it was full of water and in the water was the sky. 'Take this,' he said. 'It is the power to make live, and it is yours.'

Now he had a bow in his hands. 'Take this,' he said. 'It is the power to destroy, and it is yours.'

Then he pointed to himself and said: 'Look close at him who is your spirit now, for you are his body and his name is Eagle Wing Stretches.'

And saying this, he got up very tall and started running toward where the sun goes down, and suddenly he was a black horse that stopped and turned and looked at me and the horse was very poor and sick; his ribs stood out.

Then the second Grandfather, he of the north, arose with a herb of power in his hand and said: 'Take this and hurry.' I took it and held it toward the black horse yonder. He fattened and was happy and came prancing to his place again and was the first Grandfather sitting there.

The second Grandfather, he of the north, spoke again: 'Take courage, younger brother,' he said, 'on earth a nation you shall make live, for yours shall be the power of the White Giant's king, the cleansing wing.' Then he got up very tall and started running towards the north, and when he turned towards me, it was a white goose wheeling. I looked about me now and the horses in the west were thunders and the horses in the north were geese. And the second Grandfather sang two songs that were like this:

They are appearing, may you behold!
They are appearing, may you behold!
The Thunder nation is appearing, behold!

They are appearing, may you behold!
They are appearing, may you behold!
The white geese nation is appearing, behold!

And now it was the third Grandfather who spoke, he of where the sun shines continually. 'Take courage, younger brother,' he said, 'for across the earth they shall take you.' Then he pointed to where the daybreak star was shining, and beneath the star two men were flying. 'From them you shall have power,' he said, 'from them who have awakened all the beings of the earth with roots and legs and wings.' And as he said this, he held in his hand a peace pipe which had a spotted eagle outstretched upon the stem, and this eagle seemed alive, for it was poised there, fluttering, and its eyes were looking at me. 'With this pipe,' the Grandfather said, 'you shall walk upon the earth and whatever sickens there you shall make well.' Then he pointed to a man who was bright red all over, the colour of good and of plenty, and as he pointed, the red man lay down and rolled and changed into a bison that got up and galloped towards the sorrel horses of the east and they too turned to bison, fat and many.

And now the fourth Grandfather spoke, he of the south, the place you are always facing, the place whence comes the power to grow: 'Younger brother,' he said, 'with the powers of the four quarters you shall walk, a relative. Behold, the living centre of a nation I shall give you, and with it many you shall save.' And I saw that he was holding in his hand a bright red stick that was alive and as I looked it sprouted at the top and sent forth branches and on the branches many leaves came out and murmured and in the leaves the birds began to sing. And then for just a little while I thought I saw beneath it, in the shade, the circled villages of people and every living thing with roots or legs or wings and all were happy. 'It shall stand in the centre of the nation's circle,' said the Grandfather, 'a cane to walk with and a people's heart, and by your powers you shall make it blossom.'

Then when he had been still a little while to hear the birds sing, he spoke again: 'Behold the earth.' So I looked down and saw it lying yonder like a hoop of peoples and in the centre bloomed the holy stick that was a tree and where it stood there crossed two roads, a red one and a black. 'From where the Giant lives (the north) to where you always face (the south) the red road goes, the road of good,' the Grandfather said, 'and on it shall your nation walk. The black road goes from where the Thunder Beings live (the west) to where the sun continually shines (the east), a fearful road, a road of troubles and of war. On this also you shall walk and from it you shall have the power to destroy a people's foes. In four ascents you shall walk the earth with power.' Then he rose very tall and started running toward the south and was an elk, and as he stood among the buckskins yonder, they too were elks.

Now the fifth Grandfather spoke, the oldest of them all, the Spirit of the Sky. 'My boy,' he said, 'I have sent for you and you have come. My power you shall see!' He stretched his arms and turned into a spotted eagle hovering. 'Behold,' he said, 'all the wings of the air shall come to you, and they and the winds and the stars shall be like relatives. You shall go across the earth with my power.' Then the eagle soared above my head and fluttered there; and suddenly the sky was full of friendly wings all coming towards me.

Now I knew the sixth Grandfather was about to speak. He who was the spirit of the earth, and I saw that he was very old, but more as men are old. His hair was long and white, his face was all in wrinkles and his eyes were deep and dim. I stared at him for it seemed I knew him somehow. As I stared, he slowly changed, for he was growing backwards into youth, and when he had become a boy, I knew that he was myself with all the years that would be mine at last. When he was old again he said: 'My boy, have courage, for my power shall be yours, and you shall need it, for your nation on earth shall have great troubles. Come.' He rose and tottered out through the rainbow door, and as I followed I was riding on the bay horse who had talked to me at first and led me to that place.

Then the bay horse stopped and faced the black horses of the west and a voice said: 'They have given you the cup of water to make live the greening day, and also the bow and arrow to destroy.' The bay horse neighed and the twelve black horses came and stood behind me, four abreast.

The bay horse faced the sorrels of the east and I saw that they had morning stars upon their foreheads and they were very bright. And the voice said, 'They have given you the sacred pipe, and the power that is peace, and the Good Red Day.' The bay horse neighed and the twelve sorrels stood behind me, four abreast. Then I knew that there were riders on all the horses there behind me, and a voice said: 'Now you shall walk the black road with these and as you walk all the nations that have roots or legs or wings shall fear you.'

So I started riding toward the east down the fearful road and behind me came horses and riders four abreast, the blacks, the whites, the sorrels and the buck-skins, and far away above the fearful road the daybreak star was rising very dim.

I looked below me where the earth was silent in a sick green light, and saw the hills look up afraid and the grasses on the hills and all the animals; and every-where about me were the cries of frightened birds and sounds of fleeing wings. I was the chief of all the heavens riding there, and when I looked behind me all the twelve black horses reared and plunged and thundered and their tails and manes were whirling hail and their nostrils snorted lightning. And when I looked below again I saw the slant hail falling, and the long, sharp rain, and where we passed, the trees bowed low and all the hills were dim.

Now the earth was bright again as we rode. I could see the hills and valleys and the creeks and rivers passing under. We came above a place where three streams make a big one, a source of mighty waters, and something terrible was there. Flames were rising from the waters and in the flames a blue man lived. The dust was floating all above him in the air, the grass was short and withered, the trees were wilting, two-legged and four-legged beings lay there thin and panting, and wings too weak to fly. Then the black horse riders shouted 'Hoka Hey!' and charged down upon the blue man, but were driven back. And the white troop shouted, charging, and was beaten; then the red troop and the yellow.

And when each had failed, they all cried together: 'Eagle Wing Stretches, hurry!' And all the world was filled with voices of all kinds that cheered me, so I charged. I had the cup of water in one hand and in the other was the bow that turned into a spear as the bay horse and I swooped down, and the spear's head was sharp lightning. It stabbed the blue man's heart and as it struck I could hear the thunder rolling and many voices that cried 'Un-hee!', meaning I had killed. The flames died. The trees and grasses were not withered any more and murmured happily together and every living being cried in gladness with whatever voice it had. Then the four troops of horsemen charged down and struck the dead body of the blue man, counting coup; and suddenly it was only a harmless turtle.

You see, I had been riding with the storm clouds and had come to earth as rain and it was drought that I had killed with the power that the six Grandfathers gave me. So we were riding on the earth now down along the river flowing full from the source of waters, and soon I saw ahead the circled village of a people in the valley. And a voice said: 'Behold a nation, it is yours. Make haste, Eagle Wing Stretches.'

I entered the village, riding, with the four horse troops behind me, the blacks, the whites, the sorrels and the buckskins, and the place was filled with moaning and mourning for the dead. The wind was blowing from the south like fever and when I looked around I saw that in nearly every tepee the women and the children and the men lay dying with the dead.

So I rode around the circle of the village, looking in upon the sick and the dead, and I felt like crying as I rode. But when I looked behind me, all the women and the children and the men were getting up and coming forth with happy faces.

And a voice said: 'Behold, they have given you the centre of the nation's hoop to make it live.' So I rode to the centre of the village, with the horse troops in their quarters round about me, and there the people gathered. And the voice said: 'Give them now the flowering stick that they may flourish, and the sacred pipe that they may know the power that is peace and the wing of the white giant that they may have endurance and face all winds with courage.'

So I took the bright red stick and, at the centre of the nation's hoop, I thrust it into the earth. As it touched the earth it leaped mightily in my hand and was a waga chun, the rustling tree, very tall and full of leafy branches and of all birds singing. And, beneath it all, the animals were mingling with the people like relatives and making happy cries. The women raised their tremolo of joy and the men shouted all together: 'Here we shall raise our children and be as little chickens under the mother sheo's wing.'

Then I heard the white wind blowing gently through the tree and singing there, and from the east the sacred pipe came flying on its eagle wings, and stopped before me there beneath the tree spreading deep peace around it.

Then the daybreak star was rising …

The fox we followed into Altamira.

The dog we followed into Lascaux.

And now, empowered by the Sacred Six, the universe working with him, an Aurignacian boy of nine has released the bound or restrained waters, has freed the source, an event that brings us back to beginnings as we ourselves have mythically imagined them. It brings us back to the Adityas and the Danavas, the Releasers and the Restrainers, of Indo-European mythology. In the beginning, according to a story in the Rig Veda, a most awful dragon called Vritra, a Danava, captured the waters of life and held them within his coils. This being so, the universe couldn't come to be. The Gods were desperate. They went to Indra, the Vajrin or wielder of the thunderbolt among them, asking him to do battle with Vritra. Indra's price was the kingship of the world. The Gods acceded to his demand. It was a titanic battle, Indra, the releaser, hurling thunderbolt after thunderbolt after thunderbolt into the coils of Vritra, the restrainer. Indra won the day and the universe as we know it emerged.

Indra and Vritra.

Black Elk and Blue Man.

Empowered by the six Grandfathers, Black Elk is the Indra of our day, he is the great Aditya who has released the waters and as such we can culturally appropriate both him and his achievement. No longer is there weeping in Eanna. He has, in his own words, killed the drought.

In India, Indra is known as Vajrin, the wielder of the thunderbolt and as Vritrahan, the slayer of Vritra.

Black Elk didn't slay Blue Man. Rather did he release him from his bad dream of himself, from his identification with his bad dream of himself, as a Danava, as a Vritra.

Black Elk didn't only release the waters. He released the restrainer of the waters.

To what extent are we Danavas to ourselves, are we Vritras to ourselves?

Clenched fist, clenched heart, clenched eyes, clenched mind, clenched imagination, clenched life.

Black Elk and Blue Man, Indra and Vritra, Aditya and Danava: the continuing and sometimes suddenly irruptive struggle between release and restraint within us all, and within the world, if not also within the universe.

It is because of the struggle of Aditya and Danava in us that life in so many of us is a rough river not a canal.

Being the primal power that he is, being it cosmologically and psychologically, Vritra will always survive his own total destruction at the hands of Indra. Revived, the old desire to imprison the waters revives in him also, and so it was that he once imprisoned the seven rivers of India. The result, within weeks, was a Waste Land. And, although not without violence to both, we might think of it as an analogue of the Waste Land Eliot leads us through, the one an Aurignacian boy, chosen and empowered by the sacred powers of the universe, has redeemed. Now again, therefore, affairs are soul size.

Vritra in our day. Vritra in his form as Blue Man.

Indra in our day. Indra in his form as Black Elk.

To think of Black Elk as an Aditya, to think of him as Indra, is not to claim him in any exclusive way as an Indo-European hero. What Black Elk did, he did for the whole Earth. And the Horsedance in which he ritually reenacted his redemption was a sacrament of healing for the whole Earth. Even to re-tell the whole thing with theurgic intent, indeed even to hear it re-told, cannot be without beneficent efficacy.

A many-splendoured theurgy of healing, first in the heavens and then on a bank of the Tongue River. A Kleje Hataal for our times. And it might be that the dry, sterile thunder that Eliot led us to has already been followed as indeed it has been preceeded by Wakinyan Tanka Thunder rolling westwards over the mountains of Turtle Island. In Turtle Island, there are thunder dreamers who, like Wolf Collar and Black Elk, are able to endure it.

It isn't of course the thunders that are sterile and dry. It is our European way of hearing it, our Ulro-European way of hearing it, that is sterile and dry. It is in our ears and eyes that the Waste Land is.

> In their weathering too
> The cliffs had shown
> His hands were now
> No affair of his,
> His skull was no more
> Than an outcrop of bone.

There were corporal works
Of mercy then;
Every breath was a fight
Between gravity and grace;

In the hard hills
Around his house,
The lightning spat
In the thunder's face.

To draw the sword from the stone is to draw our European way of seeing the stone out of the stone.

And might we not dream a dream, might we not dream with the dreaming Earth: in our efforts to heal the Waste Land, Black Elk takes over at the point where, having done what he could, our European hero leaves off. Indeed, knowing that in order to go forward we must first go back, might we not also imagine, again with the imagining Earth, that Black Elk is an Aurignacian ancestor, in a spiritual sense, of Galahad. Only an Aurignacian medicine man can go down into the crypt under Corbenic and draw the spear out of the bison bull's sexuality, out of male sexuality. Only a thunder dreamer who has been chosen and empowered by the powers of the universe can release the waters that will save the Waste Land. All of this accomplished, the woolly rhinoceros will return and among us there will once again be those who are owl dreamers, auroch dreamers, eohippus dreamers, trilobite dreamers, thunder dreamers, morning star dreamers. Their dreams will be dreams out of commonage consciousness, out of commonage unconsciousness. Their dreams will be dreams out of the *harmonia praestabilita* that so deeply and so calmly and so wisely underlies life lived asleep, life lived awake. Their dreams will be dreams out of *Anima Mundi*.

Vritra will not imprison the rivers forever. He will not imprison the clouds and the rain and springtime forever. A day will come when wailing for what Vritra has done will give way to rejoicing for what Indra or Black Elk has done. In the Rig Veda we read:

Thou hast set loose the seven rivers to flow.
Thou causest water to flow on every side.
Indra set free the waters.
Thou, Indra, hast slain Vritra by thy vigour,
Thou hast set free the rivers.
Thou hast slain the slumbering Ali for the release of the waters, and hast marked out the channels of the all-delighting rivers.
Indra has filled the rivers, he has inundated the dry land.
Indra has released the imprisoned waters to flow upon the earth.

Aditya and Danava.

Black Elk and Blue Man.

Indra and Vritra.

Could it be, though, that Vritra will one day awake from his age-old dream of himself as a Danava? Instead of preventing, will he one day protect, the birth of a world within his coils?

Atum in the coils of Iru-To.

'All is well,' Atum says, in the Book of Two Ways.

'All is well, be of good cheer!'

'I will repeat to you the four good deeds which mine own heart contrived when I was still in the midst of the serpent coils, in order that evil should be silenced.'

Atum within the coils of Iru-To.

Vishnu recumbent and asleep on the supporting coils of Ananta.

Buddha protected by the coils of Mucalinda.

Converting our Serpents, our Sea Dragons:

> Marduk recumbent on the coils of Tiamat,
> Apollo recumbent on the coils of Python,
> Jesus recumbent on the coils of Leviathan.

Psalm seventy-four celebrates the old heroic way:

For God is my King of old, working salvation in the midst of the earth. Thou didst divide the sea by thy strength; thou brakest the heads of the dragons in the waters. Thou brakest the heads of Leviathan in pieces and gavest him to be meat to the people inhabiting the wilderness.

And Isaiah looks forward to a great day:

On that day the Lord with his sore and great and strong sword shall punish Leviathan the piercing serpent, even Leviathan the crooked serpent, and he shall slay the dragon that is in the sea.

Lobotomizing the earth, lobotomizing the sea, lobotomizing the psyche. Lobotomy isn't the answer. It is trouble. Trouble altogether greater than the trouble it sought to eradicate. We must come forward from, must grow from, new beginnings. And in this maybe the God we encounter in Deutero Isaiah will be on our side: 'Remember ye not the former things,' he says, 'neither consider the things of old. Behold, I will do a new thing; now it shall spring forth.'

New beginnings from which to come forward springing forth. Beginnings in which integration not suppression becomes prototypical. And so, instead of Yahweh slaying Leviathan, we have

Jesus recumbent, like Vishnu, on the coils of Leviathan.

Jesus protected, like Buddha, by the coils of Rahab.

> The world's great age begins anew
> The golden years return.

Another Altamira. Another Lascaux.

A brush hogan for Lucy. A brush hogan for Lyca. A brush hogan for Europa.

Another Black Elk. An Aurignacian Black Elk. A European Black Elk.

Black Elk carried his vision, remembering every wonder of it, for seven or eight years, and in his own words:

A terrible time began for me then, and I could not tell anybody, not even my father and mother. I was afraid to see a cloud coming up, and whenever one did, I could hear the thunder beings calling to me, 'Behold your grandfathers! Make haste!' I could understand the birds when they sang and they were always saying, 'It is time! It is time!' The crows in the day and the coyotes at night all called and called to me, 'It is time! It is time! It is time!' Time to do what? I did not know. Whenever I awoke before daybreak and went out of the tepee, because I was afraid of the stillness when everyone was sleeping, there were many low voices talking together in the east and the daybreak star would sing this song in the silence:

> In a sacred manner you shall walk
> Your nation shall behold you.

I could not get along with people now, and I would take my horse and go far out from camp alone and compare everything on the earth and in the sky with my vision. Crows would see me and shout to each other as though they were making fun of me:

> Behold him! Behold him!

When the frosts began, I was glad because there would not be any more thunderstorms for a long while and I was more and more afraid of them at the time, for always there would be voices crying, 'Oo oohey! It is time! It is time!'

The fear was not so great all the time in the winter, but sometimes it was bad. Sometimes the crying of coyotes out in the cold made me so afraid that I would run out of the tepee into another and I would do this until I was worn out and fell asleep.

I wondered if maybe I was only crazy, and my father and mother worried a great deal about me ...

When the grasses were beginning to show their tender faces again, my father and mother asked an old medicine man by the name of Black Road to come over and see what he could do for me. Black Road was in a tepee all alone with me and he asked me to tell him if I had seen something that troubled me. By now I was so afraid of being afraid of everything that I told him about my vision and when I was through he looked at me and said, 'Ah-h-h!', meaning that he was much surprised. Then he said to me, 'I know now what the trouble is! You must do what the bay horse in your vision wanted you to do. You must do your duty and perform this vision for your people upon earth. You must have the horse dance first for your people to see. Then the fear will leave you, but if you do not do this, something very bad will happen to you.'

And so it was. Black Road and a wise old man called Bear Signs took over. East of the Rockies, on bank of the Tongue River, they set up a sacred tepee of bison hide and on it they painted the sacramenta of the vision.

On the west side they painted the bow and a cup of water; on the north, white geese and the herb; on the east, the daybreak star and the pipe; on the south, the flowering stick and the nation's hoop. Also they painted horses, elk and bison. Then over the door of the sacred tepee they painted the flaming rainbow. It took them all day to do this and it was beautiful.

And to stand in the west, four thunders there, four black horses were found. And to stand in the north, four thunders there, four white horses were found. And to stand in the east, four thunders there, four sorrels were found. And to stand in the south, four thunders there, four buckskins were found. The four riders of the four black horses in the west were painted black with blue lightning stripes down their legs and arms and with white hail spots on their legs. And the horses' legs were painted with blue streaks of lightning. And in the north, the riders of the white horses were painted white all over with red streaks of lightning on their arms and legs and on the legs of the horses there were streaks of red lightning, and all the white riders wore plumes of white horsehair on their heads to look like geese. In the east, the riders of the sorrels were painted red all over with straight black lines of lightning on their limbs and across their breasts, and there was straight black lightning on the limbs and breasts of the horses too. In the south the riders of the buckskins were painted yellow all over and streaked with black lightning. The horses were black from the knees down and their upper legs and breasts were streaked with black lightning. The bay horse Black Elk was riding had red streaks of lightning on his limbs, and on his back, where he sat, a spotted eagle outstretching was painted. Black Elk himself was painted red all over with black lightning in his limbs. He wore a black mask and·across his forehead a single eagle feather hung.

Sacramentally now, or liturgically and ritually now, horses and riders were Thunder Beings.

Thunder Horses.

Thunder Riders.

Thunder Beings.

Four Thunder Beings in the east, four Thunder Beings in the west, four Thunder Beings in the north, four Thunder Beings in the south. Again and again, thundering inwards from their quarters, they touched the flowering tree at the centre.

'Any great thing the universe does, it does in a circle.' So declared Black Elk.

Could it be that the universe did a great thing, working with circle and centre, on a bank of the Tongue River?

Did you ever have second thoughts, Democritus? Did it ever occur to you that the atoms the universe is composed of are liturgies? Liturgies as simple and tremendous as the Horsedance beside the Tongue River. Did it ever occur to you that the universe at large is a beautifully choreographed dance of liturgies, atomic and galactic?

The atom's hierophany of itself by the Tongue River.

The atom's hierophany of itself in vajra mandalas.

The atom's hierophany of itself in Gothic rose windows.

Until the bleached lens of our Mount Palomar telescope has blossomed into a Gothic rose window, or into a vajra mandala, or into the vajra-asva dance by the Tongue River, we won't be seeing the universe for what it is.

A vajra mandala of Thunder Horses and Horse Lightnings. The bindu, or centre, a flowering tree.

Flowering tree. Flowering retina. Flowering lens. Flowering atom.

Res Extensa René rewriting his philosophy by the Tongue River.

René Descartes and Black Elk.

Black Elk, our Aurignacian Thunder Dreamer.

The fox, the dog and the bay horse.

Bay horse. Horse who is hierophant.

The dog didn't stray. Wholly astray ourselves, we cannot see that, seeming to stray, the dog was psychopompos.

Old Man was right:

Now if you are overcome you may go to sleep and get power. Something will come to you in your dream and that will help you. Whatever those animals that appear to you in your sleep tell you to do, you must obey them. If you want help, are alone and travelling and cry aloud for aid, your prayer will be answered – perhaps by the eagles, or by the buffalo or by the bears. Whatever animal answers your prayer you must listen.

Might it not be that it is in answer to a prayer prayed palaeolithically long ago in the Dordogne that the fox, the dog and the horse have come to our aid? Or could it be that they have come to our aid in answer to a prayer that would be prayed on a mountain peak in Paha Sapa? An old Pleistocene medicine man of our day, it is Black Elk who prays:

Hey-a-a-hey! Hey-a-a-hey! Hey-a-a-hey! Hey-a-a-hey! Grandfather, Great Spirit, once more behold me on earth and lean to hear my feeble voice. You lived first, and you are older than all need, older than all prayer. All things belong to you – the two-leggeds, the four-leggeds, the wings of the air and all green things that live. You have set the powers of the four quarters to cross each other. The good road and the road of difficulties you have made to cross; and where they cross, the place is holy. Day in and day out, forever, you are the life of all things. Therefore, I am sending a voice, Great Spirit, my Grandfather, forgetting nothing you have made, the stars of the universe and the grasses of the earth.

You have said to me, when I was still young and could hope, that in difficulty I should send a voice four times, one for each quarter of the earth, and you would hear me. Today I send a voice for a people in despair –

Black Elk's prayer and Ahab's prayer, if such it was:

Oh! Thou clear spirit of clear fire, whom on these seas I as Persian once did worship, till in the sacramental act so burned by thee, that to this hour I bear the scar; I now know thee, thou clear spirit, and I now know that thy right worship is defiance. To neither love nor reverence wilt thou be kind; and e'en for hate thou canst but kill; and all are killed. No fearless fool now fronts thee. I own thy speechless, placeless power; but to the last gasp of my earthquake life will dispute its unconditional, unintegral mastery in me. In the midst of the personified impersonal, a personality stands here. Though but a point at best; whencesoe'er I came; wheresoe'er I go; yet while I earthly live, the queenly personality lives in me, and feels her royal rights. But war is pain, and hate is woe. Come in thy lowest form of love, and I will kneel and kiss thee; but at thy highest, come as mere supernal power; and though thou launchest navies of full-freighted worlds, there's that in here that still remains indifferent. Oh, thou clear spirit, of thy fire thou madest me, and like a true child of fire I breathe it back to thee.

Black Elk and Ahab.
Black Elk's Pleistocene Horsedance on the bank of the Tongue River, Ahab's eucharist on board our modern *Nave*.
Black Elk's spear, Ahab's harpoon.
The flowering tree of Black Elk's vision, the mainmast of the *Pequod*.
A peak in Paha Sapa, the quarterdeck of our whaleship.
The good red road and the black road.

Haven't we already encountered Black Elk's flowering tree? Isn't it the great tree at Ta'doiko, the tree called Hu'kimtsa, in the Maidu story of origins, the tree under which Turtle, Earth-Initiate and Father-of-the-Secret-Society, sat for four days?

The choice is simple:

Hu'kimtsa or the mainmast.

About which of these will modern humanity attempt to cohere?

From which of these will modern humanity attempt to draw life?

The prayer of an Aurignacian thunder dreamer.

The prayer of someone who once looked about him and saw that 'the horses of the west were thunders and the horses of the north were geese.'

The prayer of an Aditya who, riding at the head of a heavenly host, had killed a great drought with the powers the six Grandfathers had given him.

To stand with Black Elk on a bank of the Tongue River is to stand with him, now in our day, in the ancient Dordogne.

Crypt-deep in Lascaux, Black Elk is our guide to Pleistocene healing in our Pleistocene past.

Crypt-deep in Lascaux, Black Elk is our guide to Pleistocene healing in a present more primitive than the primordial.

Bay horse. Horse who is hierophant.

Heal us, bay horse, of single vision.

Heal us, horse who is hierophant, of the Waste Land in our minds and eyes.

Heal us now in our ancient present. Heal us now in a present that is as ancient as our ancient past.

To inherit our Oglala present is to inherit our Pleistocene past.

The Horsedance of the Oglala, the horse sacrifice of Indo-Europeans.

A vajra mandala of thunder horses by the Tongue River, a king of the Ulster Ui Neill dressed in the skin of a white horse by the Foyle River.

Among the Navajo, the Son of Turquoise Woman stands for his horse:

> I am the Turquoise Woman's son.
> On top of Belted Mountain
> beautiful horses – slim like a weasel!
> My horse with a hoof like a striped agate,
> with his fetlock like a fine eagle plume:
> my horse whose legs are like quick lightning,
> whose body is an eagle-plumed arrow:
> my horse whose tail is like a trailing black cloud.

The Little Holy Wind blows through his hair.
My horse with a mane made of short rainbows.
My horse with ears made of round corn.
My horse with eyes made of big stars.
My horse with a head made of mixed waters.
My horse with teeth made of white shell.
The long rainbow in his mouth for a bridle
and with it I guide him.
When my horse neighs, different-coloured horses follow.
When my horse neighs, different-coloured sheep follow.
I am wealthy because of him.
Before me peaceful.
Behind me peaceful.
Under me peaceful.
Over me peaceful.
Peaceful voice when he neighs.

I am everlasting and peaceful.
I stand for my horse.

D.H. Lawrence caught sight of that horse:

In Lobo, in Taos, in Santa Fe the Turquoise Horse is waving snow out of his tail, and trotting gaily to the blue mountains of the far distance. And in Mexico his mane is bright yellow on his blue body, so streaming with sun, and he's lashing out again like the devil, till his hoofs are red.

Turquoise horse. And Uffington horse. Our horse lashing out.

Lashing out, surely, at single vision and Newton's sleep. Lashing out at a way of seeing the world that hurts the world. Lashing out at a way of seeing the stone that is a sword hilt-deep in the stone.

We only need to draw the sword from the stone and there it is! The stone as it naturally is, tremendously is, is the Grail seen more openly than we are for the moment able for in the river below Camelot.

The whyght samyte having fallen from his eyes or never having grown in his eyes, Blake saw Tyger. Saw him much as the Navajo saw Black Bear:

My moccasins are black obsidian,
My leggings are black obsidian,
My shirt is black obsidian.
I am girded with a black arrowsnake.
Black snakes go up from my head.
With zigzag lightning darting from the ends of my feet I step,
With zigzag lightning streaming from my knees I step,
With zigzag lightning streaming from the tip of my tongue I speak.

Now a disk of pollen rests on the crown of my head.
Grey arrowsnakes and rattlesnakes eat it.
Black obsidian and zigzag lightning stream out of me
in four ways,
Where they strike the earth, bad things, bad talk does
not like it.
It causes the arrows to spread out.
Long life, something frightful I am.
Now I am.

There is danger where I move my feet.
I am whirlwind.
There is danger when I move my feet.
I am a grey bear.

When I walk, where I step, lightning flies from me.
Where I walk, one to be feared I am.

Where I walk, long life.
One to be feared I am.
There is danger where I walk.

Did he who made the lamb make thee? The answer of the Navajo, as
indeed the biblical answer in the Book of Job, is yes.

Time is eternity living dangerously. But without the danger life would
be inert.

How tremendous the universe is. It is as tremendous in a daisy as it is
in a galaxy.

> To see a world in a grain of sand,
> And a heaven in a wild flower;
> Hold infinity in the palm of your hand,
> And eternity in an hour.

Boehme declares: 'He to whom time is the same as eternity and eternity the same as time, is free of all adversity.'

Is certainly free to meet adversity in a different way.

Uffington horse, Turquoise horse, horse who is hierophant showing us
the Oglala horsedance that is the liturgical structure of every atom.

Poor Democritus!

Let Dylan sing to you:

> All the sun long it was running, it was lovely, the hay
> Fields high as the house, the tunes from the chimneys, it was air
> And playing, lovely and watery
> And fire green as grass.

And nightly under the simple stars
As I rode to sleep the owls were bearing the farm away,
All the moon long I heard, blessed among stables, the nightjars
    Flying with the ricks, and the horses
        Flashing into the dark.

And then to awake, and the farm, like a wanderer white
With the dew, come back, the cock on his shoulder: it was all
    Shining, it was Adam and maiden,
        The sky gathered again
And the sun grew round that very day.
So it must have been after the birth of the simple light
In the first, spinning place, the spellbound horses walking warm
    Out of the whinnying green stable
        On to the fields of praise.

Maybe one night as we ride to sleep on Uffington horse, or on Turquoise horse, or on horse who is hierophant – maybe one night riding to sleep we will see the owls and the nightjars carrying the forms of our European sensibility and the categories of our European understanding away. Coming back to us transformed, a cock crowing on the shoulder of every form, of every category, we will walk, walking behind the spellbound horses, out

                on to the fields of praise.

A Pleistocene horsedance in the Dordogne.

A vajra mandala dance of thunder horses and horse lightnings in the Pleistocene Dordogne.

A bodhi mandala dance of thunder horses and horse lightnings and above it in the fabulous depths of the night sky a thunder horse neighing; *yatra na anyat pasyati, na anyat srinoti, na anyad vijanati, sa bhuma.*

Horsehead Nebula and horse who is hierophant: a religion that is hospitable to both horses. A religion that knows what the Mandukya Upanishad knows. A religion that knows that all is Brahman.

        The world's great age begins anew,
        The golden years return.

A religion that knows that the gold of the golden years is a state of mind not a metal.

A religion that knows that the gold of the golden age is a willingness to listen to the neighings of two horses; the neighing of the horse who is hierophant and the neighing of the Horsehead Nebula.

Horsedance.

Aditya dance.

An Aditya dance in the Dordogne.

An Aditya dance that would release us from philosophical hard bondage, from hard bondage of eye and mind, in our Cartesian-Newton-ian Tiere Gaste.

A vajra mandala dance in Ulropa.

A garbha mandala dance in Ulropa.

A bodhi mandala dance in Ulropa.

Time to launch another *Argo*. Time to bring home a Golden Fleece of Upanishads and Sutras.

During the sixth moon of 804, I, Kukai, sailed for China aboard the Number One Ship, in the party of Lord Fujiwara Ambassador to the T'ang court. We reached the canst of Fukien by the eight moon, and four months later arrived at Ch'ang-an, the capital, where we were lodged in the official guest residence. The ambassadorial delegation started home for Japan on March 15, 805, but in obedi-ence to an imperial edict I alone remained behind in the Hsi-ming Temple where the abbot Yung-chung had formerly resided.

One day, in the course of my calls on eminent Buddhist teachers of the capi-tal, I happened by chance to meet the abbot of the East Pagoda Hall of The Green Dragon Temple. This great priest, whose Buddhist name was Hui-kuo, was the chosen disciple of the Indian Master, Amoghavajra. His virtue aroused the rever-ence of his age; his teachings were lofty enough to guide emperors. There sover-eigns revered him as their master and were ordained by him. The four classes of believers looked up to him for instruction in the esoteric teachings.

I called on the abbot in the company of five or six monks from the Hsi-ming Temple. As soon as he saw me he smiled with pleasure and he joyfully said, 'I knew that you would come! I have been waiting for such a long time. What pleasure it gives me to look on you to day at last. My life is drawing to an end and until you came, there was no one to whom I could transmit the teachings. Go without delay to the ordination altar with incense and a flower.' I returned to the temple where I had been staying and got the things which were necessary for the ceremony. It was early in the sixth moon, then, that I entered the ordi-nation chamber. I stood in front of the Garbha [womb] Mandala and cast my flower in the prescribed manner. By chance it fell on the body of the Buddha Vairochana in the centre. The master exclaimed in delight, 'How amazing! how perfectly amazing!' He repeated this three or four times in joy and wonder. I was then given the fivefold baptism and received the instruction in the three myster-ies that bring divine intercession. Next I was taught the Sanskrit formulas for the Womb Mandala and learned the yoga meditations on all the honoured Ones.

Early in the seventh moon I entered the ordination chamber of the Vajra [diamond] Mandala for a second baptism. When I cast my flower, it fell on

Vairochana again and the abbot marvelled as he had before. I also received ordination as an acharya early in the following month. On the day of my ordination, I provided a feast for five hundred of the monks. The dignitaries of the Green Dragon Temple all attended the feast and everyone enjoyed himself.

I later studied the Diamond Crown Yoga and the five divisions of the True Words teachings and spent some time learning Sanskrit and the Sanskrit Hymns. The abbot informed me that the Esoteric Scriptures are so abstruse that their meaning cannot be conveyed except through art. For this reason he ordered the court artist Li Chen and about a dozen other painters to execute ten scrolls of the Womb and Diamond Mandalas, and assembled more than twenty scribes to make copies of the Diamond and other important esoteric scriptures. He also ordered the bronzesmith Chao Wu to cast fifteen ritual implements. One day the abbot told me, 'Long ago, when I was still young, I met the Great Master Amoghavajra. From the first moment he saw me, he treated me like a son, and on his visit to the court and his return to the temple I was as inseparable from him as his shadow. He confided to me, "You will be the receptacle of the esoteric teachings. Do your best!" I was then initiated into the teachings of both the Womb and the Diamond, and into the secret mudras as well. The rest of his disciples, monks and laity alike, studied just one of the mandalas on one Honoured One or one ritual, but not all of them as I did. How deeply I am indebted to him I shall never be able to express.

'Now my existence on earth approaches its term, and I cannot long remain. I urge you, therefore, to take the two mandalas and the hundred volumes of the esoteric teachings, together with the ritual implements and these gifts which were left to me by my master. Return to your country and propagate the teachings there.

'When you first arrived I feared I did not have time enough left to teach you everything, but now my teaching is completed, and the work of copying the Sutras and making the images is also finished. Hasten back to your country, offer these things to the court, and spread the teachings throughout your country to increase the happiness of the people. Then the land will know peace, and everyone will be content. In that way you will return thanks to the Buddha and to your teacher. That is also the way to show your devotion to your country and to your family. My disciple I-ming will carry on the teachings here. Your task is to transmit them to the Eastern Land. Do your best! Do your best!'

These were his final instructions to me, kindly and patient as always. On the night of the last full moon of the year he purified himself with a ritual bath and, lying on his right side and making the mudra of Vairochana, he breathed his last. That night, while I sat in meditation in the hall, the abbot appeared to me in his usual form and said, 'You have long been pledged to propagate the esoteric teachings. If I am reborn in Japan, this time I will be your disciple.'

An Oriental *Argo*.

An *Argo* coming West, its argosy a golden fleece of Upanishads and Sutras.

An *Argo* whose Argonauts are monks, heirs to the initiations and teachings of Amogavajra. Wherever they land, they will build a Green Dragon Temple.

The hope is of course that they will go ashore at Colchis, and Colchis will then be Colonus to our dragon-slayers.

Imagine it: Beowulf undergoing the initiations of the womb and diamond mandalas.

Imagine Ahab, looking like Glaucus, and led by Pip, coming there.

Will we call the rock he sets foot on our new Plymouth Rock?

The choice once again is simple:

A Whaleman's Chapel or A Green Dragon Temple.

A canonical and an apocryphal Book of Job. In the apocryphal account of his latter days, Job is abbot in the East Pagoda Hall of a Green Dragon Temple.

The canonical and the apocryphal Job: the Job in and through whom Western civilization crashed, the Job in and through whom ancient and modern history would find its way to Buddh Gaia. Migrating, the agon deepened itself in Jonah and Jesus. In them the karmic residua of old but not extinct savannahs and sea-floors were uncovered as they were in Nietzsche. Uncovered inwardly in much the same way as Darwin discovered and uncovered them outwardly at Punta Alta.

Job beholding Behemoth. Darwin beholding Mylodon. The difference is that Job's was as much an inner as an outer beholding:

When I say my bed shall comfort me, my couch shall ease my complaint, then thou scarest me with dreams and terrifiest me through visions, So that my soul chooseth strangling and death rather than my life.

I have said to corruption, thou art my father, to the worm thou art my mother and my sister.

I am a brother to dragons and a companion to owls.

Apocryphally, Job's was an inner voyage of an inner *Beagle*. A Mesektet *Beagle*, ancient Egyptians might call it.

In man is all whatsoever the sun shines upon or heaven contains, as are also hell and all the deeps.

It was onto an inner, ancient Punta Alta that Job came ashore.

Job's Galapagos wasn't just a change of scientific paradigm. It was an enantiodromia. An enantiodromia not just in himself, but in ancient and modern Western history. It was a terrible transition from European tall ship to Maidu Raft:

Argo, Nave, Mayflower, Beagle, Pequod, Wreckage, Raft
Age of the world's night.
A'noshma Jesu slipping over the side.

Ta'doiko

Earth-Initiate calling constellations into our night sky

Calling them, he names them:
Jesus Grand-Canyon-deep in the world's karma
Jesus on the Hill of the Koshaless Skull
A'noshma Jesu slipping over the side of psyche and universe
Jesu anadyomene
Jivamukta Messiah preaching his first Evangelanta sermon

It is only by undergoing a ragnarok in our minds and eyes that we can come to or wake up in Ta'doiko, or, meaning the same thing, that we can come to or wake up in what ancient Egyptians called Tep-zepi and Tai-wer.

In its first coming forth the Earth came forth by day. It came forth as Buddh Gaia and, voyaging towards it, modern humanity has come ashore at Punta Alta, which means that our first task is to acknowledge and integrate our inner ancient regime, our inner, phylogenetic ancient regime. That integration is our coming ashore. Our coming ashore is our Gethsemane.

At Punta Alta, a low cliff and gravel beach on the Argentine coast, Darwin came upon a fossil bed which, in his own words, 'is highly interesting from the number and extraordinary character of the remains of gigantic land-animals embedded in it'. Known hereabouts as Don Carlos Darwin or as El Naturalista, he and Covington, his assistant, set to work with pickaxes, releasing some old obtruding bones and some not yet obtruding from the cliff face. After only a couple of days and nights, for they worked also at night, they had assembled quite a heap of antediluvian enormities on the beach, a heap that would soon reappear, causing annoyance there, on the deck of the *Beagle*. Darwin himself describes the find:

First, parts of three heads and other bones of the Megatherium, the huge dimensions of which are expressed by its name. Secondly, the Megalonyx, a great allied animal. Thirdly, the Scelidotherium, also an allied animal, of which I obtained a nearly perfect skeleton. It must have been as large as a rhinoceros; in the structure of its head it comes, according to Mr Owen, nearest to the Cape Anteater, but in some other respects it approaches to the armadillos. Fourthly, the Mylodon Darwinii, a closely related genus of little inferior size. Fifthly, another gigantic edental quadruped. Sixthly, a large animal with an osseous coat in compartments, very like that of an armadillo. Seventhly, an extinct kind of horse. ... Eightly, a tooth of a Pachydermatous animal, probably the same with the Machrauchenia, a huge beast with a long neck like a camel .... Lastly, the Toxodon, perhaps one of the strangest animals ever discovered; in size it equalled an elephant or Megatherium, but the structure of its teeth, as Mr Owen states, proves indisputably that it was intimately related to the Gnawers ... .The remains of these nine great quadrupeds and many detached bones were found embedded on the beach within the space of about 200 yards square. ... The remains at Punta Alta were embedded in stratified gravel and reddish mud, just such as the sea might now wash up on a shallow bank. ... The great size of the bones of the Megatheroid animals including the Megatherium, Megalonyx, Scelidotherium and Mylodon, is truly wonderful.

Inland, in the Pampas, he found

the osseous armour of the gigantic armadillo-like animal, the inside of which, when the earth was removed, was like a great cauldron; I found also the teeth of the Toxodon and Mastodon, and one tooth of a horse, in the same stained and decayed state. The latter tooth greatly interested me, and I took scrupulous care in ascertaining that it had been embedded contemporaneously with the other remains ...

Six weeks later, his excursions across the Pampas continuing, he was still discovering the remains of an extinct fauna:

I set out on my return in a direct line for Monte Video. Having heard of some giant's bones at a neighbouring farm-house on the Sarandis, a small stream entering the Rio Negro, I rode there accompanied by my host, and purchased for the value of eighteen pence the head of the Toxodon. When found, it was quite perfect; but the boys knocked out some of the teeth with stones, and then set up the head as a mark to throw at. By a most fortunate chance I found a perfect tooth, which exactly fitted one of the sockets in this skull embedded by itself on the banks of the Rio Tercero, at a distance of about 180 miles from this place. I found remains of this extraordinary animal at two other places, so that it must formerly have been common. I found here also, some large portions of the armour of a gigantic armadillo-like animal, and part of the great head of a Mylodon. The bones of this head are so fresh, that they contain, according to the analysis of Mr T. Reeks, seven per cent of animal matter, and when placed in a spirit-lamp they burn with a small flame. The number of the remains embedded in the great estuary deposit which form the Pampas and covers the granitic rocks of Banda Oriental, must be extraordinarily great. I believe a straight line drawn in any direction through the Pampas would cut through some skeleton or bones. Besides those which I found through my short excursions, I heard of many others, and the origin of such names as 'the stream of the animal', 'the hill of the giant', is obvious. At other times I heard of the marvellous property of certain rivers which had the power of changing small bones into large; or, as some maintained, the bones themselves grew.

As far as I am aware, not one of these animals perished, as was formerly supposed, in the marshes or muddy river beds of the present land, but their bones have been exposed by the streams intersecting the subaqueous deposit in which they were originally embedded. We may conclude that the whole area of the Pampas is one wide sepulchre of these extinct, gigantic quadrupeds.

After much reflection Don Carlos concludes:

Certainly, no fact in the long history of the world is so startling as the wide and repeated extermination of its inhabitants.

Darwin at Punta Alta: although not just yet, not consciously yet, evolution looking back on itself.

Did the looking cause a funeral not just in his brain, but of his brain, of some of it? Of himself he writes:

Poetry of many kinds ... gave me great pleasure, and even as a schoolboy I took intense delight in Shakespeare, especially in the historical plays. I have also said that formerly pictures gave me considerable and music very great delight. But now for many years I cannot endure to read a line of poetry. I have tried lately to read Shakespeare, and found it so intolerably dull that it nauseated me. I have also lost almost any taste for pictures or music. ... My mind seems to have become a kind of machine for grinding general laws out of large collections of facts, but why this should have caused the atrophy of that part of the brain alone, on which the higher tastes depend, I cannot conceive. The loss of these tastes is a loss of happiness, and may probably be injurious to the intellect, and more probably to the moral character, by enfeebling the emotional part of our nature.

Was Darwin's calamity unique to him? Or is it something that is happening to increasing numbers of us who live in the West? Is mind in us becoming a kind of machine? And if it is, what is the remedy? I think of the *Beagle* sailing towards Lemuy, an island off southern Chile. Darwin himself supplies the details:

We steered for the island of Lemuy. I was anxious to examine a reported coal-mine, which turned out to be lignite of little value, in the sandstone (probably of an ancient tertiary epoch) of which these islands are composed. When we reached Lemuy we had much difficulty in finding any place to pitch our tents, for it was spring-tide, and the land was wooded down to the water's edge. In a short time we were surrounded by a large group of nearly pure Indian inhabitants. They were much surprised at our arrival, and said one to the other, 'This is the reason we have seen so many parrots lately; the cheucau (an odd red-breasted little bird, which inhabits the thick forest, and utters very peculiar noises) has not cried 'beware' for nothing.'

Our encounter with cheucau, the little redbreast of the thick forest, might be the real meaning of our encounter with Toxodon and Mylodon or indeed with the finches of Galapagos. It recalls Black Elk's encounter with the kingbird:

It was when I was five years old that my Grandfather made me a bow and some arrows. The grass was young and I was on horseback. A thunderstorm was coming from where the sun goes down, and just as I was riding into the woods along a creek, there was a kingbird sitting on a limb. This was not a dream, it happened. And I was going to shoot at the kingbird with the bow my Grandfather made, when the bird spoke and said, 'The clouds all over are one-sided.' Perhaps it meant that all the clouds were looking at me. And then it said: 'Listen! A voice is calling you.'

The fox who led us into Altamira, the dog who led us into Lascaux, the kingbird who asked us to listen, and the cheucau who warned a traditional people that Western science was coming ashore.

Did cheucau fear that exposure to our Western way might turn the minds of these people into machines? Did cheucau know that a way of being in the world and with the world could give way to a way of being on it and against it? Did cheucau know that what happened to Darwin could happen to humanity?

Do the animals know we are in trouble? Are they trying to help us? Are they opening old trails for us? Trails to possibilities and depths of nature inside and outside ourselves that we have lost contact with? Are they calling us back into commonage consciousness not just with themselves but with all that exists?

Is it time and is it now again safe for us to inherit the shamanic mandate that Job emerged from his initiation with:

For thou shalt be in league with the stones of the field and the beasts of the field shall be at peace with thee.

A sense I have is that kingbird and cheucau have something altogether more important, altogether more stupendous, to say to us than the finches of Galapagos. Not that the finches aren't also saying it. The trouble is, so much of our Pleistocene minds having atrophied, we cannot hear them.

All of this notwithstanding, we should of course remain sympathetic to Darwin, because there is a price to be paid for cutting our moorings to a world view with which, by education and general culture, we have become identified. To threaten my world view is to threaten my identity.

We don't only have a physical immune system. We also have a psychological immune system which, even more aggressively and successfully perhaps, fights off all ideas and world views which, if admitted, would inwardly destabilize and disorient us. A psychic immune system that is badly breached, either from within or without, will leave us wide open to what we might call Daniel's sickness. In Daniel, particularly in his dreams, the apocalyptic end of an old world and the visionary glimmerings of a new world were imagining themselves, and he fell ill. In his own words:

I Daniel was grieved in my spirit in the midst of my body, and the visions of my head troubled me.

As for me Daniel, my cogitations much troubled me, and my countenance changed in me; but I kept the matter in my heart.

And I Daniel fainted, and was sick certain days; afterward I rose up, and did the king's business; and I was astonished at the vision, but none understood it.

Therefore, I was left alone, and saw this great vision, and there remained no strength in me; for my comeliness was turned in me into corruption, and I retained no strength.

In this regard also, we might recall Descartes' night of big dreams and his vow on the following day to go on a pilgrimage to Our Lady of Loreto.

Might it not be that Darwin could have done with any comfort Our Lady of Loreto might have given him when, taking a pick-axe as any Aditya would, he released a new, and, to some, a troublesome vision of ourselves and our world from the fossilferous rocks?

Galahad releasing the Ulro Rock. Black Elk releasing the waters. Darwin releasing a cosmology which evolving life may not refuse.

Could it be that in Darwin, too, Aditya and Danava fought their old immemorial battle? Could it be that, just as he once imprisoned the seven rivers of India, so did he imprison the more poetic, more musical, lobes of Darwin's mind?

Armed as she was in her faith, could Emily Brontë have been an Our Lady of Loreto to Darwin?

> Though earth and man were gone,
> And suns and universes ceased to be,
> And Thou went left alone,
> Every existence would exist in Thee.

Looking with him at the heap of bones on the beach at Punta Alta, would it have meant anything much to him to hear her say, would it indeed have meant anything much to herself to hear herself say:

There is not room for Death,
Nor atom that his might could render void,
Thou – Thou art being and breath,
And what Thou art may never be destroyed.

Could it be that here on the beach of Punta Alta we have to go deeper than what we biologically are? And could it be that this is the next great step in evolution? And could it furthermore be that this great step was taken when, crossing the Kedron, Jesus karmically integrated all of evolved and evolving life, and then, letting go of it all, looked down into Adam's empty skull?

Golgotha has prepared us for Punta Alta. The Hill of the Koshaless Skull has prepared us for the Toxodon's empty skull, the one El Naturalista bought for eighteen pence.

And the Buddha, surely, has something to say to us on Punta Alta:

There is an unborn, an unbecome, an unmade, an uncompounded. And if there was not an unborn, an unbecome, an unmade, an uncompounded, there would be no escape for what is born, has become, is made, is compounded. But because there is an unborn, an unbecome, an unmade, an uncompounded, there is an escape for what is born, has become, is made, is compounded.

I proclaim, Friend, that in this fathom-sized, feeling-afflicted, ascetic's body dwell the world and the origin of the world and the annulment of the world and the path that leads to the annulment of the world.

On the morning of his enlightenment, the Buddha spoke a famous *udana*, an *udana* the skull of Toxodon might echo back to us on board the *Beagle*, on board the *Nave* that has, at Christmas, stood out into heavy south-western gales:

Housebuilder! I behold thee now.
Again a house thou shalt not build.
All thy rafters are broken now.
The ridgepole also is destroyed.
My mind, its elements dissolved,
The end of craving has attained.

Buddha's *udana*. Christ's cry of dereliction.

Argo, Nave, Mayflower, Beagle, Pequod and now again, our European voyage itself sea-changed, an Oriental *Argo* coming home with a golden fleece of Upanishads and Sutras, coming home with the Narada story and the ropesnake parable, coming home with Good Friday Good News.

*Yatra na anyat pasyati, na anyat srinoti, na anyad
vijanati, sa bhuma.*

The only good way to inherit what we biologically are is to go beneath and beyond what we biologically are.

The glorious way, the Good Friday way, to inherit what we biologically are is to look down into Adam's, into Toxodon's, *sa bhuma* skull.

Oh dichosa ventura.

Beach at Punta Alta.

Dover Beach.

The Ulro roar of Dover Beach that Matthew Arnold, and with him much of modern Western humanity, has turned away from.

But things have changed, Matthew. Galahad has liberated the rocks from our Ulro perceptions of them. Black Elk has released the waters. Darwin, like Turtle, was gone a long time but he has, having the courage for the beach at Punta Alta, released a cosmology that can house us.

Come back with your wife to the window, Matthew. Come with her out of doors and call out Godspeed to our new *Nave* standing out into heavy south-western gales.

Can you hear them, Matthew? Punta Alta horse and Bay horse calling to each other across the glorious fatalities of space and time, across the uneventful fatalities of extinction and fossilization.

Then all the horses went into formation, four abreast – the blacks, the whites, the sorrels and the buckskins – and stood behind the bay, who turned now to the west and neighed; and yonder suddenly the sky was terrible with a storm of plunging horses in all colours that shook the world with thunder, neighing back.

The thunder that shook the world, awakened the world, out of its Ulro dream of itself.

The thunder that shook the funeral out of every human brain.

The krakynge and the cryynge of thundir that announced the accomplishment of the Grail Quest.

Well indeed might her votaries sing her litany to Our Lady of Loreto:

> Mirror of justice
> Seat of wisdom
> Cause of our joy
> Spiritual vessel
> Vessel of honour
> Singular vessel of devotion
> Mystical rose
> Tower of David
> Tower of ivory
> House of gold

Ark of the covenant
Gate of heaven.

Are you ready to join them, René?
Are you ready to be bhakta to Bhudevi?
Are you ready to be bhakta to Buddh Gaia?
And you, El Naturalista, are you ready to follow the fox and the dog
into old, Palaeolithic ways of hearing in you? Are you ready to sail out
once again into heavy south-western gales? Are you ready to listen, as a
Lemuy Indian would listen, to cheucau and finch? Would you be able for
it if a Galapagos finch said 'Listen! A voice is calling you'? Are you able
for the fossil horse of the Pampas, are you able for the Bay horse?
A *Nave* standing out.
Standing out as if in fulfilment of an ancient prophecy:

Venient annis
Saecula seris, quibus Oceanus
Vincula rerum laxet, et
Patent Tellus, Tiphysque novos
Detegat orbes, nec sit terris
Ultima Thule.

Englished it reads: In years to come, Oceanus will unloose the chains
that bind things, revealing the vast earth, Tiphys will discover new lands,
and Thule will not be the limit of the world.

Tiphys was pilot of the *Argo* on its voyage to Colchis to recover the
Golden Fleece. Jason was captain. On board were many heros thirsting to
win yet more glory by slaying yet another dragon. Among them were
Orpheus and Herakles, Orpheus presumably with his lyre, Herakles with
his club. It was with club and lyre that Greeks would have cleared and
tamed the first, savage world, making it inhabitable to humankind.

How different European culture would be if the Argonauts had set sail
for Colchis intending not to slay or tame the dragon but to build a Green
Dragon Temple there.

The Golden Fleece was to Argonauts what whyght samyte was to
knights of the Grail Quest. Like a cataract in an eye, it blinded them to
the most holy, most sacred thing in the world. It blinded them to ordinariness.

Indra, Black Elk, and now Oceanus.

Oceanus unloosing the chains that bind things.

But it isn't things that are bound. It is our ways of seeing things and
knowing things that are bound.

Ultima Thule is an inner, psychological, not an outer, cosmological limit. It limits our awareness of reality, of kingbird and checau, of daisy and galaxy.

There is, however, a place of transformation. It is known to the owls and the nightjars. So, who knows! We might wake up one morning having somehow or somewhere acquired both the courage and the capacity to see what is there, to be blessed by what is there, when we open our Fern Hill door and the whole world tells us, in its ordinariness tells us, that the Grail Quest is accomplished.

Fern Hill regained. Paradise regained. Within our eyes and minds regained.

No, not forever. Thule will not be the limit of our world. Especially will it not be so if we think of Thule as the kind of seeing which, while remaining ordinary, can be but isn't vision.

Our Nave standing out.

Our greatest and most dangerous voyage it is, this voyage to where we are.

Could it be that Moby-Dick, a twisted harpoon protruding from his back, will be our pyschopompos?

Nave into which no one has brought a harpoon or crossbow.

A long, long voyage to bring home the rungless ladder that will leave us exactly where we were before we set out, standing on Buddh Gaia.

In Buddh Gaia we will still have to deal with those portions of eternity that Blake on occasion was so intensely aware of:

The roaring of lions, the howling of wolves, the raging of the stormy sea and the destructive sword are portions of eternity too great for the mind of man.

Even if the wolf at the gate is Fenris Wolf, however, we should nonetheless go ahead and take down our defensive city wall and rebuild it as a Green Dragon Temple. This after all is the transition, spiritually and historically vast, that enacted itself in Job.

In Buddh Gaia we will still have to deal with Nietzsche's discovery, and the only good way to do that is in an egressus trans torrentem, the angel who offers us the cup on our side and our God not just on our side but suffering with us. Deriving confidence in this most awful situation from the lamb of God will be those who consciously forgo the development of an inner psychological osseous coat to protect them from what they inwardly are as indeed they will also forgo the development of an outer osseous carapace or coat to protect them from the devouring dangers around them. In this regard they will be choosing to go by another evolutionary way than that of the armadillo. And this they will do, and continue to do, even if in some analagous sense the landbridge between the Americas is restored and the predators are coming south.

The Tao Te Ching is emphatic:

When he is born, man is soft and weak; in death he becomes stiff and hard. The ten thousand creatures and all plants and trees while they are alive are supple and soft, but when they are dead they become brittle and dry. Truly, what is stiff and hard is a 'companion of death'; what is soft and weak is a 'companion of life'. Therefore 'the weapon that is too hard will be broken, the tree that is the hardest will be cut down'. Truly, that hard and mighty are cast down; the soft and weak set on high.

The osseous armadillo or the stripped and wholly vulnerable Lamb of God. Inevitably, and wisely perhaps, many of us will compromise. But having done so, we might remember that in one of his incarnations the Buddha offered himself to the uncompromising jaws of a lioness who, having found no prey for almost a month, was returning now, the first staggers of death in her, to her cubs. In another version of this story, there were two prospective Buddhas, the one who so unhesitatingly sacrificed himself and another who, anxiously concerned for his spiritual development, was most careful to preserve himself. When, after innumerable further incarnations, this latter Buddha finally arrived at his goal, the other was already there waiting for him. Had been waiting for him for aeons. It reminds us of Standing Mouse who, although he sacrificed his eyes, one to a blind buffalo and the other to a blind wolf, so that they might see, nonetheless found his way to Medicine River, found his way to the Great Sun Door above and beyond the eagles who, governed almost totally by instinct, were still looking down.

In Buddh Gaia, when we finally come home to it, there will be fear, there will be terror. Even some there will be who will experience Pascal's terror:

Le silence éternel de ces espaces infinis m'effraye.

The only good answer to Pascal's night of terror is Pascal's night of fire:

L'an de grâce 1654
Lundi, 23 novembre, jour de Saint Clément, pape
et martyr et autres au martyrologe
Veille de Saint Chrysogone, martyr, et autres,
Depuis environ dix heures et demie du soir jusques environ minuit et demie,

Feu

Dieu d'Abraham, Dieu d'Isaac, Dieu de Jacob,
Non des philosophes et des savants.
Certitude. Certitude. Sentiment. Joie. Paix. …
Oubli du monde et de tout, hormis Dieu. …
'le monde ne t'a point connu, mais je t'ai connu.'
Joie, joie, joie, pleurs de joie.

Pascal's night of fire.
And Suso's noon of heavenly lightnings.

In the first days of his conversion, it happened upon the feast of St Agnes, when the convent had breakfasted at midday, that the Servitor went into the choir. He was alone, and he placed himself in the last stall on the prior's side. And he was in much suffering, for a heavy trouble weighed upon his heart. And being there alone, and devoid of all consolations – no one by his side, no one near him – of a sudden his soul was wrapt in the body, or out of his body. Then did he see and hear that which no tongue can express. That which the Servitor saw had no form, neither any manner of being; yet he had of it a joy such as he might have known in the seeing of the shapes and substances of all joyful things. His heart was hungry yet satisfied, his soul was full of contentment and joy; his prayers and hopes were all fulfilled. And the friar could do nought but contemplate this Shining Brightness; and he altogether forgot himself and all other things. Was it day or night? He knew not. It was as it were a manifestation of the sweetness of Eternal Life in the sensations of silence and rest. Then he said, 'If that which I see and feel be not the Kingdom of Heaven, I know not what it can be: for it is very sure that the endurance of all possible pains were but a poor price to pay for the eternal possession of so great a joy.'

This ecstasy lasted from half an hour to an hour and whether his soul were in the body or out of the body he could not tell. But when he came to his senses it seemed to him that he returned from another world. And so greatly did his body suffer in this short rapture that it seemed to him that none, even in dying, could suffer so greatly in so short a time. The Servitor came to himself moaning, and he fell down upon the ground like a man who swoons. And he cried inwardly, heaving great sighs from the depth of his soul, and saying, 'Oh my God, where was I and where am I?' And again, 'Oh my heart's joy, never shall my soul forget this hour!' He walked, but it was but his body that walked, as a machine might do. None knew from his demeanour that which was taking place within. But his soul and his spirit were full of marvels; heavenly lightnings passed and repassed in the deeps of his being and …

Pascal's night of fire.
Suso's noon of heavenly lightnings.
Teresa of Avila's transverberation.

It pleased the Lord that I should sometimes see the following vision. I would see beside me, on my left hand, an angel in bodily form – a type of vision which I am not in the habit of seeing, except very rarely. Though I often see representations of angels, my visions of them are of the type which I first mentioned. It pleased the Lord that I should see this angel in the following way. He was not tall, but short, and very beautiful, his face so aflame that he appeared to be one of the highest types of angel who seem to be all afire. They must be those who are called Cherubim; they do not tell me their names but I am well aware that there is a great difference between certain angels and others, and between these and others still of a kind that I could not possibly explain. In his hands I saw a long golden spear and at the end of the iron tip I seemed to see a point of fire. With this he seemed to pierce my heart several times so that it penetrated to my entrails. When he drew it out, I thought that he was drawing them out with it, and he left me completely afire with a great love for God. The pain was so sharp that it made me utter several moans; and so excessive was the sweetness caused me by this intense pain that one can never wish to lose it, nor will one's soul be content with anything less than God. It is not bodily pain, but spiritual, though the body has a large share in it – indeed a great share. So sweet are the colloquies of love which pass between the soul and God that if anyone thinks I am lying, I beseech God, in his goodness, to give him the same experience.

A heavenly spear, fire at the point of it, in Black Elk's hand.

A heavenly spear, fire at the point of it, in the angel's hand.

Teresa transverberated and, dare we say it, the Blue Man transverberated.

Vritra transverberated.

Suso, St Teresa and Pascal telling us that neither inwardly nor outwardly is our Ultima Thule the limit.

All Danavas, all restrainers of life, restraining it so tightly that none of us now can hear the roaring of Medicine River.

All Danavas transverberated, all Danavas become bhaktas, become Gopis, their love of him compelling their high God to be lovable, their love of him compelling their high God to become incarnate as Krishna, their love for her compelling Buddh Gaia to become Bhudevi.

Krishna, the Blue God, playing flute music in Vrindavan.

Radha and Krishna.

Shepherd and Shulamite.

I am the rose of Sharon, and the lily of the valleys. As the lily among thorns, so is my love among the daughters. As the apple tree among the trees of the wood, so is my beloved among the sons. I sat down under his shadow with great delight, and his fruit was sweet to my taste. He brought me to the banqueting house, and his banner over me was love. Stay me with flagons, comfort me with apples, for

I am sick of love. His left hand is under my head, and his right hand doth embrace me. I charge you, O ye daughters of Jerusalem, by the roes, and by the hinds of the field, that ye stir not up, nor awake my love, till he please. The voice of my beloved! Behold, he cometh leaping upon the mountains, skipping upon the hills. My beloved is like a roe or a young hart; behold, he standeth behind our wall, he looketh forth at the windows, showing himself through the lattice. My beloved spoke, and said unto me, Rise up, my love, my fair one, and come away. For, lo, the winter is past, the rain is over and gone, the flowers appear on the earth, the time of the singing of birds is come, and the voice of the turtle is heard in our land. The fig tree putteth forth her green figs and the vines with the tender grape give a good smell. Arise, my love, my fair one, and come away.

Black Elk has stabbed the Blue Asura, has transverberated the great and terrible Danava, and, lo, we can hear the roaring of Medicine River.

Black Elk has stabbed the Blue Asura, has transverberated the Vritra who is doing to us what he did to Darwin and, lo, 'the fig tree putteth forth her green figs' in Tiere Gaste. But neither Parsifal nor Galahad nor Gawain can see that. And they cannot see it because they haven't yet realized that the everyday light of their minds and eyes is the whyght samyte that eclipses the Grail. Eclipse, they haven't yet realized, is from within themselves. Tiere Gaste, they haven't yet realized, is from within themselves. And so it must be that Sir Gawain will come to Chateau Merveil. It must be that, invited to stay for the night, he will lie on a bed called Liz de la Mervoille, his chonyid bardo bed.

As with Job, so with Sir Gawain: 'When I say my bed shall comfort me, my couch shall ease my complaint, then thou scarest me with dreams, and terrifiest me through visions, so that my soul chooseth strangling and death, rather than my life.'

Night when the King of Terrors is given a free hand to do as he wills with us.

Night when, with the Psalmist, we say, 'Fearfulness and trembling are come upon me, and horror hath overwhelmed me.'

Night when, pliant and compliant, we take the shape whatever nightmare is nightmaring us.

Night when, like the phoenix, we catch fire.

Night when, karmically, our psyches come to the boil, boil over.

> At midnight on the Emperor's pavement flit
> Flames that no faggot feeds, nor steel has lit,
> Nor storm disturbs, flames begotten of flame,
> Where blood-begotten spirits come
> And all complexities of fury leave

> Dying into a dance
> An agony of trance
> An agony of flame that cannot singe a sleave.

There are, William, purifying fires that aren't imaginary, aren't figments of our guilt. They are real, and purifying us, they bring us to the boil, so much so that sometimes our room is filled with vapourized moral pollution, filled as it were with the steam from an inner witch's cauldron. It might indeed be that the flames that boil this karmic cauldron cannot singe a material sleave, but they are real. Spiritually, they are real. And they do cause nightsweats.

> Double, double, toil and trouble;
> Fire burn, and cauldron bubble.

The cauldron bubbled in John Bunyan:

But my original and inward pollution, that, that was my plague and my affliction; that I saw at a dreadful rate always putting forth itself within me, that I had the guilt of to amazement; by reason of that, I was more loathsome in mine own eyes than was a toad, and I thought I was so in God's eyes too; sin and corruption, I said, would as naturally bubble out of my heart, as water would bubble out of a fountain ...

Shoeing a horse, a farrier will apply the red–hot, iron shoe to the hoof and hold it there till it burns a shallow bed for itself, the burning hoof all the while giving off a smoke that smells like burning hair. Sometimes, and particularly when we have come as far as the emperor's pavement, it will seem that plague after plague are laid, as by a farrier, to the quick of our soul, and then we will know, by the smoke we will know, that it is above all in the golden smithies of Byzantium that we are likely to experience our *Walpurgis Nacht*.

When our karmic appendix bursts, any bed we happen to be lying on will be our chonyid bardo bed, will be our Liz de la Mervoille, and any house we happen to be in will be our Chateau Merveil, and any chapel we seek shelter in will be our Chapel Perilous.

One evening, at this stage long inured to the quest, Sir Gawain was riding through a dark forest. Night had only just fallen when he saw candlelight in front of him. Dismounting when he reached it, he crossed its threshold into Chapel Perilous. In it there was a bier, with a corpse very richly draped lying upon it. At the four corners of the bier there were four tall candles, their flames not flickering, not even when a gust of wind blew through the door. Still marvelling, he was suddenly alarmed to defensive posture when a hand, nothing but a hand holding a dagger, reached from a wall. Fight it he must, defeat it he must, or die. Approaching it to engage with it, it was suddenly a hand holding a halter or was it a bridle? But what wild horse would it fit? Into what wild worlds would that wild horse take him? Defeat it he must or go mad. Sir Gawain had crossed a very dangerous threshold. The least awful thing that could happen to him is that he would be the next corpse lying on the bier.

Chapel Perilous, Chateau Merveil and Liz de la Mervoille: terror that knights of the Grail Quest talk about are not at all comparable in awe-ful-ness to the terror and pure dread that some mystics experience. There is an Emptiness, a Dark, a No-thing-ness, a Void, that doesn't phenomenal-ize itself into this or that, into angel or demon, into hand holding a dagger or hand holding a halter, and it is precisely this fact, that it doesn't phe-nomenalize itself, that there is in it nothing for eye or ear, for touch, taste or smell, that there is in it nothing the mind can engage with, it is this emptiness, this not-anythingness, that induces such terror and dread in us. And yet, as time goes on, we begin to see, but not with our eyes, not with our minds, beyond our cry of Good Friday dereliction we see, that this not-anythingness isn't negative, isn't privative – it is Tenebrae, the con-templative dark in which, koshaless like Adam's skull at the foot of the cross, we wait upon God. Calling it a dark night, St John of the Cross says of it, that it is more lovely than the dawn.

And there is good news in this not just for Sir Gawain, there is good news in it for Captain Ahab. Although in different ways, both Gawain and Ahab are running the risk of the frightful calamity that engulfed Actaeon. Laying his head on the block more surely than he did at the green chapel, Gawain yearns for a vision of the uncovered Grail, he in other words yearns for the removal of the veil of whyght samyte that protects us from too sudden and too naked a vision of the Divine Effulgence. Believing that the visible world is a pasteboard mask, Ahab, harpoon in hand, sets out to rend it, and all the more vengefully will he rend it because he sometimes thinks that behind it he will find the great Nihil, the great Naught. And there we have it: the medieval quest and, since Kant, the modern quest. And thinking of this latter quest: in what way or ways does Ahab differ from Schopenhauer? In what way or ways does he differ from Wagner and the young Nietzsche, the somnambulist who is afraid to wake up? In what way or ways does he differ from Coleridge sitting in post-Kantian dejection, from Arnold turning away? Only in this perhaps: believing in the living act, the undoubted deed, he vengefully forged a diabolical harpoon.

Gotterdammerung on a stage in Bayreuth, ragnarok on the quarter-deck of the *Pequod*.

Ahab emerging from his cabin. Hitler emerging from his bunker.

And fate we might say – 'and fate is heard in the note of the Gjallarhorn'.

And Goldcomb crows from the birdwood, and Rustred crows from the bars of Hel, and Fjalar crows from the crossbeam of a gibbet.

The *Pequod* sails into Ginnungagap.

But which is it, we must now ask: is it whyght samyte covering a divine effulgence or is it a pasteboard mask covering a great Nihil, a great Naught?

A Christianity that has its source in the Triduum Sacrum can answer that question: to Semele and Actaeon, to Gawain and Ahab, to questing humanity in all ages and in all cultures, and to the questing Earth itself, it opens the door of a Tenebrae Temple.

There is no single evolutionary event since the Precambrian that can compare in importance with Tenebrae.

In the presence of the Tenebrae harrow we can estimate evolution. Journeying with it, following it through its nocturnes, we can estimate our own dignity, discovering, as we quench the candles, that it lies in our willingness to be divinely guided into the dereliction of Good Friday, and being in it and finding ourselves so totally without resource, there is now a chance that we will discover in ourselves a yearning and a willingness to be as out of God's way awake as we are in dreamless sleep. In a final surrender to the Divine invitation, we have crossed into the passive dark night of the spirit.

> O the mind, mind has mountains, cliffs of fall
> Frightful, sheer, no-man-fathomed. Hold them cheap
> May who ne'er hung there.

Following the Tenebrae harrow into and through its nocturnes, we come to see that for all its mountains and chasms and falls-frightful, mind itself is a kosha. To say this, though, is not to cheaply disregard the mountains and the chasms of our dreaming and waking. It is at our peril, particularly once we've set out on the spiritual journey, that we will ignore them.

Conscious and unconscious, psyche is the blind not the window.

Having considered the varieties of religious experience, William James concluded that 'there should be no premature closing of our account with reality.'

Think of Job and Jonah. Before catastrophe engulfed him, Job would not have known what Sir Thomas Browne was saying when he said, 'there is all Africa and her prodigies in us'. Neither, prior to the catastrophe that swallowed him, would Jonah have known what Jacob Boehme was saying when he said, 'In man is all whatsoever the sun shines upon or heaven contains, as are also hell and all the deeps'.

Had Moses, coming down from Mount Sinai, said only that, had he simply said, there should be no premature closing of our account with reality, and had we in every generation taken what he said seriously, then, surely, we wouldn't now be experiencing, as some say we are, the age of the world's night.

In the age of the world's night the abyss of the world must be experienced and endured.

In the age of the world's night someone willingly becomes nothing and in this nothing the world re-enacts its beginnings. This, surely, is what happened to, and in, Jesus.

In the age of the world's night someone returns to the beginning, becomes so inwardly empty as to be available to the beginning.

In the age of the world's night the Christian Nave stands out, as the *Beagle* did, into heavy south-westerlies. Out beyond Land's End and Finis Terre. Out, out, out into its Good Friday dereliction, out into the dark that was in the beginning, a dark in which there is no starboard and no larboard.

In the age of the world's night, we shouldn't be talking at all, maybe, about the Christian *Nave*, the tall ship that Chartres is, the tall ship that Cologne is. We should be talking rather about this tall ship becoming our Maidu raft:

In the beginning there was no sun, no moon, no stars. All was dark and every-where there was only water. A raft came floating on the water. It came from the north and in it were two persons – Turtle (A'noshma) and Father-of-the-Secret Society (Pelieipe). The stream flowed very rapidly. Then from the sky a rope of feathers, called Pokelma, was let down, and down it came Earth-Initiate. When he reached the end of the rope, he tied it to the bow of the raft, and stepped in. His face was covered and was never seen, but his body shone like the sun. He sat down, and for a long time said nothing. At last A'noshma said, 'Where do you come from?' and Earth-Initiate answered, 'I come from above.' Then A'noshma said, 'Brother, can you not make for me some good dry land, so that I may some-times come up out of the water?' Then he asked another time, 'Are there going to be any people in the world?' Earth-Initiate thought awhile, and then he said, 'Yes'. A'noshma asked, 'How long before you are going to make people?' Earth-

Initiate replied, 'I don't know. You want to have some dry land; well, how am I going to get any earth to make it of?' A'noshma answered, 'If you will tie a rock about my left arm, I'll dive for some.' Earth-Initiate did as Turtle asked, and then, reaching around, took the end of a rope from somewhere, and tied it to Turtle. When Earth-Initiate came to the raft, there was no rope there; he just reached out and found one. Turtle said, 'If the rope is not long enought, I'll jerk it once, and you must haul me up; if it is long enough, I'll give two jerks, and then you must pull me up quickly, as I shall have all the earth that I can carry.' Just as Turtle went over the side of the boat, Father-of-the-Secret Society began to shout loudly.

Turtle was gone a long time. He was gone six years; and when he came up he was covered in green slime, he had been down so long. When he reached the top of the water, the only earth he had was a very little under his nails; the rest had all washed away. Earth-Initiate took with his right hand a stone knife from under his left armpit, and carefully scraped the earth out from under Turtle's nails. He put the earth in the palm of his hand, and rolled it around till it was round; it was as large as a small pebble. He laid it on the stern of the raft. By and by he went to look at it; it had not grown at all. The third time he went to look at it, it had grown so that it could be spanned by the arms. The fourth time he looked, it was as big as the world, the raft was aground, and all around were mountains as far as he could see.

When the raft had come to land, Turtle said, 'I can't stay in the dark all the time. Can't you make a light, so that I can see?' Earth-Initiate replied, 'Let us get out of the raft, and then we will see what we can do.' So all three go out. Then Earth-Initiate said, 'Look that way, to the east! I am going to tell my sister to come up.' Then it began to grow light, and day began to break; then Father-of-the-Secret Society began to shout loudly, and the sun came up. Turtle said, 'Which way is the sun going to travel?' Earth-Initiate answered, 'I'll tell her to go this way, and go down there.' After the sun went down, Father-of-the-Secret Society began to cry and to shout again, and it grew very dark. Earth-Initiate asked Turtle and Father-of-the-Secret Society 'How do you like it?' and they both answered, 'It is very good.' Then Earth-Initiate answered, 'No, I am going to do more yet.' Then he called the stars each by its name, and they came out. When this was done, Turtle asked, 'Now, what shall we do?' Earth-Initiate replied, 'Wait and I'll show you.' Then he made a tree grow at Ta'doiko – the tree called Hu'kimtsa; and Earth-Initiate and Turtle and Father-of-the-Secret Society sat in its shade for two days. The tree was very large and had twelve different kinds of acorn growing on it. After they had sat for two days under the tree, they all went off to see the world that Earth-Initiate had made ....

Turtle was gone a long time. So was Jesus. Seeking to allow the universe to reenact its beginnings in the nothingness that he would become, seeking to allow the universe to remember and re-enact its highest intuitions of itself in him, he crossed the Kedron. There was green slime on him when he came back and now the Christian rosary, the Great Biography, has blossomed into five new mysteries, five mystical mysteries:

> Jesus Grand-Canyon-deep in the world's karma.
> Jesus on the Hill of the Koshaless Skull
> A'noshma Jesu
> Jesu Anadyomene
> Jivanmukta Jesus preaching his first Evangelanta sermon.

Ananta coiling herself into a raft for Vishnu.
Tiamat coiling herself into a raft for Marduk.
Tannin coiling herself into a raft for Baal.
Typhon coiling herself into a raft for Zeus.
Leviathan coiling herself into a raft for Jesus.

Jesus, our A'noshma, slipping over the side. Jesus going down. Going down, down, down into the Abyss that was before world was or psyche was. Down in search of the Divine, Night-of-Brahma intuitions, myths, metaphors and mahavakyas with which, in the age of the world's night, we can once again come ashore.

In the depths, becoming nothing, he became song, the song of the world's return, of our return:

> Te Kore
> Te Kore tua-tahi
> Te Kore tua-rua
> Te Kore-nui
> Te Kore-roa
> Te Kore-para
> Te Kore-whiwhia
> Te Kore-rawea
> Te Kore te tamaua
> Te Po
> Te Po-teki
> Te Po-terea
> Te Po-whawha
> Hine-Make-moe
> Te Ata
> Te Au-tu-roa
> Te Ao-marama
> Whai-Tua
> Maku
> Mahora-nui-a-rangi
> Rangi potiki
> Papa

New heavens, new earth.

Jesus sowing the new earth with the intuitions, metaphors, myths, mahavakyas of the Mandukya Yuga.

A hand, still green with the slime of the pre-cosmic Abyss, sowing the earth with the seeds of a new culture.

Mouths, still green with the slime of the pre-cosmic Abyss, singing the Mandukya Om in Ta'doiko.

And what else but Om vibrations, vibrating light, are the stars that shine above Ta'doiko.

Ta'doiko; our new Tep Zepi, our new Tai-wer.

In and from Ta'doiko we can begin again.

Then he [Earth-Initiate] made a tree grow at Ta'doiko, the tree called Hu'kimtsa: and Earth-Initiate and Turtle and Father-of-the-Secret Society sat in its shade for two days. The tree was very large and had twelve different kinds of acorns growing on it. After they had sat for two days under the tree they all went off to see the world that Earth-Initiate had made. ... While they were gone Coyote and his dog Rattlesnake came out of the ground ...

So now, even now, here in Ta'doiko, we must come to terms with Rattlesnake. And there are, maybe, only two ways in which to do this. We might call them the Christian way and the Hopi way. Setting its religiously hoofed heel on his head, Christianity would crush him. The Hopi, on the other hand, would accommodate him, would enter into religious, into mystic, communion with him in a snake dance.

The Christian way, the biblical way, hasn't worked. But the biblical way isn't a homogeneous way. Within the biblical way is the way of Job, the way of a man who, at the invitation of his God, learned to stand psychically unlobotomized on the unlobotomized earth.

Job's way. A reversal of the biblical way. A reversal of the way of Gilgamesh.

In the beginning of our Western white way, Gilgamesh, a culture hero, and Enkindu, a tamed wild man of the steppes, went east, intending murder, to Huwawa's cedar forest. It was a long journey. As we in the west understand things, it was a heroic journey. And as we would expect, Huwawa was vanquished. Huwawa died. No one mourned him. No one wept for him. It occurred to no one to stand up in Uruk and call out that lobotomizing the earth, lobotomizing the psyche, isn't the good way. No sibyl foresaw that, in the person of Nebuchadnezzar, Gilgamesh would regress to a state of brutality from which, in his condition of natural wildness, Enkidu was altogether exempt. Nebuchadnezzar is portent. Like a Goya's Giant, he haunts the horizons of our history.

Confronted as we now are by the calamities, cultural and psychological, of our ancient Middle-eastern, Mediterranean way, maybe we should be hospitable to an alternative way, the way, perhaps, of the Kwakiutl.

Traditionally, the Kwakiutl lived between the cedar forest and the sea's entrall. And in their winter ceremonies called Tsetsekia, they welcomed the Huwawas of the one and the Leviathans of the other into their firelight.

Job's Tsetsekia. Job beholding Behemoth. And we must remember that when his God invited Job to behold, he was inviting him not only to look, he was inviting him to psychologically accommodate, to cosmologically accommodate what he was seeing. He was inviting him to adjust to heads, his own head included, that he would never bridle.

Job beholding Leviathan. The Kwakiutl beholding the Great Iakim:

> The Great Iakim will rise from below;
> He makes the sea boil, the Great Iakim,
> And we are afraid.

The story of Job. Job being, to begin with, not unlike the New England colt that Melville talks about in *Moby-Dick*:

Tell me, why this strong, young colt, foaled in some peaceful valley of Vermont, far removed from all beasts of prey – why is it that upon the sunniest day, if you but shake a fresh buffalo robe behind him, so that he cannot even see it, but only smells its wild, animal muskiness – why will he start, snort, and with bursting eyes paw the ground in phrensies of affright? There is no remembrance in him of any gorings of wild creatures in his green northern home, so that the strange muskiness he smells cannot recall to him anything associated with the experience of former perils; for what knows he, this New England colt, of the black bisons of distant Oregon?

No; but here thou beholdest, even in a dumb brute, the instinct of the knowledge of the demonism of the world. Though thousands of miles from Oregon, still when he smells that savage musk, the rending, goring bison herds are as present as to the deserted, wild foal of the prairies, which this instant they may be trampling into dust.

The colt and the chicks.

The experiment on the chicks was simple. The chicks that were chosen had been hatched out under an infrared lamp. They had no contact at any time with adults of their own species. They had, therefore, learned nothing from them. And yet, when the experimenter moved his model of a hawk above them, they scurried in terror for cover. Slightly deforming his model, he moved it above them again, and again they scurried. Deforming his model till it looked like a pigeon, not like a hawk, he moved it above them yet again, but now it evoked no terrified reaction, it evoked no response at all. The conclusion was obvious; the image of hawk and the response that it triggers are innate in the chick.

'For what knows he, this New England colt, of the black bisons of distant Oregon?'

Oregon isn't distant. Oregon is where we are. The valley in Vermont that is grazed by the colt and the valley in Oregon that is grazed by bison are the same valley, the same Frazer canyon, for, as Nietzsche has it, 'the old human and animal world, indeed the entire prehistory and past of all sentient being, works on, loves on, hates on, thinks on, in me'.

The colt and the chick. And the professor of Greek at Basle university whose religion and culture left him, as they have left the rest of us, 'helpless before the contents of our own minds'.

Oregon, Olduvai Gorge and the Grand Canyon are suburbs we live in. We live in them without the hospitalities of Kwakiutl firelight to all that borders the little clearing of consciousness, without the hospitalities of Tsetsekia firelight to all that lives in the cedar forest and in the sea's entrall.

The Tsetsekia in which the Kwakiutl integrated their canyon. The Tsetsekia in which we must integrate ours.

Job's Tsetsekia.

The Tsetsekia that enacted itself in a modern city: I am walking in Soho, in London. But it could be Aristotle walking in Athens. It could be Isaiah walking in Jerusalem. It could be Nebuchadnezzar walking in Babylon. It could be Gilgamesh walking in Uruk. It could be Nietzsche walking in Basle. It could be Kurtz walking in Brussels, the sepulchral city. Indeed, it could be Kurtz ascending the primeval river. It could be a colt following a hidden geological fault-line in his green valley in Vermont. Under that valley, as under Old Compton Street, is Bright Angel Trail.

I am walking in Soho. I am walking, that is, in the red-light area of my own psyche. I turn in to Old Compton Street. A little way down it, drawing gaudy attention to itself on the other side, I see a striptease club I used to visit when I was younger. I cross the street and go in. I am immediately as if were becalmed. I am in a state of silent wonder. The wonder is altogether older and bigger than I am. The individual I am, or was, is somehow dissolved in the eternal sea of it. Only the most ghostly suggestion of who or what I am survives in the wonder. And, independently of me, the wonder is wondering at the marvellous and great transformation that has taken place here. The old, dark, dingy atmosphere is gone. Gone also are the lurid allurings to priapic delight. It's as if an underworld had come overground. Or, rather, it is as if a cathedral crypt had come up into the choir, had become a choir. Vaguely, I am aware of striptease music upstairs, but it is the Salome veils in my mind and eyes that are falling away. They do fall away, all of them, and now I see. On the bright, sunlit ground floor where I am is rack after rack after rack of seaside, summer clothes. Like garments of light they are. Garments of paradisal light. All living instincts in me are becalmed in the wonder of them. It is wonder beyond words to me that they are all unisexual. I walk out into the street. Walking towards Wardour Street, I am aware that I have a four-pronged farm fork in my hand. On the prongs are scales of dry cow dung. I walk up Wardour Street. Naturally, like one state of mind replacing another, I am in an eighteenth-century park. Again, naturally, as I am walking in it, manure fork in hand, this park becomes a savannah. I do not see them, but maybe there are hominids in the bushes. Maybe Lucy is watching me. Crossing the savannah, I notice a patch of ground that looks different from its surroundings. I begin to dig, using the manure fork. I uncover three granite steps. Climbing down, I stand on the lowest of them. Below me, vastly, an oceanarium opens out. Altogether vaster than it physically is, it is here beside me, here, just here, below me, and yet, how far, far away, how unreachably far away, in both space and time, it is. On the far granite embankment of it there is a man. Bending forward, very slowly and very deliberately, from his hips, he reaches with both hands down into the water. The merest gesture of lifting on his part is sufficient. An immense iron grid rises up from underneath the water, upwards and backwards towards me, until, eventually, it is flush with the high embankment I am standing on. Something tremendous is happening in the water. Up from the depths a stupendous ocean boiling, green and blue, breaking to turquoise, is rising. Even before it breaks the surface, I see that it is an immense confusion or tangle of sea zoas, zoas of the benthos. Draped across them all, undulating downwards out of view, upwards into view, is a great snake-form. Seeing it, I call it a dogfish. Such a plenoma of insurgent aliveness in any one being I had never seen. Taigas and thunders bloomed from within him. Under his skin, shimmering there, were tundras and tropical rainforests. Everything outrageous and gorgeous that eyes have seen in time and eternity teemed there. Somehow, I took my eyes off him. But it can't have been me who broke the spell of pure beholding. It must have been the dream that was dreaming me that broke it. I was standing, far away, below, on the lower embankment, where the man who lifted the grid had stood. I was barefoot. An otter came past. I was frightened, afraid he would bite my small toe. Then I was sitting on the water, exactly where the tangle of sea zoas had emerged. Behind me, eyeing me, its mouth agape and watering for me, was a Mesozoic monster. Without looking around, I could see that it was getting ready to lunge at me. Suddenly it steadied itself, backing back so as to have a better run at me. Agape, his mouth was like a canyon. It was a living, gaping canyon that was coming to swallow me, but, at the last moment, it veered away to the right of me. Then again, backing furiously, he steadied himself. The chasm his mouth was, was watering for me. He came. This time, at the last moment, it veered away to the left of me. That's it, I thought, the rehearsals are over. Bottomlessly gaping, with a gaping that had perditions unheard of in it, he came. Surrendered to my fate, I waited. I was already in the valley of the shadow of death, or worse, when the great, swallowing thing became a harmless, small thing swimming away. I woke up.

The Tsetsekia in which the Kwakiutl ascended their river.

The Tsetsekia in which we must ascend ours.

'How beautiful upon the mountains are the feet of him that bringeth good tidings, that publisheth peace; that bringeth good tidings of good, that publisheth salvation; that saith unto' *homo habilis*, holding a manure fork in his hand, have no fear of the sea's entrall, have no fear of your mind's entrall.

> Eftsoones they saw an hideous host arrayed,
> Of huge sea monsters, such as living sense dismayed.
>
> Most ugly shapes, and horrible aspects,
> Such as Dame Nature selfe mote feare to see,
> Or shame, that ever should so fowle defects
> From her most cunning hand escaped bee;
> All dreadful pourtraicts of deformitie;
> Spring-headed Hydraes, and sea-shouldering whales,
> Great whirlpooles, which all fishes make to flee,
> Bright Scolopendraes, armed with silver scales,
> Mighty Monoceroses, with immeasured tayles
>
> The dreadful Fish, that hath deserv'd the name
> Of Death, and like him lookes in dreadful hew,
> The griesly Wasserman, that makes his game
> The flying ships with swiftnesse to pursew,
> The horrible sea-satyre, that doth shew
> His fearful face in time of greatest storme,
> Huge Ziffius, whom mariners eschew
> No lesse than rockes (as travellers informe)
> And greedy Rosmarines with visages deforme.

All these, and thousand thousands many more,
And more deformed monsters thousand fold
With dreadful noise, and hollow rombling rore,
Came rushing in the foamy waves enrold,
Which seemed to fly for feare, them to behold;
Ne wonder, if these did the knight appall;
For all that here on earth we dreadful hold,
Be but as bugs to fearen babes withal,
Compared to creatures in the sea's entrall.

The New England colt. Sir Guyon, the appalled knight. And Nietzsche.

In the absence of Kwakiutl firelight in his culture, Nietzsche didn't survive, didn't safely or sanely survive, the shaking of the fresh buffalo robe behind him. He didn't survive the lifting of our inner suppressing grid.

Dionysus is in a sense the God who shakes the fresh buffalo robe behind us.

Robe of all our terrors. Terrors of the colt. Terrors of the chick.

Robe of every terror that was ever experienced.

Robe, however deeply buried they might be, of Palaeozoic, Mesozoic and Cainozoic terrors.

When as Bullman, or as effeminate and smiling boy, Dionysus shakes that robe behind us, the conventions of everyday, ordinary living are swept away and without knowing why, we are on the mountain, dancing wildly. *Oreibasia* it used to be called, this mountain dancing, and it was the first act in a play of five acts, the others being *sparagmos, omophagia, enthusiasmos* and *ekstasis.*

Not a good way to deal with your own discovery, Friedrich. Not a good way to deal with the 'hollow, rombling rore' from the cedar forest, from the sea's entrall. Not a good way to deal with Wordsworth's awareness of human inwardness:

> Not chaos, not
> The darkest pit of lowest Erebus
> Nor aught of blinder vacancy scooped out
> By help of dreams – can breed such fear and awe
> As fall upon us often when we look
> Into our minds, into the Mind of Man ...

The terrible epopteia.

The epopteia that becomes agon. In Job it became agon. In Jesus Transtorrentem it became an agony of redemptive integration. And even

though the sufferings of the Greek tragic stage were in a sense re-enact-
ments of the sufferings of Dionysus, in neither himself nor in his suffering surrogates or epigonoi did Dionysus cross the Ilissus as Jesus crossed
the Kedron.

A great, hopeful hush fell upon the Greek tragic stage the day Jesus
crossed the Kedron. Dionysus, its divine sponsor and patron, was suddenly
an old God. He had a choice: either to follow where Jesus led or become
a historical curiosity.

In Gethsemane, Jesus wasn't a colt in a green valley in Vermont when,
suddenly, someone shook a fresh buffalo robe behind him. In Jesus, the
robe emerged from within. Integrated and redeeemed, it came to the surface in him. And so, never again would it be merely the backdrop to a
tragic stage.

Jesus having left his Good Friday face in it, Christianity doesn't throw
in the towel this side of the Ilissus, this side of the Kedron.

Putting up the hero's sword, Jesus walked into the cedar forest. Not
playing a taming lyre, he walked into the sea's entrall. Cedar forest and
sea's entrall; between them we live.

'This is what I believe', D.H. Lawrence says:

'That I am I.'
'That my soul is a dark forest.'
'That my known self will never be more than a little clearing in the forest.'
'That gods, strange gods, come forth from the forest into the clearing of my
known self, and then go back.
'That I must have the courage to let them come and go.'
'That I will never let mankind put anything over me, but that I will try always
to recognize and submit to the gods in me and the gods in other men and
women.'

The Kwakiutl would suggest that it isn't only gods who come out of
the forest into the clearing. Dzoonokw comes out. Bukwus comes out.
From the forest at the northern end of the world Hohokw comes out.
Hohokw and his horde. Out of it comes Baxbakualanuxiwae. Out of the
sea's entrall comes Gomogwa, comes Numxilexiu. Numxilexiu throws a
big wave before him. Out of it comes the Great Iakim:

> The Great Iakim will rise from below;
> He makes the sea boil, the Great Iakim,
> And we are afraid.

From the sea's entrall, the Great Iakim. From the entrall of the cedar
forest, Huwawa.

Huwawa and Dzoonokw.

Here comes the Great Dzoonokw who carries off humans in her arms, who gives us nightmares, who makes us faint. Great Bringer of Nightmares! Great Lady who makes us faint. Terrible Dzoonokw!

Think of them, Sion and Athens. Sion in which we sing Psalm eight. Athens in which we sing the second stasimon. For all their deinanthropic glories, however, what else but Kwakiutl villages are these cities? What else after evensong are they but sea-level settlements as open as ever the Sumerian night-mind was to Huwawa emerging from the cedar forest, as open as ever the Kwakiutl night-mind was to Gomogwa emerging from the sea's entrall?

Which will best protect us, city wall or Tsetsekia?

In which will we find good guidance, in the strophes of the second stasimon or in the nocturnes of Tenebrae?

Exchanging our city wall for the ceremonial welcome of the sea-level settlement, exchanging the *yu wei* of the strophes for the *wu wei* of the nocturnes, we might indeed build another Sion, we might indeed build another Athens.

The excluding wall going down, as it did in Job. The repressing grid going up.

In Job the grid and the wall gave way to Tsetsekia.

What happened in Job happened in Jesus. In Jesus also, however, the strophes fell away, unable to watch, unable to stay awake, during the nocturnes.

Dare we imagine it? At the point where *Pequod* culture went under, *Tehom uttered his voice and lifted up his hands on high.* In the voice and in the hands a last biblical book. In the voice and in the hands a Tehom Te Ching.

The snake we project into the rope. The Abyss we project into Tehom.

In St John of the Cross, our rock of faith dissolves into what he calls the Abyss of faith. It would be altogether more true to what happens, however, had he called it not the abyss of faith but the Tehom of faith, or, having the ritual mind, the Tenebrae of faith.

Tsetsekia we need, and Tenebrae.

It will sometimes seem right and appropriate to sing Psalm eight in Sion. It will sometimes seem right and appropriate to sing the second stasimon in Athens. But how arrogantly odd it would seem were Sir Gawain to sing either one or the other of them as he crosses its threshold into Chapel Perilous. How arrogantly odd it would seem were

Tutankhamen to sing either one or the other of them when, archetypally deep in his psyche, he lies on the bed of the Divine Cow. How arrogantly odd it would seem were Ishmael to sing either one or the other of them when, washed up at last, he hears Huwawa coming from the cedar forest, Ziffius coming from the sea's entrall.

It isn't only modern, naturalistic literature that has left us helpless before the contents of our own minds. Christianity, relying on its 'thou shalt nots', hasn't watched with us, hasn't walked to the end below of Bright Angel Trail with us. Having refused Gethsemane, in its modern form, Christianity cannot therefore speak comfortably to us.

Having their Red Cedar Bark ceremonies, their Tsetsekia, having their hospitable, if terrifying, firelight, the Kwakiutl are less helpless, perhaps, than we are.

Red Cedar Bark ceremonies we need, Tsetsekia we need, not peremptory banishment to eternal punishment in an eternal hell. Milton's final solution hasn't worked. The *malleus maleficarum* that he put in the 'dredded' hand of the Christ child only means that, built like Knossos above a labyrinth, our civilization is seismically unsafe.

In the city, savannah.

In the city, *homo habilis* holding a farm fork in a hand that is structurally homologous to the fin of a shark, to the foot of a crocodile.

In the city, *homo regressus* uncovering an inner Bright Angel Trail of three stone steps. A step called the Cainozoic, a step called the Mesozoic, a step called the Palaeozoic.

Regression and return.

Homo regressus bringing back Good News from a canyon in Lucy's savannah. Good News about our prospects as a species. Good News from within his nature for Anthropus.

Healing an individual, psychoanalytically, in his or her past.

Healing a people culturally in their cultural past.

Tsetsekia in Athens. Tsetsekia in Jerusalem. Tsetsekia in Babylon. Tsetsekia in Uruk.

Gilgamesh, King of Uruk, inviting Huwawa, Lord of the cedar forest, into his city.

Huwawa, Hohokw, Dzoonokw, Bukwus.

Great Iakim, Shalyat, Yam, Tannin, Tiamat, Typhon, Leviathan,

Inviting all who inhabit the cedar forest and the sea's entrall into our city.

Letting the repressing grid go up, sacredly, for a sacred few days.

The holy fear of the uncontrollable forces in human nature and the consequent strict resistance to the animal instincts and energies, which characterize the common history of man from the earliest taboo to the latest moral tract, can be explained as the result and residue of devastating experiences in the past of the race and the by-product of the successful, historical struggle for independence of a higher, 'purer', spiritual principle. The primitive forces out of the depths of which this principle arose, like the victorious sun, Sol Invictus, climbing the heavens out of the stormy sea (the turbulent abode of the monsters of the deep), had to be checked, held at bay and tied back, like the Greek Titans imprisoned under volcanic Aetna, or like the Great Dragon of the Revelation of St John. The very real peril of an elementary upheaval and rocking outburst led to the construction of dichotomic systems, such as those not only of Jainism and the Shankhya, but also of the Persian Zoroastrian ethical religion, the Gnosis of the Near East, Christianity, Manichaeism, and the usual codes of manners of primitive and civilized mankind.

In India, in the ancient world, and among most of the people known to anthropologists and historians, there has been, however, an institutionalized system of festivals – festivals of the gods and genii of vegetation – whereby, without danger to the community, the conventional fiction of good and evil could be suspended for a moment and an experience permitted of the mighty Titan-powers of the deep. Carnival, the day of masks, revealing all the odd forms that dwell in the profundities of the soul, spills forth its symbols, and for one dream-like, nightmarish, sacred day, the ordered timid consciousness freely revels in a sacramentally canalized experience of its own destruction. The masks are dream-like. Dreamlike also are the carnival events. Indeed, the world of sleep into which we descend every night, when the tensions of consciousness are relaxed, is precisely that from which the demons, elves, divine and devilish figures of the world mythologies have all been derived. All the gods dwell within us, willing to support us, and capable of supporting us, but they require the submission of consciousness, on abdication of sovereignty on the part of our conscious wills. In so far, however, as the little ego regards its own plans as the best, it resists rigorously the forces of its divine substratum. The gods thereupon become dangerous for it, and the individual becomes his own hell. The ancient peoples made peace with the excluded forces by holding them in worship and allowing them their daemonic carnival – even while cultivating, simultaneously, under the forms of sacrifices to the higher gods, a fruitful relationship with the forces implicated in the social system. And by this means they won the permission, so to speak, of their own unconscious to continue in the conventional conscious attitude of profitable virtue.

Tsetsekia or Carnival?

Given that it is to beings such as Tiamat and Huwawa that we would be culturally hospitable, surely it is Tsetsekia, rather than Carnival, that is called for.

Tsetsekia for the great beings, Carnival for the lesser beings.

Tsetsekia for Tiamat, for Huwawa. Carnival for Centaur and sea-satyre.

The great calamity: our Old Testament hostility to her turned Leviathan into Rahab.

Ahab's hostility to him turned the White Whale into Moby-Dick:

Days, weeks passed, and under easy sail, the ivory *Pequod* had slowly swept across four several cruising grounds; that of the Azores; of the Cape De Verdes; on the Plate (so called) being off the mouth of the Rio de La Plata; and the Carrol Ground, an unstaked, watery locality, southerly from St Helena.

It was while gliding through these latter waters, that one serene and moonlight night, when all the waves rolled by like scrolls of silver; and, by their soft ,suffusing, seethings, made what seemed a silvery silence, not a solitude; on such a silent night a silvery jet was seen far in advance of the white bubbles of the bow. Lit up by the moon, it looked celestial; seemed some plumed and glittering God uprising from the sea.

Moment when their veil of biblical whyght samyte fell from our eyes.

Moment when their veil of secular whyght samyte fell from our eyes.

Moment when we saw divinity in the depths.

Argo, Nave, Mayflower, Beagle, Pequod.

Moment when our Western voyage might have sailed into and through a crisis of re-appraisal, a crisis of conversion.

That Carrol cruising-ground was our other Galapagos, our Atlantic Galapagos, a Galapagos altogether greater in its consequences for our understanding of ourselves and our voyage than the Galapagos of iguanas and finches that Darwin walked in.

Let us tack and tack again towards the Carrol Ground. Let us cruise there in the hope that we might be awakened, from waking and sleeping, by Fedallah's cry:

Days, weeks passed, and under easy sail, the ivory *Pequod* had slowly swept across four several cruising-grounds; that off the Azores; off the Cape de Verdis; on the Plate (so called) being off the mouth of the Rio de La Plata; and the Carrol Ground, an unstaked, watery locality, southerly from St Helena.

It was while gliding through these latter waters that one serene and moonlight night, when all the waves rolled by like scrolls of silver; and by their soft, suffusing seethings, made what seemed a silvery silence not a solitude; on such a silent night a silvery jet was seen far in advance of the white bubbles of the bow. Lit up by the moon, it looked celestial; seemed some plumed and glittering god uprising from the sea. Fedallah first descried this jet. For of these moonlight nights, it was his work to mount to the main-mast head, and stand a look-out there, with the same precision as if it had been day. And yet, though herds of whales were seen by night, not one whaleman in a hundred would venture a lowering for them. You may think with what emotions, then, the seamen beheld this old Oriental perched aloft at such unusual hours; his turban and the moon, comparisons in one sky. But when, after spending his uniform interval there for several successive nights without uttering a single sound; when, after all this silence, his unearthly voice was heard announcing that silvery, moon-lit jet, every reclining mariner started to his feet as if some winged spirit had lighted in the rigging, and hailed the mortal crew, 'There she blows.'

Silent night on the Carrol cruising-ground.

Silent night, holy night, when all the waves rolled by like scrolls of silver.

Night when, the whyght samyte fallen from his eyes, Fedallah cried.

Night when the Arthurian phase of the Grail Quest was accomplished.

Night when the turn among mortals that Hölderlin talks about might have taken place:

> ... The heavenly powers
> Cannot do all things. It is mortals
> Who reach sooner into the abyss. So the turn is
> With these. Long is
> The time, but the true comes into
> Its own.

There are two ways of reaching into the Abyss; the way of Jesus and A'noshma; and the way of Ahab and his crew – the way, that is, that Western culture is now reaching into it:

But, at last, when turning to the eastward, the Cape winds began howling around us, and we rose and fell upon the long, troubled seas that are there; when the ivory-tusked *Pequod* sharply bowed to the blast, and gored the dark waves in her madness, till, like showers of silver chips, the foam-flakes flew over her bulwarks; then all this desolate vacuity of life went away, but gave place to sights more dismal than before.

Close to our bows, strange forms in the water darted hither and thither before us; while thick in our rear flew the inscrutable sea-ravens. And every morning, perched on our stays, rows of these birds were seen; and in spite of our hootings, for a long time obstinately clung to the hemp, as though they deemed our ship some drifting, uninhabited craft; a thing appointed to desolation, and therefore fit roosting place for their homeless selves. And heaved and heaved, still unrestingly heaved the black sea, as if its vast tides were a conscience; and the great mundane soul were in anguish and remorse for the long sin and suffering it had bred.

Pequod culture: our culture a thing appointed to desolation.

A ghostly *Argo*, its only sail the buffalo robe of all our terrors.

A ghostly *Pequod*, its only argosy the ghostly voice of Ahab:

But do I look very old, so very, very old, Starbuck? I feel deadly faint, and bowed, and humped, as though I were Adam staggering beneath the piled centuries since Paradise.
God! God! God!

We all stagger beneath them, to some extent, don't we, Ahab?

Having taken them on consciously, seeking to redeem them, Jesus staggered under them.

The cedar forest
The sea's entrall
The buffalo robe of all our terrors
The piled centuries since paradise.

All of these Jesus took on. All of these he endured. His endurance of them is called his passion. There are those who say that his passion is an unfinished symphony. Some there are, therefore, who, given a share in it, seek to complete it with him.

A Holy Thursday Tsetsekia is one way in which we might ritually participate with him in his passion.

Tsetsekia and Tenebrae.

The Christian raft coming home with two rituals; Tsetsekia and Tenebrae; and with five new mysteries in its rosary; Jesus Grand-Canyon-deep in the world's karma, Jesus on the hill of the koshaless skull, A'noshma Jesus, Jesus Anadyomne, Jivamukhta Jesus preaching his first Evangelanta sermon.

Calvary and Golgotha are one and the same summit of one and the same hill, and yet an astounding gulf, in depth and height, yawns between them. And it might be that Jesus carried the cross, had to carry it, only as far as the summit we call Calvary. On the summit called Golgotha, the summit of the koshaless skull, the cross would have been an unhelpful distraction.

The Holy Week of Evangel and the Holy Week of Evangelanta are one and the same Holy Week, and yet, a stupendous gulf, in both height and depth, yawns between them. In evangel we have Holy Thursday in the Garden of Olives, Good Friday on Calvary, and Easter in the Garden of the Sepulchre. In Evangelanta we have Holy Thursday in Gethsemane, Good Friday on Golgotha, Easter on the shore of Turiya-Tehom.

Jesus in Gethsemane. Jesus at the end below of Bright Angel Trail. Jesus staggering under the piled centuries since Paradise.

Jesus, our A'noshma, slipping over the side. Jesus going down in search of forms for our sensibility, categories for our understanding.

Our Holy Week ragnarok of the old categories, the old forms.

We don't need new heavens and a new earth, we only need new eyes and minds with which to see and know the earth and the heavens we already have.

Their Salome veils of whyght samyte falling from a dreamer's eyes in Soho.

Primarily, the Grail is a way of seeing things. Only secondarily is it any particular thing that we happen to be looking at.

Coming forth by day in a striptease club in Solo.

Our Grail Quest is a quest to come forth by day:

Will you see the infancy of this sublime and celestial greatness? Those pure and virgin apprehensions I had from the womb, and that divine light wherewith I was born are the best unto this day, wherein I can see the universe. By the gift of God they attended me into the world, and by his special favour I remember them till now. Verily they seem the greatest gifts his wisdom could bestow, for without them all other gifts had been dead and vain. They are unattainable by book and therefore, I will teach them by experience. Pray for them earnestly; for they will make you angelical and wholly celestial. Certainly Adam in Paradise had not more sweet and curious apprehensions of the world than I when I was a child.

All appeared new and strange at the first, inexpressibly rare and delightful and beautiful. I was a little stranger, which at my entrance into the world was saluted and surrounded with innumerable joys. My knowledge was divine. I knew by intuition those things which since my apostasy I collected again by the highest reason. My very ignorance was advantageous. I seemed as one brought into the estate of innocence. All things were spotless and pure and glorious; yea, and infinitely mine, and joyful and precious. I knew not that there were any sins, or complaints, or laws. I dreamed not of poverties, contentions or vices. All tears and quarrels were hidden from my eyes. Everything was at rest, free and immortal. I knew nothing of sickness or death or rents or exaction either for tribute or bread. In the absence of these I was entertained like an angel with the worke of God in their splendour and glory. I saw all in the peace of Eden; heaven and earth did sing my Creator's praises, and could not make more melody to Adam than to me. All time was eternity and a perpetual Sabbath. Is it not strange that an infant should be heir of the whole world, and see those mysteries which the books of the learned never unfold?

The corn was orient and immortal wheat, which never should be reaped, nor was ever sown. I thought it had stood from everlasting to everlasting. The dust and stones of the street were as precious as gold; the gates were at first the end of the world. The green trees when I saw them first through one of the gates transported and ravished me, their sweetness and unusual beauty made my heart to leap, and almost mad with ecstasy, they were such strange and wonderful things. The men! Oh what venerable and reverend creatures did the aged seem! Immortal cherubims! And young men glittering and sparkling angels, and maids strange seraphic pieces of life and beauty! Boys and girls tumbling in the street, and playing, were moving jewels. I knew not that they were born or should die; but all things abided eternally as they were in their proper places. Eternity was manifest in the light of the day, and something infinite behind everything appeared, which talked with my expectation and moved my desire. The city seemed to stand in Eden, or to be built in heaven … I knew no churlish proprieties, nor bounds, nor divisions, but all proprieties and divisions were mine; all treasures and the possessors of them. So that with much ado I was corrupted, and made to learn the dirty devices of the world, which now I unlearn, and become, as it were, a little child again that I may enter into the Kingdom of God.

Coming forth by day. Coming forth out of the dirty devices of our builded world. Devices which aren't outside of us only; they are inside us as forms of our sensibility, categories of our understanding.

Our builded world. A world of rents and exactions and churlish proprieties and divisions. A world built with a *techne* derived from the fire that we stole from heaven.

Our builded world. Our builded land of Goshen. Land of hard bondage. Land of hard philosophical and epistemological bondage.

Our builded world. A world that is too much with us:

> The world is too much with us; late and soon,
> Getting and spending, we lay waste our powers;
> Little we see in nature that is ours;
> We have given our hearts away, a sordid boon!
> The sea that bares her bosom to the moon;
> The winds that will be howling at all hours,
> And are up-gathered now like sleeping flowers;
> For this, for everything we are out of tune;
> It moves us not. Great God! I'd rather be
> A Pagan suckled in a creed outworn;
> So might I, standing on this pleasant lea,
> Have glimpses that would make me less forlorn;
> Have sight of Proteus rising from the sea;
> Or hear old Triton blow his wreathed horn.

Proteus rising from the sea. Tehom uttering his voice and lifting up his hands on high. Is the face of Tehom a new face of God? Are our images of God as King of kings and Lord of lords giving way to an imageless image of God as Divine Ground, to an imageless image of God as En-Sof? Are we ready after two thousand years of the Sermon on the Mount for a Tehom Te Ching? Are we ready for the Mandukya Om of Tehom? The Om the whole universe is a blossoming of?

Could it be that, empowered from the heart of the Triduum Sacrum, we can chant the *anahata shabda* Om?

Tehom om om om om.

Are we ready to cross from Evangel to Evangelanta? Are we ready, that is, for the land into which we've already come? Are we ready for Tenebrae?

And Fedallah, our look-out, he who first saw Cetus Psychopompos rising from the sea, will he, in a moment of preternatural silence at the heart of the storm, hear what cannot be heard, the first om out of Tehom?

Argo, Nave, Mayflower, Beagle, Pequod, Raft.

Turtle was gone a long time. So long was he gone, there was green slime on him when he returned. And the song of origins he heard on the floorless floor of the Abyss, he taught us that song:

> Te Kore
> Te Kore-tua-tahi
> Te Kore-tua-rua …

And there it was, all around us now, the stupendous, great and sacred Earth we had come ashore on. And we could hear it. We could hear the roaring of Medicine River, and we knew we were healed. All the way back to the pit in Lascaux and beyond we were healed. It was, to begin with, a Pleistocene morning we walked abroad in.

In a thunderstorm one night, struck perhaps by lightning, Wolf Collar fell unconscious. In a dream, Thunderbird came to him, coming first as a bird, then as a woman. She took him to her Blue Thunder tipi. Terror of her didn't turn him inside out or back to front. Sitting there with her, he remained who he was. She gave him a drum and four songs. Also, as a sign of her particular favour, she gave him leave to live in a Blue Thunder tipi. Later that night he dreamed again; Young Thunder, whose name was Iron Voice, said: 'I am the one that strikes; I am going to make a great medicine man of you; you will surprise the people. I will come many times when you are sleeping and each time I will teach you something new.' He gave Wolf Collar a shield and two songs.

Out hunting, a few years later, a wounded Buffalo charged and gored Wolf Collar, yet he felt no hurt. At another time he caught and killed a grizzly bear. In a dream, the grizzly bear came to him and gave him a medicine bundle that had a grizzly bear claw in it.

Wolf Collar and Black Elk: Pleistocene medicine men singing their Pleistocene medicine songs among us.

Imagine it: Wolf Collar's Blue Thunder tipi pitched among the great herds of our lost Serengeti between Altamira and Lascaux.

Imagine it: Wolf Collar singing his medicine songs in our lost Serengeti before Europa, fleeing from the bull, came into it before our biblical mandate to rule over the earth and subdue it.

Imagine it: Wolf Collar opening his Pleistocene medicine bundle, singing his Pleistocene medicine songs, in the pit in Lascaux. Wolf Collar healing what is, perhaps, the oldest wound in the European unconscious. The open Ice Age wound we suffer most terribly from. The wound on the one side of which is the speared Bison, on the other side of which is the prostrate Birdman.

Imagine it: Wolf Collar, himself gored by a buffalo bull, healing the wound between birdman and bull, healing the wound in commonage consciousness.

Imagine it: Wolf Collar, Birdman, Bisonman, Rhinocerosman reinstituting commonage consciousness in the pit in Lascaux.

Imagine it: Wolf Collar, Birdman, Bisonman, Rhinocerosman dancing the masked dance, the dance of commonage consciousness, in the pit in Lascaux.

Healed as far back as the pit in Lascaux.

Healed as far back as Lucy's savannah.

Healed as far back as the end below of Bright Angel Trail.

Healed as far back as Tep Zepi and Tai'wer.

Healed as far back as the coils of Iru-To.

Healed at all levels of consciousness and unconsciousness.

At a sun dance once, Wolf Collar sat in his Blue Thunder tipi. On his left sat a man called Iron Pipe, on his right a man called Running Wolf. Wolf Collar sang his thunder songs. Then he got up and drew jagged lines from the feet of the two men to the door. He came back and sat down. Lightning flashed along the lines, but no one was hurt.

Before he died, Wolf Collar told Many Shots, his son, about the powers given to him by the thunders. He vomited a small stone and said, 'That's what has kept me powerful.' Back in his mouth, it was buried with him.

There was a blizzard of blue and yellow lightning when Wolf Collar died. He died at a time when, following a fox and a dog, we were already re-entering Altamira and Lascaux.

Prometheus following a fox. Following him all the way back into Blue Thunder tipi. In Blue Thunder tipi Wolf Collar tells him a story:

In the beginning there was no fire, and the world was cold, until the Thunders, who lived up in Galun'wati, sent their lightning and put fire into the bottom of a hollow sycamore tree which grew on an island. The animals knew it was coming out of the top, but they could not get to it because of the water, so they held a council to decide what to do. This was a long time ago. Every animal that could fly or swim was anxious to go after the fire. Raven offered and because he was so large and strong, he thought he could surely do the work, so he was sent first. He flew high and far across the water, and alighted on the sycamore tree, but while he was wondering what to do next, the heat had scorched all his feathers black and he was frightened, and came back without the fire. Screech Owl volunteered to go and reached the place safely, but while he was looking down into the hollow tree a blast of hot air came up and nearly burned out his eyes. He managed to fly home, but it was a long time before he could see well, and his eyes are red to this day. Hooting Owl and Horned Owl went, but by the time they got to the hollow tree the fire was burning so fiercely that the smoke nearly blinded them and the ashes carried up by the wind made white rings about their eyes. They had to come home again without the fire, but for all their rubbing they were never able to get rid of the white rings. Now, no other bird would venture, and so the little Uksu'hi snake, the black racer, said he would go through the water and bring back the fire. He swam across to the island and crawled through the grass to the tree, and went in by a small hole at the bottom. The heat and smoke were too much for him. After dodging about blindly over the hot ashes, until he was almost on fire himself, he managed by good luck to get out again, but his body had been scorched black and ever since he has the habit of darting and doubling on his tracks as if trying to escape from close quarters. Gule'gi, the great black snake, offered to go. He swam over to the island and, true to his climbing habits, he climbed up the tree on the outside but when he put his head down into the hole the smoke choked him so that he fell into the burning stump and before he could climb out again he was as black as Uksu'hi. Now the animals held another council, for there was still no fire and the world was cold, but birds, snakes and four-footed animals all had some excuse for not going. They were all afraid to venture near the burning sycamore. At last Kanane'ski Amai'yehi, the water spider, said she would go. This is not the water spider that looks like a mosquito, but the other one, she who has black downy hair and red stripes on her body. She can run on top of the water or dive to the bottom, so it would be easy for her to go to the island, but the question was, how could she possibly bring back the fire? I'll manage that, said Kanane'ski

Amai'yehi. She spun a thread from her body and wove it into a tutsi bowl which she fastened on her back. Walking water, she walked to the island. She walked through the grass to the hollow tree. In it the fire which the Thunders had sent was still burning. Putting a small coal of it in her bowl, Kanane'ski Amai'yehi set out, walking water, walking home.

Having finished his story, Wolf Collar went to the door and called out into the night. Coming back, he sat on the floor and waited. In a while Kanane'ski Amai'yehi came in, bringing a coal. Soon there was a fire of pine cones and spruce logs in Blue Thunder tipi and sitting about it in a wide circle were Spider, Fox, Wolf Collar and Prometheus.

New fire. Fire sent down, not fire stolen.

Pleistocene fire.

Kwakiutl firelight.

Light into which we welcome the terrors of the cedar forest and the sea's entrall.

Tsetsekia firelight, forest-clearing firelight, into which we can welcome the Great Iakim who, rising from its depths, makes the sea boil, who, rising from its depths, makes the psyche boil.

It boiled in Daniel:

And I Daniel fainted and was sick certain days

Tsetsekia firelight, forest-clearing firelight, into which we can safely welcome Numxilexiu.

When he is in the mood to do so, Numxilexiu can throw an overwhelming wave of the sea or of the psyche before him. He did it in Job:

I will speak in the anguish of my spirit, I will complain in the bitterness of my soul. Am I a sea, or a whale, that thou settest a watch over me? When I say my bed shall comfort me, my couch shall ease my complaint, then thou scarest me with dreams and terrifiest me through visions, so that my soul chooseth strangling and death rather than my life.

Tsetsekia firelight, forest-clearing firelight, into which we can safely welcome Draco.

Many times slain, as many times more violently reborn, we can welcome Tiamat, Python, Leviathan.

Tsetsekia firelight, forest-clearing firelight, into which we can welcome Ropesnake, the most sea-shaking, earth-shaking, mind-shaking, soul-shaking of all Zoas.

Tsetsekia firelight, forest-clearing firelight, into which we can welcome Narada.

Tsetsekia firelight, forest-clearing firelight, in which we can listen to the wisdom stories of the First Peoples of the world.

> In the very earliest time
> when both people and animals lived on earth
> a person could become an animal if he wanted to
> and an animal could become a human being.
> Sometimes they were people and sometimes animals
> And there was no difference.
> All spoke the same language.
> That was the time when words were like magic.
> The human mind had mysterious powers.
> A word spoken by chance might have strange consequences.
> It would suddenly come alive
> and what people wanted to happen could happen –
> all you had to do was say it.
> Nobody can explain this: that's the way it was.

And at some level of sea and psyche that's how it still is.

Ancient Egyptians knew that words were like magic. They knew that particular words spoken in a particular way had power. They called them *hekau*. Knowing the power that was in them, they inscribed them on the walls of their tombs and on their coffin boards.

Our words also would be words of power if, on the far side of Job's agon, we lived from those *Anima Mundi* moods in which the stones of the field are in league with us, and the beasts of savannah and field are at peace with us.

Think of Earth-Initiate calling the stars into existence. Think of him calling five new constellations into existence.

Think of him calling *Pert em hru* culture out of the wreckage of *Pequod* culture.

After Auschwitz, Ta'doiko.

The story of Job is the story of someone who became an Earth-Initiate. Instead of Job sitting civically in the city gate we have Job as initiating abbot in the East Pagoda Hall of a Green Dragon Temple.

Green Dragon Temple, Blue Thunder Tipi, Kwakiutl Big House, and, yet to be built, the hope of it not yet sown like a seed in the earth, a Tenebrae Temple.

After the collision, A'noshma Dei descending to the floor of the Abyss.

After Auschwitz, Ta'doiko.

After Hiroshima, the Navajo cradle.

In us, not after us, Job's enantiodromia.

At the end of a century of fantastic technologial tricks, Prometheus undergoing radical re-education in a Pleistocene tipi.

Stolen fire or fire sent down?

The screams of a screaming eagle or the medicine songs of Thunder Bird?

Songs that will heal Prometheus. Heal him of his *protarchos ate*, heal him of original *tolma*, heal him of Titanic *techne*.

In present day reckoning, the earth is four thousand six hundred million years old, a reach of time too vast to imagine. Reducing it to pictureable proportions, let us think of it as forty-six years old. About its first seven years hardly anything is known. Of its next thirty-five years we know but a little. At forty-two, it began to bloom biologically. A year ago, when it was forty-five, dinosaurs appeared. Mammals showed up eight months ago. In the middle of last week human-like apes evolved into ape-like humans. Modern humans have been around for four hours. During the last half hour we discovered agriculture. Sixty seconds ago we left the crofts and gave our energy to the thing we call the industrial revolution, and now, sitting in Hiroshima or sitting under a hole in the ozone layer, we owe it to the earth to ask two simple questions: Are we the iceberg into which the earth has crashed? Have we, as a species, lost evolutionary legitimacy? At the foot of a Caucasus rock wall, an eagle screaming above us, let us ask them.

Prometheus Agonistes.

Prometheus undergoing what Job underwent.

Ancient and modern Western history finding its way, not through Prometheus, but through Job.

The breakthrough to the voice of Old Man that occurred in Job.

Job unbound. Job walking through his ancient city, manure fork in hand.

Prometheus unbound.

Prometheus walking free of his Erinyes. An Erinys called Harpoon. An Erinys called Tryworks. An Erinys called Turbine. An Erinys called GNP. An Erinys called Becherels. An Erinys called Nerve Gas. An Erinys called Lost Serengeti. An Erinys called Chain Saw. An Erinys called Ozone Hole.

Guided by his daughter, Oedipus came to Colonus, to metamorphic encounter with Thunder there.

Guided by the fox that guided us back into commonage consciousness, Prometheus came to Blue Thunder tipi.

Prometheus healed, Prometheus set free, by a Pleistocene Thunder Dreamer singing the songs that were given to him by Thunder, drumming the drum that was given to him by Thunder, in his Blue Thunder tipi.

Not one of our heroes but needs to come to Blue Thunder tipi.

Blue Thunder tipi and brush hogan.

Europa's four nights in the brush hogan.

First Man and First Woman making a cradle for Europa, for Little Girl Lost, lost long ago in Western Asia, lost in the culture she gave her name to:

> We make a cradleboard for you, our foster child,
> May you grow to a great old age
> Of the sun's rays we make the back
> Of black clouds we make the blanket
> Of rainbow we make the bow
> Of sunbeams we make the side loops
> Of lightning we make the lacings
> Of river mirrorings we make the footboard
> Of dawn we make the covering
> Of earth's welcome for you we make the bed.

'The world's great age begins anew' – in a Navajo cradle.

The death of *Pequod* culture. The birth of Navajo cradle culture.

Time to sing! Time to sing the song of commonage consciousness. Time to sing the song Uvavnuk sings in Ice-age igloo:

> The great sea has set me in motion,
> Set me adrift,
> Moving me as the weed moves in a river.
> The arch of sky and mightiness of storms
> Have moved the spirit within me,
> Till I am carried away,
> Trembling with joy.

Blue Thunder tipi. Brush hogan. Ice-age igloo.

The fire the Thunders gave us.

The drum and the songs the Thunders gave us.

Poor Tom is no longer acold.

Sitting in a Blue Thunder tipi, sitting by the fire the Thunders gave us, Poor Tom, if he wishes, can listen to Black Elk when he speaks, to Yajnavalkya when he speaks, to Buddha when he speaks, to Lao Tze when he speaks, to Jesus when he speaks.

Black Elk speaks:

I looked below me where the earth was silent in a sick green light, and saw the hills look up afraid and the grasses on the hills and all the animals; and everywhere about me were the cries of frightened birds and sounds of fleeing wings. I was the chief of all the heavens riding there, and when I looked behind me, all the twelve black horses reared and plunged and thundered and their manes and tails were whirling hail and their nostrils snorted lightning. And when I looked below again, I saw the slant hail falling and the long, sharp rain, and where we passed, the trees bowed low and all the hills were dim.

Now the earth was bright again as we rode. I could see the hills and valleys and the creeks and rivers passing under. We came above a place where there streams made a big one – a source of mighty waters – and something terrible was there. Flames were rising from the waters and in the flames a blue man lived. The dust was floating all about him in the air, the grass was short and withered, the trees were wilting, two-legged and four-legged beings lay there thin and panting, and wings too weak to fly.

Then the black horse riders shouted 'Hoka ley' and charged down upon the blue man, but were driven back. And the white troop shouted, charging, and was beaten, then the red troop and the yellow.

And when each had failed, they all cried together, 'Eagle-Wing-Stretches, hurry!' And all the world was filled with voices of all kinds that cheered me, so I charged. I had the cup of water in one hand and in the other was the bow that turned into a spear as the bay and I swooped down, and the spear's head was sharp lightning. It stabbed the blue man's heart, and as it struck I could hear the thunder rolling, and many voices that cried 'Un-hee!' meaning I had killed. The flames died. The trees and grasses were not withered anymore and murmured happily together and every living thing cried in gladness with whatever voice it had. Then the four troops of horsemen charged down and struck the dead body of the blue man, counting coup and suddenly it was only a harmless turtle.

Jesus speaks:

Seek ye first the Kingdom of God and all things else shall be added unto you.

The Kena Upanishad speaks:

There goes neither the eye, nor speech, nor the mind; we know It not; nor do we see how to teach one about It. Different It is from all that is known, and beyond the unknown It also is.

Yajnavalkya speaks:

The Self is not this, not that. It is unseizable, for it cannot be seized; indestructible, for it cannot be destroyed; unattached, for it does not attach itself; it is unbound, it does not tremble, it is not injured.

Buddha speaks:

I proclaim, friend, that in this fathom-sized, feeling-afflicted, ascetic's body dwell the world and the origin of the world and the annulment of the world and the path that leads to the annulment of the world.

There is suffering, there is a cause of suffering, there is a path that leads to the end of suffering, there is an end of suffering.

Lao Tze speaks:

Heaven is eternal, the Earth everlasting.
How come they to be so? It is because they do not foster
Their own lives;
That is why they live so long.
Therefore the sage
Puts himself in the background, but is always to the fore,
Remains outside, but is always there.
Is it not just because he does not strive for any personal end
That all his personal ends are fulfilled.

He who knows the male, yet cleaves to what is female
Becomes like a ravine, receiving all things under heaven;
And being such a ravine
He knows all the time a power that he never calls upon in vain.
This is returning to the state of infancy.
He who knows the white yet cleaves to the black
Becomes the standard by which all things are tested
And being such a standard
He has all the time a power that never errs,
He returns to the limitless
He who knows glory, yet cleaves to ignominy
Become like a valley that receives into it all things under Heaven
And being such a valley
He has all the time a power that suffices;
He returns to the state of the Uncarved Block.

Great Tao is like a boat that drifts;
It can go this way, it can go that.
The ten thousand creatures owe their existence to it and it
does not disown them;
Yet having produced them, it does not take possession of them.
Tao, though it covers the ten thousand things like a garment
Makes no claim to be master over them.
Therefore, it may be called the Lowly.
The ten thousand creatures obey it

Though they know not that they have a master;
Therefore it is called the Great
So too the Sage just because he never at any time makes
A show of greatness in fact achieves greatness.

Jesus speaks:

Abba, Father, all things are possible unto Thee; take away this cup from me; nevertheless not what I will, but what Thou wilt ... My God, my God, why hast thou forsaken me ...

Farid Al-Din'Attar speaks:

In the deep waters of the ocean of annihilation I would seek to be, for though I aspire to the Sun, yet, since one is powerless to attain to Thy great height, I would aspire to sleep at Thy feet. Behold what grief I suffer without Thee! But now, since I have become nothing, I know that in the end I shall attain again to my desire. I said unto Thee: 'I have passed away, as I was asked to do.' Thou saidst unto me: 'I will bring thee unto Eternal Life, as thou hast wished, for when thou dost see thyself as nothing, then will I give unto thee such an existence as thou hast desired.'

Every moment now I spend in loving adoration of Another than myself. Long ago I died to mine own existence and if now I live it is in the existence of Another. I sacrificed all tranquillity and ease and renounced all hope of fame, so that I might attain to complete annihilation. I laid down my life and sacrificed my soul, and all humankind became as nothing to me. Now I have arisen and I am free from all grief of soul, for I am set free from the world of Existence and Non-Existence and I dwell beyond both. I have taken my flight from phenomenal existence to non-entity.

I am without body and soul and surely these are necessary to me. Without these, what am I? I am that which I was meant to be. Within myself, I have no knowledge of myself, for self-less I was meant to be. Happy is the one who has thus passed away from mortality, for passing away is the essence of abiding in immortality. This I know, that self-annihilation is a glorious thing, but that which I do not know is what I am yet to be.

Eckhart speaks:

Comes then the soul into the unclouded light of God. It is transported so far from creaturehood into the nothingness that, of its own power, it can never return to its agents or its former creaturehood. Once there, God shelters the soul's nothingness with his uncreated essence, safeguarding its creaturely existence. The soul has dared to become nothing, and cannot pass from its own being into nothingness and then back again, losing its own identity in the process, except God safeguarded it. This must needs be so.

And so, even if our Western voyage, our *polla ta deina* voyage, our Genesis, chapter 1, verses 26 and 28 voyage, even if that impious voyage has foundered, as Sophocles half suspected that it would, we are, nonetheless, not destitute: Galahad has released the rocks, so that Ulro is Uluru; Black Elk has released the waters, healing the Waste Land; a fox has guided us back into commonage consciousness; we have fire – not stolen fire, fire sent down as a gift from above; we have a Pleistocene medicine song; we have a Navajo cradle; we have a brush hogan; we have a Blue Thunder tipi; we have heard the roaring of Medicine River; coming with a new diagnosis of what ails us, Narada has walked through the Pass at Thermopylae, a re-educated Prometheus is sitting in the lotus position in Ta'-doiko, we have heard the voice of Old Man, we have drawn the spear out of the Bison Bull; we have ceremonies, called Tsetsekia, in which we open a great communal door to whatever might come among us from the cedar forest and the sea's entrall.

Tsetsekia we have and Tenebrae.

In Tsetsekia Ishmael will deal with Zeuglodon. In Tenebrae Ahab will deal with his diluvian insight.

New constellations there are by which to navigate our way to where we are.

Having all of this, we have as much perhaps as Aeneas had leaving the burning town, as Abraham had leaving a jaded age.

And that's not all. Like Darwin harrowing the beach at Punta Alta, Jesus has harrowed our inner, phylogenetic ancient regime which, as Nietzsche discovered, lives on, thinks on, dreams on in us. In this, here at Punta Alta and in the Grand Canyon, we are beginning to acquire evolutionary legitimacy. The wake of the *Pequod* has given way to Bright Angel Trail.

Then shall come Jesus and a clamour shall be made, or a loud sound of things striking together, and let Jesus say: Lift up your heads, O ye gates, and be ye lift up ye everlasting doors; and the King of Glory shall come in.

> JESUS: Open hell gates, anon,
> You princes of pain, every one,
> That God's Son may in gone,
> And the King of bliss!
>
> SATAN: Say, what is he, that King of bliss?
>
> JESUS: That Lord, the which almighty is.
> There is no power like to his;
> Of all joy he is the King.

And to him is none like, iwis,
As is soothly seen by this,
For man that sometime did amiss,
To his bliss he will bring.

Coming forth by day, ancient Egyptians called it.

A great day it is, the day we are willing to be Earth-Initiates.

A great day it is, the day our raft runs aground and we come ashore, coming home to where we always have been.

A great day it is, the day we come ashore knowing that sooner or later, walking in his black moccasins, Black Bear will walk towards us. He won't speak soft words to us. And yet, walking sometimes into our dreams, he will leave a medicine bundle.

A great day it is, the day we come ashore and go walkabout in Buddh Gaia.

GLOSSARY

Acallamh Irish word meaning colloquy or dialogue.

Actaeon In Greek mythology, a hunter who surprised the virgin goddess Artemis bathing with her nymphs in a pool. In punishment Artemis turned him into a stag; not recognizing him, his hounds gave chase and tore him asunder.

Adarsana Sanskrit word meaning without vision.

Adityas In Indo-European mythology adityas are releasers, while danavas are restrainers.

Aeon Greek word meaning an age.

Agon A conflictive dialogue as encountered in Greek tragic drama. The Christian word agony derives from it.

Akhty Of the horizon.

Al Hallaj Muslim mystic, crucified in a square in Baghdad in 922.

Altamira Palaeolithic cave in northern Spain.

Anadyomene From the Greek, rising, or coming in from, the sea.

Anahata Shabda (mantra) Metaphysical sound of any two things striking together.

Anantasayin Recumbent on the coils of the great snake Ananta, a figuration of infinity.

Anaximenes (d. *c.* 500 BC) Pre-Socratic philosopher, born in Miletus.

Angelo of Foligno (1248-1309) Italian mystic.

Anima Mundi The world's soul.

A'noshma Turtle, in the Maidu story of origins.

Antanabhavic Sanskrit word meaning the state between death and rebirth.

Araranaskakti A projecting power of the mind, which obscures or conceals.

Archaeornis First or most ancient bird as it evolved out of Mesozoic reptile.

Areopagus Rock Rock of the Acropolis in Athens where a famous court was held.

Argo Ship in which many Greek heroes, including Orpheus and Herakles, sailed to Colchis to bring home the Golden Fleece.

Arjuna Character in the great Indian epic *The Mahabharata*.

Asparsaya Sanskrit word meaning without contact or touch.

Asura In Hinduism, an anti-god, of whom there were many.

Atum Ancient Egyptian god.

Aufklarung German word meaning enlightenment.

Aurignacian One of the Palaeolithic ages. In this age some of the cave paintings of southern France (*q.v.* Lascaux) and northern Spain (*q.v.* Altamira) were executed.

Ayahuasca Hallucinogenic drink brewed from the yaje vine in Amazonia.

Baqa Arabic word used by sufis meaning abiding in the godhead.

Baxbaknalanuxiwre Monster known to the Kwakiutl (*q.v.*).

Beagle Ten-gun brig in which Darwin spent five years as a naturalist sailing around the world, calling at the Galapagos in the Pacific where he made the observations that would finally give rise to the theory of evolution.

Beowolf Scandinavian who slew Grendel.

Berkeley, George (1685-1753) Irish bishop and idealist philosopher born in Kilkenny.

Bhagavad Gita Sacred book in Hinduism.

Bhairave Terror form of the Hindu god Shiva (*q.v.*).

Bhakta Passionate devotee of a goddess or god in Hinduism.

Bhu Devi Earth-goddess in Hinduism.

Bhuvaneshvat Temple complex in India.

Black Elk Oglala medicine man of the Sioux tribe who, at the age of nine, was assumed into the heavenly world. There he participated in a great healing drama, which released the waters. This he and his people later re-enacted on the bank of the Tongue River (*q.v.*) in Montana in the 1880s.

Blake, William (1757-1827) English poet, painter and mystic, born in London to an Irish hosier.

Blue Thunder tipi Tipi that the chief of the Thunder Bears permitted Wolf Collar (*q.v.*) to erect and live in.

Boehme, Jacob (1575-1624) German Protestant mystic.

Bohdi Tree Tree under which the Buddha found enlightenment. The word *bodhi* suggests enlightenment.

Brahma One of the three great gods of Hinduism (Brahma, Vishnu and Shiva).

Bright Angel Trail One of the winding trails that leads down to the floor of the Grand Canyon in Arizona.

Browne, Thomas (1605-82) English physician and author of *Religio Medici* (1635).

Bruno, Giordano (1548-1600) Christian mystic, burnt at the stake in Rome.

Buddh Gaia Where the Buddha won enlightenment there is a temple called Buddh Gaya. The word *buddh* is from a root suggesting enlightenment. The ancient Greeks thought of the Earth as a goddess called Gaia. Buddh Gaia therefore suggests that the Earth itself is already enlightened, or is capable of being enlightened.

Bullman See Minotaur.

Bunyan, John (1628-88) English Dissenter and author of *The Pilgrim's Progress* and *Grace Abounding to the Chief of Sinners*.

Cadmus In Greek mythology, a man who came west out of Asia and built Thebes (*q.v.*).

Calderon (1600-81) Spanish dramatist schooled under the Jesuits.

Camelot Seat of King Arthur and his court.

Catherine of Genoa (1447-1510) Italian mystic.

Catherine of Siena (1347-80) Italian mystic.

Cetus Dei As in Agnus Dei, the lamb of God, Cetus Dei means the whale of God.

Chalcedon Small town on the Bosphorus, where a Christological definition about Jesus's two-natures-in-one-person was elaborated at a Council of the Church in AD 451.

Chandogya Title for one of the great Upanishads (*q.v.*).

Chapel Perilous Chapel of terrors that Sir Gawain enters on his way to encounter the Green Knight.

Chateau Merveil Castle of marvels and terrors in the Grail quest.

Chonyid Bardo In Tibetan Buddhism, a phase or state of the soul's journey between death and rebirth.

Chuang Tzu Great sage who gave his name to one of the classics of Taoism.

Cittametra Epistemological doctrine of radical idealism, in Mahayane Buddhism. See the Lankavatara Sutra.

Coatlicue Aztec earth-goddess.

Colonus Grove sacred to the Erinyes (*q.v.*) in ancient Attica.

Corbenic One name for the castle in which the Grail is housed.

Dame Julian of Norwich (1343-c.1413) English anchoress and author of *Revelations of Divine Love*.

Danavas See Adityas.

De Caussade French Christian mystic of the seventeenth century.

Democritus (c. 460-c.370 BC) Pre-Socratic philosopher born in Abdera in Thrace. The subject of Karl Marx's PhD thesis.

Desert of Zin Desert into which the children of Israel came, having passed through the Red Sea. See Book of Numbers, 20.

Deucalion In Greek mythology, the survivor of the Flood.

Dichosa Ventura Line from a poem by St John of the Cross (*q.v.*), meaning 'Oh happy venture'.

Dionysius the Areopagite Syrian Christian mystic writing between 475 and 525 BC.

Dionysus Greek god of wine, called Bacchus by the Romans. Son of Zeus.

Diotima Wise woman from Mantineia (*q.v.*) quoted by Socrates (*q.v.*) in Plato's dialogue, *The Symposium*.

Divine (Un) Grund Ground out of which all things emanate. German word meaning no ground, the no-ground that grounds.

Dover Beach Poem by Matthew Arnold.

Dreupadi Character in the Indian epic *The Mahabharata*.

Drona Character in the Indian epic *The Mahabharata*.

Duat Egyptian underworld.

Dumuzi Abzu God of the Abyss in Sumerian and Babylonian mythology.

East Pagoda Hall See Green Dragon Temple.

Eckhart (1260-1327) Rhineland mystic.

Ekstasis Literally, 'standing outside oneself': our word ecstasy.

El Shaddai A name for the god of the Old Testament.

Elend Antelope of southern Africa.

Elora Complex of rock-cut caves in central India.

Enantiodromia A turning around of the road that one is on.

Enthusiasmos Greek word meaning invasion or possession by a god.

Epoptai Greek word meaning viewers of sacred things.

Equus Dei Literally, the horse of God, as in Agnus Dei.

Erebus Greek underworld.

Erinyes Terrible furies in ancient Greek mythology.

Esagila Great temple in ancient Babylon.

Europa Abducted Asian maiden who gave her name to Europe.

Evangelanta Newly coined word. In Hinduism there are collections of sacred texts called the Vedas. They are, so to speak, a first revelation, heard in times long past. Other texts, called the Upanishads, constituting a further 'revelation', were written later. Collectively these latter texts are called Vedanta, a compound of veda and anta, literally 'after the Vedas'. In Christianity we have the initial Good News, the Greek word for which is Evangel. As in Hinduism there is Veda and Vedanta, so in Christianity there is Evangel and Evangelanta. Coming as they do, after the Evangel, the writings of the Christian mystics constitute Evangelanta.

Fama Arabic word used by sufis meaning our passing away into the godhead.

Farid, Al-Din Attax (1140-1233) Muslim mystic born near Nishapur.

Fénelon, Francois de (1651-1715) French prelate, writer and champion of Madame Guyon (*q.v.*).

Fjalar One of the three cocks whose crowing announces ragnarok (*q.v.*) in Nordic mythology.

Gamow, George Russian author of the Big Bang Theory.

Ghora Murti Terrible face or form of the goddess or god in Hinduism.

Glaucus Sea-god in Greek myth who figures in Plato's dialogue, *The Republic*.

Gnostic Literally, somone who knows. Historically, Gnostics were active in the east Mediterranean at the beginning of the Christian era.

Goldcomb One of the three cocks whose crowing announces ragnarok (*q.v.*) in Nordic mythology.

Golgotha-Borobudur Literally, a place of the skull, the hill on which Christ was crucified on Good Friday; and a Buddhist temple in Java: an amalgamation of the Christian and the Buddhist pyramidal temple.

Great Iakim Sea-monster that the Kwakiutl (*q.v.*) welcomed among them during their winter ceremonies called Tsetsekia (*q.v.*).

Green Dragon Temple Temple in China.

Guernica Basque town bombed by the Germans during the Spanish Civil War in 1936; title of a painting by Picasso.

Guyon, Madame (1648-1717) French Christian mystic.

Gyrans gyrendo spiritus radii Spiralling in a spiral, the spirit moves.

Hadewyck of Antwerp Dutch mystic.

Harmonica Praestabilita Pre-established harmony.

Harrowing of Hell Medieval belief that on the night of Good Friday, Jesus went down into Hell and led out all souls of the pre-Christian dispensation who had lived good or exemplary lives. This episode in the great drama of Christian redemption was frequently enacted on the medieval stage. The version quoted here is from the Chester cycle of mystery plays.

Heidegger, Martin (1889-1976) German philosoper, born in Messkirch, Baden, to a Catholic sexton.

Heilgeschichte German word meaning sacred history, as the Bible understands it.

Hekau Ancient Egyptian term meaning words of power.

Hilton, Walter (d. 1396) English mystic.

Hogan Circular house made from brushwood, or wattle-and-daub, among the Navajo (*q.v.*).

Hohokw Monster known to the Kwakiutl (*q.v.*).

Hölderlin, Johann (1776-1843) Romantic poet and Hellenist, born in Lauffen, Germany.

Horakhty Hoves of the Horizon, the sun god emerging victoriously over the horizon in the morning.

Horsehead Nebula In galaxy M83 there is a nebula which has in it an aura of fire and cloud that looks astonishingly like a horse's head. In this book we have imagined that it was from such a nebula that our own solar system evolved.

Hosonji Type of song sung by the Navajo (*q.v.*). It is believed that it transports the singer to the paradisal place it sings of.

Hui Neng Sixth patriarch of Buddhism in China.

Huichol Indian people living in the Sierra Occidental mountains in Mexico.

Ilissus River that flows beside Athens. See Plato's *Phaedrus*.

Indra King of the gods, in the Hindu pantheon. The greatest of the adityas (*q.v.*).

Iru-To The great earth-snake in ancient Egyptian mythology.

Ishmael Narrator of Melville's *Moby-Dick*.

Jivanmukta Sanskrit word meaning one who is liberated in this life.

Jnana Yoga Hindu word cognate to the Greek word *gnosis*, meaning a particular kind of knowledge concerning the divine and our relationship to it.

Jnegararana Obscuration or veiling caused by thought.

Job Fictional protagonist in the biblical Book of Job.

Kalkin Hindu god Vishnu (*q.v.*) in his next incarnation, in horse form.

Kant, Immanuel (1724-1804) German philosopher and critical idealist born in Königsberg, Prussia, to a saddler.

Karma Character in the Indian epic *The Mahabharata*.

Kedron Stream in a valley outside Jerusalem. See John, 18:1.

Kithairon Mountain in Greece on which the votaries of the god Dionysus (*q.v.*) used to celebrate their biennial trance dancing.

Kleje Hataal Nine-night healing rite among the Navajo (*q.v.*).

Krak des Chevaliers Crusaders' castle in the Near East.

Krishna Character in the Indian epic *The Mahabharata*.

Kunti Character in the Indian epic *The Mahabharata*.

Kwakiutl Indian people, living on the north-west coast of North America.

Laius Father of Oedipus (*q.v.*).

Land of Goshen Israelite name for the Egypt in which they were enslaved.

Lascaux Palaeolithic cave in southern France.

Law, William (1686-1761) English clergyman from Kingscliffe, Northamptonshire, born to a grocer. Refused to take an oath of loyalty to King George I. Disciple of Boehme (*q.v.*).

Leviathan Great monster of the deep in the Bible.

GLOSSARY

Linga-sharirn Among Hindus, a ritual for the dead.
Little Girl Lost See Lyca.
Liz de la Mervoille Bed of wonders and terrors in Chateau Merveil (*q.v.*).
Loman, Willie Hero in Arthur Miller's play *Death of a Salesman*.
Longinus Roman soldier who speared Jesus on Good Friday.
Los Character in Blake's prophetic poems.
Lucy Gray Young woman about whom Wordsworth wrote a poem of that name.
Lyca Name of 'Little Girl Lost'; title of a poem by Blake.

Maenads Followers of votaries of the god Dionysus (*q.v.*).
Maidu Raft The Maidu are a Indian tribe living in California. The raft in question is the one which appears in their story of origins 'Turtle Was Gone a Long Time'.
Mahavakya Sanskrit word meaning great saying. According to Shankara (*q.v.*), there are six such great sayings in the Upanishads (*q.v.*).
Malleus Maleficarum Hammer of witches; name of a medieval treatise on demonology.
Mantineia Place in ancient Greece from which Diotima (*q.v.*) comes.
Marasena The hordes of Mara, lord of sensual desire and death in Buddhism.
Marathon Plain in ancient Greece on which a decisive battle between Persians and Greeks, Asians and Europeans, was fought.
Marduk One of the great Babylonian gods, slayer of Tiamat (*q.v.*). His name means son of the sun.
Mayashakti Hindu goddess who is the source of maya, or the world illusion.
Mayflower Ship in which the Puritan pilgrim fathers sailed to the New World, making landfall at Plymouth Rock in Massachusetts, New England.
Maymed Kynge Fisher king in the Grail legend.
Medicine River River to which Standing Mouse journeys in a Native American story.
Mesehtiu An adze-shaped sacred instrument used in the ritual called the Opening of the Mouth in ancient Egypt.
Metanoesis As metaphysics means beyond the physical, so does metanoesis mean beyond mental activity, beyond mind.
Minotaur Half-bull, half-man that Pasiphae (*q.v.*) gave birth to.
Mona Melencolia Europa Conflation of Leonardo's *Mona Lisa* and Durer's *Melencolia*.
Moses and Aaron Brothers who led the children of Israel out of Egypt.
Mount Abu Temple mount sacred to the Jains in India.
Mount Athos Peninsula in northern Greece famous for the number and importance of its monasteries.

Mouscron Madonna Sculpture of mother and child by Michaelangelo.

Narada Protaganist in a Hindu parable.

Navajo Tribe of Indians living in the south-west of North America.

Nave Technically, the body of a Christian church, from the Latin word meaning boat, and therefore thought of as the ship, or ark, that would take us through the turbulent waters of time to the shore of Eternity.

New Canaan Town in Connecticut, New England.

Newton, Isaac (1642-1727) English author of the laws of gravity, his most famous book being *Philosophiae Naturalis Principia Mathematica* (1687).

Nicea Town in Asia Minor where a famous Council of the Church was held. The Nicene Creed was formulated there.

Nierikayes Huichol (*q.v.*) word meaning a portal or doorway into non-ordinary worlds.

Nietzsche, Friedrich (1844-1900) German philosopher, born in Röcken, Saxony, to a Lutheran pastor.

Night of Brahma According to Hindus there is a night of Brahma during which the whole universe is re-absorbed without trace, and a day of Brahma in which the universe re-emanates.

Nirguna Brahman The Brahman without attributes.

Nirvikalpasemadhi State of contemplation in which there is no object of awareness. In it, we have gone beyond the subjective and objective divide.

Numxilexiu Great sea-monster known to the Kwakiutl (*q.v.*).

Nunataks Eskimo word meaning that portion of a mountain which protrudes above the ice.

Oedipus King of Thebes (*q.v.*) in ancient Greece, who discovered that he had killed his father and married his mother.

Oglala Sept of the Sioux.

Olduvai Gorge in the Rift Valley in Africa.

Omophagia Greek word meaning eating raw flesh.

Oothoon Character in Blake's prophetic poems.

Orc Character in Blake's prophetic poems.

Orestes Son of Clytemnestra and Agamemnon. See *The Oresteia* by Aeschylus.

Osiris (Ani) God of the dead in ancient Egyptian religion.

Outre Mere Literally, 'over the seas' in medieval French romance.

Ozymandias Greek name of an ancient Egyptian pharaoh; subject of a sonnet by Shelley.

Padmasambhava Sanskrit word meaning lotus-born.

Paha Sapa Sioux name for the Black Hills of South Dakota.

Pascal, Blaise (1623-62) French philosopher-mystic and mathematician, born in Clermont-Ferrand.

Pasiphae (calving ground) Wife of Minos, king of Crete. She mated with a bull from the sea and gave birth to the Minotaur (*q.v.*).

Pequod Whale ship in which Captain Ahab and his crew pursued the great white whale called Moby-Dick. Also, a tribe of Indians from the Massachussetts region, massacred by white settlers in 1639.

Peyote Small desert cactus whose fruits are hallucinogenic. Mescalin is an extract.

Pico della Mirandola (1463-94) Florentine scholar and humanist of the Renaissance. His most famous essay is on the dignity of man (1486).

Pleroma Greek word meaning fullness.

Polla ta deina First three words of Sophocles' second stasimon (*q.v.*) in *Antigone*.

Porete, Marguerite Mystic from Hainault, Belgium, burnt at the stake in 1360.

Protarekos ate Greek term meaning the primal act of madness. See *The Oresteia* by Aeschylus.

Psalm eight Psalm in which a biblical definition of man is elaborated.

Purama Hindu mythic tale.

Pythia Prophetess at the earth oracle in Delphi in ancient Greece.

Queequeg One of the three harpooners on board the *Pequod* (*q.v.*).

Ragnarok In Nordic mythology, the cataclysmic end of the world.

Ratnasambhava Sanskrit word meaning jewel-born.

Rig Veda Collection of Hindu sacred texts.

Rustred One of the three cocks whose crowing announces ragnarok (*q.v.*) in Nordic mythology.

Ruysbroeck, Johaness (1293-1381) Flemish mystic.

St John of the Cross (1542-91) Spanish mystic.

St Teresa of Avila (1515-82) Spanish mystic and Carmelite from Old Castile.

Salamis Site of a sea battle in ancient Greece between Persians and Greeks.

Sea of Typhoons Eastern sea into which the *Pequod* (*q.v.*) sailed and foundered.

Second stasimon Ode in the play *Antigone* by Sophocles (*q.v.*), in which is elaborated a definition of man.

Semele In Greek mythology, the mother of the god Dionysus (*q.v.*). Zeus, in the form of a mortal, became her lover. Hera, the wife of Zeus, became jealous and persauded Semele to ask Zeus to show himself in his true form. Zeus, knowing the consequences, refused, where-upon Semele denied him access to her bed. In anger Zeus revealed himself in his thunder-and-lightning form. Semele was consumed in the conflagration and for a long, long time afterwards her palace in Thebes still smouldered.

Serengeti Great plain in Kenya, famous for its wild animals.

Shankara One of the great philosopher-mystics of the Hindu tradition.

Shiva Among Hindus, one of the great trinity of gods (Brahma, Vishnu and Shiva).

Shulamite The woman, the beloved in the Song of Songs in the Bible.

Sidpa Bardo In Tibetan Buddhism, one of the states through which the soul journeys between death and rebirth.

Siduri Name given to a wife of Noah in this book.

Sikharas Spire or tower of a Hindu temple, representing the central mountain of the world.

Simeon The man who, when he saw the Christ-child presented in the temple, uttered the words 'Now lettest thou thy servant depart in peace' – in Latin, *Nunc dimittis*. See Luke 2.

Sinan Great architect of mosques in the Ottoman empire.

Smoking mirror Aztec god named Tezcatlipoca, meaning smoking mirror.

Socrates (469-399 BC) Founding father of Greek philosophy, born in Athens.

Sophocles (*c.* 496-05 BC) One of the great Athenian tragedians.

Spakana Seeress in Nordic mythology.

Sparagmos Greek term meaning tearing the captured live animal asunder.

Suger (*c.* 1081-1151) French bishop responsible for the building of St Denis, outside Paris, the inception of Gothic architecture.

Sumpatheia ton hollon Stoic phrase meaning the sympathy of all things with all things.

Sunda Straits Straits in an eastern sea through which the *Pequod* (*q.v.*) sailed to its doom.

Sundara Murti Beautiful face or form, of the goddess or god in Hinduism.

Suso (1295-1365) Rhineland mystic.

Sutra Sacred book purporting to record sayings or discourses of the Buddha.

Ta'doiko First ground onto which, in the Maidu story of origins, Turtle, Earth-Initiate and Father-of-the-Secret-Society, emerged.

Tai-wer In ancient Egyptian mythology, the first land or mound out of primordial waters.

Tairbfheis Vatic bullfeast among the ancient Irish.

Tao Te Ching Translated by Arthur Waley (1934) as *The Way and Its Power*, a Taoist sacred text attributed to Lao Tzu (*c.* 604-523 BC) consisting of eighty-one short chapters of poetry and philosophical reflection.

Tatei Hikuri Among the Huichol (*q.v.*), grandmother Peyote.

Tauler (1300-1361) Rhineland mystic.

Te Kore Maori word meaning the Void.

Techne Greek word for the manufacture and use of tools.

Tehom Ancient Hebrew word for the Great Deep.

Tenebrae Ritual re-enactment of the darkness of Good Friday, and the passion and death of Christ.

Teonanaeatl Psilocybin mushroom, thought of as a god in ancient Mexico.

Tep-Zepi In ancient Eyptian mythology, the First Time.

Thales First of the pre-Socratic philosophers, who lived in Ionia on the coast of Asia Minor.

Thebes Troubled city in ancient Greece, which, more than most, illustrates our difficulties in attempting to civilize ourselves, in attempting to live civically. Oedipus (*q.v.*) was the most famous of its kings.

Thel Character in Blake's prophetic poems.

Tiamat Dragoness of the Abyss in Babylonian and Sumerian mythology. Slain by the god Marduk (*q.v.*).

Tmolus Mountain in Asia Minor from which the god Dionysus (*q.v.*) and his Bacchantes came west into Greece.

Tolma Greek word meaning an act of audacity tending to rashness.

Tongue River River that flows into the Yellowstone through Wyoming and Montana.

Traherne, Thomas (1637-74) English mystic and poet, born to a shoemaker in Hereford. Author of *Centuries of Religious Meditations*.

Triduum Sacrum Three sacred days of Holy Week, Holy Thursday, Good Friday and Easter Sunday.

Tsetsekia Winter ceremonies of the Kwakiutl (*q.v.*).

Tsurunga Sacred ritual object among Australian Aborigines.

Turiya Literally, the fourth, referring in the Mandukya Upanishad to Divine Ground (*q.v.*) which is beyond all duality.

Udana Hymn or song – especially as spoken by Buddha on the morning of his enlightenment.

Upanishads Sanskrit word meaning a sitting-down (at another's feet); sacred Hindu texts on the nature of man and the universe, part of Vedic writings dating back two and a half millennia.

Ur of the Chaldees Mesopotamian city out of which God called Abraham.

Urizen Character in Blake's prophetic poems.

Utnapishtun Sumerian survivor of the Flood (of Noah and Deucalion).

Uvavnuk Inuit medicine woman.

Vala Character in Blake's prophetic poems.

Veronica's napkin Napkin offered by a woman named Veronica to Jesus on his way to his crucifixion on Golgotha.

Viksepashakti Mental power by which we project something illusory onto reality. 'Shakti' signifies female power in a goddess or god.

Vishnu Major Hindu deity, the second member, with Brahma and Shiva, of a triad of gods manifesting cosmic functions of the Supreme Being.

Vishvarupa Hindu god Vishnu (*q.v.*) as Omniform – the form that contains all forms

Vishvayuga Form that contains all ages.

Vritra In Hindu mythology, a great dragon who imprisoned the waters in his coils.

Vyasa Supposed author of the great Indian epic *The Mahabharata*.

Waters of Nun Primordial waters of Egyptian mythology.

Whaleman's Chapel Located in New Bedford, Connecticut, mentioned in Melville's *Moby-Dick*.

Whyght Samyte White silk in which the Grail was covered when it entered the hall of the round table on Pentecost Sunday.

Wirikuta Mexican desert in which the Huichol (*q.v.*) seek peyote (*q.v.*).

Wolf Collar Blackfoot medicine man.

Wounded Knee Site of a massacre of Sioux Indians by American soldiers in South Dakota *c.*1889.

Wu-hsin Chinese word of Zar Bhuddist provenance meaning no mind, or beyond mind.

Wu Wei In Taoist philosophy, action by inaction.

Xerxes Persian king. His efforts and those of King Darius to conquer Greece were defeated at the battles of Marathon (*q.v.*) and Salamis (*q.v.*). As a consequence, the Greek Enlightenment could and did continue to flourish.

Yahweh One of the personal names for the God of the Old Testament. See Psalm seventy-four, verse fourteen.

Yakut People of Siberia.

Yam Canaanite Leviathan (*q.v.*).

Yana Vessel, in the sense of ship or ferry. A Sanskrit word in Buddhism.

Yatra na anyat pasyati, na anyat srinoti na anyad vijanati, sa bhuma Where nothing else is seen, nothing else is heard, nothing else is thought about, there is the Infinite. *Chandogya Upanishad*, vii, xxiv.

Year One Reed In the Aztec calendar, the year in which Cortez came and destroyed their empire and religion (1519, in our calendar).

Yenessi River in Siberia.

Yenisei Ostyaks People of Siberia.

Yojo Cultic divinity worshipped by Queequeg (*q.v.*).

Yu Wei In Taoist philosophy, deliberate, self-conscious action.

Yudishtina Character in the Indian epic *The Mahabharata*.

Zeuglodon Prehistoric whale, a fossil of which was unearthed in Alabama in the 1840s. See *Moby-Dick*, chapter 104. As Job was down-cast by Leviathan, so was Ishmael down-cast by Zeuglodon: 'I am horror-struck at this antemosaic, unsourced existence of the unspeakable terrors of the whale, which, having been before all time, must needs exist after all humane ages are over.'